THE COMPETITION ACT 1998:
A PRACTICAL GUIDE

AUSTRALIA
LBC Information Services
Sydney

CANADA and the USA
Carswell
Toronto

NEW ZEALAND
Brooker's
Auckland

SINGAPORE and MALAYSIA
Sweet and Maxwell (S.E. Asia)
Singapore

THE COMPETITION ACT 1998:
A PRACTICAL GUIDE

By

Dorothy Livingston
MA (Oxon.), Solicitor,
Partner, Herbert Smith

LONDON · SWEET & MAXWELL · 2001

Published in 2001 by Sweet & Maxwell Limited of
100 Avenue Road,
London NW3 3PF
Typeset by J&L Composition Ltd, Filey, North Yorkshire
Printed in England by
MPG Books Ltd, Bodmin,Cornwall

No natural forests were destroyed to make this product; only farmed
timber was used and replanted

ISBN 0–752 00622–3

A CIP catalogue record for this book is available from the British Library

Foreword

The Competition Act 1998 amounts to more than just another evolutionary step in the development of an increasingly important branch of the law. It embodies a new conceptual approach towards crucial aspects of competition law, which is fundamentally different from that contained in the pre-existing law, and it lays down the detailed procedural arrangements for giving effect to that new approach. An experienced pilot is therefore needed, if practitioners are to understand the change in approach and find their way through the new arrangements.

That is what this book provides. Dorothy Livingston has both great practical experience of competition law and the intellectual and academic background needed to write an authoritative and comprehensive guide to the new Act, which is clear, well ordered and eminently comprehensible, even to those who have not hitherto bathed deeply in these waters.

I naturally welcome not only the appearance of this book, but the legislation which it analyses. When I became the Commissioner responsible for competition policy at the beginning of 1989 it had already for some time been the hope of the European Commission that those Member States which had strong and effective competition policies would want increasingly to align those policies with European Community legislation and practice, even when they were not legally required to do so. In some countries there would have been a political predisposition to do this, but the domestic framework of competition policy was so weak that it was not a practical proposition to take aboard the more rigorous and substantial provisions of E.U. law. In this country the position was very different. The United Kingdom had its own substantial and well-developed corpus of law, but there was certainly no politically based inclination to take on E.U. rules for their own sake. The E.U. system had to win its spurs on its own merits.

Over the years that is just what happened. The pressure to switch over to a prohibition-based system gradually grew because it was increasingly felt that the Restrictive Trade Practices Act and the Resale Prices Act were procedurally cumbersome, and the remedies they provided were less effective than those provided for by the Treaty, as it was applied by the European Commission. It was gratifying to see a consensus for change emerge in the United Kingdom, not because of any political pressure but because the business community and the legal community saw what was being done in Brussels and came to prefer it. The Competition Act 1998 is the result.

The ultimate irony is that it is now the European Commission which is trying to devolve the exercise of some of its own powers to the Member States, because it is overwhelmed by the sheer volume of casework, and the business community in the United Kingdom and elsewhere, that is reluctant for this to happen. How that will pan out it is too early to say. If the Commission's proposals are implemented this will certainly lend to a further important evolution in the practice, if not the law, relating to a European competition policy. But that is for the future and another distinguished book from the pen of Dorothy Livingston? I cannot make any promises on her behalf!

The Rt Hon. The Lord Brittan of Spennithorne Q.C.

Table of Statutory Instruments

Preface

This book has evolved over the period since 1997, when the Competition Bill started its parliamentary process. It now deals with not only the Competition Act 1998, but the mass of subsidiary legislation and Guidelines that have been issued in the course of its implementation. It also deals with the interrelation with EC competition law, including the new Vertical Agreements Block Exemption and the proposed reforms.

The Act has been in force since March 1, 2000. Although the OFT has been busy since then, there is as yet little in the public domain. What is evident is that the OFT have been successful in keeping down the number of formal notifications and are able to concentrate on enforcement measures, as well as continuing work on their Guidelines. The first proposed block exemption, covering public transport ticketing agreements is the subject of a consultation process.

The book states the law at October 6, 2000. Already more reform of competition law is in the pipeline and this is covered briefly in Chapter 17.

The book is my sole responsibility and the views expressed are my own and should not be regarded as the views of my firm or of any other person.

This book owes a great deal to the support I have had from Herbert Smith and colleagues at the firm throughout its preparation, starting with the Hansard monitoring carried out by Francesco Lamanna and ending with the detailed checking and research carried out by Helena Camacho assisted by Melanie O'Brien. Many members of the European and Competition Law Department have contributed in one way or another, some with extensive research work and others with a most useful "peer group review". I will mention particularly my partners, Elizabeth McKnight, Stephen Wisking and James Quinney and (on property matters), Patrick Robinson; colleagues, Kristien Geeurickx, Victoria Ripley, Claire Leek, James Wynn-Evans, Genevieve Johnston, Kyriakos Fountoukakos, Tim Briggs and Giles Warrington; former colleagues, Mark Maurice-Jones, Andrea Appella, Patricia Carvill and Matthew O'Regan; and, especially, my secretary, Isabella Frimpong and the rest of our secretarial team for wrestling with my handwriting and habit of underestimating the space needed to write any addition to the text.

I owe a debt of gratitude for encouragement and practical support to my Head of Department, Jonathan Scott, and Senior Partner, Richard Bond, and especially, to Lord Brittan of Spennithorne for doing me the honour of writing as he has done in his very generous foreword.

Finally, and not least, I should thank my daughters, Katherine and Alice, for their patience as the demands of the book were juggled with family life, from weekend to weekend, and even when the holiday cottage kitchen table became a temporary desk.

Dorothy Livingston

Exchange House,
London.

October 6, 2000

Table of Contents

Chapter 3

Role of the Principal Regulators

Chapter 4

Regulators with Concurrent Powers

Chapter 7

Exclusions from the Prohibition of Anti-competitive Agreements

Chapter 8

Exemptions from the Chapter I Prohibition

Chapter 10

Consequences of Infringing the Chapter I Prohibition

Chapter 12

Exclusions from the Prohibition of Abuse of Dominant Position

Chapter 13

Procedure in Relation to the Chapter II Prohibition

Chapter 14

Consequences of Infringing the Chapter II Prohibition

Chapter 15

Retention of Existing Monopoly Investigation Regime

Chapter 16

Transitional Arrangements

Chapter 17

Reform Provisions

Table of Cases

Table of Statutes

Table of Statutory Instruments

European Legislation: Treaties

Please note that the Treaty of Amsterdam, 1997, renumbered some of the Articles of the Treaty establishing the European Communities. Where applicable, the old numbering is shown, after the new numbering, in brackets.

1951 Paris. Treaty establishing the European Coal and Steel Community (April 18): (1998) O.J. 98/C9/03 5.2.1, 12.4.3, 12.4.6
   Art.65(5) 10.3.5
   Annex 1 7.6.7

1957 Rome. Treaty Establishing the European Economic Community (March 25): 298 U.N.T.S. 11 3.5.3, 5.2.1, 5.2.7, 5.3.2, 5.4.1, 7.6.4, 7.6.7
   Art.10 12.4.2
   Art.39 7.6.8
   Art.81(ex 85) 1.1.1, 1.1.3, 1.1.11, 1.1.13, 1.1.13, 1.2.3, 1.3.2, 1.3.4, 2.1.2, 2.3.1, 3.2.1, 3.2.15, 3.3.4, 4.4.1, 4.4.8, 5.1.2, 5.1.5, 5.2.4, 5.2.5, 5.2.6, 5.3.4, 5.3.6, 5.4.2, 5.5.1, 6.1.1, 6.1.2, 6.2.1, 6.3.1, 6.4.1, 6.4.2, 6.4.4, 6.5.1, 6.5.4, 6.6.2, 6.7.1, 6.7.2, 6.7.3, 6.8.1, 6.8.3, 7.2.2, 7.3.1, 7.6.5, 8.1.3, 8.1.6, 8.2.3, 8.2.10, 8.2.13, 8.2.16, 8.3.8, 8.3.9, 8.4.1, 8.4.4, 8.4.5, 8.4.6, 8.4.9, 8.5.1, 8.5.2, 9.2.4, 9.5.3, 9.12.1, 9.14.1, 10.1.2, 10.1.3, 10.1.4, 10.1.5, 10.2.1, 10.2.2, 10.2.3, 10.2.4, 10.2.5, 10.3.1, 10.3.2, 10.3.10, 11.1.3, 11.2.2, 11.3.2, 11.4.3, 11.6.1, 14.1.1, 14.2.2, 17.7.1, 17.7.2, 17.7.3, 17.7.4
   Art.81(1) (ex 85(1)) 3.2.5, 8.1.3, 8.1.4, 8.2.9, 8.3.1, 8.4.1, 8.4.2, 8.4.3, 8.4.4, 8.4.5, 8.4.8, 8.4.9, 8.4.13, 8.5.1, 8.5.2, 10.1.3, 10.2.5, 10.3.10
   Art.81(1)(a)–(e) 6.1.2
   Art.81(2) 1.1.4, 10.1.2
   Art.81(3)(ex 85(3)) 1.1.3, 1.1.8, 1.1.10, 1.1.11, 3.2.2, 7.2.1, 7.2.2, 7.2.7, 7.2.8, 8.1.3, 8.1.4, 8.1.6, 8.2.3, 8.2.4, 8.2.7, 8.2.11, 8.4.6, 8.4.7, 8.4.9, 8.4.10, 10.3.10, 11.8, 17.7.1, 17.7.2
   Art.82(ex 86) 2.1.1, 2.1.2, 2.2.2, 2.2.3, 2.2.4, 2.3.1, 2.3.2, 2.3.4, 3.2.15, 3.3.4, 4.4.1, 5.1.2, 5.1.5, 5.2.4, 5.2.5, 5.2.6, 5.3.4, 5.3.5, 5.3.6, 5.4.2, 5.5.1, 6.2.1, 6.6.2, 7.6.5, 8.2.16, 8.5.1, 9.2.5, 9.5.3, 9.12.1, 9.14.1, 10.1.5, 10.2.1, 10.2.2, 10.2.3, 10.2.4, 10.2.5, 10.3.1, 10.3.2, 11.1.1, 11.1.2, 11.1.3, 11.1.4, 11.2.1, 11.2.2, 11.3.2, 11.3.4, 11.4.1, 11.4.3, 11.5.1, 11.5.2, 11.6.1, 11.6.2, 13.1.1, 13.1.2, 13.2.3, 14.1.1, 14.2.2, 15.1.2, 17.7.1, 17.7.2, 17.7.3, 17.7.4
   Art.82(1) 7.6.3
   Art.83(ex 87) 8.5.1
   Art.84(ex 88) 3.3.4, 8.1.3, 8.5.1, 8.5.2
   Art.85(ex 89) 8.1.3, 8.5.1, 10.1.3, 10.2.5
   Art.86 10.2.5
   Art.86(2)(ex 90(2)) 4.4.3, 7.6.3, 12.4.2
   Art.177 5.5.1
   Art.230(ex 173) 9.8.1
   Art.295(ex 222) 5.3.4
   Annex II 8.3.8

1992 Oporto. Agreement on the European Economic Area (May 2) [1994] O.J. L1/523 12.4.3
   Art.53 8.4.2
   Art.53(1) 8.4.2, 8.4.13

1997 Amsterdam. Treaty of Amsterdam (October 2) [1999] O.J. L114/56 1.1.1

European Legislation: Regulations, Directives, Decisions

Sections and Schedules of the Competition Act in Force

Taking into account:

Statutory Instrument 2000 No. 344 (C.9) The Competition Act 1998 (Commencement No. 5) Order 2000 ("No. 5")

Statutory Instrument 2000 No. 2859 (C.74) The Competition Act 1998 (Commencement No. 4) Order 2000 ("No. 4")

Statutory Instrument 2000 No. 505 (C.74) The Competition Act 1998 (Commencement No. 3) Order 2000 ("No. 3")

Statutory Instrument 2000 No. 3166 (C.74) The Competition Act 1998 (Commencement No. 2) Order 2000 ("No. 2")

Statutory Instrument 2000 No. 2750 (C.74) The Competition Act 1998 (Commencement No. 1) Order 2000 ("No. 1")

Sections and Schedules in force	Commencement Order
PART I	
Chapter I	
Agreements	
Section 1: Enactments repealed	
(b)–(d)	No. 5
Section 2: Chapter I Prohibition	
Entire Section	No. 5
Section 3: Excluded Agreements	
1(b)	Partially No. 2
	Remainder No. 5
1(a)(c)(d)	No. 2
(2)–(6)	No. 2
Section 4: Individual exemptions	
Entire section	No. 5
Section 5: Cancellations of individual exemptions	
Entire section	No. 5
Section 6: Block exemptions	
Entire section	No. 5
Section 7: Block exemptions: opposition	
Entire section	No. 5
Section 8: Block exemption: procedure	
Entire section	No. 5
Section 9: Exemption criteria	
Entire section	No. 5
Section 10: Parallel exemptions	
Entire section	No. 5
Section 11: Exemption for certain agreements	
Entire section	No. 5

Sections and Schedules in force	Commencement Order
PART IV	
Sections 70–76: Supplemental & Transitional	
Section 70: Contracts as to patented products	
Entire section	No. 5
Section 71: Regulations, orders and rules	
Section 72: Offences by bodies corporate	
Entire section	No. 5
Section 73: Crown application	
Entire section	No. 5
Section 74: Amendments, transitional provisions, savings & repeals	Partially Nos. 2 and 3
	Insofar as it relates to provisions in Schedule 10 in force No. 5
Section 75: Consequential and supplementary provision	
Section 76: Short title, commencement and extent	
SCHEDULES	
Schedule 1: Exclusions, mergers and concentrations	
Entire schedule	No. 2
Schedule 2: Exclusions: other competition scrutiny under other statutes	
Paras: (1)–(5)	No. 5
(6)	No. 2
Schedule 3: General exclusions	
Entire schedule	No. 2
Schedule 4: Professional rules	
Entire schedule	No. 2
Schedule 5: Procedure for notification under Chapter I	
Paras: (1)–(6)	No. 5
Schedule 6: Procedure for notification under Chapter II	
Paras: (1)–(6)	No. 5
Schedule 7: The Competition Commission	
Entire schedule	No. 3
Schedule 8: Appeals	
Paras: (1) (Part II)	No. 3
(2)–(4)	No. 5
Schedule 9: Director's rules	
Entire schedule	No. 1
Schedule 10: Regulators	
Paras: (2)–(8)	Partially No. 1, for all remaining purposes No. 5
9(7)(b)	No. 2
10 (6)(b)	No. 2
11(b)	No. 2
12(7)(b)	No. 2
13(10)(b)	No. 2

Sections and Schedules in force	Commencement Order
10(a)	No. 5
11	No. 5
12	No. 5
13	No. 5
14(2)	No. 5
16	No. 5
17	No. 5
18(a)	No. 5
19	No. 5
20(3)–(6)	No. 5
21	No. 5

Schedule 13: Transitional provisions and savings
Paras:

10(5)	No. 2
19(3)	No. 2
11	No. 2
12(1)	Partially No. 2, for all remaining purposes No. 5
40	No. 4
41	No. 4
8	No. 5
9	No. 5
10	No. 5
12(2)	No. 5
13–18	No. 5
19(1)–(2)	No. 5
20–34	No. 5
36–39	No. 5
42–46	No. 5

Schedule 14: Repeals

OFT Guidelines

The Major Provisions OFT 400, published March 1999	1.1.7, 1.3.3, 4.5.1, 5.4.3, 9.1.1, 9.7.2–9.7.3, 9.16.4, 13.2.3, 13.4.2, 13.4.9, 15.1.2–15.1.3, 16.6
The Chapter I Prohibition OFT 401, published March 1999	1.1.11, 5.4.3, 6.3.1, 6.5.4, 6.6.1, 6.8.1, 8.2.4, 8.4.10
The Chapter II Prohibition OFT 402, published March 1999	2.3.3, 11.2.3, 11.4.2–11.4.3, 11.5.2–11.5.3
Market Definition OFT 403, published March 1999	6.7.4, 8.2.8, 11.3.1–11.3.3, 15.2.1
Powers of Investigation OFT 404, published March 1999	9.9.1–9.9.3, 9.10.1–9.10.3, 9.12.2 9.13.5, 9.14.4
Concurrent Applications to Regulated Industries OFT 405, published March 1999	4.1.2, 4.3.2, 4.3.4, 4.3.7, 4.5.1
Concurrent Applications to Regulated Industries – revised consultation draft version, OFT 433, March 2000	4.1.2, 4.3.2–4.3.4, 4.3.7, 4.5.1
Transitional Arrangements OFT 406, published March 1999	7.5.4, 16.4.5, 16.7.3, 16.8
Enforcement OFT 408, published March 1999	9.5.1, 10.3.3, 10.3.5, 10.3.7, 10.5.2
Trade Associations, Professions and Self-Regulating Bodies OFT 408, published March 1999	6.3.4, 6.4.2–6.4.3
Assessment of Individual Agreements and Conduct OFT 414, published September 1999	11.5.3
Assessment of Market Power OFT 415, published September 1999	11.4.2
Exclusions for Mergers and Ancillary Restrictions OFT 416, published September 1999	7.4.7
The Application of the Competition Act in the Telecommunications Sector OFT 417, published February 2000 OFTEL publication	4.4.1, 4.4.4
Vertical Agreements and Restraints OFT 419, published February 2000	7.2.3
Land Agreements OFT 420, published February 2000	7.3.2–7.3.3, 7.3.7–7.3.8
The Application of the Competition Act in the Water and Severage Sectors OFT 422, published January 2000 OFWAT publication	4.4.7, 12.4.2

Useful Web Addresses

Civil Aviation Authority (CAA)   http://www.caa.co.uk
Competition Commission   http://www.competition-commission.gov.uk
Court Service   http://www.courtservice.gov.uk
Department of the Environment, Transport and the Regions
                                        http://www.detr.gov.uk
Department of Trade and Industry   http://www.dti.gov.uk
European Union (access to information on the E.C. Commission)
                                        http://europa.eu.int
Independent Television Commission (ITC)
                                        http://www.itc.org.uk
Office of Fair Trading (OFT)   http://www.oft.gov.uk
Office of Gas and Electricity Markets (Ofgem)
                                        http://www.ofgem.gov.uk
Office of the Rail Regulator (ORR)   http://www.rail-reg.gov.uk
Office of Telecommunications (Oftel)
                                        http://www.oftel.gov.uk
Office of Water Services (Ofwat)   http://www.ofwat.gov.uk
United Kingdom Parliament   http://www.parliament.uk

Chapter 1

The United Kingdom's Version of Article 81

1.1 The New Law
1.2 History
1.3 What it Means for Business

1.1 The New Law

1.1.1 Alignment with E.C. Law

The aim of the reform contained in The Competition Act 1998 was to introduce a prohibition against anti-competitive agreements closely based on Article 81 (Article 85 prior to the Treaty of Amsterdam taking effect in 1999) of the E.C. Treaty, thus replacing the current system of control under the Restrictive Trade Practices Act 1976 ("RTPA") (which consolidated earlier legislation) and the Resale Prices Act 1976, which have both been repealed. This major reform sweeps away the previous United Kingdom system for controlling anti-competitive agreements in force since 1956. It took effect on March 1, 2000. The Competition Act 1998 also introduces a prohibition of abuse of a dominant position, based on E.C. law (see Chapter 2).

The jurisdiction of the competition authorities over an agreement under the new Act arises from the anti-competitive nature of the agreement in its effects or intended effects on competition and is to be judged accordingly. This sweeps away the old system under the RTPA in which jurisdiction was form based; the RTPA took account of effects only in consideration of those agreements which fell within its scope. The RTPA was extensively criticised for controlling many innocuous agreements and missing many anti-competitive agreements because of this jurisdictional approach.

The reform also introduces a more extensive investigative regime and much stiffer penalties superficially in line with Article 81, but in reality owing more to the feared investigative powers of HM Customs and Excise and the punitive approach of United States anti-trust law, with the level of fines potentially about three times that anticipated when the legislation passed through Parliament.

Just as the new system in the United Kingdom is coming into operation major changes are being proposed to the administration of E.C. competition law. These will give national authorities the power to apply the whole of Article 81 directly, but will prevent the application of national competition laws in cases where the agreement or practice concerned affects trade between Member States. Under the proposed changes the United Kingdom would be able to apply its own procedure and penalty regime in cases related to Article 81, but some adaptations of the Competition Act 1998 would be needed to make the E.C. and United Kingdom regimes operate as a harmonious whole. The proposed E.C. regime, which would apply to many of the most important cases dealt with by the United Kingdom authorities, is discussed further in Chapter 17 at 17.7.

1.1.2   Subsidiary Legislation and Guidelines

Much of the detail of the reform was left to subsidiary legislation and to the development of policy by the Secretary of State for Trade and Industry ("Secretary of State") and by the Director General of Fair Trading ("Director") who, assisted by his staff at the Office of Fair Trading ("OFT"), is given primary responsibility for enforcement subject to the appellate process described in Chapter 9. The OFT has produced a major body of policy Guidelines and individual utility Regulators who enjoy concurrent powers have produced additional guidance for their industries. A list appears at [p. l]. These will be revised as policy develops (indeed some were in the course of revision within weeks of the legislation coming into force). The Guidelines should be considered alongside the legislation itself, the starting point when applying the Chapter I Prohibition.

1.1.3   Scope of Prohibition

The Competition Act 1998 section 2 prohibits agreements, decisions by associations of undertakings and concerted practices which may affect trade within the United Kingdom and which have the object or effect of preventing, restricting or distorting competition within the United Kingdom.

As with Article 81 there are a series of exemptions, including the recognition of exemptions granted under Article 81(3) E.C. Treaty as exemptions under the Act (see below at 1.1.11 and Chapter 8). The legislation, unlike previous legislation, expressly covers agreements with the Crown (s. 73).

Unlike Article 81 there are, in addition, a number of exclusions from the scope of the prohibition (see Chapter 7). These identify types of agreement where the prohibition simply cannot be applied except in some exceptional circumstances. The most important exclusions are for vertical agreements, that is agreements between traders at different levels in the supply chain, for land agreements and for mergers (which will continue to be regulated either under the Fair Trading Act 1973 ("FTA") or the E.C. Merger Regulation (see Chapter 7). The vertical agreements exclusion follows in principle (but with differences in application) moves in E.C. legislation, in the shape of the vertical agreements block exemption from the Article 81 prohibition (Commission Regulation (E.C.) No. 2790/99, [1999] O.J. L336/21) which took effect in June 2000 (see 1.1.8 below). In practice, however, whether an exclusionary or an exempting legislative technique is used, the uncertainties in the scope of exclusions and exemptions mean that the Regulators and the Courts will be kept busy analysing whether the conditions for exclusion or exemption are satisfied in borderline cases.

1.1.4   Agreements in Breach are Void

Agreements affected by the prohibition are void in so far as not exempted or excluded (s. 2(4)). Section 2(4) is intended to be interpreted by the courts in the same way as Article 81(2) so as to apply only to the affected provisions and not to the agreement as a whole. The legislators and Regulators believe this to be one of the effects of section 60 which, broadly, requires the courts and Regulators to follow E.C. jurisprudence. Whether an agreement is wholly or partly void is likely to depend upon whether the remainder constitutes a viable agreement (see more detailed discussion at Chapter 10).

1.1.5 Fines and Damages for Breach of the Prohibition

In addition to voidness, fines may be imposed by the Director of up to 10 per cent of the United Kingdom turnover of each infringing undertaking for a period equal to the length of the infringement, but limited to the turnover for the three business years preceding the date on which the infringement ended: the Competition Act 1998 (Determination of Turnover for Penalties) Order 2000 (S.I. 2000 No. 309) discussed in Chapter 10. Parties to "small agreements" are generally immune from fines (see 1.1.6 below).

This level of penalty is permissible within the legislation, although it could be three times that indicated in the passage of the Bill, where fines were described as modelled on the E.C. system (which is limited to one year's turnover) but confined to United Kingdom turnover (*Hansard*, H.L., Vol. 593, No. 210, col. 1374 (October 20, 1998)).

An interesting feature is the Director's leniency policy (discussed at Chapter 10, para. 10.3.7) which is modelled on that of the United States Department of Justice. It may give a "whistle blower" party to an infringing agreement full protection from fines in certain circumstances.

The Director also has the ability to impose final "cease and desist" orders and take interim measures pending his decision.

It is Government policy that there should be private rights of action for breach of statutory duty open to aggrieved third parties but, unlike most United Kingdom statutes which intend to create such rights alongside penalties laid down in the statute (*e.g.* RTPA, s. 35), there is no express provision in the Act (see Chapter 10). Findings of fact made by the Director in his decisions will be prima facie binding in court proceedings (see s. 58).

1.1.6 Small Agreements

In order to ensure that small and medium sized companies ("SMEs") are not unduly burdened by the prohibition, parties to an agreement termed in the Act as a "small agreement" are protected from the risk of fines (s. 39). They are not, however, immune from action by the Director to prevent the continued operation of the agreement. The protection from fines also can be withdrawn (but only on a prospective basis). Price fixing agreements do not benefit from this protection from fines in any event (s. 39(1)(b)).

Section 39 provides that small agreements can be defined by reference to thresholds based on the parties' turnover or market share. The Government indicated during the legislative process that it was considering a turnover related criterion only, namely aggregate United Kingdom turnover of between £20 million and £50 million (*Hansard*, H.L., Vol. 583, No. 64, col. 434 (November 17, 1997)). The Competition Act 1998 (Small Agreements and Conduct of Minor Significance) Regulations 2000 (S.I. 2000 No. 262) sets the threshold at a maximum combined annual worldwide turnover of £20 million for all the parties to the relevant agreement or arrangement. The details of calculation are discussed at Chapter 10, para. 10.3.8, but it is worth noting that any agreement involving a member of a substantial group of companies is unlikely to qualify as a small agreement.

1.1.7 Appreciability

The Director has announced his intention to adopt a much broader "rule of reason" appreciability test for the application of the Chapter I Prohibition than has the

E.C. Commission. Generally he does not intend to apply the Chapter I Prohibition to agreements which do not involve price-fixing or market sharing agreements where the parties' combined market share does not exceed 25 per cent (OFT Guideline, *The Chapter I Prohibition*, OFT 401, March 1999, para. 2.19). This may not apply, however, where a large number of small agreements of the same type have a network effect, such as occurred with the brewery tied house agreements for public houses. This approach should nevertheless benefit agreements, both large and small. Except where, in a discrete local market, genuinely small businesses have a market share of over 25 per cent, the Director's rule of reason may be of more assistance to smaller business activities than the small agreements exclusion. The "rule of reason" is, of course, not set in stone and a decision applying the prohibition to a non price fixing term below the Director's intended appreciability threshold could produce a deluge of notifications to the OFT.

1.1.8   Vertical Agreements

One aim of the reform is to remove most vertical agreements, that is agreements between traders at different levels in the supply chain, from the scope of the prohibition of anti-competitive agreements. Intellectual property licences, except to the extent that they are ancillary to the supply of goods or services, are not covered. It was not possible for the Government to settle on a suitable definition of vertical agreements in time for it to be incorporated in the Act. However, section 50 provides that the Secretary of State may legislate by statutory instrument to restrict the application of the prohibition to vertical agreements. The Competition Act 1998 (Land and Vertical Agreements Exclusion) Order 2000 (S.I. 2000 No. 310) excludes vertical agreements, to the extent that they come within its scope, from the Chapter I Prohibition. The exclusion does not apply to "price fixing agreements" such as those which provide for resale price maintenance. Price ascertainment mechanisms agreed between the parties in relation to the prices the supplying party will charge the other party for goods or services supplied under the vertical agreement itself will normally fall outside the definition of "price fixing". Where an agreement has elements which are not related to the vertical relationship, these are not excluded from the prohibition (see more detailed discussion in Chapter 7). There is an overall power for the Director to "clawback" and consider agreements which fall within the exclusion but which give rise to concerns under the Chapter I Prohibition.

The United Kingdom has adopted a much broader approach to vertical agreements than the E.C. Commission, whose block exemption contains complex (and uncertain) market share thresholds for its application, as well as a prescriptive approach to non-compete restrictions and a more comprehensive "black list" of prohibited provisions (Regulation on the application of Article 81(3) of the Treaty to categories of vertical agreements and concerted practices, Commission Regulation No. 2790/1999, [1999] O.J. L336/21). This exclusion will help to ensure that the OFT is not swamped with notifications of distribution agreements whose effects on competition are generally benign.

1.1.9   Land Agreements

The RTPA and most other United Kingdom competition legislation historically has not applied to economic activity unrelated to the supply of goods or services. The Competition Act 1998, however, applies to agreements dealing with property; both land and incorporated property such as intellectual property rights. Many land agreements will benefit from exclusion from The Competition Act 1998 (Land and

Vertical Agreements Exclusion) Order 2000 (supra). The details are discussed in Chapter 7.3. The Competition Act 1998 also provides (at s. 68) for the possibility of the monopoly and merger control jurisdiction under the FTA being extended to cover land agreements more generally by statutory instrument made under a new FTA, section 137(3A). No steps have been taken to extend the FTA jurisdiction.

1.1.10 Individual and Block Exemptions and Related Guidance

Agreements which breach the prohibition are capable of individual exemption by the Director where they provide countervailing benefits, with exemption criteria which follow closely those of Article 81(3) (s. 9). The Director may also give confidential guidance on the availability of an individual exemption.

There may also be block exemptions covering particular categories of agreement. Any area to be covered by a block exemption will be recommended by the Director to the Secretary of State following public consultation (s. 6). No block exemptions had been adopted prior to the Act coming into force, no doubt because the existence of "parallel exemptions" enables United Kingdom businesses to benefit from the block exemptions promulgated by the E.C. Commission (see 1.1.11 below), and because of the scope of the exclusions discussed above.

The Director is now consulting on a proposed block exemption for public transport ticketing schemes. As a result of the fragmented ownership of the transport businesses which provide public service transport, the provision of through ticketing and multi-modal ticketing for the convenience of passengers generally requires agreements between operators on the price and terms of these tickets. Since these schemes operate within the United Kingdom it is unlikely that they will raise concerns under E.C. competition law and they are therefore suitable for a block exemption at national level. Air transport is excluded from the proposed block exemption.

1.1.11 Value of E.C. Exemptions and Comfort Letters

Agreements which have individual or block exemption under Article 81(3) will be automatically exempt from the United Kingdom domestic prohibition (s. 10). This "parallel" exemption will also cover agreements which fall within the terms of an E.C. block exemption but are not subject to Article 81 because they do not affect inter-state trade. The Director has the power to impose conditions or obligations subject to which such parallel exemptions are to have effect. He can also cancel a parallel exemption in certain circumstances.

Agreements which have been notified to the E.C. Commission and have obtained a comfort letter will not be able to benefit from these parallel exemption provisions. The OFT Guideline, *The Chapter I Prohibition*, OFT 401, March 1999, Part 7 sets out how the Director intends to treat agreements which have been given a comfort letter. The Director will not, as a general policy, depart from the E.C. Commission's assessment as set out in an E.C. comfort letter. Comfort letters do not always, however, address the substance of an agreement or points specifically relevant to a market within the United Kingdom.

Proposals for reform of E.C. competition law enforcement would prevent the Director imposing additional requirements in any case affecting trade between Member States. In these cases, however, the Director will become the primary regulator for the enforcement of Article 81 in cases involving United Kingdom parties. These proposals are contained in a draft Council Regulation. This regulation will replace Council Regulation 17/62 published by the E.C. Commission on September 27, 2000 and is discussed further in Chapter 17 at 17.7.

1.1.12   Decisions by the Director and Guidance

The Director has power to take decisions :

- giving an individual exemption from the prohibition;
- stating that an agreement is outside the prohibition (similar to a negative clearance by the E.C. Commission);
- finding that an agreement infringes the prohibition and either requiring it to be brought to an end (in whole or in part) or imposing conditions and obligations in relation to its future performance.

A decision will take the form of a reasoned statement by the Director following a full assessment of the market and the comments of third parties (s. 14 and Sched. 5, para. 5).

The Director may also give guidance in confidence without consulting third parties. This is a less complex procedure which will be sufficient, in most cases, to give the parties protection from fines (ss. 13 and 15). Guidance will, however, be of doubtful value in the event of a later dispute as to the application of the prohibition, particularly where the dispute is with a third party who had no opportunity to comment at the guidance stage.

1.1.13   Processes Leading to a Decision

A notification, complaint or an own initiative investigation by the Director or a Utility Regulator may all lead to a decision. Guidance may only follow notification specifically requesting guidance.

Notification

The notification procedure, where parties apply for a decision or guidance, is laid down in the Director's Rules: The Competition Act 1998 (Director's rules) Order 2000 (S.I. 2000 No. 293) made pursuant to section 51 and Sched. 9. The notification form, Form N, which is similar to Form A/B used for notifying agreements under Article 81, is to be found at Annex 1 to the Director's Rules. The Act provides for fees to be charged for notifications (s. 53) and the Director's Rules set these at £5,000 for guidance and £13,000 for a decision (see r. 6 and Annex 2).

Complaints and Third Party Rights

Third parties may complain to the Director and also make observations in his public consultation processes in relation to agreements submitted for exemption or negative clearance. They may ask the Director to review a decision which he has taken within one month of publication of the decision (s. 47 and the Director's Rules, r. 28). It is intended that third parties will have a right to claim damages or injunctive relief in the courts when they are adversely affected by a prohibited agreement. This is not, however, expressly provided for in the legislation.

Investigative powers – Own Initiative Investigation

The Director may also undertake investigations on his own initiative (e.g. based on information reported in the press). The Director has extensive powers to request information and carry out investigations at business and other premises, which in some ways go beyond those powers in Regulation 17/62 for the enforcement of Article 81 by the E.C. Commission. Failure to co-operate may be a criminal offence (see Chapter 10).

1.1.14 Utilities Regulators

Certain Utilities Regulators (water, gas and electricity, rail and telecommunications) have concurrent jurisdiction with the Director in their respective areas of competence. There are procedures laid down in the Competition Act 1998 (Concurrency) Regulations 2000 (S.I. 2000 No. 260) to deal with jurisdictional overlap and all Regulators will work to firm guidelines agreed with the Director (see Chapter 4). The Independent Television Commission ("ITC") is not given concurrent powers, although it has competition regulatory functions covering all television services except the BBC. The Civil Aviation Authority ("CAA") will be given concurrent powers in relation to some activities under proposals in the Transport Bill, presently before Parliament (see Chapter 17).

1.1.15 Appeals

There is a right of appeal from certain decisions of the Director or a Regulator with concurrent jurisdiction (s. 46 and s. 47(6)). Appeals are heard by an appeal tribunal of the Competition Commission, a new body created to replace the Monopolies and Mergers Commission ("MMC") (s. 45(3)). There are further rights of appeal to the Court of Appeal and House of Lords on points of law and level of penalties. In cases where an appeal tribunal sits in Scotland, appeals will be initially to the Court of Session and where it sits in Northern Ireland to the Northern Ireland Court of Appeal (see further Chapter 3, para. 3.5.2).

1.2 History

1.2.1 White Paper in 1989

For many years the RTPA (which consolidated legislation dating back to 1956) had been universally regarded as in need of reform. In 1988 the Government published a Green Paper, *Review of Restrictive Trade Practices Policy*, (Cm. 331, March 1988), followed by a White Paper, *Opening Markets: New Policy on Restrictive Trade Practices*, (Cm. 727, July 1989), which indicated that legislation to reform control of restrictive trade practices in the United Kingdom was imminent. In the event, no parliamentary time was found by successive Conservative administrations. It was the Labour Government, elected in 1997, which found time in their first full parliamentary session. The Competition Act 1998 in so far as it deals with anti-competitive agreements largely reflects the reforms originally proposed in the 1989 White Paper.

1.2.2 Further Consultation in March 1996

In March 1996 the Conservative Government published a Consultation Document, *Tackling Cartels and the Abuse of Market Power: Implementing the Government's Policy for Competition Law Reform* (DTI, March 1996 (URN 96/760)). This set out once again the underlying principles for reform and detailed proposals to implement the Government's policy to replace the RTPA with a prohibition of anti-competitive agreements.

1.2.3   1996 Draft Bill

The process was taken a stage further by the publication of a draft Bill in August 1996, which proposed the introduction of a prohibition of anti-competitive agreements. Although the 1996 draft Bill followed the broad framework of Article 81, the prohibition was intended to be narrower, focusing on agreements which were likely to have a detrimental effect on the economy and which had, or were likely to have, a "significant" effect on competition. This draft Bill formed the basis on which the Act was developed.

1.3   What it Means For Business

1.3.1   Crackdown on Cartelistic Behaviour

The thrust of the legislation and guidelines reflects its aim to stamp out true cartelistic behaviour, such as price fixing arrangements between competitors and bid-rigging. Strong investigative powers, harsh penalties and encouragement of "whistle blowers" are the prime tools to achieve this and the OFT is well resourced to carry out this task.

The level of penalties means that no businesses, even small ones, may ignore the legislation. All should be aware that participation in price fixing arrangements will be heavily penalised. At the time of writing, the OFT have indicated that they will shortly make their first announcement of success in stopping a cartel with the assistance of a whistle blower, who will benefit from immunity from fines.

All businesses would benefit from using the OFT's small guide *How your business can achieve compliance*. Those who have identified particular problem areas or have a "track record" of investigation under other competition legislation will require more specialised training. A programme aimed at achieving a shift in corporate culture in a business used to cartelistic practices requires major effort led by senior management.

1.3.2   Burdens on Business

Despite the abolition of the tedious registration requirements under the RTPA, the Competition Act 1998 seems likely to result in considerably heavier compliance costs. Government estimates range from a reduction of £2.7 million to an increase of £1.2 million per annum in United Kingdom recurring competition law compliance costs. The Confederation of British Industry ("CBI") thought this certainly underestimated the true cost, while the opposition in the House of Commons claimed the true compliance cost could be £1 billion (*Hansard*, (Standing Committee G) col. 60 (May 21, 1998)).

The small number of notifications since the Act came into force indicate the range of exclusions and exemptions (as well as the Director's statement on appreciability) has been successful in persuading business that there is no need for a high level of individual notifications. As decisions come out, however, some companies will recognise a significant number of agreements requiring individual exemptions. These companies may bear very heavy burdens particularly if their competitors, suppliers, or customers make tactical use of the complaints procedure as a business strategy.

"Competition defences" can give substantial leverage to defendants in contractual disputes, even in what were previously straightforward debt collection exercises (*e.g. Oakdale (Richmond) Ltd v. NatWest Bank plc*, [1997] Eu. L.R. 27, in which allegations were made that a standard form mortgage was unenforceable for breach of Article 81). The long running saga of litigation between publicans and breweries in relation to individual leases and the application of the detailed block exemption for beer exclusive purchase agreements illustrates the potential costs well. The cases run from *Inntrepreneur Estates v. Mason* [1993] 2 C.M.L.R. 293, [1993] 45 EG 130, right up to 1999, when the Court of Appeal made a reference to the European Court of Justice in *Crehan v. Courage Ltd* [1999] E.C.C. 455–530 and [2000] O.J. C47/26 (for the preliminary reference) which seems likely to prolong the saga for at least another two years.

The extent to which the prohibition will introduce additional contractual uncertainties into English, Scottish and Northern Irish law will depend upon the efficiency of administration by the Director and Regulators with concurrent jurisdiction, as well as the ability of the courts to develop effective procedures for detecting and dealing swiftly with purely tactical competition defences.

1.3.3 Dangers of Multiple Regulation

There are some procedures to limit multiple regulation under the Act by the Director and other United Kingdom Regulators with concurrent jurisdiction in the arrangements they adopt for co-ordinating their operations under the Competition Act 1998. However, the Director and utility Regulators retain the ability to use the complex monopoly provisions of the FTA to investigate parallel behaviour by a number of businesses together having a market share in excess of 25 per cent. The Government also intends to limit the use of the scale (individual market share over 25 per cent) monopoly provisions of the FTA to cases where the Director has found breaches of the Act and requires consideration of a structural remedy, except in relation to the regulated utilities where use of these powers independently is considered necessary (See OFT Guideline, *The Major Provisions*, OFT 400, March 1999, para. 3.5). In addition, there are currently separate licence provisions (*e.g.* the predatory pricing condition in electricity licences) and other regulators with separate competition functions (*e.g.* ITC, CAA and the E.C. Commission). This means that businesses may be exposed to re-regulation of the same matters.

The OFT's statement (OFT 400, Supra) that "it is not intended that the prohibitions in the Competition Act and the retained complex monopoly and scale monopoly provisions in the Fair Trading Act should be used in parallel to investigate the same matters" seems likely in practice to be strained. In part this is because the FTA powers of investigation prior to a monopoly reference to the Competition Commission (FTA s. 44 amended by the Competition Act 1998 s. 66) could be used to look for evidence of breach of the Competition Act where the OFT would not have sufficient evidence of infringement of the Competition Act to use its investigative powers under that Act. Also a monopoly investigation before the Competition Commission may uncover breaches of the Competition Act and, unless the terms of reference to the Competition Commission are then altered, parallel proceedings seem inevitable.

No other business community in the world has such complex and multiplicitous regulation in the field of competition law.

1.3.4 Benefits for Business and the Public

The principal benefit for established businesses is the similarity of this legislation to Article 81 and to the laws for controlling anti-competitive agreements in many other countries, both within and outside the European Community, which have modelled their laws on Article 81. Business is also relieved of the tedious formalities of the RTPA, but also of its relative certainties. The anticipated benefits for the United Kingdom and ultimately for consumers, are discussed in 1.3.6 below.

1.3.5   Benefits for Complainants

Complainants who may be able (as in the United States) to use the complaining process as part of the competitive process against their leading competitor(s) will have a formidable battery of regulatory media. A number of utilities Regulators will have concurrent powers with the Director. In some circumstances, complainants will be able to seek review by an appeal tribunal of the Competition Commission of a refusal by the Director or a Regulator to change a decision with which they are dissatisfied. A decision of the Competition Commission may then be reviewed by an appellate court and the House of Lords on points of law. In addition there is a range of other regulatory mechanisms that may apply concurrently, including complaint to the E.C. Commission, private actions in the United Kingdom courts, the complex monopoly and (in limited circumstances) the scale monopoly jurisdictions under the FTA.

1.3.6   Policy Aims

The overall policy aim of the Act is summed up by the statement of Margaret Beckett (the then Secretary of State for Trade and Industry) at the time the Bill was published for consultation in August 1997:

> "Present competition law is not working well. Its reform is long overdue . . . Consumers need a better deal, we need to prevent and remedy anti-competitive behaviour more effectively. We also need to do so efficiently, avoiding placing unnecessary burdens on business." (Foreword to the draft Bill published in August 1997).

The new Act will provide a welcome new deterrent and remedy against horizontal cartels, which, other than in the most exceptional cases, do serious harm to the interests of business and consumers. The weak investigation powers and limited sanctions of the RTPA have provided no real deterrent and only limited remedies against these harmful agreements.

The other benefits of more independent, fairer and more transparent competition will be difficult to judge and are intangible in nature. The McKinsey report *Driving Productivity and Growth in the United Kingdom Economy,* October 1, 1998 advocates an ever more aggressive competition policy, as promoting efficiency, while citing "red tape" as a drag on efficiency. Whilst the benefits of the new legislation for tackling cartels are clear, the red tape created by the extended application of competition policy in the field of, for example, innovative joint ventures and research and development agreements seems to be ignored. The rigid application of competition theory to new businesses on the basis of the identity of proposed participants appears to be a particular feature of European regulation, as opposed to that of the United States, and is to be followed in the United Kingdom. A more aggressive competition policy that focuses on these targets will bring more, not less, red tape and is unlikely to realise the benefits envisaged by McKinsey.

Chapter 2

The United Kingdom's Version of Article 82

2.1 The New Law
2.2 History
2.3 What The Reform Means for Business

2.1 The New Law

2.1.1 Aim of Reform

The aim of the reform contained in Chapter II of the Competition Act 1998 is to introduce a new prohibition based closely on Article 82 (formerly Article 86) of the E.C. Treaty, which is aimed at anti-competitive behaviour by dominant firms. It addresses conduct which affects trade within the United Kingdom and which amounts to the abuse of a dominant position held by one or more undertakings within the United Kingdom (either as a whole, or in a distinct local or regional market). The prohibition is set out in full in section 18 of the Competition Act. Any behaviour which infringes the Chapter II Prohibition will be unlawful and subject to penalties.

The Director General of Fair Trading ("Director") with his staff at the Office of Fair Trading ("OFT") will investigate suspected infringements of the prohibition, either after receiving a complaint or on his own initiative and has powers to obtain information and to halt alleged anti-competitive behaviour. Breach of the prohibition will be assessed on competition grounds. There are very limited exclusions from the Chapter II prohibition, one such exclusion being mergers, which continue to be regulated either under the Fair Trading Act 1973 ("FTA") or the E.C. Merger Regulation (see Chapter 12). A *de minimis* provision for conduct of minor significance, providing some protection from fines, applies in favour of small businesses, as under the prohibition of anti-competitive agreements (See Chapter 10, para. 10.3.8 and Chapter 14, para. 14.2.3).

Changes proposed in September 2000 by the E.C. Commission in the administration of E.C. competition law would give the Director power to apply Article 82 directly, but would exclude the application of the Chapter II Prohibition in cases which affect trade between Member States. The proposals would allow the application of United Kingdom procedure and penalties (see Chapter 17 at 17.7).

2.1.2 Procedure

The Director's decisions about whether or not the prohibition has been breached and the penalties to be imposed will be made public in the form of fully reasoned decisions. In support of his regulatory functions the Director will have extensive powers of investigation and the power to impose interim measures (see Chapter 9). As with Article 82, it is possible to obtain a decision that the prohibition does not apply (negative clearance), but there are no exemptions. It is also possible to obtain guidance (ss. 20–22). The Director has a duty to issue general advice by way of guidelines on how he intends to apply the prohibition in practice. As with the United Kingdom's version of Article 81, several utility sector regulators have concurrent jurisdiction with the Director. There is a right of appeal from decisions of the Director or a sector Regulator to the Competition Commission and thence to the Court of Appeal and the House of Lords on points of law and level of penalty.

2.1.3   Penalties

Financial penalties may be imposed by the Director of up to 10 per cent of United Kingdom turnover for a period equal to the length of the infringement, but limited to the turnover for the three business years preceding the date on which the infringement ended (see The Competition Act 1998 (Determination of Turnover for Penalties) Order 2000 (S.I. 2000 No. 309)). Immunity from fines is given to smaller businesses (see 2.3.5 below). The Director also has the ability to require conduct in breach of the prohibition to be stopped or changed so that it no longer infringes and to take interim measures pending his decision. It is intended that third parties will have the right to claim damages but the legislation does not specifically provide for this (see Chapter 10 at 10.2 and Chapter 14 at 14.1).

2.1.4   Retention of Existing Monopoly Investigations Regime

The provisions of the Competition Act 1980 dealing with anti-competitive practices were repealed when the 1998 Act came into force. The complex monopoly provisions of the FTA were retained as it was felt that the two prohibitions alone would not be able to deal with some of the competition problems which arise from the structure and operation of markets, where there are a small number of strong players (so called oligopolistic markets). The scale monopoly provisions, which apply where a single business has a market share of over 25 per cent, were also retained, but are to be limited in application, as explained at 2.1.5 below. See Livingston, *Competition Law and Practice* (Sweet and Maxwell, 1995) Chapter 20 for a detailed discussion of the monopolies regime.

2.1.5   Application of Monopolies Regime

In cases where the complex monopoly provisions of the FTA apply, FTA investigations could lead to structural remedies, such as divestment, which could reduce the market power of two or three leading market players with joint dominance. Use of the complex monopoly provisions could also allow behavioural remedies across a larger number of market participants with similar practices, for example, the three statutory instruments following the MMC's report, *Credit Card Services* (1989) Cm. 718.

The scale monopoly provisions of the FTA are largely replaced by the prohibition of abuse of a dominant position. The Department of Trade and Industry ("DTI") proposes, except in the case of regulated utilities, to limit scale monopoly investigations to cases where a breach of the prohibition has already been proven, so as to attack the market position itself. However, this limitation of FTA powers will be achieved not by amendment but rather by informal agreement between the Secretary of State and the Director, which may easily be departed from on a case by case basis.

The risks of multiple regulation under FTA and the Competition Act 1998 are discussed in Chapter 1, para. 1.3.3.

2.2 History

2.2.1 Change of Policy

The adoption of the prohibition in respect of abuse of a dominant position in the Competition Act 1998 represents the major change by the new Labour administration from the policy of the previous Conservative Government (see 2.2.2 below). The European Commission had been encouraging the adoption of an Article 82 look-alike for some time.

2.2.2 Green Paper 1992

In November 1992, the Government published a Green Paper: *Abuse of Market Power: A Consultative Document on Possible Legislative Options* (Cm. 2100). This proposed three options in respect of the Competition Act 1980 (which dealt with unilateral anti-competitive practices by an investigative process without provision for penalties) and the monopolies provisions of the FTA:

(1) strengthening of existing legislation;

(2) a prohibition system similar to that under Article 82, but covering practices by businesses with much lower levels of market power than "dominance";

(3) the operation of some form of the two systems side by side, probably involving the maintenance of the system of monopolies investigations but replacing the Competition Act 1980 with a prohibition of anti-competitive practices.

At that time the Conservative Government abandoned options (2) and (3). The consultation process had raised a number of concerns about the imposition of a wide-ranging prohibition system. The risk that the uncertainties created could inhibit rather than strengthen competition, as well as the compliance cost for companies, made options (2) and (3) unattractive. The Competition Act 1998, however, in effect adopts option (3).

2.2.3 Further Consultation in March 1996

Following the deregulation initiative, the Government published in March 1996 a Consultation Document: *Tackling Cartels and the Abuse of Market Power*, (URN 96/760) which again proposed to strengthen the powers of the Director to deal with abuse of market power under the FTA and the Competition Act 1980. The consultation document stated that the Government remained of the view that no compelling case had been made that a prohibition of abuse of market power would bring benefits for the economy at large. In assessing the balance of advantage and disadvantage its preference for a strengthened existing system over a prohibition was a fine judgement.

The consultation in 1996 did not reach consensus as to the best approach by controlling the abuse of market power. Views were divided between those who wanted to see:

(1) a full Article 82 style prohibition of abuse of a dominant position;

(2) a more limited prohibition of serious abuse;

(3)   a strengthening of the existing system under the FTA and the Competi-
       tion Act 1980 by introducing greater powers of investigation and powers
       to impose interim measures.

2.2.4   Draft Bill of August 1996

As a result of the consultation, the Government remained concerned that the risks
of inhibiting genuinely competitive behaviour might outweigh the potential benefits
of the greater deterrence that a prohibition system might bring.

The Government decided to maintain the system for dealing with unilateral practices on a case-by-case basis without introducing a general prohibition and to
proceed to strengthen existing legislation on abuse of market power. The Draft Bill
of August 1996 therefore contained clauses which proposed to strengthen the FTA
and the Competition Act 1980 by introducing stronger investigatory powers,
interim measures and greater coverage of property rights. Apart from interim
measures these proposals survived and were enacted in the Competition Act 1998
sections 66, 67 and 68.

The DTI continued to promote further debate on the prohibition-based
approach and sought views on the case for a more limited, tightly defined prohibition. This debate was superseded by the change of Government and the final adoption of the United Kingdom's version of Article 82 in section 18 of the Competition
Act 1998.

2.3   What the Reform Means for Business

2.3.1   High Level of Regulation

The new prohibition combined with the retention of the monopoly investigation powers under the FTA make the United Kingdom one of the most regulated economies,
in terms of competition law, in the world. This is coupled with the burden of multiple regulation and risk of re-regulation of the same issues not only under the Competition Act 1998, the FTA and Articles 81 and 82, but also, for a number of
businesses, under additional or concurrent powers of sector Regulators. While such a
regime may be good news for the legal profession and for economic advisers, as well
as being enjoyable for Regulators, the cost to both the public purse and to the country's more successful businesses, especially those subject to several United Kingdom
Regulators, is substantial.

2.3.2   Importance of Economic Analysis and its Effects

As regards the specific elements of the United Kingdom's version of Article 82, it
is important to note that the analysis of what constitutes a dominant position is
largely an economic one in which the definition of the relevant product or service
market is key. It involves consideration of a large number of complex facts, some of
which will be disputed or at least open to differing assessments. It is a subject
where, particularly for those without training in economics, first impressions and
prejudices are difficult to set aside. Cases will often be promoted by complainants,
who will urge upon the Director the injustice and oppression, real or otherwise,
they feel that they are suffering. In many cases complainants will rouse a genuine
sympathy in the officials with whom they deal, whether or not their difficulties are
correctly attributed to the behaviour of the allegedly dominant undertaking.

2.3.3 Establishing Dominance

The Director has announced a policy intention, based on E.C. practice, to use a 40 percent individual market share threshold above which a business may have dominance, although it will be a matter of fact and degree in every case: OFT Guideline, *The Chapter II Prohibition*, OFT 402, March 1999, para. 3.13.

2.3.4 Compliance — Small Businesses

The OFT has embarked on an extensive training programme in both economics and relevant law, which should ensure that officials are well equipped to work with these disciplines and to recognise when they might be falling into the "subjectivity" trap.

A company who only has a strong market position in a geographically small area of the United Kingdom (say a bus company serving a small local town) will have to review carefully whether any business decision, such as a price change, may expose it to a fine for breach of the new prohibition. There is no requirement that the dominant market position be in a "substantial" part of the United Kingdom This appears tougher than Article 82, which only applies if the dominant market position is in a substantial part of the common market, a term which has been interpreted by the ECJ as involving a large geographic area with distinct economic characteristics, *i.e.* where "the objective conditions of competition are the same for all traders" (*United Brands v. Commission* (Case 27/76) [1978] E.C.R. 207, [1978] 1 C.M.L.R. 429). The House of Lords, in a competition context (the merger provisions of the FTA) has given the word "substantial" a very different meaning as no more than an area in respect of which there is a sufficient public interest in exercising the jurisdiction (see *South Yorkshire Transport Ltd v. MMC* [1993] 1 W.L.R. 23, [1993] 1 All E.R. 289 at 292(g)).

The omission of the word "substantial" allows the prohibition to apply in parts of the United Kingdom which do not have the characteristics of a separate economic market and which are even below the threshold set by the House of Lords in the South Yorkshire case. It is to be expected, however, that the Director will maintain a sense of proportion when dealing with businesses with high market shares in a very restricted locality, even where they do not benefit from the exclusion from fines discussed in 2.3.5.

2.3.5 Conduct of Minor Significance

The Competition Act 1998 (s. 40(3)) provides for an undertaking responsible for conduct of minor significance to be excluded from the risk of fines. The meaning of "conduct of minor significance" was left to be defined by the Secretary of State by reference to turnover or market share of the perpetrator.

The Competition Act 1998 (Small Agreements and Conduct of Minor Significance) Regulations 2000 (S.I. 2000 No. 262) defines as conduct of minor significance for the purposes of section 40, conduct by an undertaking whose "applicable turnover" in the business year ending in the calendar year preceding the one during which the infringement occurred does not exceed £50 million (see reg. 4). This "applicable turnover" is the worldwide turnover (which reflects an undertaking's real economic strength and ability to get appropriate advice). As a result, the full force of the law will not generally fall on small businesses, whether operating in local or national markets. Immunity may be withdrawn, but not with retrospective effect.

2.3.6 Compliance: Guiding Principle

If a business recognises, with the benefit of legal and economic advice, that it is at risk of being considered dominant, then it should recognise the risks that it runs if it does not exercise the care in its business conduct that goes with the responsibility of dominance. Even where it does exercise such care, it may be called to justify its conduct to one or more Regulators or a court. Such businesses, large or small, are in particular need of strong internal compliance programmes. The OFT's small guide *How your business can achieve compliance* is a useful starting point, but businesses which are likely to be judged dominant require additional specialist training, since they must learn to monitor routine commercial behaviour, including behaviour which, in a business without market power, would be regarded as beneficial competitive behaviour, but which may be regarded as abusive when carried out by a dominant business.

Chapter 3

Role of the Principal Regulators

3.1 Overview
3.2 The Director General of Fair Trading
3.3 The Secretary of State
3.4 The Competition Commission
3.5 The Role of the Courts

3.1 Overview

3.1.1 The Director

The Director General of Fair Trading ("Director") assisted by his staff at the Office of Fair Trading ("OFT"), is the main enforcement body under the Competition Act 1998 for the prohibition against anti-competitive agreements, the "Chapter I Prohibition", and the prohibition against abuse of a dominant position, the "Chapter II Prohibition". Further reform relating to the constitution of the OFT is in contemplation (see Chapter 17 at 17.1).

3.1.2 The Utility Regulators

Certain of the utility Regulators are given concurrent jurisdiction under the Competition Act 1998 with that of the Director in their respective sectors. The telecommunications, gas and electricity, water and rail Regulators have been given concurrent powers (see Chapter 4).

3.1.3 The Secretary of State

The role of the Secretary of State for Trade and Industry is largely legislative, with limited powers to create exclusions from the prohibitions and to resolve jurisdictional disputes among the Director and the sector Regulators. The Secretary of State does not have the final say, as he currently does in relation to monopolies and mergers.

3.1.4 The Competition Commission

A new body, the Competition Commission, replaces the Monopolies and Mergers Commission (the "MMC") and is given two distinct and separate functions. First, the Competition Commission, as an appeals tribunal, will hear appeals against the decisions of the Director and, second, it will carry on the previous activities of the MMC as a reporting body under the Fair Trading Act 1973 ("FTA") in respect of monopolies and mergers and under the utilities legislation.

Further reform affecting the monopolies and mergers regime is in contemplation (see Chapter 17 at 17.6).

3.1.5   The Courts

Decisions of the Competition Commission as an appeal tribunal under the Competition Act 1998 are open to further appeal on points of law and level of penalties to the Court of Appeal and the House of Lords. The courts will also deal with enforcement in any case where a direction of the Director is breached or a penalty is not paid.

The courts may also have the power to judicially review certain decisions of the Director and of the Competition Commission of a procedural nature not covered by the appeal process.

Finally, it was the intention of the legislators that the courts should deal with civil claims arising from breach of the prohibitions. Certainly they will deal with disputes about the enforceability of contractual provisions, but the exact basis on which the Courts would deal with third party claims for damages or injunctive relief is unclear.

3.2   The Director General of Fair Trading

3.2.1   Role and Position of the Director

The role of the Director under the Competition Act 1998 is to enforce the prohibitions in Chapters I and II and to facilitate this by laying down procedural rules and issuing guidelines. Notification may be made to the Director for either guidance (which is normally confidential) or a decision in respect of the prohibitions. Appeals against the Director's decisions can be made to the Competition Commission and then to the Court of Appeal and House of Lords on points of law and level of penalties by parties to affected agreements and, in limited circumstances, by third parties (ss. 46–49). The general structure of the Director's powers reflects the fact that the prohibition and grounds for exemption are closely modelled on Article 81 of the E.C. Treaty. Thus, the Director may rule that the prohibition does not apply (negative clearance), give exemptions and also give more informal indications of his views.

The Director heads the OFT, which is a non-ministerial government department staffed by civil servants (FTA s. 1 and Sched. 1). The Director has power to delegate his statutory functions, other than the making of a statutory instrument (FTA Sched. 1, para. 7). The Director's sponsoring department is the Department of Trade and Industry ("DTI"). The Director also has functions under the FTA in relation to monopolies and mergers and a number of consumer related functions (for example, under the Consumer Credit Act 1974 and the Unfair Terms in Consumer Contracts Regulations 1999 (S.I. 1999 No. 2083)) which are outside the scope of this book. Proposals for changes in the status of the OFT which would end the individual position of the Director are discussed in Chapter 17 at 17.1.

3.2.2   Decisions by the Director

The Director may take a decision:

(a)   that either or both of the Chapter I and the Chapter II Prohibitions do(es) not apply;

(b)   in the case of an agreement, that it is exempt from the Chapter I Prohibition;

(c)   that an agreement infringes the Chapter I Prohibition;

(d)   that conduct infringes the Chapter II Prohibition.

The Director also has the power to bring certain agreements and conduct which benefit from exclusions from the application of one or both prohibition back within the scope of the prohibitions by a process called "clawback" (see Chapter 7 at 7.1). Once clawed back, the Director may take one of the decisions described above.

Decision that Prohibitions do not Apply

(a)   If a party to an agreement applies to the Director for it to be examined under section 14 or if a business that fears it is dominant applies to have its conduct reviewed under section 22, the Director may make a decision that the relevant agreement or conduct falls outside the prohibitions. This is equivalent to a negative clearance decision by the E.C. Commission under Regulation 17/62. Power to consider notifications for guidance or a decision in respect of excluded agreements (where the Director is considering withdrawal of the exclusion) and those benefiting from a transitional period has been added by the Competition Act 1998 (Notification of Excluded Agreements and Appealable Decisions) Regulations 2000 (S.I. 2000 No. 263) (the "Excluded Agreements Order"). Its purpose is to allow the parties to obtain a ruling where an exclusion may cease to apply: this is particularly beneficial where an agreement may benefit from a short-term transitional period of exclusion (see Chapter 16) and the parties may need to know where they stand when the exclusion expires. There would rarely be any benefit in delaying consideration until the exclusion runs out, either from a commercial or a regulatory perspective.

Exemption from Chapter I Prohibition

(b)   The Director is also empowered to make a decision granting an individual exemption from the Chapter I Prohibition in respect of a particular agreement, if two conditions are met. First, a party to the agreement must notify the Director of the agreement and include in the application for a decision a request for the agreement to be given an individual exemption (ss. 4 and 14). Second, the agreement must satisfy the section 9 criteria, namely, that the agreement improves production or distribution or promotes technical or economic progress whilst sharing resulting benefits with consumers, but does not impose unnecessary restrictions on the undertakings or enable them to significantly eliminate competition in respect of the relevant products. These exemption criteria are closely modelled on Article 81(3) and E.C. jurisprudence will apply in the interpretation of the domestic criteria (see Chapter 5). The Director is able to attach conditions or obligations to any grant of an individual exemption and may provide that the exemption has effect for a limited period. The Director may also take such a decision prospectively when considering an agreement which benefits from an exclusion and which he has power to consider under the Excluded Agreements Order.

Infringement Decisions

(c) and (d)

> When taking a decision that an agreement infringes the Chapter I Prohibition or that conduct infringes the Chapter II Prohibition, it is the role of the Director to give such directions "as he considers appropriate" to bring the infringement to an end (ss. 32 and 33). Failure to comply with such directions may result in the Director applying to the court for an order (s. 34). A suggested amendment to change the words "as he considers appropriate" to "as are requisite" was resisted in the Report stage in the House of Lords (see *Hansard*, H.L., Vol. 586, No. 107. col. 349 (February 19, 1998)) on the basis that the Director is not expected to give directions that exceed what is necessary: "if we are not to place some faith in [the Director's] judgement, we should not be proposing to give him the powers which the [Act] proposes to give to him" (Lord Simon of Highbury). The Director may also impose financial penalties (see 3.2.7 below).

Interim Measures Decisions

The Director also has the power to take interim measures, by giving directions before the relevant investigation has been completed (s. 35), where he has a reasonable suspicion that one of the prohibitions has been infringed and where it is necessary to act as a matter of urgency to prevent serious irreparable damage to a person or to protect the public interest.

3.2.3   Guidance on Individual Agreements or Conduct

The Director may give formal guidance on an application under section 13 (Chapter I Prohibition) or section 21 (Chapter II Prohibition) and may also (without any statutory basis) give guidance more informally. While formal guidance limits the ability of the Director to take further action, it does not provide protection against third party challenges. If guidance indicates that an exemption is needed, it will only serve to establish that the agreement is wholly or partially unenforceable. In the event of a dispute arising, one of the parties to an agreement may need to ask the Director to take a decision on the matter.

3.2.4   Block Exemptions

If the Director considers that a certain category of agreements are likely to meet the section 9 criteria, the Director may recommend to the Secretary of State that a block exemption order is made, specifying that the particular category is exempt from the Chapter I Prohibition (s. 6(1)). In certain circumstances, the Director may cancel a block exemption in respect of a particular agreement. No exemptions are available in relation to the Chapter II Prohibition. Block exemptions are dealt with in further detail in Chapter 8. At the time of writing, one block exemption has been proposed in respect of public transport ticketing schemes (Consultation Document, *Block Exemption Order* July 2000).

3.2.5   Parallel Exemptions

An agreement is exempt from the Chapter I Prohibition if it is exempt from the prohibition contained in Article 81(1) by virtue of a Regulation of the E.C.

Commission or the Council of Ministers providing for block exemptions; or because it has been granted individual exemption by the E.C. Commission, or through the operation of the opposition procedure set out in an E.C. block exemption (s. 10(1)). It will also be exempt if the agreement would fall within the scope of an E.C. block exemption but for the fact that it does not affect trade between Member States (s. 10(2)). Such exemptions are called parallel exemptions.

Under section 10(5), the Director may impose, vary, or remove conditions or obligations subject to which a parallel exemption is to have effect, or cancel the exemption, in accordance with the circumstances specified in rules made under section 51. Under these provisions the Director also has the power to require information from the parties to the agreement in question. The Competition Act 1998 (Director's rules) Order 2000 (S.I. 2000 No. 293) (the "Director's Rules"), Rule 21 deals with these matters. The application of section 10 would be affected by proposed reforms to the E.C. system discussed in Chapter 17 at 17.7.

3.2.6 Small Agreements and Conduct of Minor Significance

The Act was intended to give smaller businesses a good deal of protection from the risk of fines.

"Small agreements" are generally subject to the Chapter I Prohibition and "conduct of minor significance" to the Chapter II Prohibition. However, these agreements and conduct normally enjoy immunity from the financial penalties, which could be imposed by the Director (although they do not have immunity from voidness and third party actions). A "small agreement" is defined in section 39 and is one which falls within a category prescribed for the purposes of the section, but which is not a price-fixing agreement. Conduct of minor significance is defined in section 40. These definitions are expanded upon in The Competition Act 1998 (Small Agreements and Conduct of Minor Significance) Regulations 2000 (S.I. 2000 No. 262), which lay down turnover thresholds for the businesses involved which are to be used to identify qualifying agreements and conduct (see Chapter 10 at 10.3.8 and Chapter 14 at 14.2.3).

The Director has the power to withdraw the limited immunity for small agreements (s. 39(4)) and conduct of minor significance (s. 40(4)) if, after investigating, he considers that the agreement or conduct is likely to infringe the relevant prohibition.

3.2.7 Penalties

The Director may also impose financial penalties in respect of an intentional or negligent infringement of the prohibitions and it is his role to fix a penalty (up to 10 per cent of United Kingdom turnover of the undertaking concerned over a period of up to 3 years, discussed at Chapter 10, para. 10.3.5) and to recover unpaid penalties as civil debts (ss. 36–39). The calculation of the turnover to be taken into account is set by the Secretary of State by statutory instrument (see 3.3.6 below). The Director is also responsible for publishing guidance in respect of the appropriate amount of penalties, subject to the approval of the Secretary of State (s. 38).

The guidance on penalties was published shortly before the Act came into force: *Director General of Fair Trading's Guidance as to the Appropriate Amount of a Penalty*, OFT 423, February 2000. When setting the amount of a penalty, the Director must have regard to this guidance, which includes a statement of the Director's policy of giving immunity to early "whistleblowers" in relation to cartels (see Chapter 10, 10.3.7). When setting the amount of a penalty in relation to an agreement or conduct, the Director, and also an appeal tribunal or the appropriate court, must take into account penalties or fines already imposed by the E.C. Commission, or by an authority in another Member State of the European Community in relation to the same agreement or conduct (s. 38(9)).

3.2.8 Investigations

It is the Director's role to conduct an investigation if there are reasonable grounds for suspecting an infringement of either the Chapter I Prohibition or the Chapter II Prohibition (s. 25). For the purpose of such investigations, the Director is given the power to require any person to provide specified documents and/or specified information. Further, any officer, authorised by the Director to do so, may enter premises (in appropriate circumstances), both with and without a warrant (ss. 26 to 30). The Director's officers have extensive powers to carry out "dawn raids", to require production of documents, to require on-the-spot explanations of documents and to take copies of documents (see Chapter 9 at 9.9).

3.2.9 Rules of Procedure

Section 51 provides for the Director to make rules in respect of procedure and other matters to facilitate the carrying into effect of Part I of the Act, which deals with the Chapter I and the Chapter II Prohibitions and their enforcement. Sched. 9 specifies in more detail the ambit of the rules to be made by the Director, but it is expressly provided that the Schedule is not intended to restrict the powers of the Director under section 51.

When making rules (including new rules by way of variation), the Director must consult with such persons as he considers appropriate (s. 51(3)), which must include the appropriate Regulator where the proposed rules relate to a matter in respect of which that Regulator exercises concurrent jurisdiction (s. 51(4) and see Chapter 4). The current rules are contained in the Director's Rules. The Director's Rules will be followed by the Director and any Regulator that exercises concurrent jurisdiction. The rules of the Director and any variations are also subject to the approval of the Secretary of State (see 3.3.5 below).

Schedule 5 provides for rules to be made by the Director in respect of the procedure for notification of agreements in accordance with section 51. Schedule 6 makes similar provisions in relation to notification of conduct under Chapter II. The Director has obligations under Scheds. 5 and 6 to follow the procedure specified in the rules and to arrange for the publication of applications for decisions and the decisions themselves, together with his reasons. The Director's Rules also provide for the payment of fees pursuant to section 53.

The nature of the procedural rules was discussed in the context of a debate in the House of Lords regarding the obligation on the Director to give notice to affected persons before making a decision (s. 31) and the enforcement of decisions (s. 31 to 35), (see *Hansard*, H.L., Vol. 586, No. 107, cols. 343–348 (February 19, 1998)). The debate concerned the balance between the need for procedural safeguards to appear on the face of the statute and the requirement that the primary legislation remain as flexible as possible. It was agreed that the benefit of procedural rules is to maintain such a balance: the rules provide the details which are not explicitly set out in the statute. The fact that the rules are themselves subject to Parliamentary scrutiny acts as a safeguard. It is clear that the overriding concern was to avoid unnecessarily limiting the powers of the Director in enforcing the prohibitions, or weakening the effectiveness of the Act by amending the words of the statute, where it is more appropriate to leave matters to rules and guidelines.

3.2.10 General Advice

Section 52 provides for the Director to prepare and publish general advice and information about the application and enforcement of the prohibitions. The Director is obliged to carry out a consultation process before finalising his advice and must include the utilities Regulators with concurrent jurisdiction in the process. The guidelines published by the OFT are issued in performance of this statutory obligation (see list at p. 1).

As regards guidance on penalties, see 3.2.7 above and Chapter 10, para. 10.3.5.

3.2.11 Confidential Information and the Public Interest

Provisions for restrictions on the disclosure of confidential information are set out in sections 55 and 56. Generally, confidential information cannot be disclosed unless consent has been obtained from the person from whom the information was obtained and, if different, the person to whom the information relates. However, there are a number of exceptions to this. Principally, disclosure is permitted for the purpose of facilitating the performance of various administrative functions of the Director and other Regulators (set out in Sched. 11), or the functions of the E.C. Commission, or to facilitate criminal proceedings, or for the purpose of civil proceedings under Part I of the Act.

In addition, in considering whether to disclose (*e.g.* in a published decision) any information acquired under or as a result of any provision of Part I of the Act, the Director must have regard to the need to exclude, as far as practicable, information which if published would, in his opinion, be contrary to the public interest. Also information the disclosure of which would, or might, in his opinion, significantly harm the legitimate business interests of the relevant undertaking or, in respect of information relating to the private affairs of an individual, significantly harm that individual's interests. The Director must also consider the extent to which such disclosure is necessary for the purposes for which it is proposed to be disclosed. Confidentiality is discussed further in Chapter 9, para. 9.2.7.

3.2.12 Exclusions: Power to Disapply

Schedule 1 provides for the exclusion of merger agreements, within the meaning of Part V of the FTA, from the Chapter I Prohibition. The Director is empowered to give directions that this exclusion does not apply to a particular agreement in certain circumstances (Sched. 1, para. 4).

Similar powers exist in relation to the exclusion for vertical agreements, land agreements and agreements relating to agricultural products (see Chapter 7).

The Director also has power to shorten transitional periods under Sched. 13 in certain circumstances (see Chapter 16, para. 16.5.2).

3.2.13 Liaison with Regulators with Concurrent Powers

The functions of the Director under Part I of the Act are to be exercised concurrently with certain utility Regulators (telecommunications, gas and electricity, water and rail). The Director's functions of co-ordination and ensuring consistency of approach in relation to these concurrent powers are described in Chapter 4 at 4.3.

3.2.14   Consistency with European Community Law

The Director also plays a role in securing the consistency of competition law applied within the United Kingdom with the treatment of corresponding questions arising in the European Community. Section 60 provides for the Director to act, so far as is compatible with the provisions of Part I, with a view to ensuring that there is no such inconsistency (see Chapter 5 at 5.3).

3.2.15   Investigations in Relation to Articles 81 and 82

Part II of the Act gives the Director additional powers of entry and investigation which will assist him when he is operating as the United Kingdom's competent authority in connection with E.C. competition cases. He will use these powers when assisting the E.C. Commission in carrying out its tasks under Council Regulation (EEC) No. 17/62 in obtaining evidence of infringements of Articles 81 and 82.

3.2.16   Monopoly and Merger Investigations: The FTA 1973

As explained in Chapter 15 below, the existing monopoly investigation regime under the FTA is retained. Part III of the Act strengthens the existing investigative powers of the Director in respect to these investigations (s. 66).

     The Director's powers in relation to the merger control regime to review and advise the Secretary of State in relation to mergers that qualify for investigation under the FTA are unchanged. There are, however, proposals for reform (summarised in Chapter 17 at 17.6).

3.3   The Secretary of State

3.3.1   General

The Secretary of State for Trade and Industry is responsible for competition matters. The role of the Secretary of State is largely legislative and he is also responsible for approving the exercise of many of the powers of the Director described above. The Secretary of State also has a significant role in connection with the establishment and membership of the Competition Commission.

3.3.2   Excluded Agreements and Conduct

Section 3 provides that the Chapter I prohibition does not apply where it is excluded as a result of Scheds. 1 to 4. Section 19 similarly provides that the Chapter II Prohibition does not apply in any case excluded by, or as a result of, Scheds. 1 or 3.

     The Secretary of State is empowered by order to amend Sched. 1 by adding or removing exclusions or varying their scope. He may also in more limited respects amend Sched. 3. Sched. 1 provides for exclusions of mergers and concentrations. Sched. 3 provides for a number of more general exclusions from the prohibition. The Secretary of State is also given various powers under the schedules themselves. Under Sched. 3, it is the role of the Secretary of State to exclude certain agreements and conduct if he is satisfied that it will be appropriate for the relevant prohibition not to apply in order to avoid a conflict with an international obligation of the United Kingdom Further, the Secretary of State is empowered to exclude a particular agreement or conduct or any agreement or conduct of a particular description if he is satisfied that there are "exceptional and compelling reasons of public policy" why the prohibition ought not to apply (Sched. 3, para. 7).

The Secretary of State also has a duty to maintain a list of rules which will constitute "designated professional rules" for the purposes of Sched. 4 which provides for the exclusion of such rules from the Chapter I Prohibition (Sched. 4, para. 2).

Exclusions are discussed in greater detail in Chapters 7 and 12.

3.3.3 Block Exemption Orders

The Secretary of State may make a block exemption order from the Chapter I Prohibition under section 6(2), following a recommendation from the Director that agreements falling within a particular category are likely to be agreements to which section 9 applies (see 3.2.4 and Chapter 8). The Secretary of State may modify recommendations from the Director but must inform the Director and take into account any of his comments (s. 8(2)). The power to vary or revoke a block exemption order is given to the Secretary of State with or without a recommendation from the Director but, in the case where the Secretary of State has acted on his own initiative, he must inform the Director and take into account any comments made by him (s. 8(5)).

Block exemptions are discussed in more detail in Chapter 8 at 8.3. At the time of writing only one block exemption has been put out for consultation. This relates to public transport ticketing schemes.

3.3.4 Article 84 E.C. Treaty

The Secretary of State is empowered under Section 11 to grant exemptions from the Chapter I Prohibition to certain agreements by means of regulations (section 11 exemptions).

A section 11 exemption may be granted to any of the very small number of agreements which fall within the situation provided for in Article 84 (formerly Article 88) E.C. Treaty. Article 84 relates to those agreements which are not covered by Council Regulations giving the E.C. Commission power to enforce Article 81 (and Article 82); it provides for the relevant Member States to have a residual jurisdiction to apply Article 81 to such agreements directly. In the United Kingdom these agreements are dealt with under the EC Competition Law (Articles 88 and 89) Enforcement Regulations 1996 (S.I. 1996 No. 2199). These regulations were made at a time when a proposed joint operation agreement between British Airways and American Airlines on trans-Atlantic routes required investigation because it fell within such a lacuna. The section 11 exemption therefore complements the parallel exemptions granted to agreements under section 10.

3.3.5 Approval of Director's Rules

The rules made by the Director about procedural and other matters in connection with the carrying into effect of the provisions of Part I of the Act must be approved by an order made by the Secretary of State before they are to come into operation (s. 51(6)). The Secretary of State may modify the rules as he considers appropriate, although he must inform the Director of any proposed modifications and take into account any comments of the Director. After consulting with the Director, the Secretary of State may also vary or revoke any rules made under section 51. The Secretary of State may also direct the Director to make rules about a particular matter.

3.3.6 Levels of Penalties

As explained in para. 3.2.7 above, it is the role of the Director to prepare and publish guidance as to the appropriate amount of any penalty under Part I of the Act (s. 38).

However, no such guidance is to be published without the approval of the Secretary of State, who must also be consulted by the Director in respect of how the guidance is published. Following the Secretary of State's approval, the Director issued guidance shortly before the Act came into force (see 3.2.7 above and Chapter 10, para. 10.3.5).

Section 36(8) provides that no penalty fixed by the Director may exceed 10 per cent of the turnover of the relevant undertaking, but the extent of the turnover and the period for which it is to be calculated is not specified in the Act. The definition of turnover is set out in an order made by the Secretary of State (The Competition Act 1998 (Determination of Turnover for Penalties) Order 2000 (S.I. 2000 No. 309)), which permits fines of up to 10 per cent of United Kingdom turnover over a period of up to three years (see discussion at Chapter 10, para. 10.3.1).

3.3.7   Establishment of the Competition Commission

The Secretary of State has a significant role to play in respect of the membership of the Competition Commission and the funds provided for it to perform its functions. These details are set out in Sched. 7 and are explained more fully below at 3.4.

The Secretary of State has the power to make rules with respect to appeals and appeal tribunals, after consulting with the President of the Competition Commission Appeal Tribunals (s. 48(2)). Part II of Sched. 8 details the scope of such rules, but it is expressly stated in section 48(4) that the detailed provisions in the Schedule are not to be taken as restricting the powers of the Secretary of State. These rules are to be found in the *Competition Commission Appeal Tribunal Rules 2000* (S.I. 2000 No. 261).

3.3.8   Confidentiality and the Public Interest

As for the Director (see above, at 3.2.11), in deciding whether to disclose any information acquired, the Secretary of State must have regard to the need to exclude, so far as is practicable, information which if disclosed would, in his opinion, either be contrary to the public interest, or significantly harm the legitimate business interests of a relevant undertaking or, where such information relates to the private affairs of an individual, significantly harm his interests (s. 56). The Secretary of State must also consider whether such disclosure is necessary for the purposes for which it is proposed to be disclosed.

3.3.9   Investigations at Crown Premises

It is the responsibility of the Secretary of State to consider, in the interests of national security (s. 73(8)), whether powers of entry conferred under the provisions relating to investigations should be exercisable in relation to premises held or used by or on behalf of the Crown. If he considers that the powers should not be used as regards any premises, he will issue a certificate which specifies the excluded premises.

3.3.10   Resolution of Disputes between Regulators with Concurrent Powers

The Secretary of State has reserved to himself the power to settle jurisdictional squabbles between the Director and the many Regulators with concurrent powers by Regulation 6 of the Competition Act 1998 (Concurrency) Regulations 2000 (S.I. 2000 No. 260) (see further Chapter 4).

3.3.11 General Powers

Section 75 confers upon the Secretary of State the power to make by order such incidental, consequential, transitional or supplemental provisions as he thinks necessary or expedient for the general or particular purposes of the Act, in consequence of any of its provisions, or for giving full effect to it. The Competition Act 1998 (Transitional, Consequential and Supplemental Provisions) Order 2000 (S.I. 2000 No. 311) and The Competition Act 1998 (Competition Commission) Transitional, Consequential and Supplemental Provisions Order 1999 (S.I. 1999 No. 506) rely in part on section 75, *e.g.* in relation to savings from repeals in S.I. 2000 No. 311, which are authorised by section 75(2)(b).

3.4 The Competition Commission

3.4.1 General

The Act provides for a Competition Commission to be established, to hear appeals from decisions related to the application of the prohibitions and in order to carry out the functions of the dissolved MMC. The appellate function is organised so that each individual appeal tribunal is drawn from a panel of members from a mix of backgrounds, headed by a person with legal training, so as to deal effectively with the cases before it. Importantly, an appeal lies against decisions of the Director, not only on points of law, but in respect of the substance of the decisions and on any penalties imposed. Each appeal tribunal is empowered to make any decisions the Director himself could have made. Detailed rules provide for the establishment and constitution of the Commission, in respect of which the Secretary of State has a significant role to play.

3.4.2 Establishment of the Competition Commission

The Competition Commission is established by section 45 as a statutory body corporate. All functions of the MMC, which is dissolved by section 45(3), are transferred to the Competition Commission. Schedule 7 makes further provisions about the structure and function of the Competition Commission. Section 45(3) was brought into force on April 1, 1999 by The Competition Act 1998 (Commencement No. 3) Order 1999 (S.I. 2000 No. 344) and transitional provisions are contained in The Competition Act 1998 (Competition Commission) Transitional Consequential and Supplemental Provisions Order 1999 (S.I. 1999 No. 506).

The Competition Commission has two distinct and separate functions: first, to hear appeals against decisions of the Director and, second, a reporting function, comprising those activities transferred from the MMC. The detailed rules regarding the latter functions of the Competition Commission are outside the scope of this book (see *Competition Law and Practice,* Chapter 24 at 24.25).

Schedule 7, para. 5 also provides for a management board, the Competition Commission Council, which may determine its own procedure in carrying out its functions in relation to the administration of the Competition Commission under Sched. 7 para. 3 and paras 7 to 12.

The Secretary of State must provide to the Competition Commission such funds as he considers appropriate to enable it to perform its functions, subject to the approval of the Treasury (Sched. 7, para. 7). The Secretary of State is also to determine the salaries and other remuneration that the Competition Commission may pay to its members, subject to Treasury approval.

Subject to provisions made by or under the Act, the Competition Commission sets its own procedure and must keep proper accounts and records. It is expressly stated that the Competition Commission is not a servant or agent of the Crown, nor is its property to be considered as Crown property (Sched. 7, para. 13).

3.4.3 Membership of the Competition Commission

The Competition Commission has two panels of members appointed by the Secretary of State to fulfil its two functions: the "appeal panel" and the "reporting panel". The Commission also has "specialist panel members" appointed under various utilities statutes. A separate panel is maintained to deal with newspaper merger references (Sched. 7, paras 1, 2 and 22).

All members of the panels are members of the Competition Commission. The Secretary of State appoints the Chairman of the Competition Commission from among the reporting panel members and the President of the Competition Commission Appeal Tribunals from among the appeal panel members.

The Competition Commission Council comprises the Chairman, the President, the Secretary and such other members as the Secretary of State may appoint (Sched. 7, para. 5). Schedule 7 also provides for limits on the term of office of the members of the Competition Commission, the procedure for resignation and the grounds for removal by the Secretary of State.

The nature of the membership of the Competition Commission was described in the House of Lords at Report stage (see *Hansard*, H.L., Vol. 586, No. 107, cols 367–375 (February 19, 1998)), in the context of a proposal (that was resisted) that the functions of the Competition Commission appeal tribunals would be better carried out by a branch of the High Court, or a "Competition Court". It was considered "essential that the tribunal panel contains the necessary breadth of experience and expertise to be able to deal effectively and efficiently with the complex commercial, economic and legal issues involved in competition cases" (Lord Haskel) and that this would be preserved by the tribunal approach, in which cases are heard by both legal and lay members. The necessary legal qualifications for the appeal tribunals chairmen would ensure sufficient legal supervision. These require at least seven years professional qualification and appropriate experience and knowledge of competition law and practice.

In a debate on similar issues in the House of Commons (*Hansard*, H.L., Vol. 589, No. 150, cols 112–113(May 11, 1998)) it was acknowledged that a separation of investigative and decision-making roles is essential to ensure a fair appeals process: this was considered to be achieved by placing the appellate function in the Competition Commission, a separate body from the primary investigation body, the OFT.

Paragraph 2(2) of Sched. 7 provides that three kinds of members (the appeal panel members, reporting panel members and specialist panel members) can be appointed as a member of either or both of the other kinds. This was also the subject of some debate in the House of Lords (see above *Hansard* reference). Concern was expressed that, since the Commission has both executive and judicial functions, an individual may be able to exercise more than one function and be "tainted" by performing both responsibilities at the same time. However, it was concluded that there would be benefits from this "cross fertilisation" and that in fact this would "facilitate the transference of expertise" and promote a consistent approach (Lord Haskel).

The members regarded as suitable for the panel dealing with newspaper merger references (which include considerations of editorial freedom as well as competition issues) do not form part of this "transfer arrangement". Paragraph 22 does not, however, expressly bar the Secretary of State from including in that panel a person who is a member of one of the other panels, leaving it unclear whether a prohibition is to be implied. In any event, the validity of proceedings is not affected by a defect in the appointment of a member (Sched. 7, para. 2(5)).

There is at the time of writing little overlap, with only one individual on both the appeal panel and the reporting panel (see Competition Commission Annual Review 1999/2000).

A *Notice on Arrangements for Constituting Appeal Tribunals* was issued by the Competition Commission on March 1, 2000. Published by the President of the Competition Commission Appeal Tribunals, pursuant to Rule 4 of the Competition Commission Appeal Tribunals Rules 2000 (S.I. 2000 No. 261), the Notice provides for the constitutional organisation of appeal tribunals to hear individual cases. Each appeal tribunal is headed by a chairman (either the President or a person appointed by him (Sched. 7, para. 27(2)). The Notice explains the system of rotation and certain prescribed requirements. This Notice reflects the considerable degree of inconsistency in the legislative and official publication references which include "Appeal Tribunal", "Appeals Tribunals" and "Appeal Tribunals" with use of both lower and upper case.

3.4.4 The Appeal Function of the Competition Commission

Any party to an agreement in respect of which the Director has made a decision and any person in respect of whose conduct the Director has made a decision may appeal to the Competition Commission (s. 46) (for discussion see 9.16). A "decision" includes a direction given under sections 32, 33 or 35 (relating to enforcement and interim measures).

Under section 47, a third party who is not the subject of a decision may apply to the Director for withdrawal or variation of a decision on the application of the prohibitions (but not a penalty decision). If the Director decides that the third party does not have sufficient interest or has not shown sufficient reason for the Director to take such action, the third party may appeal to the Competition Commission against this decision (s. 47(6)).

3.4.5 Conduct of Appeals

Part I of Sched. 8 sets out the procedure for the conduct of appeals. This is amplified by rules set out in Part II of Sched. 8 and The Competition Commission Appeal Tribunal Rules 2000 (S.I. 2000 No. 261). These include: the appointment of a Registrar of Appeal Tribunals; notice of appeals and the response; pre-hearing reviews and preliminary matters; the conduct of the hearing; orders for interest; fees; the withdrawal of an appeal; interim orders and the consolidation of appeals or joinder of parties. The Competition Commission has also published a Guide To Appeals under the Competition Act 1998 (June 2000). All these are discussed in more detail in Chapter 9 at 9.16.

The President in his statement in the Competition Commission Annual Review 1999/2000 describes the Appeal Tribunals as "courts of law" and stresses that the rules of procedure, based on those of the European Court of First Instance and taking account of recent changes to high court civil procedure (the Woolf reforms), are designed to meet an appropriate standard.

3.4.6 Outcome of Appeals

It is the role of an appeal tribunal to determine each appeal it hears on the merits, by reference to the grounds of appeal set out in the notice of appeal (Sched. 8, para. 3(1)).

The decision of the tribunal must contain a statement of the reasons for the decision and should be published as the President considers appropriate (Sched. 8, para. 4).

The tribunal may confirm or set aside the decision which is the subject of the appeal or any part of it and may:

(a) remit the matter to the Director;

(b) impose or revoke, or vary the amount of, a penalty;

(c) grant or cancel an individual exemption or vary any conditions or obligations imposed in relation to the exemption by the Director;

(d) give such directions, or take such other steps as the Director could himself have given or taken, or;

(e) make any other decision which the Director could himself have made (Sched. 8, para. 3(2)).

Any decision of the tribunal on an appeal has the same effect, and may be enforced in the same manner, as a decision of the Director. If the Director's decision is confirmed the tribunal may still set aside findings of facts upon which the relevant decision was based.

3.4.7 Consistency with E.C. Law

Appeal tribunals have the same obligations as courts in this regard (see 3.5.3 below).

3.5 The Role of the Courts

3.5.1 General

Appeals from the appeal tribunals of the Competition Commission are possible on a point of law or as to penalties. The Courts also have a role to play in respect of judicial review of decisions for which no right of appeal exists (see 3.5.9 below), enforcement in disputes between private parties and in relation to enforcement of directions given by the Director and the collection of penalties. All courts and tribunals determining questions under Part I of the Act must act to ensure consistency with E.C. law (see Chapter 5).

3.5.2 Appeals from the Competition Commission

An appeal lies on a point of law arising from the decision of an appeal tribunal of the Competition Commission or from any decision of an appeal tribunal as to penalties.

An appeal must be made to an appropriate court, with leave of the tribunal in question or of the court. An "appropriate court" is the Court of Appeal in England and Wales, the Court of Session in Scotland and the Court of Appeal in Northern Ireland. The ultimate Court to hear appeals from any of those Courts will be the House of Lords.

3.5.3 Consistency with E.C. Law

It is the role of the court to ensure, so far as is possible, that competition law within the United Kingdom is dealt with in a manner which is consistent with corresponding questions arising in Community law in relation to competition within the Community (s. 60). In this context "court" means any court or tribunal.

At any time when determining a question arising under Part I of the Act, the court must act, so far as is compatible, with a view to securing that there is no inconsistency in its determination of that question with the principles laid down by the Treaty and the European Court, and any relevant decision of that court, as applicable at that time in determining the corresponding question arising in E.C. law. The Court must also have regard to any relevant decision or statement of the E.C. Commission. This is explained in more detail in Chapter 5.

3.5.4 Findings of Fact by the Director

Section 58 provides that a finding of fact by the Director which is relevant to an issue arising in Part I proceedings is binding on a court, except where it is the subject of an undecided appeal or is under review by the Director himself. The Court of Appeal is able to direct otherwise.

3.5.5 Enforcement of Directions

Section 34 provides that the Director may apply to the court where a person fails, without reasonable excuse, to comply with a direction of enforcement made under sections 32 or 33.

The court may make an order requiring the defaulter to make good his default within a specified time or, if the direction is related to anything to be done in the management or administration of an undertaking, requiring the undertaking or its officers to do it; breach would be punishable as a contempt of court. The court may also make an order for costs in respect of the application.

3.5.6 Recovery of Penalties

It is the role of Director to recover from an undertaking any amount payable under a penalty notice which remains outstanding on the expiry of the specified date, if no appeal is pending (s. 37). Penalties are recoverable as civil debts due to the Director and will be enforceable through the courts according to the normal procedure.

3.5.7 Delay by the Director

Paragraph 7 of Sched. 5 provides that, where the Director fails to determine an application for a decision in accordance with the specified procedure and the court is satisfied that there has been undue delay on the part of the Director, the court may give such directions to the Director as it considers appropriate to secure that the application is determined without unnecessary further delay. There is no comparable provision in respect of applications for guidance. This provision is not yet in force (see Chapter 9).

3.5.8 Third Party Claims for Damages

There is no express right in the Act to bring a private enforcement action. The OFT Guideline: *Enforcement*, OFT 407, March 1999 at para. 5.1 states that third parties who consider that they have suffered loss as a result of any unlawful agreement or conduct, have a claim for damages in the courts. The questions which this raises are discussed in more detail in Chapter 10 at 10.2.

3.5.9   Judicial Review

There is a potential role for the High Court in judicial review proceedings that may be taken in respect of action by the Director or Competition Commission. This was expressly acknowledged by Lord Simon of Highbury in the House of Lords (*Hansard*, H.L., Vol. 586, No. 107, col. 381 (February 19, 1998)). Judicial review may be available in relation to administrative matters, in particular where a decision has consequences which are not open to review in the appeal process. These proceedings would be pursued and conducted in accordance with the usual procedure for judicial review, which is outside the scope of this book.

Chapter 4

Regulators with Concurrent Powers

4.1 Sector Regulators
4.2 Functions Retained by Director
4.3 Co-Ordination of Functions
4.4 Regulators' Statutory Sectoral Duties
4.5 Application of The Monopoly Provisions of the Fair Trading Act 1973

Note: The OFT has proposed alterations to the Guideline: Concurrent Application to Regulated Industries *(OFT 405) and started consultation on the Revised Guideline:* Concurrent Application to Regulated Industries *(OFT 433). Due to this reference is made in this Chapter to both the original Guideline and the Revised Consultation Draft.*

4.1 Sector Regulators

4.1.1 Regulators with Concurrent Powers

The functions of the Director under Part I of the Act are to be exercised concurrently in a number of regulated sectors by the relevant Regulator (see Competition Act 1998 s. 54), both in relation to the Chapter I Prohibition on agreements which restrict, distort or prevent competition and the Chapter II Prohibition on abuse of a dominant position.

The industry sectors concerned are telecommunications, gas and electricity, water and rail. The regulators with concurrent powers are: the Director General of Telecommunications, the Director General of Electricity Supply, the Director General of Gas Supply, the Director General of Electricity Supply for Northern Ireland, the Director General of Gas Supply for Northern Ireland, the Director General of Water Services and the Rail Regulator.

The Regulation of Gas and Electricity is currently carried out by a single individual holding both positions for Great Britain and another individual holding both Northern Ireland offices. Their administrative staffs have been combined, in Great Britain under the title "Office of Gas and Electricity Markets" ("OFGEM") and in Northern Ireland under the title "Office for the Regulation of Electricity and Gas" ("OFREG"). This change has been effected on an extra-statutory basis. In relation to Great Britain the Utilities Act 2000 provides for the two existing Directors General to be replaced by the Gas and Electricity Markets Authority ("GEMA"). This new Authority which is likely to be in place by December 2000, will assume the powers of the Directors General in relation to the Competition Act 1998. It is unclear whether, in day-to-day parlance, GEMA will replace OFGEM as the name used for the regulator. Statutory reform in respect of Northern Ireland awaits the outcome of a consultation paper to be issued during 2000.

Initial proposals for the Utilities Act 2000 to extend concurrent powers to the Civil Aviation Authority ("CAA") in relation to airports were not taken forward. However, the Transport Bill, currently before Parliament, extends concurrent powers to the CAA in relation to air traffic control (see Chapter 17, para. 17.3.1).

Section 54 of the Competition Act introduces Schedule 10 which sets out the requisite amendments to the relevant sector-specific legislation in order to establish concurrency and the specific areas in which each Regulator is to exercise concurrent jurisdiction.

4.1.2 Scope of Concurrent Powers

Regulators have the power to deal with infringements of the Chapter I and II Prohibitions in their designated sector. Generally, the Regulator will deal with the case where it falls within his jurisdiction (see below at 4.3.2).

The areas over which the Regulators are to have current jurisdiction are widely drafted. The current concurrent powers are set out below:

Agreements or conduct relating to:	Statute	Regulatory body
Commercial activities connected with telecommunications	The Telecommunications Act 1984	OFTEL
Shipping, conveyance or supply OFGEM/GEMA	The Gas Act 1986 of gas and activities ancillary thereto (in Great Britain)	
Commercial activities connected OFGEM/GEMA electricity (in Great Britain)	The Electricity Act 1989 with the generation, transmission or supply of	
Commercial activities connected with the generation, transmission or supply of electricity in Northern Ireland	The Electricity (Northern Ireland) Order 1992	OFREG
Conveyance, storage or supply of gas in Northern Ireland	The Gas (Northern Ireland) Order 1996	OFREG
Commercial activities in England and Wales connected with the supply of water or securing a supply of water, or with the provision or securing of sewerage activities	The Water Industry Act 1991	OFWAT
Supply of railway services	The Railways Act 1993	ORR

The above table follows that contained in the OFT Guideline, *Concurrent Application to Regulated Industries*, OFT 405, March 1999 and maintained in the Revised Consultation Draft Version of the Guideline, OFT 433, March 2000. These are subsequently referred to in this chapter as the "Concurrency Guideline" and distinguished by reference to their OFT reference numbers.

4.1.3   Regulators Not Given Concurrent Powers

The inclusion of the CAA as a Regulator with concurrent jurisdiction has been the subject of some discussion: it is possible that it will be given concurrent jurisdiction at a later date. It is interesting to note that the Independent Television Commission ("ITC") has not been granted concurrent powers in relation to its regulation of the broadcasting industry (other than the BBC), but maintains its powers to act in respect of competition matters by licence provisions (see s. 2(2)(a)(ii), Broadcasting Act 1990). This exposes broadcasting businesses to up to three different United Kingdom regulators with competition powers: OFT, ITC and, on the technical transmission side of operations, OFTEL.

4.1.4   Powers of Regulators

Within its sector, each Regulator has almost all of the powers of the Director to apply and enforce the prohibitions. These include:

- giving guidance on the application of the Act;

- considering complaints about breaches;

- imposing interim measures to prevent serious and irreparable damage;

- considering notifications for a decision and giving decisions on the application of the Act;

- granting exemptions to the Chapter I Prohibition (and imposing conditions, where appropriate);

- carrying out investigations (on the Regulator's own initiative and in response to complaints) with the same powers to require the production of documents and information and to search premises;

- imposing financial penalties (taking into account the Director's statutory guidance on penalties);

- giving and enforcing directions to end infringements; and

- issuing general advice and information on the application of the Competition Act in the relevant sector.

The relationship of these powers to those which the Regulators enjoy under their respective statutes is discussed at 4.4 below.

4.2   Functions Retained by Director

The Director alone retains responsibility for making and amending the procedural rules and issuing guidance on penalties.

However, when the Director prepares or alters guidance in respect of the appropriate levels of a penalty (s. 38), or lays down procedural rules (s. 51), or prepares advice or information (s. 52) in connection with a matter over which a Regulator exercises concurrent jurisdiction, the Director must consult the relevant Regulator(s).

4.3   Co-ordination of Functions

4.3.1   Regulations Made by the Secretary of State

Under section 54(4), an amendment made to the Bill at the Third Reading in the
House of Commons (*Hansard*, H.C., Vol. 315, No. 202, cols 1199–1200 (July 8,
1998)), the Secretary of State has the power to make regulations for the purpose of
co-ordinating the performance of functions under Part I of the Act which are exercisable concurrently by two or more "competent persons". For these purposes
"competent person" means the Director or any of the Regulators but the OFT
Guidelines use the word "authority" in the same sense. This book follows the OFT for
the sake of simplicity, even when referring to the Regulations.

The Competition Act 1998 (Concurrency) Regulations 2000 (S.I. 2000 No.
260) (the "Concurrency Regulations") make provision for the following:

- the procedure for determining who is to exercise the functions in a particular case;

- the steps to be taken before an authority exercises such functions;

- the avoidance of "double jeopardy" by ensuring that only one authority can
  carry out the substantive tasks of investigation and decision making in relation to a particular matter, even though this may cause some delay in the
  commencement of an investigation under sections 25 *et seq.* or of interim
  measures proceedings;

- the procedure for determining disputes as to which authority is to exercise
  the functions: the Secretary of State has reserved the decision to himself
  where agreement cannot be reached between the Director and the
  Regulators;

- transfer of the exercise of functions from one authority to another;

- the use of staff for an investigation by another authority; and

- the service of notices.

4.3.2   Guiding Principle

The methodology for dealing with cases where there is concurrent jurisdiction is set
out in the Concurrency Guideline. This explains (at para. 3.1 of OFT 405 and
para. 3.8 of OFT 433) that an agreement or conduct which falls within the jurisdiction of a Regulator will normally be dealt with by that Regulator, although in
some cases the Director will deal with such a case.

The general principle is that "a case will be dealt with by whichever of the Director General of Fair Trading or the relevant regulator is better, or best, placed to do
so". The Concurrency Regulations have opted quite clearly for a single authority
dealing with each case and have rejected the possibility of joint case handling (contemplated in section 54(5)(d) of the Act).

The factors that will be taken into account in deciding which authority should exercise concurrent powers include the sectoral knowledge of a Regulator, any previous
contacts between the parties or complainants and a Regulator, or with the Director,
and any recent experience in dealing with any of the undertakings or similar issues
which may be involved in the proceedings. Irrespective of which authority formally
deals with a case, the Director and other Regulators will be consulted, as appropriate.

4.3.3 Deciding Which Authority Will Act

Applicants will be notified as soon as is practicable as to the authority handling the relevant notification, (Concurrency Regulations, Regulation 5(4)(b)). If it is appropriate for the case to be transferred subsequently to another authority, an applicant or the undertaking(s) under investigation will be given an opportunity to make representations and then notified of any such change with reasons (Concurrency Regulations, Regulation 8(2) and 8(4)). The procedure on transfer after an investigation has commenced recognises that the applicant or undertaking under investigation may face additional costs and delays, as well as an element of double jeopardy, from a transfer. As this type of decision is not an appealable decision under section 46, the transfer process could be open to judicial review (although the Secretary of State has the power to add to the list of decisions that may be appealed).

The same rights to be informed and make representations do not arise when a transfer is made at the initial stages before the first agreement or determination of the authority which will handle the case under the Concurrency Regulations, Regulation 5(3) or 6(3)(a), or where the parties concerned have not had notice that the transferor has taken any steps (Regulation 8(5)(a) and (b)). In the case where an application has been made for a decision only the applicant, but not other parties to the agreement or conduct, are entitled to notice (Regulation 8(5)(c)). Other persons such as complainants or other parties with a legitimate interest in the outcome have no legal right to be informed. The Concurrency Guideline in its proposed revision makes it clear that the Director and Regulators will keep complainants advised "as soon as practicable" (OFT 433, para. 3.13). There are no fixed time limits, except:

- on a determination of a dispute by the Secretary of State, which must be made within eight working days of request (Concurrency Regulations, Regulation 6(3)); and

- on a subsequent transfer between authorities, when the applicant or the subject of the investigation is to be afforded a period of seven working days to make representations (Concurrency Regulations, Regulation 8(2)).

4.3.4 Applications and Complaints

The Concurrency Guideline (OFT 405, paras 3.3–3.6 and OFT 433, paras 3.11–3.13) indicates how concurrency will work in practice in respect of the submission of notifications and complaints.

Notifications for guidance or a decision must, in all cases, be sent to the Director (Concurrency Regulations, Regulation 4) and an extra copy of the Form N should be provided for each relevant Regulator (in the opinion of the applicant) (Directors' Rules, Rule 3(2)). A copy may also be sent direct to such Regulator(s) if the matter falls within one of the relevant industry sectors. A notification will not be incomplete where an additional copy is not provided or sent to the relevant Regulator.

In contrast, a complaint may be made *either* to the Director *or* direct to the relevant Regulator, although the same general principles regarding case-handling will apply. Complainants should not, however, send a copy of the complaint to a second authority. If a complaint concerns licence conditions as well as alleged breaches of the Competition Act 1998, it should be sent to the relevant Regulator. If substantial new factual evidence comes to light, this should be submitted to the same authority that dealt with the initial complaint. Applications for interim measures are to be dealt with in a similar way to complaints.

4.3.5   Concurrency Working Party

The Concurrency Working Party was formed in 1997 to ensure co-ordination between the Director and the Regulators, to consider the way in which concurrency would work in practice and to prepare guidelines. The Working Party is chaired by a representative of the OFT, and the OFT and each Regulator are represented. The Working Party continues, after the implementation of the Act, to look at issues related to information sharing, updating of guidelines and allocation of jurisdiction.

4.3.6   Disclosure of Information — General Principle

Section 55 of the Act provides for restrictions on disclosure of information obtained under the Act which relates to the affairs of any individual or any particular business of an undertaking. However, the provisions restricting the disclosure of information do not apply to disclosures of information made for the purpose of facilitating the performance of any "relevant functions" of a "designated person" (as defined in Schedule 11). The definition of relevant functions includes functions under the Act as well as under all the statutes referred to above (at 4.1.2) and the definition of designated persons includes the Director and all the Regulators. It should be noted that the definition also covers a wider range of statutes and persons: including statutes such as the Airports Act 1986, the Broadcasting Acts 1990 and 1996 and additional authorities such as the ITC, the CAA and the Financial Services Authority.

The confidentiality provisions also do not apply to a disclosure of information which is, *inter alia*, made for the purpose of facilitating the performance of the functions of the E.C. Commission under Community competition law, or criminal proceedings in the United Kingdom, or made with a view to the institution of, or for the purposes of, civil proceedings under Part I of the Act, or which is required to meet a Community obligation (s. 55(3)).

4.3.7   Sharing of Information between Authorities with Concurrent Powers

Information about complaints and investigations will be shared between the Regulators and Director in order to ascertain whether or not there is concurrent jurisdiction (Concurrency Regulations, Regulation 3). The Concurrency Guideline, OFT 405, para. 3.8 and OFT 433, para. 3.4, state:

> "Information about cases in progress, including matters of general policy and the way in which the Act is interpreted and applied, will also be shared, in each case with a view to ensuring consistency in decision making."

The ensuring of consistency can probably be regarded as part of the relevant functions of the Director and each of the Regulators with concurrent powers, given the nature of the legislation, although not specifically provided for.

4.4   Regulators' Statutory Sectoral Duties

4.4.1   Statutory Duties

The statutes listed in the table (in para. 4.1.2 above) set out the duties of the Regulators. In general, each Regulator's statutory duty will include the duty to promote competition, as well as the obligation to ensure that there is sufficient provision of the regulated service throughout the United Kingdom and to protect the interests of consumers and customers.

Some of the Regulators had imposed specific licence conditions on some or all of their licensees in furtherance of their duty to promote competition. The leading example is OFTEL's "fair trading condition" which closely follows Articles 81 and 82. OFTEL believes that this does not apply now the Competition Act 1998 has come into force (see OFTEL/OFT Guideline: Competition Act 1998, Application in the Telecommunications Sector, OFT 417, February 2000 (the "Telecommunications Guideline") para. 4.8.4). In any event, the condition expires on July 31, 2001. Other licence conditions touching on competition may remain in place (see 4.4.4 below).

4.4.2   Primacy of Competition Act Duties

An amendment made during the reading of the Bill in the House of Lords altered the original drafting so that, when exercising their concurrent jurisdiction under the Act, the Regulators' statutory duties under the sector-specific statutes do not apply. Originally, it was intended that the statutory duties were to come second to the competition issues which were to be "paramount". However, sector Regulators may "have regard" to the subject matter of their sectoral duties when using their Competition Act powers, if it is a matter to which the Director could also have regard in exercising his powers under the Act (see, for example, Sched. 10, para. 5(4) introducing s. 2(6A) and 2(6B) into the Water Industry Act 1991).

4.4.3   Exceptions for "General Economic Interest"

One exclusion from the prohibitions of the Act (Sched. 3, para. 4), modelled on Article 86(2) (formerly Article 90(2)) of the E.C. Treaty, provides that neither of the prohibitions applies to an undertaking entrusted with,

> "the operation of services of general economic interest or having the character of a revenue-producing monopoly in so far as the prohibition would obstruct the performance, in law or in fact, of the particular tasks assigned to that undertaking."

This exclusion is discussed further in Chapter 7, para. 7.6.3. However, in the context of concurrent jurisdiction, it is important to note that where this exclusion covers a particular activity of a regulated business, the relevant Regulator will still be able to apply his powers under the relevant utility statute to that activity. In fact, as the Concurrency Guideline (OFT 405, para. 4.6) states

> "it is precisely in these situations that the regulators' ability to ensure that services are available to consumers throughout the United Kingdom on reasonable terms by using their sector powers is particularly relevant".

4.4.4   Use of Sectoral Powers on Competition Related Matters

A particular agreement or practice may fall within the scope of a Regulator's powers under the Competition Act 1998 and his sector specific powers: for example, a breach of the prohibition of undue discrimination in the licence of a public telecommunications operator could also involve a breach of the Chapter II Prohibition if the operator is dominant and, possibly an agreement in breach of the Chapter I Prohibition. OFTEL, in the Telecommunications Guideline paras 4.3–4.7 states a preference for applying the Competition Act first, but points out that the Regulator cannot fetter his discretion and must decide on a case by case basis. Regulatees will no doubt prefer the application of the licence provision, which only carries financial penalties for repeated breach after a provisional or final enforcement order has been made, but complainants will argue for the application of the Competition Act powers, or, possibly, the use of a combination of powers.

4.4.5   Sector Specific Guidelines

Issues for particular sectors vary according to their particular legislation and the state of development of competition in the relevant sector. Most of the Regulators have published guidelines or draft guidelines in association with the OFT to highlight these issues and explain their own approach (see list at [p. l]). All can be expected to maintain guidelines for their sectors.

4.4.6   Telecommunications

The Telecommunications Guideline contains a comprehensive review of competition policy for that sector. The Director General of Telecommunications draws on E.C. precedent to show how he will have regard to regulatory rules when applying the Competition Act (see 4.4.2 above). At para. 3.6 he quotes from the E.C. Commission Notice on the application of the competition rules to access agreements in the telecommunications sector, [1998] O.J. C265/02 (the "Access Notice").

> "When appropriate, legislation such as the ONP [Open Network Provision] framework will be used as an aid in the interpretation of the competition rules. Given the duty resting on the National Regulatory Authority to ensure that effective competition is possible, application of the competition rules is likewise required for an appropriate interpretation of the ONP principles".

Section 60 requires the Regulator to have regard to relevant statements by the E.C. Commission, such as the Access Notice.

4.4.7   Water and Sewerage

The Guideline, *The Competition Act 1998, The Application in the Water and Sewerage Sectors*, OFT 422, January 2000, sets out the approach of the Director General of Water Services. He has consciously used the Act to promote the adoption of principles for common carriage of water and shared use of treatment plants by licensed undertakers (paras 4.16 – 4.20), although (unlike other "network industries") there is no statutory framework for this and the industry structure is not ideally suited to wide scale sharing of infrastructure by licensed undertakers and other suppliers. The Director General has drawn on the E.C. essential facilities doctrine and seeks to develop it beyond present E.C. authorities (paras 4.21 *et seq,*).

The Guideline also shows the intention to use the Competition Act to achieve better enforcement of a number of regulatory objectives, including in relation to pricing, non-price terms and connections to water mains. Because of the regulatory framework of exclusive territorial appointment, many businesses in these sectors are at risk of action under the Chapter II Prohibition since many of them are likely to enjoy local or regional dominant positions.

4.4.8 Railway Services

The Railway Regulator and the Director have published a draft Guideline, *The Competition Act 1998, The Application to Railway Services*, OFT 430, February 2000 Consultation Draft (the "Rail Guideline"), with a consultation period that ended on the March 31, 2000.

The Regulator intends to take a case by case approach to the use of his regulatory or Competition Act powers where both may apply (paras 2.1–2.3). He intends, in relation to the Competition Act 1998, to have particular regard to the views of the Railways Franchising Director and other public bodies who contribute to the cost of railway companies, fulfilling their public service obligations (para. 3.1). The proposed strategic Rail Authority (to be established by the Transport Bill currently before Parliament and already operating on a "shadow" basis) will promote agreements to secure cross-industry co-operation: the Rail Regulator will have to review these agreements under the Chapter I Prohibition (para. 3.2 and relevant criteria are discussed at paras 5.12 *et seq,*). In an industry where co-operation brings benefits (*e.g.* quality of information for travellers, greater efficiency) the assessment of such agreements will be particularly important.

In relation to market definition, the Director recognises that rail services are not necessarily operating in a rail market but may be in the same market as other forms of passenger transport on the same route (*e.g.* inter-city coach service) or other methods of moving freight (road, sea or inland waterways). Transport service markets are, however, likely to be route specific (see discussion in s. 4 of the Rail Guideline). The Regulator may also examine input markets: for example, in relation to Rolling Stock Leasing, it is noted that the leasing companies (ROSCOS) enjoy market power and may be dominant for the purposes of the Chapter II prohibition. Breach of their voluntary code of conduct (published February 10, 2000) could also amount to a breach of the Prohibition (Rail Guideline, s. 7).

The OFT consultation on the proposed block exemption for Public Transport Ticketing Schemes (consultation period July 6, to August 18, 2000) deals specifically with the railway industry's Ticketing and Settlement Agreement (TSA) and also the relationship with the proposed competition test for statutory ticketing schemes set out in the Transport Bill, Sched. 10. It is not clear whether the TSA will benefit from the proposed Block Exemption or be dealt with individually. Parallel exemptions in the rail sector may arise under Regulation 1017/68 rather than Article 81 and the Rail Regulator notes his ability to add conditions or obligations to such exemptions (Rail Guideline, paras 5.6 to 5.8).

It should be noted that the Rail Regulator's concurrent jurisdiction covers railway services operating in Great Britain as defined in section 82 of the Railways Act 1993 (including services which do not require licences under the Act — see para. 1.22 and, in relation to international services, para. 8.2). His concurrent jurisdiction does not cover activities carried out by a rail link undertaker in relation to the Channel Tunnel Rail Link or services in Northern Ireland (para. 1.21). This is affected by changes in the Transport Bill (see Chapter 17 at 17.3.3).

4.4.9 Gas and Electricity Markets

The OFT/OFGEM published in draft the Guideline: *The Application of the Competition Act to the Energy Sectors*, OFT 428, Consultation draft version in May 2000, consultation on which closed on July 7, 2000. This follows on from an earlier draft published by OFGEM alone in late 1999. The consultation is linked to consultation on the "good market behaviour" licence condition. OFGEM identifies at para. 3.4 particular characteristics of the industries which will affect its approach, including:

- the importance of "unbundling" business activities in order to promote competition;

- the existence of long term monopolies in transportation, transmission and distribution where the costs of replication are prohibitive;

- the market power of some of the former nationalised industries;

- the constraints of product and market characteristics, such as the limited storability of electricity, low elasticity of demand for electricity and gas and, at some periods, of supply;

- the number and complexity of codes and agreements related to security of supply and safety;

- the existence of price controls in parts of industries where market power is particularly strong;

- the existence of economic linkages between different parts of the networks, resulting in market power in one set of activities or markets having a substantial effect on other activities or markets.

OFGEM intends to be rigorous in the application of the Act, in particular in satisfying itself that agreements achieve their ends in the least restrictive way possible (para. 3.37).

4.5   Application of the Monoploy Provisions of the Fair Trading Act 1973

4.5.1   Scale Monopoly Powers Remain Fully Available

The Government has decided that Regulators should have the ability to use the scale monopoly powers under the FTA alongside their Competition Act powers in relation to regulated industries. This is because of "the special circumstances of the utility sectors and the difficulty of establishing competition": OFT Guideline, *The Major Provisions*, OFT 400, March 1999 and para. 13.5 and the Concurrency Guideline (unchanged), para. 4.8. Many utility businesses have inherited previous nationalised industry monopolies at national or regional level and therefore qualify for investigation under the scale monopoly provisions: indeed in the past, these provisions have been the basis for achieving re-organisation of the gas industry, which was privatised as a single nationwide business *Gas* (1988) Cm. 500, *Gas and British Gas plc* (1993) Cm. 2314–2316, coupled in 1993 with a licence modification reference.

Network businesses such as Transco (gas), National Grid (electricity) and Railtrack, whose national networks are not replicated by competitors, are most suited to examination under the scale monopoly regime, if problems should arise.

4.5.2   Complex Monopoly Powers

The similar nature and structure of regulated businesses within a utility sector, as well as the common regulatory structure, mean that regulated industries are likely to be suitable for investigation under the complex monopoly provisions of the FTA.

In industries such as water and electricity these provisions, which remain freely available, would be a valuable tool for tackling structural problems in the industry as a whole. No other investigative tool would be suitable for this purpose: a scale monopoly reference or licence condition reference of, for example, a single water and sewerage undertaking could only deal with that individual company's activities in its own region or that company's structural organisation; a Chapter I investigation could only address a particular agreement or concerted practice and a Chapter II investigation could only examine a particular type of abusive behaviour (even if it was carried out by a number of industry participants who together enjoyed joint dominance).

4.5.3   The FTA Regime

Chapter 15 deals more fully with the operation of the FTA regime alongside the Competition Act 1998. All the Regulators who presently have concurrent powers under the Competition Act 1998, also have concurrent powers to make references under the monopoly provisions of the FTA. None of them have any powers under the merger provisions of the FTA.

4.5.4   Other References to the Competition Commission

The same Regulators may also make licence modification references to the Competition Commission under their respective statutes in cases where a licence modification cannot be agreed. In some sectors (*e.g.* water, electricity and gas) the Competition Commission is effectively an appellate body in respect of each Regulator's periodic price control reviews. Some other Regulators, notably the CAA in relation to designated airports, make references to the Competition Commission as part of the regulatory process.

Chapter 5

The Governing Principles Section

5.1 Overview

5.1.1 Alignment with E.C. Competition Law

One of the Government's primary aims behind the Competition Act 1998 is to align United Kingdom domestic competition law with E.C. competition law. As Lord Simon (the Government minister responsible for the passage of the Bill through the House of Lords) said at Third Reading in the House of Lords:

"As far as possible, we want to achieve a seamless web so that agreements and practices which are prohibited under one regime are prohibited under the other and those that are permitted are permitted under both". (*Hansard,* H.L., Vol. 586, No. 116, col. 1363 (March 5, 1998)).

5.1.2 Not Enough to Copy Wording

Simply copying the wording of Articles 81 and 82 E.C. Treaty would not have been enough to ensure this alignment. It is also critical that the domestic prohibitions are *interpreted* in the same way as Articles 81 and 82. The governing principles section of the Act, section 60, is designed to achieve consistency of interpretation by, in effect, importing E.C. jurisprudence into the domestic system. The Act, therefore, starts life with a ready made 38 year history of E.C. case law which will assist in its interpretation. The language of this section, which expresses its application to be to "questions in relation to competition" will give rise to a debate as to the extent to which principles of E.C. law of more general application are to be followed in cases involving the prohibitions. This writer believes that the Courts will resolve the debate in favour of a wide interpretation but only time will tell (see discussion below in ss. 5.2 and 5.3).

5.1.3 Governing Principles Key to Interpretation

When interpreting the new provisions of the Act, it will be essential to consider the application of the governing principles clause (s. 60). Sections of the Act should not be read literally since they must be interpreted in accordance with E.C. jurisprudence — the words in the Act do not necessarily mean what they say! For example, the Chapter I Prohibition, read literally, would appear to catch agreements which had any restrictive effect on competition, however negligible that may be. However, one of the intended results of the governing principles section is to import the E.C.

doctrine of "appreciability": only agreements which have an "appreciable" effect on competition will be caught by the Chapter I Prohibition (see Chapter 6 at 6.2). The Government resisted various opposition attempts in the Lords and the Commons to insert an express appreciability test on the basis that it was already imported via the governing principles clause.

5.1.4   Praise and Criticism

The principle of seeking alignment with E.C. competition law has been broadly welcomed by the business community and by many in the Lords and the Commons. However, the governing principles clause was one of the most criticised aspects of the Bill during its Parliamentary passage. The criticism was mainly directed at its drafting and the assorted qualifications and conditions to the importation of E.C. jurisprudence, which are likely to result in considerable uncertainty as to its application. Lord Fraser, the Opposition front bench spokesman in the House of Lords, described this provision as:

> "The El Dorado clause in the Bill which will provide a gold mine for lawyers for at least the next decade" (*Hansard,* H.L., Vol. 586, No. 108 col. 510 (February 23, 1998)).

5.1.5   Conclusion

The principle of seeking to align United Kingdom competition law with E.C. competition law is welcome. It is unfortunate that the drafting of the governing principles clause has left so much uncertainty which will need to be resolved by the courts. In particular, the drafting appears to take no account of matters which the ECJ has held to be matters of national law (see 5.2.6 below) or of the inapplicability of certain Treaty provisions in a national context (see 5.3.5 below). This difficulty would be partly eliminated if E.C. law is changed, as proposed by the E.C. Commission, so that only Articles 81 and 82 themselves can be applied by national authorities and courts in cases where there is an effect on trade between Member States. These proposals for reform are discussed in Chapter 17 at 17.7.

An opportunity to clarify the private remedies available for breach of Articles 81 and 82 as well as for breach of the prohibitions has been missed. This is discussed at 5.2.6 below and in Chapters 10 and 14.

5.2   Structure and Application of the Governing Principles Section

5.2.1   Novel Structure

The structure of section 60, the governing principles section, is novel for a United Kingdom statute. It starts with a "purpose" clause (s. 60(1)), which is designed to shape the interpretation of the operative provisions in sections 60 (2) and (3). Section 60(1) states that the purpose of section 60 is:

> "to ensure that so far as is possible (having regard to any relevant differences between the provisions concerned) questions in relation to competition within the United Kingdom are dealt with in a manner which is consistent with the treatment of corresponding questions arising in Community law in relation to competition within the Community".

The Director, the sector Regulators, courts and tribunals when determining a question arising under Part I of the Act must act (so far as is compatible with the provisions of that Part) with a view to securing that there is no inconsistency between:

- the principles applied and the decisions reached in determining that question; and

- the principles laid down by the E.C. Treaty and the European Court of Justice and Court of First Instance, and any relevant decision of such courts in determining any corresponding question arising in Community law (s. 60(2)).

Those applying the prohibitions are also under a duty to "have regard" to any relevant decision or statement of the E.C. Commission (s. 60(3)). Notices by the E.C. Commission giving guidance on the interpretation of block exemptions, for example, are likely to fall into the category of "statements" as are many comfort letters and some observations in the E.C. Commission's annual competition reports. Note that the "Treaty" referred to is the E.C. Treaty and any potentially relevant case law under the competition provisions of the ECSC Treaty has no special status.

5.2.2 Approach to Interpretation

The drafting of the section does not involve a simple unqualified transposition of E.C. law into the domestic system. In determining whether E.C. law is applicable in the interpretation of any particular part of the Competition Act, it is important to consider two questions:

(1) What E.C. law is imported?

(2) Has the importation of E.C. law been disapplied for the relevant section, or is its importation qualified?

5.2.3 What E.C. Law is Imported?

The Government has made clear on several occasions that it is not the intention of the Competition Act to "import the E.C. system lock, stock and barrel". Three types of law can be considered:

(1) Substantive;

(2) High level principles; and

(3) Detailed procedural matters.

The observations of the Government during the passage of the Bill are mentioned below, but for the courts and administrative authorities, the starting point is section 60 itself. The section pins the application of E.C. principles to issues where the court or administrator is considering "a question relating to competition within the United Kingdom", and the identification of the principles which would be applied in determining a corresponding question under E.C. law. This question is discussed below in relation to each of substantive law, high level principles and detailed procedural matters.

5.2.4 Substantive Law

There can be no doubt that when applying the prohibitions themselves, substantive E.C. law on the meaning of Articles 81 and 82, for example whether an agreement can be said to "restrict, prevent or distort competition", or whether a company has a "dominant" position is meant to be imported into the United Kingdom system, subject to the impact of exclusions which may prevent the application of the prohibition.

5.2.5 High Level Principles

The Government has confirmed that "high level" principles are also intended to be imported under the governing principles clause. As Lord Simon said at Third Reading in the House of Lords:

> "The very fact that Articles 85 and 86 [now Articles 81 and 82] now have an internal dynamic means that they have to be understood in the context of the general principles which apply to them as part of Community law. These, which one might call high level principles, may impinge upon the meaning and effect of the prohibitions as a question of law. They range from the principle of legal certainty which carries with it the proposition that contracts should not be lightly set aside, to the principles of fairness in administrative action." (*Hansard*, H.L., Vol. 586, No. 116, col. 1363 (March 5, 1998)).

The Government did not elaborate on what principles it regarded as qualifying as "high level" principles, but the courts would seem likely to regard as a relevant principle, those of general application which would affect the application of the substantive law. One that is likely to qualify is the principle of proportionality under which, for example, the Director's actions must be proportionate to the harm they are designed to remedy. This would put a limit on the conditions which the Director could attach to the grant of an exemption: they would have to be "proportionate" to the harm they were seeking to address. In other contexts, proportionality is a procedural concept and, as discussed below, it is much less clear how far E.C. principles applicable to procedure can or should affect the matters which English law or the law of other United Kingdom jurisdictions regards as procedural, in particular where domestic legislation lays down the procedure to be followed.

5.2.6 Remedies

The governing principles section was also intended to import the E.C. law relating to the entitlement to injunctions and damages for persons suffering from breaches of Articles 81 and 82. This is not done expressly but simply by providing that the decisions to which the Director, the Regulators and the courts are to have regard include decisions as to the civil liability of an undertaking for harm caused by its infringement of Community Law (see section 60(6)(b)). However this in turn brings its own problems since the law relating to private remedies for breach of E.C. prohibitions is, according to the decisions of the ECJ, largely dependent on national and not E.C. law and the relevant English law is far from clear (a problem discussed more fully in Chapter 10, para. 10.2.1). An opportunity was missed to clarify the law relating to private remedies for breach of Article 81 or Article 82, as well as the prohibitions. There is likely to be much expensive litigation before the courts (or further legislation) to clarify the extent of third party rights.

5.2.7 Procedural Rules

Detailed procedural rules set out in Commission/Council Regulations are not intended to be imported. As Lord Simon said at Third Reading in the Lords:

"At the Community level, much of the detailed procedure for the administration of the E.C. prohibition system is set out in Commission or Council regulations. The governing principles clause will not import any of these detailed procedures. This is especially so since the Commission is made up of a college of Commissioners and many of its procedures would simply not be appropriate for the Director." (*Hansard*, H.L., Vol. 586, No. 116, col. 1364 (March 5, 1998)).

Instead the detailed procedure for the administration of the United Kingdom prohibitions is set out in Rules of Procedure adopted by secondary legislation. (The Competition Act 1998 (Director's rules) Order 2000 (S.I. 2000 No. 293) (the "Director's Rules") and The Competition Commission Appeal Tribunal Rules 2000 (S.I. 2000 No. 261)) (the "Appeal Rules"). The Government explained that the adoption of the Director's procedural rules will not constitute "determining a question in relation to competition" for the purposes of section 60 and therefore relevant E.C. rules on this issue would not be imported. The form of the Director's Rules confirms that he sees no reason to be bound by the Commission's procedural practices. Similarly, the legislation on penalties and guidance (including the leniency policy) are quite independent of E.C. law (see Chapter 10 at 10.3).

It seems obvious that Community law principles will be irrelevant in relation to procedural matters specifically provided for under United Kingdom legislation.

There is, however, another route by which procedural concepts employed by the E.C. institutions may emerge: this arises from the general obligations of the United Kingdom Government under the E.C. Treaty. These would import certain basic requirements affecting procedure, notably the requirement to comply with the European Convention on Human Rights which applies as a matter of E.C. law. Following implementation of the Human Rights Act 1998 in October 2000, these principles also have a source in domestic law. Where there are gaps in United Kingdom procedural rules, courts or regulators are not bound by section 60 to adopt E.C. procedural principles of the "lowest common denominator" nature, which underpin Community competition case procedure, including the procedural concept of proportionality. Of course, United Kingdom regulators may be influenced by such matters and the Appeal Rules of the Competition Commission are heavily influenced by the procedures of Court of First Instance.

5.3   Departures From E.C. Jurisprudence

5.3.1   Corresponding Questions

The first basis on which there is to be a departure from E.C. jurisprudence is where the question arising under the Competition Act 1998 cannot be said to be "corresponding" to any question which has been decided under E.C. law. The term "corresponding question" is a critical term designed to qualify the E.C. law which is to be imported, but it is undefined and its scope is uncertain, although it would be clear that it applied when considering, for example, what amounts to dominance for the purposes of the Chapter II Prohibition. The courts and Regulators would naturally look to the ECJ definition (see Chapter 11 at 11.4).

5.3.2   Not a "Corresponding Question" — the Single Market Example

The Government gave the E.C. single market objectives as an example of an aspect of E.C. law which could not be said to be "corresponding" to an issue which was relevant for competition within the United Kingdom As Lord Simon said at Committee stage in the House of Lords:

> "The Community objective of ensuring a common internal market for 15 different national states simply does not make sense in a purely domestic context. Therefore, those applying the prohibitions must be able to produce a sensible translation of the E.C. rules into the domestic system." (*Hansard*, H.L., Vol. 583, No. 69, col. 961 (November 25, 1997)).

The Government expanded on and qualified its earlier statements in the Lords on the issue of E.C. single market objectives in the House of Commons. The intention of the Government appears to be that where an agreement does not restrict inter-State trade, E.C. jurisprudence relating to territorial restrictions will not be relevant to the domestic system. However, where the agreement in question does restrict inter-State trade, E.C. jurisprudence on territorial restrictions will be relevant, since agreements which seek to exploit the practical barriers to trade which continue to exist between different national states will raise competition concerns. As Nigel Griffiths, the then Minster for Competition and Consumer Affairs, said at Committee stage in the House of Commons:

> "The fact that the single market objectives will not be relevant for many agreements which come within the scope of the Chapter I Prohibition does not mean that the European Commission and the United Kingdom prohibitions are different. For example, it does not mean the single market considerations must be dissected out of an E.U. decision before applying clause 60.

> Under each prohibition, what is important is whether the agreement can be said to have the object or effect of restricting, preventing or distorting competition. As the general rule, agreements which seek to divide markets along national lines raise serious competition concerns. That is because barriers to trade still exist between Member States." (*Hansard*, H.L., Vol. 314, No. 189, col. 545 (June 18, 1998)).

In any event, in cases where the agreement affects inter-State trade, the Government is under an obligation, as one of its basic Community obligations under the E.C. Treaty, to give effect to the principle of the single market and any interpretation of the Competition Act 1998 which was inconsistent with that obligation would seem to be improper and open to challenge. This would be so even if the United Kingdom case in which the interpretation was given, raised no question precisely corresponding to a decided question of E.C. law relating to competition.

5.3.3 Criticisms

Many commentators, including the CBI, criticised the use of the term "corresponding" as being too imprecise and claimed that it would in turn lead to great uncertainty as to the E.C. jurisprudence which was to be imported. Some have argued that the courts would give the term a very narrow interpretation, confining the application of the governing principles clause to specific agreements or conduct being considered under the domestic system, which had previously been the subject of a decision by the E.C. authorities. Such a narrow interpretation is unlikely even though the imprecise nature of the term "corresponding" will lead to uncertainty as to what is to be imported. This will need to be resolved by the courts.

5.3.4 Position if the Act Contains No Equivalent Provision

Other unanswered questions on the meaning of the term "corresponding" include the issue of whether relevant E.C. Treaty principles are disapplied if there is no equivalent provision in the Act. For example, the Government claimed (*Hansard*, H.L., Vol. 586, No. 116, col. 1366 (March 5, 1998)) that, just as Article 81 and 82 are qualified by Article 295 (formerly Article 222) E.C. Treaty so the domestic prohibitions would be similarly qualified. Article 295 provides that the E.C. Treaty (and legislation made under it) shall in no way prejudice the national systems of property ownership of Member States. However, the fact that there is no equivalent in the Act to Article 295 may mean that it is not a "corresponding" issue for the domestic system and that, therefore, there is no such qualification on the domestic prohibitions. If that were correct, then decisions under the Competition Act could negate intellectual property rights, although a decision under Article 81 or Article 82 could only affect their exercise, but not their existence.

A number of countervailing considerations arise where intellectual property rights themselves reflect mandatory requirements of E.C. law or international treaties binding on the United Kingdom (such as the Berne Convention on copyright). The balancing of these laws with the prohibitions should provide considerable protection against the Director taking a sustainable decision which effectively extinguishes an intellectual property right which is validly existing and which the United Kingdom is bound to recognise as a matter of E.C. law. While theoretically a later statute could be given effect so as to put the United Kingdom in breach of an earlier adoption of an international treaty (in particular one not the subject of any Community obligation) the courts would be sensitive to the issues involved. In addition, the Secretary of State has power to create an exclusion where the application of one of the prohibitions would create a conflict with an international obligation of the United Kingdom (Sched. 3, para. 6).

5.3.5 Position Where There Are Material Differences in United Kingdom Law

Another basis on which the Competition Act departs from E.C. jurisprudence is where the relevant E.C. law would not be "compatible" with the provisions of the Act. For example Article 82 applies only where the firm in question has a dominant position within a "substantial part" of the common market, but the equivalent Chapter II Prohibition may apply even if the dominant position is not in a substantial part of the United Kingdom (see discussion in Chapter 11 at 11.3.4). E.C. jurisprudence on the concept of "substantial part" is therefore, quite simply, irrelevant.

5.3.6 Attempt to Create Equivalence in Approach to Mergers within United Kingdom Jurisdiction

The Government came under considerable pressure in the Parliamentary stages to spell out where the Act was meant to apply E.C. jurisprudence (*e.g.* see *Hansard*, H.L. Vol. 586, No. 108, col. 514 (February 23, 1998)) and where it was intended to depart from it so as to provide certainty for business. The Schedule 1 exclusion for mergers provides an example of a case where confusion could arise:

- Under E.C. competition law, the E.C. Commission does not have powers to apply Articles 81 and 82 to mergers which amount to a concentration as defined in the Merger Regulation. (Council Regulation (EEC) 4064/89 as amended). This restriction applies also to ancillary restraints, that is provisions which are "directly related and necessary" to the concentration (Merger Regulation, Article 8(2)).

- The exclusion under the Competition Act 1998 Sched. 1, Part I of mergers within the meaning of the FTA from the scope of the prohibitions appears to have no relation to E.C. law, since the concept of a merger under the FTA is significantly different from that of a concentration under the Merger Regulation (*e.g.* many joint ventures which are concentrations are not FTA mergers, while acquisitions which confer material influence over policy falling short of decisive influence could be FTA mergers but not concentrations). Previous United Kingdom legislative policy was to examine ancillary restraints separately from merger approval and, approval of a merger under the FTA provided no legal protection for the agreements effecting that merger from the provisions of the RTPA 1976.

- It might therefore be thought that E.C. law on the application of Articles 81 and 82 to concentrations would not be relevant to the exclusion of FTA mergers. However, Sched. 1, Part I, para. 1(2) to the Act expressly excludes from the application of the Chapter I Prohibition provisions which are "directly related and necessary" to the merger situation (within the meaning of the FTA). These words were deliberately copied from the E.C. Merger Regulation, Article 8(2) with the intention that the E.C. doctrine of ancillary restraints will govern the application of the domestic prohibitions to provisions related to FTA mergers (including those that fall outside the Merger Regulation definition of a concentration) such as non-competition covenants on a vendor.

When considering the application of the Act it will therefore be very important to study the relevant sections of the Act in great detail to establish whether phrases from E.C. law could trigger the application of the governing principles clause.

5.4 Differences Between Jurisprudence of the ECJ/CFI and that of The European Commission

5.4.1 Greater Flexibility in Approach to E.C. Commission Rulings

Those applying the prohibitions are under a duty to act with a view to securing there is no inconsistency with principles of the E.C. Treaty, or a decision of, or principle laid down by, the ECJ/CFI. There is a considerably greater degree of flexibility where statements or decisions of the E.C. are in issue. The governing principles section merely imposes a duty "to have regard" to relevant decisions and statements of the E.C. Commission. This weaker obligation is explained by the fact that the E.C. Commission is an executive body and its decisions and views on the application of the law are subject to the decision of the CFI/ECJ. In practice, the E.C. Commission's interpretation of E.C. law is quite capable of diverging from that of the European Courts, but may go unchallenged unless examined by a court. For example, the English Court of Appeal has adopted an interpretation of Commission Regulation (EEC) 1984/83 related to the exclusive purchasing of beer which is inconsistent with the Commission's explanatory notice of June 22, 1983: *Crehan v. Courage; Byrne v. Inntrepreneur Beer Supply Co Ltd; Langton v. Same; Smith v. Greenalls Management Ltd; McGaughey v. Cain CA* [1999] E.C.C.

455–555. It was therefore sensible for the legislation not to impose a binding obligation to achieve consistency with E.C. Commission jurisprudence.

5.4.2 Persuasive Authority

Nevertheless it is hoped that E.C. Commission jurisprudence will provide highly persuasive authority for the application of the domestic prohibitions. E.C. Commission decisions, practices and notices provide a valuable guiding source for business wishing to comply with Article 81 and 82. Much of the value of the domestic law alignment with E.C. competition law principles would be lost if those applying the prohibitions ignored E.C. Commission practice.

5.4.3 Commission Statements

There is no definition of what counts as an E.C. Commission "statement". However, it would seem that the authority of the E.C. Commission must be behind the statement for it to qualify. Therefore comments of DG IV officials on their own should not come with the scope of section 60(3). Statements which should count include E.C. Commission Notices (*e.g.* its notice on ancillary restraints), Annual Reports on Competition Policy and comfort letters which have been preceded by an Official Journal Notice under Article 19(3). The OFT Guidance: *The Major Provisions*, OFT 400, March 1999 at para. 6.2 gives the Director's view that a relevant statement should have the authority of the E.C. Commission as a whole and gives as an example statements about its policy approach which the E.C. Commission has published in its Annual Report on Competition Policy. Explanatory notices on the application of Regulations fall into the same category.

In dealing with E.C. "comfort letters", the Director has indicated that he will not normally depart from the European Commission's assessment. In the final version of the OFT Guideline, *The Chapter I Prohibition*, OFT 401, March 1999 no distinction is made between informal administrative comfort letters and those preceded by the publication of a notice under Article 19(3) of Regulation 17/62 (para 7.12). The Director remarks that the Act does not make provision for the informal procedures of the E.C. Commission (para. 7.11) and therefore this statement of policy by the Director appears to be made independently of section 60. However, an Article 19(3) notice indicating a preliminary intention by the E.C. Commission to take a favourable view and a subsequent comfort letter confirming that view, appear to carry the authority of the E.C. Commission to a far greater degree than a comfort letter written without such a notice, or communicated to only some of the affected parties.

5.5 Possibility of References to The European Court Of Justice

5.5.1 ECJ Approach to Equivalent National Laws

The European Court of Justice decision of *Leur Bloem v. Inspecteur Der Belastingdienst/ondernemingen* (Case C–28/95 [1997] E.C.R. I–4161) provides some support for the Government's hope that references under Article 177 E.C. Treaty will be possible where Article 81 or 82 is not directly in issue. In practice, however, E.C. competition law may often be jointly pleaded with domestic competition law allowing the court to make a reference directly under Article 81 or 82.

Chapter 6

Prohibition of Agreements Which Restrict, Distort or Prevent Competition

6.1   The Chapter I Prohibition
6.2   Interpretation
6.3   Undertakings
6.4   Agreements, Decisions and Concerted Practices
6.5   Object or Effect of Preventing, Restricting or Distorting
      Competition
6.6   Agreements which Affect Trade in the United Kingdom
6.7   Appreciability
6.8   Conduct which will be Caught by the Chapter I Prohibition

6.1   The Chapter I Prohibition

6.1.1   Prohibition of Anti-Competitive Agreements

Section 2(1) in Chapter I of the Competition Act 1998 prohibits (unless benefiting from an exemption or exclusion):

> "agreements between undertakings, decisions by associations of undertakings or concerted practices, which:
> (a) may affect trade within the United Kingdom, and
> (b) have as their object or effect the prevention, restriction or distortion of competition within the United Kingdom".

The new Chapter I Prohibition and the associated provisions of the Act replace legislation designed to control restrictive trading agreements in The Restrictive Trade Practices Act 1976 ("RTPA"), Restrictive Practices Court Act 1976, the Resale Prices Act 1976 and the Restrictive Trade Practices Act 1977. These are repealed by section 1 of the Act (brought into force on March 1, 2000 by the Competition Act 1998 (Commencement No. 5) Order 2000 (S.I. 2000 No. 344) (c.9). The Chapter I Prohibition, by mirroring the wording of Article 81 E.C. Treaty and by introducing into United Kingdom competition law a more "effects-based" approach to the control of restrictive practices, aims to ensure greater consistency in the treatment of such practices at the hands of domestic and European competition authorities. Provisions in an agreement which infringe the prohibition will be void, unless the agreement falls within the terms of one of the general exclusions or exemptions (see Chapters 7 and 8), or is notified to the Director and granted an individual exemption.

6.1.2   Agreements to which the Prohibition Applies

Like Article 81 E.C. Treaty, the Chapter I Prohibition includes a list of the types of agreements or practices that will be caught by the prohibition, namely:

"agreements decisions or practices which:

(a)   directly or indirectly fix purchase or selling prices or any other trading conditions;

(b)   limit or control production, markets, technical development or investment;

(c)   share markets or sources of supply;

(d)   apply dissimilar conditions to equivalent transactions with other trading parties, thereby placing them at a competitive disadvantage;

(e)   make the conclusions of a contract subject to acceptance by the other parties of supplementary obligations which, by their nature or according to commercial usage, have no connection with the subject of such contracts."

Section 2(2) is identical to the provisions of Article 81(1)(a)–(e) and is an indication of the types of agreements that may be deemed to raise serious competition concerns. It should be considered to be in the nature of an explanation or an aid to interpretation, rather than as a provision that defines or limits the scope of the preceding prohibition.

6.2   Interpretation

6.2.1   Interpretation Consistent with Article 81 E.C. Treaty

In the notes accompanying the first draft of the Competition Bill sent out for consultation in August 1997 the Government made clear that the Chapter I Prohibition was to be interpreted so as to avoid any conflict with Article 81 E.C. Treaty and stated that, except where there were good reasons for difference, its

"objectives of effectiveness and minimum burden in operation are best served by ensuring that the domestic prohibition is interpreted in such a way as to avoid any inconsistency with the way in which Articles [81] and [82] themselves are interpreted by the European court".

This applies except were there are "clear and explicit" departures from the E.C. legislation. These objectives are incorporated into the Competition Act by means of the governing principles section at section 60, which is discussed in detail in Chapter 5. In particular, questions arising out of the Chapter I Prohibition which were, when debated, deemed to be best resolved by reference to the governing principles clause, were the question of appreciability (see 6.7.1 below) and the approach to voidness of contracts or parts of contracts in breach of the Chapter I Prohibition (see *Hansard*, H.L., Vol. 583, No. 63, cols 267–268 (November 13, 1997), Vol. 585, No. 99 cols 889–891 (February 9, 1998) and see discussion at Chapter 10, para. 10.2.5).

6.2.2   Approach of United Kingdom Authorities

In what respects and to what extent the United Kingdom competition authorities will build up a separate body of decisions remains to be seen, but guidance in respect of the basic provisions of the Chapter I Prohibition (and the other provisions of the Act) is to be found in existing E.C. case law. On this question of appreciability the Director already shows signs of adopting a somewhat more broadly based approach than the E.C. Commission (see 6.7.4 below).

6.3 Undertakings

6.3.1 Single Economic Entity

When considering what constitutes an undertaking for the purposes of Article 81 E.C. Treaty, the E.C. Commission and the ECJ look at the economic and control structure of the activities under consideration and ignore legal divisions and the nature of the entity. There is a brief consideration of the issues in the OFT Guideline, The Chapter I Prohibition, OFT 401, March 1999 (the "Chapter I Guideline") paras 2.5–2.6.

6.3.2 Parent and Subsidiary

Whether a parent company and its subsidiaries form a single economic entity or several economic units will be a question of fact in every case: *Beguelin Import v. GL Import Export* (C-22/71) [1971] E.C.R. 949, [1972] C.M.L.R. 81. Wholly owned subsidiaries will usually be regarded as forming a single economic unit with their parent, unless their business has some particular characteristic (*cf. Re the Joint Venture of Ing C Olivetti & C, SpA and Canon Inc.* [1988] O.J. L52/51, [1988] 4 C.M.L.R. 177, [1989] 4 C.M.L.R. 940 and *Metro SB-Grossmarkte GmbH & Co KG v. Commission* (C–75/84) [1986] E.C.R. 3021, [1987] 1 C.M.L.R. 118).

A partially owned subsidiary is more likely to be regarded as a separate economic entity from its parent and fellow subsidiaries if, for example, its management has been given the power to operate independent policies and it is able to finance its activities without reliance on its parent. Some partially owned subsidiaries are joint ventures in which the other shareholders may have similar powers of control to the parent. These seem likely to be treated as economic entities independent of all their shareholders.

Where a parent and subsidiary are regarded as a single economic undertaking, agreements between them do not fall within the ambit of the Chapter I Prohibition and the terms of such internal agreements will be ignored in assessing agreements made with third parties by any of them (see *Re Kodak* [1970] O.J. L147/24, [1970] C.M.L.R. D19, as amended by [1970] O.J. L159/22).

6.3.3 Partnerships and Co-operatives

In *Hydrotherm Geraatebau GmbH v. Compact del Dott Ing Mario Andreoli* (Case C–170/83) [1984] E.C.R. 2999, [1985] 3 C.M.L.R. 224 the test used in relation to partnerships was whether the parties operated as a single economic undertaking. It was held that a limited partnership and its general partner (an individual) were a single undertaking for the purpose of applying a block exemption to an agreement between the partnership and a third party. However, this case relates only to the position of members of a partnership in their dealings with third parties; it does not mean that a partnership agreement (as an agreement between individuals or businesses) falls outside the scope of the Chapter I Prohibition. Agricultural cooperatives are treated similarly in E.C. law, the body as a whole being regarded as a single economic entity in its dealings with third parties, and the members being deemed separate for the purposes of considering the agreement between the members (see *Preserved Mushrooms* [1975] O.J. L29/26, [1975] 1 C.M.L.R. D83).

6.3.4   Representative Bodies

Representative bodies such as trade and services supply associations are specifically covered by the wording of the Chapter I Prohibition and decisions by them and agreements between their members will be within its ambit (see *Re ANSEAU NAVEWA* [1982] O.J. L167/39, [1982] 2 C.M.L.R. 193. Professional bodies and self-regulating bodies also fall into the category of associations of undertakings included in the legislation. Further guidance in respect of how the new legislation applies to such bodies has been issued by the OFT in its guideline, *Trade Associations, Professions and Self Regulating Bodies*, OFT 408, March 1999 (the "Trade Association Guideline") (see also 6.4.2 below).

6.3.5   Other entities

Other entities whose status has been considered in E.C. case law and which have been regarded as separate economic units are non-profit making bodies representing the interests of a number of organisations (see *Interpar v. Gesellschaft zur Verwertung von Leistungsschutzrechen mbH* [1981] O.J. L370/49, [1982] 1 C.M.L.R. 221), individuals engaged in economic activities on their own account (for example, acting as consultants) (see *Reuter v. BASF AG* [1976] O.J. L254/40, [1976] 2 C.M.L.R. D44), persons who have the legal relationship of an agent to a principal, but who have separate economic activities or assume financial responsibility or act for several parties (see *Re Italian Cast Glass: The Community v Fabrica Pisana SpA & Others* [1980] O.J. L383/19, [1982] 2 C.M.L.R. 61) (as opposed to agents who are "true commercial agents" and, accordingly, neither undertake nor engage in the activities of an independent trader in the course of operations), and state entities or state authorised bodies (such as utilities), whether publicly or privately owned, when carrying out commercial activities (see *Re ANSEAU NAVEWA* (1982) supra at 6.3.4 above).

6.3.6   The Crown

Case law made in application of the RTPA meant that agreements with the Crown were not subject to the provisions of that legislation. In contrast, agreements with the Crown are specifically included within the scope of the Act and will be subject to the provisions of the Chapter I Prohibition, subject to a number of provisos. In particular, the Crown is not criminally liable as a result of any provision of the Act, the Crown is not liable for any penalty under the Act and nothing in the Act affects Her Majesty in her private capacity (see s. 73(1)). However, in many of its activities the Crown would not be recognised by European jurisprudence as an "undertaking", since it would be carrying out policy rather than commercial objectives.

6.4   Agreements, Decisions and Concerted Practices

6.4.1   Agreements

All types of agreement, formal and informal, express and implied are caught by Article 81 E.C. Treaty. Similarly the Chapter I Prohibition applies not only to formal, legally binding agreements, but also to informal understandings and "gentlemen's agreements" (see *Re Franco-Japanese Ballbearings Agreement* [1974] O.J.

L343/19, [1975] 1 C.M.L.R. D8). Agreement may also be implied or inferred from conduct. In *AEG-Telefunken AG v. E.C. Commission* (Case C–107/82) [1983] E.C.R. 3151, [1984] 3 C.M.L.R. 325, AEG's selective distribution system was considered, and the company's persistent refusal to appoint additional stockists was held to include an implied agreement between AEG and its existing stockists to limit the number of dealers at stockist level. Agreements linked with statutory requirements have also been deemed to be within the scope of Article 81, and may therefore be within the scope of the Chapter I Prohibition, in particular where they go beyond the requirement of the law or are fixed in agreement with the industry in question (see *Bayonox*, [1990] O.J. L21/71, [1990] 4 C.M.L.R. 930).

6.4.2　Decisions and Recommendations

As well as decisions by associations of undertakings, decisions taken by an association whose members are associations of undertakings are within the ambit of Article 81 (see *Re Milchfaorderungsfonds* [1985] O.J. L35/35 [1985] 3 C.M.L.R. 101). A professional body may also be deemed to be such an association (see *Re Consiglio Nazionale degli Spedizionieri Doganali* [1993] O.J. L203/27). Recommendations of such associations, even where they are expressed as non-binding or have been disregarded by members, may be deemed to be decisions for the purposes of Article 81 E.C. Treaty: *IAZ International Belgium NV v. Commission* (Joined Cases C96–102, 104–105, 108–110/82) [1983] E.C.R. 3369; [1984] 3 C.M.L.R. 276. In particular, the ECJ has held that non-binding recommendations by an association amount to a decision where the association's statutes allow it to regulate its members and, in practice, members quickly follow its recommendations (see *FEDETAB and others v. Commission* (Joined Cases C–209–215/78, 218/78) [1980] E.C.R. 3125, [1981] 3 C.M.L.R. 134). The fact that compliance with recommendations was voluntary has been deemed irrelevant by the ECJ in several instances, where it considered, for example, that the recommendations reflected usual practice or the wishes of an association and would therefore affect trade as if they were a binding decision, and that compliance with those recommendations had an appreciable effect on competition in the market in question.

　　The OFT's Trade Association Guideline, paras 2.2 and 2.3 also make clear that "decisions by associations of undertakings" has a wide meaning and, as in E.C. case law, may include the constitution or rules of an association of undertakings or its recommendations (whether or not they are binding) or "other activities". For example, resolutions of a management committee or decisions of the executive or rulings of its chief executive may all be "decisions" for the purposes of the Chapter I Prohibition.

6.4.3　Information Agreements

The Trade Association Guideline discusses the exchange of information and the extent to which it may give rise to the infringement of the Chapter I Prohibition. Exchange of specific price information within the context of a trade association would be caught by the Chapter I Prohibition as a decision of an association of undertakings or an agreement between its members, although an agreement relating to information which is not confidential and does not enable the identification of confidential information of individual undertakings may be acceptable: see *Bundesverband Deutscher Stahlhandel eV* 80/257/ECSC, [1980] O.J. L62/34, [1980] 3 C.M.L.R. 193.

　　The exchange of some types of non-price information may also infringe the Chapter I Prohibition, particularly in a concentrated market where the information is sufficient to limit or destroy competition between a small number of participants and to raise entry barriers for third parties: see the European decisions on the exchange of information on sales and market shares by the *United Kingdom Agricultural Tractor Registration Exchange* [1992] O.J. L68/19, [1993] 4 C.M.L.R. 358, upheld by the CFI at T 34/92 *Fiatagri and Ford New Holland v. Commission* [1994] E.C.R. II–905, *New Holland Ford Limited v. Commission* (Case C–8/95) [1998] E.C.R. I–3175, [1998] 5 C.M.L.R. 311 and *John Deere v. Commission* (Case C–7/95P) [1998] All E.R. (E.C.) 481, [1998] E.C.R. I–3111, [1998] 5 C.M.L.R. 311.

Exchanges limited to opinion and experience are unlikely to infringe the Chapter I Prohibition (*Commission Notice on Co-operation Agreements* [1968] O.J. (C75/3).

Schedule 4 of the Act provides for the exclusion from the scope of the Chapter I Prohibition of certain "designated" professional rules (notified to and designated by the Secretary of State). These include professional rules relating to services such as legal, medical and dental services, the provision of education and training and the services of Ministers of Religion. The Director is to keep a list of "designated" professional rules, which can be amended (see Chapter 7, para. 7.7.1).

6.4.4   Concerted Practices

The reference to concerted practices in Article 81 E.C. Treaty and in the Chapter I Prohibition is intended to catch the type of anti-competitive behaviour which involves tacit co-operation falling short of an agreement, for example, where several players in an industry introduce uniform pricing policies. In *ICI Ltd v. Commission* (Cases C–48–49, 51–57/69) [1972] E.C.R. 619, [1972] C.M.L.R. 557 the ECJ defined a concerted practice as "a form of co-ordination, between undertakings which, without going so far as to amount to an agreement properly so called, knowingly substitutes a practical co-operation between them for the risks of competition". This case shows that to establish a concerted practice both parallel behaviour and circumstances which suggest co-operation to remove uncertainties are needed. A concerted practice may be inferred where there is evidence which suggests that the behaviour in question is inexplicable in the market concerned as independent parallel behaviour. Concerted practices have also been inferred in cases where one or more undertakings have changed their behaviour in accordance with the wishes of another (see *Camera Care v. Hasselblad* [1982] O.J. L161/18, [1982] 2 C.M.L.R. 233) and, in the banking sector, co-operation to maintain the status quo was deemed to be a concerted practice (see *Gerhard Zuchner v. Bayerische Vereinsbank AG* (Case C–172/82) [1981] E.C.R. 2021, [1982] 1 C.M.L.R. 313). Where a formal agreement has been ended but the agreed behaviour continues, a concerted practice may also be inferred (see *Etablissements Consten SARL & Grundig Verkaufs GmbH v. Commission,* (Joined Cases C 56 & 58/64) [1966] E.C.R. 299, [1966] C.M.L.R. 418).

In *Re Woodpulp; A Ahlström Oy v. Commission* (Cases C89, 104, 114, 116–117, 125–9/85) [1985] O.J. L85/1, [1993] E.C.R. 1307, [1993] 4 C.M.L.R. 407 at para. 71 the ECJ did place limits on how far a concerted practice might be inferred in the absence of evidence of co-ordination, saying "parallel conduct cannot be regarded as furnishing proof of concentration unless concentration constitutes the only plausible explanation for such conduct. It is necessary to bear in mind that, although Article 81 of the Treaty prohibits any form of collusion which distorts competition, it does not deprive economic operators of the right to adapt themselves intelligently to the existing and anticipated conduct of their competitors."

6.5   Object or Effect of Preventing, Restricting or Distorting Competition

6.5.1   Preventing, Restricting or Distorting Competition

Examples of the types of behaviour which may be considered to prevent, restrict or distort competition are included in the legislation at section 2(2) and listed at 6.1.2 above. Conduct which is typically prohibited or deemed to be within Article 81, which will also fall within the domestic prohibition, includes cartellism, price fixing, market sharing, production/sales quotas, resale price maintenance, agreements to limit or co-ordinate investment, bid-rigging and certain types of agreements relating to the exchange of information (see 6.8.1 to 6.8.7, below). Whether the prohibition can also apply to pro-competitive agreements (on the basis that a pro-competitive effect is a distortion of competition) is discussed at 6.5.4 below.

6.5.2   Object or Effect

An agreement, decision or concerted practice may be prohibited on the grounds that it is anti-competitive either in object or in effect. This means that the relevant competition authority will examine both the purpose of the agreement or other behaviour, and its result. Therefore, if parties conclude an agreement or carry out a concerted practice for the purpose of preventing, distorting or restricting competition, they may be found to be in breach of the Chapter I Prohibition, even if their behaviour has had absolutely no effect in practice. In addition, an agreement which only incidentally has an anti-competitive effect will be caught, regardless of the parties' lack of intention.

6.5.3   Object

While the object of an agreement may be said to refer to the parties' intentions, it is more properly construed as referring to the subject matter of the agreement, including its purpose and result. The object is the purpose which can be understood from the terms laid down in the agreement in question, or which can be observed from the conduct in question, rather than from any statements which any parties may have made in relation to the purpose of the agreement or conduct. That an agreement or conduct has not attained its object is no defence to any action for breach of the prohibition.

In the courts in civil law jurisdictions an agreement will almost always be examined in its wider context, including economic factors which influence its operation (see *La Technique Minière v. Maschinenbau Ulm GmbH* (Case C–56/65) [1966] E.C.R. 235, [1966] C.M.L.R. 357 and *AEG Telefunken AG v. E.C. Commission* (Case 107/82) [1983] E.C.R. 3151, [1984] 3 C.M.L.R. 413). However in approaching the term "object" the United Kingdom courts would usually interpret an agreement in order to ascertain its purpose and there are only limited instances where the surrounding circumstances will be considered in the exercise, although there is an increasing tendency to look at these circumstances (see *Investors Compensation Scheme v. West Bromwich Building Society* [1998] 1 W.L.R. 896, [1998] 1 All E.R. 98). It may be that this difference will result in some divergent results unless a court has a proper understanding of what is meant by the object of the agreement, decision or practice, and is prepared fully to adopt the European approach. It seems clear that the United Kingdom competition authorities will adopt the European approach, and the governing principles section should be used to encourage the United Kingdom courts also to do so.

6.5.4   Effect

The effect of an agreement is its "natural and probable consequences" (*Re the IFTRA Rules for Producers of Virgin Aluminium* [1975] O.J. L228/38, [1975] 2 C.M.L.R. D20). These will also be considered in context (for example, in the context of a network of agreements, where a standard term is used widely in a relevant trade, or where the agreement will affect future manufacturing or sales patterns for a new product). In *BAT Ltd & R J Reynolds Industries Inc v. Commission* (Cases 142 and 156/84) [1987] E.C.R. 4487, [1987] 2 C.M.L.R. 551 it was made clear that it was sufficient for an agreement to have a potential (rather than an actual) effect for it to fall within Article 81. Effect may be unintentional: for example, in *Re Bayer Dental* (Decision 90/645) [1990] O.J. L351/46, [1992] 4 C.M.L.R. 61, language used to limit a manufacturer's liability in respect of resale abroad of a product which might not meet the requirements of health and safety laws in other Member States was held to have gone too far and to infringe Article 81.

The Chapter I Guideline para. 3.3 remarks that "any agreement that has an appreciable effect on competition is likely to fall within the Chapter I Prohibition." This statement may show an intention to follow the line of European cases dealing primarily with effect on trade between Member States rather than effect on competition limb of Article 81. These cases apply Article 81 to agreements which increase competition: *Establissements Consten SARL & Grundig Verkaufs GmbH v. Commission* (Joined Cases C 56 & 58/64) [1966] E.C.R. 299, [1966] C.M.L.R. 418, *R Continental Gummi-Werke and Michelin* [1988] O.J. L305/33, [1989] 4 C.M.L.R. 920. These cases were concerned to found jurisdiction to consider anti-competitive elements within an overall pro-competitive arrangement, particularly in the circumstances where it was difficult to discern any restriction on movement of goods or services between Member States (see 6.6 below). The statement in the Guideline may however be inadvertence on the OFT's part rather than an intention to assert that purely pro-competitive agreements are caught by the prohibition if they bring appreciable benefits for competition. If an agreement has an appreciable anti-competitive effect within the United Kingdom it will be caught by the Chapter I Prohibition and overall pro-competitive effect will found arguments for an exemption.

6.6   Agreements Which Affect Trade in the United Kingdom

6.6.1   Meaning of Trade

The term "trade" has been interpreted widely. The Government's intention is that the "trade test" should be read in conjunction with section 2(7) of the Act, which provides that an effect on trade in the United Kingdom means "in relation to an agreement which operates or is intended to operate only in a part of the United Kingdom, that part". The Government intends this provision to displace a presumption which might arise in E.C. jurisprudence that there must be an effect on movement of trade. Instead, under the provisions of the Act, it is clearly intended that the agreement, decision or concerted practice affects the "activity" of trade. The Chapter I Guideline remarks at para. 2.16 that "it is very unlikely that an agreement which restricts competition in the United Kingdom does not also affect trade in the United Kingdom".

6.6.2   Part of the United Kingdom

Article 81 (unlike Article 82) has no reference to parts of the common market. The introduction of a reference to part of the United Kingdom in the United Kingdom's version of Article 81 therefore invites comparison with United Kingdom rather than E.C. legislation. Section 2(7) also distinguishes the Act from the merger provisions of the FTA, where there is a requirement that all or "a substantial part" of the United Kingdom must be affected, and aligns it with the monopoly provisions of the FTA, section 9, which allow a monopoly reference to be made in relation to any part of the United Kingdom The decision of the House of Lords that "substantial part" means "of such size, character and importance as to make it worth consideration for the purposes of the Act" (see *South Yorkshire Transport Limited v. Monopolies and Mergers Commission* [1993] 1 W.L.R. 23, [1993] 1 All E.R. 289) means that, in practice, use of the word "substantial" in the merger provisions of the FTA is of little effect. However, the omission of the reference to "substantial" removes the debate in respect of the size of the geographic area which must be affected by the agreement, decision or practice. Except where the effect of an agreement is *de minimis* (see 6.7.4 below), almost all agreements between parties with business interests in the United Kingdom may affect trade in the United Kingdom Agreements where there were not two parties carrying on business in the United Kingdom for the purposes of the RTPA but which do affect trade in the United Kingdom in one way or another may be caught, and become subject to the scrutiny of the United Kingdom competition authorities for the first time (but see the jurisdictional limitations discussed at 6.6.3 below).

6.6.3   Territoriality

Under the usual rules of statutory interpretation, "United Kingdom" means Great Britain (England, Wales, Scotland and subsidiary islands but not the Isle of Man or the Channel Islands) and Northern Ireland (The Interpretation Act 1978, ss. 2 and 22(1), Sched. 1 and Sched. 2, para. 4(1)). Section 2(3) of the Competition Act 1998 states that the prohibition applies "only if the agreement, decision or practice is, or is intended to be, implemented in the United Kingdom". This is intended to reflect E.C. jurisprudence established in *Re Wood Pulp* (Cases C–89, 104, 114, 116–117, 125–129/85) [1988] E.C.R. 5193, [1984] 4 C.M.L.R. 901. The aim of the Government was to avoid creating a loophole whereby parties could escape falling within the Chapter I Prohibition by executing agreements outside the United Kingdom, while maintaining the United Kingdom's usual policy on territoriality, which is restrained and rejects a pure "effects based approach". An amendment of the provision, whereby "implemented" was replaced by "acted on" was rejected on the grounds that jurisdiction could be claimed on the basis of the economic effects felt within a State resulting from behaviour outside that State. The Government believed that to be too wide a basis for the prohibition (see *Hansard*, H.L., cols. 261–262 (November 13, 1997)).

Prior to the enactment of the Act, the Minister for Competition and Consumer Affairs (then Nigel Griffiths) stated "our policy is not to claim jurisdiction over activities outside the United Kingdom on the sole basis of the economic effects of such activities felt within the United Kingdom" (HC Official Report, SC G (Competition Bill) cols 87–88, June 2, 1998).

6.7   Appreciability

6.7.1   Importance of Appreciability

The idea that, the effect of an agreement on trade has to be "appreciable" for it to fall within the prohibition is crucial in the context of legislation which does not distinguish between actual and potential effect. Without the appreciability test it would seem that almost every commercial agreement implemented in the United Kingdom would be caught by the prohibition, however small the parties and however minor its application. The "appreciable effect" rule was developed in E.C. jurisprudence in order to introduce some reasonable limit to agreements which could be caught by Article 81. The governing principles provision at section 60 of the Act (see Chapter 5) means that a similar rule will be applied in the context of the new legislation. This intention was made clear when, at Committee Stage in the House of Lords, it was moved that the draft legislation be amended so as to include a provision to reflect that the Chapter I Prohibition would only apply if "the agreement, decision or practice has, or is likely to have, a significant effect on competition within the United Kingdom". It was stated in response that it was the intention of the bill, as drafted, that the competition regime should only be concerned with situations where the anti-competitive effects were significant or appreciable. The proposed amendment was rejected on the grounds that E.C. jurisprudence already incorporated an appreciability test. It was also considered that an explicit significance test in the body of the Act did not fit well with the approach of reliance on European case law and "could be harmful in indicating a departure from established European principles where this is not the intention". There was a risk that "in apparently departing from established European principles, we might inadvertently make so high a threshold for action that we could impede the effective tackling of anti-competitive agreements" (*Hansard*, H.L., Vol. 583, No. 63, cols 258–260 (November 13, 1997) and H.L., Vol. 585, No. 99, cols 884–888 (February 9, 1998)).

6.7.2   Operation in relation to Article 81

In deciding whether an agreement may be deemed to have an "appreciable effect" on trade between Member States, the E.C. Commission and the European Court are not bound by any particular rules and can be quite flexible. They will take into account factors such as the size of the businesses concerned and their market shares. Potential size is also taken into account, that is, how the businesses in question might develop if the agreement under consideration is successful. In *Re Service Master Limited* [1988] O.J. L332/38, [1989] 4 C.M.L.R. 581, the notification of a standard form agreement at the commencement of the development of a network was considered by reference to the size of the network if the agreement was successful. If one of the parties occupies a position as a leading manufacturer of a particular product worldwide, that may be enough for an agreement to be deemed to have an appreciable effect, even if the relevant party's market share in the E.C. is comparatively low (for example, 10 per cent, as in *Duffy Group v. Quaker Oats Limited (Fisher Price)* [1988] O.J. L 49/19, [1989] 4 C.M.L.R. 553. The Commission's notice on agreements of minor importance clarifies to some extent its position (see O.J. [1997] C372/05): it will normally treat any horizontal agreement involving parties at the same level of trade with a combined market share of under 5 per cent, and any vertical agreement involving parties at different levels of trade with a combined market share of under 10 per cent as falling outside Article 81.

6.7.3 How the Rule Might be Applied to the Domestic Prohibition

The Director will, of course, assess the effect of an agreement on competition for the purposes of the Chapter I Prohibition by looking at the market and the economic context of that agreement. Whether an agreement, decision or practice has an appreciable effect will nonetheless often depend on the extent of parties' presence in the relevant product and geographic market, as it does under Article 81.

6.7.4 De Minimis

The Chapter I Guideline states that the Director takes the view that agreements will not generally have an appreciable effect on competition if the parties' combined share of the relevant market does not exceed 25 per cent, subject to certain exceptions (para. 2.19–2.20). Market definition is the subject of a separate OFT Guideline, *Market Definition*, OFT 403, March 1999. The exceptions include agreements between undertakings which fix prices or share markets, impose minimum resale prices or are part of a network of similar agreements which have a cumulative effect on a particular market. The Director's rule of thumb suggests a more generous approach than that of the E.C. Commission (see 6.7.2 above), and makes no distinction between horizontal and vertical agreements involving vertical relationships (*e.g.* copyright licences) which do not benefit from any exclusion or exemption. It also reflects a unified approach to United Kingdom competition law, since 25 per cent market share is the basis of the monopoly jurisdiction under the Fair Trading Act 1973 and one of the bases of jurisdiction under the merger provisions of that legislation. Individual cases may be exceptions to the rule, probably creating most risk for businesses which are large and successful in their main markets (product or geographical) but are the subject of complaints about their activities in markets where they are less successful.

6.7.5 Limited Immunity for Small Agreements

The Competition Act provides, at section 39, for limited immunity from fines for the parties to "small agreements" (except for price-fixing agreements), put into effect by the Competition Act 1998 (Small Agreements and Conduct of Minor Significance) Regulations 2000 (S.I. 2000 No. 262). This is considered further in Chapter 10 at 10.3.8.

6.8 Conduct Which will be Caught by the Chapter I Prohibition

6.8.1 Two Categories of Conduct

There are two categories of conduct which fall within the scope of the Chapter I Prohibition, these being conduct which is absolutely prohibited, and conduct which is eligible for an exemption. The various types of conduct which are typically prohibited by the prohibition are set out briefly in the paragraphs below, and discussed in more detail in *Competition Law and Practice* pp. 38–44 as conduct typically prohibited by Article 81. The Chapter I Guideline also provides useful guidance in respect of the type of conduct which may typically be deemed to be in breach of the Chapter I Prohibition. The circumstances in which certain types of conduct are eligible for an exemption are discussed in Chapter 8.

6.8.2   Cartellism

Cartels (*i.e.* horizontal agreements between several natural competitors which limit competition between them) may, among other things, fix prices, limit production and set up barriers to market entry. Typical conduct is discussed below at 6.8.3–6.8.5. Cartels protect members of the cartel by protecting their markets and their profit margins, as well as dispensing with the need for them to develop new products to attract or keep customers. By virtue of all of these factors, such agreements raise the most significant barriers to competition in any market, by ensuring that the conditions which are seen to be the benefits of an open and competitive market (*i.e.* lower prices, innovation and choice) no longer play a part in the market that is the subject of the cartel. After years of adverse decisions and heavy fines, cartellism has, to a large extent, been driven underground and parties will often attempt to conceal their involvement and deny the existence of any pact.

6.8.3   Price Fixing

The E.C. Commission has, in the context of Article 81, traditionally taken a harsh view of horizontal price-fixing agreements and imposed heavy fines on the parties to them within its overall cap for each participant of 10 per cent of turnover in the most recent complete business year (Council Regulation 17/62/EEC, Article 15(2)) (see, for example, the fines imposed on the participants in a cartel in Pipes used for District Heating Systems, which totalled 92.21 million Euros (£64.5 million) (*Pre-insulated pipes cartel* (Case IV/35.691/E-4) [1999] O.J. L024/1) of which a fine of 70 million Euros was imposed on the largest of the cartel members – ABB.

6.8.4   Co-ordinated Resale Price Maintenance

The Commission has rejected attempted justifications: In *FEDETAB* [1978] O.J. L224/29 the Commission refused to grant an exemption to a joint recommendation of resale prices to retailers, and rejected the argument that the recommendation was needed to protect specialist retailers against damaging price competition. The decision was upheld by the ECJ in *FEDETAB v. Commission* (Joined Cases 209–215/78, 218/78) [1980] E.C.R. 3125, [1981] 3 C.M.L.R. 134. The last United Kingdom agreement providing for co-ordinated resale price maintenance (which was exempted from the RTPA and the Resale Prices Act 1976), is currently before the Restrictive Practices Court, which is reviewing the decision in *Re Medicaments* [1971] 1 All E.R. 12, (1971) L.R. 7 R.P. 267. If the Director succeeds in his arguments, its transitional exclusion from the Chapter I Prohibition will be lost (see Chapter 16 at 16.4). The Restrictive Practices Court has already struck down the Net Book Agreement (March 13, 1997), which also allowed for recommendation of resale prices.

6.8.5   Market Sharing

Attempting to compartmentalise a market through market-sharing agreements (typically, dividing a market geographically) will fall within the prohibition (see *Re Welded Steel Mesh* [1989] O.J. L260/1, [1991] 4 C.M.L.R. 13). Bid-rigging may involve price-fixing, but may also involve other measures to achieve the allocation of contracts, with some participants declining to quote and others offering poor terms. Bid-rigging in any form is viewed as seriously as price fixing.

6.8.6   Production and Sales Quotas

A cartel may impose production and sales quotas on its participants which reinforce agreements on prices and leave participants with no incentive to compete for customers. Limiting production maintains high prices by ensuring that there is no surplus and therefore demand remains steady; limitation of sales has a similar effect, as well as discouraging competition for new customers. Some agreements provide for financial penalties to be imposed on participants in a cartel who exceed quotas, and the proceeds shared out among those who fail to reach them (see *Re Roofing Felt: Belasco v. E.C. Commission* (Case C–246/86) [1989] E.C.R. 2117, [1991] 4 C.M.L.R. 130). All these types of agreement will fall within the Chapter I Prohibition and are very unlikely to qualify for exemption.

6.8.7   Open Cartellism

Typical features of open cartellism are product standardisation, joint advertising and the development and use of standard contractual terms. Often such practices may be deemed justifiable, for instance on safety grounds, or in certain circumstances to save costs, or because it is advantageous to customers and suppliers in certain markets to have properly understood common terms. The type of behaviour co-ordinated by trade associations may often constitute a form of open cartellism, and it is the detail of the conduct or the agreement which determines whether or not it is acceptable (provided it does not affect individual pricing, see *Re Vimpoltu* paras 35–39, [1983] O.J. L200/44, [1993] 3 C.M.L.R. 619, rather than the fact of its existence.

6.8.8   Other Conduct

An agreement between a manufacturer and a party who resells that manufacturer's products will, insofar as it limits the reseller's freedom to decide upon the price at which it will resell the product in question, fall within the ambit of the Chapter I Prohibition (see *Re Spices* [1978] O.J. L53/20, [1978] 2 C.M.L.R. 116), and an obligation to abide by recommended retail prices will not normally merit an exemption (see *Distillers Company v. Commission* (Case 30/78) [1980] E.C.R. 2229, [1980] 3 C.M.L.R. 121), although in certain circumstances it may be possible to justify a provision that keeps prices below a defined level. The exclusion from the Chapter I Prohibition for vertical agreements reflects this European jurisprudence by limiting the scope of its applicability in respect of provisions which have the object or effect of restricting the buyer's ability to determine its sale price: The Competition Act 1998 (Land and Vertical Agreements Exclusion) Order 2000 (S.I. 2000 No. 310), Article 4 is discussed in Chapter 7 at 7.2.

6.8.9   Acceptable Agreements

There are a number of types of agreements, or provisions commonly found in agreements, which, although they may appear to be anti-competitive, will not usually be regarded as in breach of the Chapter I Prohibition. In addition to certain activities of trade associations as noted at 6.8.7 above, examples of agreements or provisions which will often be considered to be justified are:

- non-compete clauses where they merely constitute an ancillary restraint essential to the attainment of an otherwise legal purpose and no more than necessary to protect the parties' legitimate business interests (see *Remia BV and Nutricia BV v. Commission* (Case 42/84) [1985] E.C.R. 2545, [1987] 1 C.M.L.R. 1); and

- licensing and distribution agreements conferring exclusive rights for the manufacture and/or distribution of goods in a particular territory.

Where a licence agreement merely restrains the licensor and licensee from competing with one another in respect of the licensed goods in the reserved territory it will normally not be in breach of the Chapter I Prohibition (see *L C Nungesser KG and Kurt Eisele v. Commission* (Case 258/78) [1982] E.C.R. 2015, [1983] 1 C.M.L.R. 278). However, if it imposes any additional territorial restraints (for example, a prohibition on the licensee on reselling the goods outside his territory), it may infringe Article 81 and the Chapter I Prohibition.

The Commission's new block exemption regulation for vertical agreements suggests, however, that non-compete provisions may require particular examination when they are co-extensive with or exceed the life of an agreement lasting more than five years: see the discussion under the heading "Single branding" at paras 137–160 of the Commission Notice, Guidelines on Vertical Restraints.

Many acceptable agreements benefit from E.C. block exemptions and United Kingdom parallel exemptions (see Chapter 8) and/or United Kingdom exclusions (see Chapter 7).

Chapter 7

Exclusions from the Prohibition of Anti-Competitive Agreements

7.1 Overview
7.2 Vertical Agreements
7.3 Land Agreements
7.4 Mergers
7.5 Exclusions for Agreements Regulated Under Other Legislation
7.6 General Exclusions
7.7 Professional Rules

7.1 Overview

7.1.1 Scope of the Chapter I Prohibition

Although it is intended that the prohibition of anti-competitive agreements should apply widely in the United Kingdom economy, it has been accepted there are a number of categories of agreements where the application of the prohibition should not apply. Some of these exclusions are very wide ranging, such as the exclusions for mergers and vertical restraints. They do, however, provide for a clawback in certain circumstances. This system of broad exclusions with the possibility of clawback has the advantage of allowing regulatory resources to concentrate on the more important issues. The broad areas where exclusion is considered to be justified are:

(1) where agreements are generally of a benign nature and do not merit scrutiny (*e.g.* vertical agreements and land agreements);

(2) where it is more efficient to consider agreements under other provisions of competition law (*e.g.* agreements ancillary to a merger);

(3) where there are or have been arrangements under other legislation to scrutinise matters for their anti-competitive effects, in order to avoid duplication (*e.g.* rules of various bodies regulated by Financial Services Legislation). This category includes agreements classified as insignificant when they were reviewed under the previous law for the purposes of section 21(2) of the Restrictive Trade Practices Act 1976 ("RTPA");

(4) where the provisions of an agreement are necessary in order to comply with legal requirements;

(5) where it is necessary to avoid conflict with international treaty obligations;

(6) where there are overriding national policy considerations; and

(7) professional rules in certain defined categories. The chosen categories recognise that such rules are somewhat in the nature of public law, and

indeed some such rules are laid down according to a statutory procedure (*e.g.* under the Solicitors Act 1974).

7.1.2 Legislative Basis — Vertical Agreements and Land

Section 50 provides that the Secretary of State may by order provide for any provision of Part I (Chapter I and Chapter II Prohibitions) to apply in relation to -

(a) vertical agreements, or

(b) land agreements

with such modifications as may be prescribed. The Order made in exercise of this power is discussed at 7.2 and 7.3 below.

Section 50(2) provides that an order may, in particular, provide for exclusions or exemptions, or otherwise provide for prescribed provisions not to apply in relation to:

(a) vertical agreements or land agreements, in general; or

(b) vertical agreements or land agreements of any prescribed description.

"Vertical agreement" and "land agreement" have such meaning as may be prescribed by an order (s. 50(5)) and no order is to be made under this section unless a draft has been laid before Parliament and approved by a resolution of each House (s. 71(4)(d)), a procedure known as the "affirmative resolution" procedure. This ensures that Parliament debates the legislation, which is not the case under the simpler "negative resolution" procedure, where a statutory instrument will become law without debate unless parliamentarians call for a debate and then reject the legislation (Statutory Instruments Act 1946, s. 4(1)).

7.1.3 Legislative Basis — Other Categories of Exclusion

Section 3 provides that the prohibition of anti-competitive agreements does not apply in any of the cases in which it is excluded by or as a result of:

Sched. 1: mergers and concentrations (discussed at 7.4);

Sched. 2: competition scrutiny under other enactments (discussed at 7.5);

Sched. 3: planning obligations and other general exclusions, including some further categories subject to competition review under other legislation, as well as categories 4, 5 and 6 above (discussed at 7.6);

Sched. 4: professional rules (discussed at 7.7).

The Secretary of State has the power by statutory instrument to add, remove or amend excluded cases in Sched. 1 (s. 3(2)). He has the power to do the same in respect of Sched. 3 (s. 3(3)). Section 3(4) provides that his power to add an additional exclusion under Sched. 3 should only be exercised if the agreements which fall within the additional exclusion do not in general have an adverse effect on competition, or, if they may have that effect, are best considered under either the Chapter II Prohibition or the FTA. The exercise of the Secretary of State's power under section 3 is subject to approval under the affirmative resolution procedure.

7.2 Vertical Agreements

7.2.1 Policy

The Government made it clear from the start that its policy would be to provide an exclusion from the Chapter I Prohibition for vertical agreements, that is, agreements between parties operating at different levels of trade (*e.g.* manufacturer and distributor or wholesaler and retailer). At the same time as the Competition Act 1998 was going through the legislative process, the E.C. Commission was undertaking the most comprehensive review of this matter for decades. In its October 1998 Communication following up from its Green Paper, the E.C. Commission proposed a single block exemption regulation, covering all vertical restraints concerning intermediate and final goods as well as services. This has come into force as Commission Regulation (EC) No. 2790/1999 of December 22, 1999 on the application of Article 81(3) of the Treaty to categories of vertical agreements and concerted practices ([1999] O.J. L336/21) which has effect from June 1, 2000 to May 31, 2010 (the "Vertical Agreements Block Exemption").

The reasons for the adoption of a policy which takes many vertical agreements out of the application of competition law at both European and United Kingdom level are twofold. First, that vertical agreements are generally benign in nature and in many cases pro-competitive, particularly in stimulating intra-brand competition. Second, because of the essential role in the distribution chain, such agreements are very numerous: individual scrutiny would take up administrative resources better used on more serious matters.

The United Kingdom has taken a more robust view of these matters and provided a wide exclusion. The E.C. Commission has taken a more restrictive view, burdened (as it is) with case law on small agreements with aggregate network effect (the special rules for beer ties and petrol station "solus" agreements in the recently expired exclusive purchasing block exemption (EC Commission Regulation 1984/83 [1983] O.J. L173/5) and cases such as *Delimitis (Stergios) v. Henninger Brau AG* (Case C-234/89) E.C.R. [1991] I-935, [1992] 5 C.M.L.R. 210). The E.C. Commission has also been heavily influenced by economists' concerns about the possible horizontal effects of vertical agreements between competitors. The resultant differences in approach are described in more detail at 7.2.8 below.

The United Kingdom Government originally expressed its intention to follow the E.C. Commission's definition of vertical agreements, but as explained above has taken a broader course in The Competition Act 1998 (Land and Vertical Agreements Exclusion) Order 2000 (S.I. 2000 No. 310) (the "Land and Vertical Agreements Order"). In both cases, however, pure intellectual property agreements are not given the same degree of freedom from the application of the competition prohibitions as are agreements concerned wholly or primarily with the provision of goods or services.

7.2.2 Practical Effects

The exclusion for vertical agreements should be extremely effective in reducing the burden on United Kingdom businesses in relation to agreements to which Article 81 does not apply.

Many United Kingdom businesses are, however, already subject to E.C. competition law and it will be burdensome for them to apply the two different tests at E.C. and United Kingdom level when deciding whether they come within the scope of the United Kingdom and E.C. prohibitions (*Hansard*, H.C., col. 632 (June 25, 1998)). Where the parties are not competitors and market shares are below 30 per cent, parties are likely to be able to tailor their agreement to qualify for either a parallel exemption (where they meet the requirements of the block exemption) or an exclusion from the Competition Act or both. Businesses with large market shares or who are actual or potential competitors may be able to bring their vertical agreements within the exclusion in the Land and Vertical Agreements Order, but will have to consider whether they need an individual exemption under Article 81(3), for any agreement which may affect trade between Member States (see also 7.2.8 below). Under proposals discussed in Chapter 17 at 17.7, the Competition Act 1998 and the exclusion would cease to apply to agreements that affect trade between Member States.

7.2.3   What is a Vertical Agreement?

The Land and Vertical Agreements Order, Article 2, defines a "vertical agreement" as:

> "an agreement between undertakings, each of which operates, for the purposes of the agreement, at a different level of the production or distribution chain, and relating to the conditions under which the parties may purchase, sell or re-sell certain goods or services and includes provisions contained in such agreements which relate to the assignment to the buyer or use by the buyer of intellectual property rights, provided that those provisions do not constitute the primary object of the agreement and are directly related to the use, sale or re-sale of goods or services by the buyer or its customers."

This definition follows closely the definitions in Articles 2(1) and 2(3) of the E.C. Vertical Agreements Block Exemption. It is explained in the OFT Guideline, *Vertical Agreements and Restraints*, OFT 416, September 1999 (the "OFT Vertical Agreements Guideline").

Each undertaking must be at a different level of the production or distribution chain "for the purposes of the agreement". Thus a distribution agreement between a supplier who also has a distribution business and an independent distributor can still benefit from the exclusion, since the agreement is concerned with their relationship at different levels in the distribution chain (OFT Vertical Agreements Guideline, paras 2.6–2.7). An agreement may have more than two undertakings as party, *e.g.* a supplier of raw materials, a manufacturer, a wholesaler and a retailer, each operating at a different level (OFT Vertical Agreements Guideline, paras 2.3–2.5).

The OFT state categorically that an agreement where more than one undertaking party is at the same level of trade cannot benefit from the exclusion (para. 2 of the Vertical Agreements Guide gives the example of an agreement between one manufacturer and six wholesalers), without any examination of their relationship for the purposes of the agreement. No doubt the courts will decide whether obligations of several and vertical nature between, in the example, each wholesaler individually and the manufacturer can benefit from the exclusion. There is no statement in the Commission Notice, Guidelines on Vertical Restraints (the E.C. Vertical Restraints Guidelines) that the similar definition in the Vertical Agreements Block Exemption has this effect (see discussion of the scope of the Block Exemption at paras 23–45, especially para. 24), and Article 2(2) reads as a limitation rather than an extension when dealing with agreements between associations and their member undertakings. The provisions on competing undertakings (see 7.2.8 below) will, however, limit the application of the Block Exemption in cases where more than one undertaking operating at the same level of trade is party to an agreement.

As mentioned above, the Block Exemption may apply to certain agreements involving an association of retailing undertakings. In contrast, all agreements involving a body acting on behalf of a number of undertakings would seem to be regarded by the OFT as outside the exclusion. A wholesaling business which buys and sells on its own account, even if it sells only to its members would not, however, seem to be distinguishable from any other undertaking and therefore would seem able to enter into excluded vertical agreements on an individual basis, with its suppliers and, with its members. The OFT's interpretation of the definition of "vertical agreement" may raise issues about the scope of the exclusion and the achievement of an interpretation consistent with the interpretation given to similar words in the E.C. Block Exemption *e.g.* in circumstances where selective distribution arrangements with a large number of distributors are subject to common changes (which may be regarded as evidencing an overall arrangement).

7.2.4   Resale Price Maintenance Agreements

The Exclusion Order provides that the exclusion for vertical agreements does not apply to any vertical agreement which directly or indirectly has the object or effect of restricting a buyer's ability to determine its sale price. This is without prejudice to the possibility of the supplier imposing a maximum sale price or recommending a sale price, provided that these do not amount to a fixed or minimum sale price as a result of pressure from, or incentives offered by, any of the parties (Land and Vertical Agreements Order, Article 4, which follows the language of Article 4(a) of the E.C. Vertical Agreements Block Exemption).

Agreements which do not benefit from the exclusion as a result of Article 4 are subject to scrutiny under the Chapter I Prohibition in respect of all their terms.

Any term providing for resale price maintenance is likely to be regarded as having an appreciable effect on competition even if the undertakings involved have less than a 25 per cent share of the relevant market (OFT Vertical Agreements Guideline, paras 1.12 and 3.3) and is unlikely to qualify for an individual exemption. In some cases, where a supplier is remunerated on a risk-sharing basis with a part of the turnover or profits of the distributor, there may, however, be a basis for justifying the involvement of the supplier in the price setting process.

7.2.5   Extent of the Exclusion

Article 3 of the Exclusion Order provides that the Chapter I Prohibition shall not apply to an agreement "to the extent that" it is a vertical agreement. The exclusion may, therefore, apply only to certain parts of an agreement rather than an agreement in its entirety. It is therefore possible for some provisions in an agreement to benefit from the exclusion for vertical agreements while others do not (OFT Vertical Agreements Guideline, para. 3.4). For example, where a supplier and a customer are also competing manufacturers, terms dealing with their joint research and development activities for a type of product they both sell would not be covered. Again, it will not always be clear which terms fall outside the exclusion because they are not vertical in nature. The OFT Vertical Agreements Guideline, para. 3.5 indicates that, where an agreement is only partly covered by the Exclusion Order and the Director has competition concerns about the object or effect of the agreement, he will have regard to the whole agreement (including that part of the agreement that benefits from the exclusion for vertical agreements) in order to assess whether the Chapter I Prohibition has been infringed.

The Director will not, however, be able to take any action against the parts which benefit from the Exclusion Order without first withdrawing the exclusion.

7.2.6 Agreements with an Intellectual Property Element

The Land and Vertical Agreements Order, like the E.C. Block Exemption, does not apply to agreements the primary purpose of which is the licensing or transfer of intellectual property rights (patents, plant breeders, design rights, copyright, secret know-how, etc) or trademark rights.

Provisions relating to the assignment to, or use by, the buyer of intellectual property rights are, however, treated as forming part of the vertical agreement if they directly relate to the use, sale or resale of the goods or services by the buyer or its customers. So, for example, a copyright licence and authority to grant copyright licences over software installed in computers would be directly related to the use of such computers by a distributor and its customers. The demarcation keeps alive the long running debate about the essential nature of some types of product *e.g.* a Compact Disk may be simply a storage medium for software and the primary object of a distribution agreement for these Compact Disks may be the authorisation of the retailer to act as agent in the grant of copyright licences to use the software (the agreement would be for the distribution of a named word processing programme or game, for example, not for the distribution of the storage medium, which is in itself of negligible value). An agreement may, however, be framed merely as one for the distribution of the physical storage medium (or even a piece of paper entitling the purchaser to apply for a licence) leaving the copyright licence as a relationship only between the end consumer and the software copyright owner: in that event, the distribution arrangements for the physical element would be vertical agreements. It is unfortunate that the exclusion could not have been clearly extended to dealing with distribution of new media products (regardless of whether the copyright element predominates). The OFT Vertical Agreements Guideline fudges the issue (see paras 2.9 to 2.13, especially para. 2.11).

7.2.7 Clawback

Section 50(3) provides that an order may empower the Director to give directions to the effect that, in prescribed circumstances, an exclusion, exemption or modification is not to apply (or is to apply in a particular way) in relation to an individual agreement. This is put into effect by Article 7 of the Land and Vertical Agreements Order.

This power of "clawback" was introduced as a *quid pro quo* for a wide-ranging exclusion. The test has two elements, the Director may direct that the exclusion does not apply if he considers:

(1)   that the agreement in question will, if not excluded, infringe the Chapter I Prohibition; and

(2)   that he is not likely to grant it an unconditional individual exemption.

The test is adapted from the test set out in Sched. 1, para. 4 of the Act and incorporated by reference. There is also the ability for the Director to withdraw the exclusion without forming a clear view, if a party fails to respond to a request for information related to a proposed withdrawal of the exclusion within 10 days (Sched. 1, para. 4(4) and Director's Rules, Rule 22 (3)).

In practice, it is likely that the Director will exercise these powers only rarely. Where he intends to give a direction withdrawing the benefit of the exclusion, he must consult the parties to that agreement (Director's Rules, Rule 22(1)). Such a direction must specify the date from which it is to take effect and it may not take effect from a date earlier than the date on which it was given. If the Director gives such a direction, he will publish it on his public register (OFT Vertical Agreements Guideline, paras 5.2 and 5.3).

Once the agreement is clawed back the parties will be able to argue the case for an individual exemption before the Director. Given the conditions for withdrawal of the exclusion, there may be a presumption that the Chapter I Prohibition is infringed, but the Director is obliged to hold an open mind until he has considered all the evidence and reached a concluded view. If he ultimately rules that an exemption is not merited, the parties can appeal against the decision to the Competition Commission. (*Hansard*, H.C., (Standing Committee G) cols 632 and 633 (June 25, 1998)).

As an anti-avoidance provision, an agreement to the like object or effect between the same parties as one from which the exclusion was withdrawn will not be excluded (Land and Vertical Agreements Order, Article 8).

One of the unanswered questions of the relationship between E.C. and national law is the extent to which national prohibitions can lawfully be applied to an agreement which benefits from an exemption under Article 81(3) (see Chapter 8). As regards vertical agreements, the E.C. Vertical Agreements Block Exemption at Article 7 gives the relevant national authority an express permission to disapply the exemption where there are adverse effects on competition in a Member State or part thereof which forms a distinct geographic market. Therefore where the Director wishes to clawback from the exclusion an agreement which is also exempt under the E.C. Vertical Agreements Block Exemption and apply the prohibition, in most cases he should be able to ensure the effectiveness of his actions and remove any possible conflict between national and Community law by also disapplying the E.C. Vertical Agreements Block Exemption.

7.2.8 Comparison with E.C. Vertical Block Exemption

Difference in Concept

Conceptually the idea of an exclusion is different from that of an exemption. An exclusion is effectively a declaration that the prohibition has no application at all, whereas an exemption raises a presumption that the prohibition does or at least may apply but the conditions for exemption are satisfied for the period of the exemption. E.C. jurisprudence is thus not relevant to the exclusion itself, although where the Land and Vertical Agreements Order adopts language used in the E.C. Vertical Agreements Block Exemption, the United Kingdom courts and authorities should interpret the words consistently. It can be expected that the ambit of the Block Exemption will assist the Director in identifying agreements which might be clawed back for consideration under the Chapter I Prohibition.

Differences in Scope

The United Kingdom exclusion is simpler in its approach. The main differences between the United Kingdom exclusion and the E.C. Vertical Agreements Block Exemption are that:

> — the E.C. Vertical Agreements Block Exemption applies only to agreements
> where the market share of the supplier (or buyer, in the case of agreements

containing exclusive supply obligations) does not exceed 30 per cent of the relevant market. There is no market share cap in order to benefit from the United Kingdom exclusion. This is the most important difference, since the E.C. Block Exemption is likely to apply to the Vertical Agreements of businesses with high market shares (unless these shares are held in narrow local markets) and the previous block exemptions for exclusive distribution and purchasing did not have market share thresholds;

— The E.C. Vertical Agreements Block Exemption does not apply to many vertical agreements between actual or potential competitors, in particular where they are competing manufacturers or service suppliers at a higher level of trade and the buyer's group turnover exceeds 100 million Euros;

— The E.C. Vertical Agreements Block Exemption contains a number of "hardcore" restrictions which, if included in the vertical agreement, have the effect of taking the agreement outside its scope altogether. The only equivalent provision affecting the United Kingdom exclusion relates to resale price maintenance (Land and Vertical Agreements Order, Article 4). This follows the language of Article 4(a) of the E.C. Vertical Agreements Block Exemption;

— The E.C. Vertical Agreements Block Exemption limits the extent to which non-compete clauses can benefit from the exemption, but the United Kingdom exclusion has no such limitation: note, however, that the common law on unreasonable restraint of trade may apply in individual cases;

— The United Kingdom exclusion operates in relation to any agreement "to the extent" that it is a vertical agreement. Thus, horizontal elements in a vertical agreement may be exposed to the Chapter I Prohibition. The E.C. Vertical Agreements Block Exemption would appear to cover horizontal elements in an agreement which meets its terms despite the parties being competitors, subject to the right of the Commission and national authorities to withdraw the benefit of the block exemption from any qualifying vertical agreement. However, the E.C. Vertical Restraints Guidelines, para. 25 third sentence, suggests that the European Commission expect the E.C. Vertical Agreements Block Exemption to be applied in the same way as the exclusion to cover the vertical elements of an agreement which contains other elements so long as the agreement has no blacklist clauses and does not fall within another block exemption. This is not, however, clear from the Block Exemption Regulation itself.

— The United Kingdom exclusion does not apply to agreements involving associations acting on behalf of their members and is apparently not intended to apply to any arrangement involving more than one party at the same level of trade: the E.C. Vertical Agreements Block Exemption may apply in these circumstances (see 7.2.3 above).

— The United Kingdom exclusion may apply to agreements that would otherwise benefit from a parallel or United Kingdom block exemption. The E.C. Vertical Agreements Block Exemption applies only so far as no other block exemption applies (Article 2(5)): this preserves, for example, the application of Commission Regulation 1475/95/EEC [1995] O.J. L145/25) to motor vehicle distribution agreements until at least September 30, 2002.

Similarities

The exclusion picks up the definition of a vertical agreement and of an agreement with resale price elements from the E.C. Vertical Agreements Block Exemption.

— Neither the exclusion nor the block exemption cover pure intellectual property agreements. Some will benefit from parallel exemption under Commission Regulation 240/96/EC on the application of Article 81(3) of the Treaty to certain categories of technology transfer agreements [1996] O.J. L31/2 which lasts until March 31, 2006. This does not cover all forms of intellectual property; copyright licences for example, do not have the benefit of any exemption or exclusion, nor do pure trademark licences.

— The E.C. block exemption does not apply to vertical agreements for rental rather than purchase of goods. The same would seem to apply to the United Kingdom exclusion. Although other United Kingdom competition legislation using the term "supply" has made no distinction between the treatment of rental and purchase arrangements, the exclusion follows the E.C. in referring to "purchase" and "sale". As operating and finance leases are common forms of vertical supply agreements in the United Kingdom (particularly for machinery, office equipment and vehicles) and are generally equally benign, the extension of the exclusion or a block exemption for such agreements would be welcome.

7.2.9   Other Possible United Kingdom Competition Scrutiny

The Chapter II Prohibition

The Exclusion Order excludes vertical agreements only from the scope of the Chapter I Prohibition. A vertical agreement which is entered into by an undertaking which holds a dominant position in a market may be subject to the Chapter II Prohibition. Abuse of a dominant position by an undertaking which takes the form of a vertical agreement or restraint is assessed in exactly the same way as any other type of conduct under the Chapter II Prohibition.

The Fair Trading Act 1973

Where combined market shares reach or exceed 25 per cent in the United Kingdom or any part of it, the complex monopoly provisions of the Fair Trading Act 1973 will continue to be available to deal with cases where the market structure is of competition concern. To a more limited extent, the scale monopoly provisions will be available against a business which on its own has a market share of over 25 per cent. A complex monopoly investigation may be appropriate where, as a result of the structure of a market, networks of vertical agreements in that market have the effect of preventing or limiting the entry of new competitors into the market, particularly if there is no evidence of an agreement or collusion between the undertakings involved which might have caused this situation to arise. (OFT Vertical Agreements Guideline, paras 6.1 and 6.2). Such an instance recently reviewed by the Competition Commission is *New Cars (A report on the supply of new motor cars within the United Kingdom)* (2000) Cm. 4666, where the report recognises considerable concerns related to exclusive dealer networks of vertical exclusive distribution agreements. These have their own E.C. block exemption in Commission Regulation 1475/EEC [1995] O.J. L145/25) which continues in force until September 2002. This may prevent the application of the prohibition meantime (see discussion at 7.2.7 last para. and 8.4.12).

7.2.10   Conclusion

The vertical agreement exclusion will reduce the burden both on business and on regulatory authorities by removing the need for the United Kingdom authorities to scrutinise essentially benign agreements which do not fall within block exemptions. It will also reduce the difficulties for business in unnecessarily restricting the form of a vertical agreement to make it fit within the conditions of a block exemption. This problem, although much reduced by the new E.C. Vertical Agreements Block Exemption, remains an issue arising from the E.C. approach.

The number of limitations on the application of the E.C. Vertical Agreements Block Exemption means that businesses, particularly larger and more international businesses, will still have some regulatory risk and burdens in relation to a number of essentially benign agreements which the United Kingdom authorities are happy to exclude, while in a few cases, agreements benefiting from the E.C. Vertical Agreements Block Exemption may not benefit from the exclusion (see discussion at 7.2.3 and comparison at 7.2.8). There are also smaller double jeopardy risks arising from the Chapter II Prohibition and the provisions of the FTA. The new powers of the E.C. Commission to "backdate" exemptions of vertical agreements to the date the agreement came into force (even if notification was made later) should however, reduce the burden on businesses, since falling outside the E.C. Vertical Agreements Block Exemption, eventually benign agreements would only need to be notified if an issue arose during their life.

7.3   Land Agreements

7.3.1   Policy and its Implementation

Land agreements are also covered by the Competition Act 1998 (Land and Vertical Agreements Exclusion) Order 2000 (S.I. 2000 No. 310). Many land agreements contain restrictions on the use of property (for example, the nature of the business which can be carried on at leased premises) which could be caught by the prohibition. Leases may also require certain services to be obtained from a particular source, *e.g.* a developer's own management company. In retail developments, restrictive covenants on the type of business to be carried on at each unit are imposed by landlords to ensure that the development offers a range of different types of shop and service outlets. A major tenant, particularly if paying turnover related rent, may be concerned to have protection from competition by another outlet of exactly the same type, especially during the first years of operation.

Following the Ravenseft decision, the RTPA was not applied to most leases and other agreements relating to land (*Re Ravenseft Properties Ltd's Application,* [1978] Q.B. 52, [1977] 1 All E.R. 47, RPC). The requirement for an effect on trade between Member States means that Article 81 is unlikely to apply except in cases where leases are used as a vehicle for an exclusive dealing or franchising network (*e.g.* tied tenancies of public houses).

In debate on the Bill in the House of Lords, concern was expressed regarding the effect of the prohibition on commercial property agreements relating to property development schemes which often contain covenants governing the use of property, and restrictions relating to insurance, maintenance services, assignment and alienation. The Government accepted that, in principle, such matters should be excluded.

During the House of Commons debate the Government stated that similar considerations arise in respect of land agreements to those relating to vertical agreements.

> "We do not believe that land agreements, so far as they relate to the creation or transfer of an interest in land, will be likely to have any appreciable effect on competition . . . If we do not treat land agreements differently, we fear that uncertainty as to the application of the Chapter I Prohibition will lead to unnecessary notification of agreements and uncertainty in the property sector . . . .We therefore believe that the powers of the new clause in relation to land agreements will enhance the clarity of the application of the prohibition, reduce the burden on business of unnecessary notifications and enable the better concentration of regulatory resources on areas of competition concern." (*Hansard*, (Standing Committee G), col. 633 (June 25, 1998)).

This apparently simple scheme of things, coupled with the Director's clear statement that "Land Agreements do not generally give rise to competition concerns" (OFT Guideline, *Land Agreements*, OFT 420, February 2000 (the "Land Guideline") is complicated by the approach taken to what is comprised in the notion of a "Land Agreement" in the Land and Vertical Agreements Order and the tortuous language of Article 6. In a number of cases it will be simpler in relation to a property agreement to form the view that there are no appreciable effects on competition than to form a clear view on the application of the land exclusion.

7.3.2 Definition of Land Agreement

The Land and Vertical Agreements Order provides that the Chapter I Prohibition shall not apply to an agreement to the extent that it is a land agreement. The exclusion is automatic and no individual notification needs to be made to the Director in order to benefit from its provisions. The Order, Article 2, defines a land agreement as:

> "an agreement between undertakings which creates, alters, transfers or terminates an interest in land, or an agreement to enter into such an agreement, together with any obligation and restriction to which Article 6 applies".

"Agreement" does not appear to be used in a strictly technical sense and therefore should include deeds and other documents which may not be contracts: for example, formal transfers of title pursuant to a contract which itself created a beneficial interest in the land transferred. The term "interest in land" is defined as including "any estate, interest, easement, servitude or right in or over land (including any interest or right created by a licence), and in Scotland also includes any interest under a lease and other heritable right in or over land including a heritable security" and land includes buildings and other structures and land covered with water. The definition does, in itself, exclude some agreements relating to land: *e.g.* an agreement between two landlords as to the rents they will charge their respective tenants or in which they agree to require their tenants to use the same services company (Land Guideline, para. 2.4). Also the definition requires that an agreement is "between undertakings". An undertaking will include an individual acting in a business capacity and should include trustees acting with a view to generating income (*e.g.* pension trustees) (see Chapter 6 at 6.3).

7.3.3   Vertical Agreement Elements of a Land Transaction

The definition of "Land Agreement", goes on to the effect that a provision of an agreement which meets the definition of a vertical agreement cannot benefit from the land exclusion, even if it forms part of the same contractual document. Thus provisions for the supply of beer in a tied tenancy or petrol to the lessee of a filling station owned by an oil company would not benefit from the land exclusion and would be considered under the vertical agreements exclusion even if they form part of a lease. The vertical agreements exclusion may well apply (Land Guideline, para. 3.4). The same may apply where a lease deals with the terms on which a landlord supplies services to his tenant *e.g.* an insurance company landlord requiring the tenant to insure with it, if not covered by the exclusion (Land Guideline, para. 2.9 discussed further at 7.3.8 below).

7.3.4   Distinction Between an Agreement and Obligations and Restrictions covered by Article 6

The vertical agreements aspect of the definition indicates that the reference to "an agreement . . . which creates [etc.] an interest in land" is not intended to refer to the whole contractual arrangement, but only to those parts actually dealing with the interest in land itself (*e.g.* transfer, grant of lease, description of the land itself). If this were not so, the provisions of Article 6 would seem to be superfluous, as they relate to normal obligations and restrictions accepted by parties to a land agreement, which will almost invariably be part of the same contractual arrangement. This is disappointingly opaque for practitioners not familiar with the debate on vertical agreements with horizontal elements and confusion is added by the use of "agreement" in the Land Guideline in the looser sense of "contractual arrangement", *e.g.* at para. 2.5. Para. 3.1 of the Land Guideline clarifies, however, that extraneous provisions, *e.g.* financing arrangements included in the same contractual arrangement, are not intended to benefit from the exclusion.

As a starting point it must be recognised that normal provisions of documents dealing with interests in land, ranging from the obligation to pay rent to restrictive covenants affecting the land dealt with or neighbouring land, benefit from the exclusion only if they are obligations or restrictions falling within Article 6 and, to the extent not covered, fall outside the exclusion (see further discussion at 7.3.6 and 7.3.7).

7.3.5   Provisions Taking Account of System of Land Ownership

It is a feature of the system of land ownership that binding obligations may arise between parties who are not in direct contractual relationship. The Order addresses this first by treating successors in title as parties to an agreement. Second, Article 6 deals with obligations and restrictions which affect a person as a holder of an interest in land. Obligations or restrictions relating to other land in which a contracting party has an interest in, "other relevant land", may in certain circumstances (see 7.3.6 and 7.3.7 below) be treated as part of a land agreement as well as those relating to the land which is the subject of the land agreement ("relevant land"). "Other relevant land" does not extend to land already in the ownership of a third party, although on subsequent transfer of the land, successors in title would be deemed to be parties to the agreement. Similarly, a purchaser may, as successor in title to the Vendor be deemed to be a party to a number of other land agreements.

7.3.6   Scope of Article 6 — Obligations

Meaning

Article 6 applies to two types of covenant "obligations" and "restrictions". There is no definition of what is meant by the term "obligations". According to the Land Guideline para. 2.5 "obligations" include basic elements of any contractual arrangement dealing with an interest in land *e.g.* covenants in a lease for payment of rent or service charge.

One category of obligations (described in 6(1)(b)(i)) constitutes types of restrictions, but generally the intent seems to be to use the term "obligation" to refer to positive obligations and to treat restrictions (or negative obligations) separately and in a more limited manner. This is not, however, entirely clear.

Capacity in which Obligations are Accepted

Obligations which qualify for the exclusion are limited by the capacity of the party accepting them. A qualifying obligation must be accepted by a party in his capacity as a holder of an interest of relevant land or other relevant land and, in the latter case be for the benefit of another party as a holder of an interest in the relevant land. This is intended to remove obligations arising from other contractual relationships between the parties from the benefit of the Land Exclusion: *e.g.* if the tenant agreed to rent office equipment from a landlord who was in business as a supplier of that type of equipment this should not be excluded (see Land Guideline; paras 2.6 to 2.9). This is because the landlord is assumed to be benefiting from the obligation in his capacity as a supplier of office equipment. It will, however, be a matter of fact, and, if the arrangement was one of convenience relating to a piece of equipment already installed in the premises, then the exclusion might apply (although such an arrangement would in any event have no appreciable effect on competition).

It should also be noted that an obligation accepted by a landlord or vendor in his capacity as a holder of "other relevant land" (*e.g.* an obligation to provide and maintain fences on his retained land) is covered, but there is not exact reciprocity in Article 6(1) and an obligation by a tenant (or purchaser) to maintain fences on the relevant land for the benefit of the landlord (or vendor) as owner of the adjoining land ("other relevant land") is not included. This seems illogical and is not explained in the Land Guideline.

An estate covenant given by a purchaser of an interest in land (relevant land), benefits owners of neighbouring property not party to a land agreement. If it is not recognised as also benefiting the vendor as the preceding holder of an interest in the relevant land, such a covenant would appear to fall outside the exclusion, unless an elaborate tracing back through a network of agreements establishes the necessary contractual nexus to the original estate contract. In the case of leasehold property, the landlord at all material times has an interest in the relevant land and this issue should not arise.

Where obligations (or restrictions) relate to "other relevant land" it seems that they need not be for the benefit of another party to the agreement, so long as they "correspond" to those accepted by a party to the agreement in his capacity as a holder of an interest in relevant land (Article 6(1)(b)). This is intended to facilitate the creation of covenants binding on a landlord/vendor and their other tenants/

successors in title which are complementary to a covenant accepted by a lessee/purchaser. The example given in the Land Guideline, para. 2.12 is of a tenant of premises at a shopping centre who is obliged to use his premises only for the sale of wet fish, while the landlord covenants that no other tenant will have the right to sell wet fish.

The word "correspond" is not defined and this may cause some difficulty. For example, if the purchaser/tenant wishes to run a newsagent and the vendor/landlord will continue to run a bookmakers in the adjoining premises, the covenants will restrict the purchaser/tenant from carrying out betting activities from the relevant land and the vendor/landlord from carrying out a newsagency business from the other relevant land. These restrictions correspond in type but not in substance; is this a sufficient correspondence for the purposes of Article 6? Paragraph 2.12 of the Land Guideline does not discuss this point.

It is also not clear if a "corresponding restriction" may be exactly the same; for example where a landlord wishes to restrict all retailers in his estate from opening on Sundays. In the Competition Act itself, section 60, the term "corresponding question" is used in the sense of the same or similar, but is again undefined.

7.3.7   Scope of Article 6 — Restrictions

Activity to which Restrictions Relate

Restrictions which benefit from Article 6 are limited to those which restrict the activity which may be carried out on, from or in connection with, relevant land or other relevant land (Article 6(2)(a) and (b)), or which restrict the freedom of a party to create or transfer an interest in the relevant land (Article 6(2)(c)). It is clear (Land Guideline, para. 2.10) that restrictions on activity whether implied from a positive formulation (only to be used for the sale of wet fish) or negative (not to be used for the sale of wet fish) are to be covered by the exclusion and the OFT suggest that any restriction as to the quality of goods would also benefit.

At para. 2.11, the OFT states that restrictions as to the conditions on which a trade or business activity may be carried out are not covered by the exclusion. They cite provisions setting minimum resale prices, quantities of goods or sources of supply. There must be considerable doubt that the language of Article 6(2)(a) and (b) actually allows for this distinction. A restriction on a source of supply may well be a restriction "on activity that may be carried out ... on, from, or in connection with the relevant land" within Article 6(2)(a). For example, the landlord may specify a particular make and design of venetian blinds to ensure a uniform appearance for his office development, or specify particular ranges of high quality branded goods to be stocked at the premises as part of his creation of a themed shopping mall. It is difficult to see why the requirement to use a particular range of blinds is not a restriction on activity carried out on, or in connection with, the land and the stocking of goods likewise.

Capacity in which Restrictions are Accepted

To benefit from the exclusion a restriction must be accepted by a party in his capacity as a holder of an interest in the relevant land or other relevant land (Article 6(2)(a)) and be for the benefit of a party in his capacity as a holder of an interest in the relevant land. The variant rules for corresponding restrictions accepted by the holder of an interest in other relevant land are the same as in the case of obligations (Article 6(2)(b)). Capacity issues are more fully discussed at 7.3.6 above.

7.3.8 Extent of the Exclusion

The Exclusion Order provides that the Chapter I Prohibition does not apply to an agreement "to the extent that" it is a land agreement. In addition to vertical agreements and obligations and restrictions not covered by Article 6 (discussed above), other extraneous provisions may therefore fall outside the scope of the exclusion. For example, if one betting shop owner used a lease to another as a repository for an agreement between them on the location of the premises in all the surrounding regions, such provisions would not fall within the exclusion. The Land Guideline para. 3.1 suggests that financing provisions will fall outside the exclusion, although if they take the form of a finance related rent (*e.g.* in a finance lease or some building leases) it is difficult to see why this should be the case. Key provisions of mortgages are financing provisions, but if not covered by the land agreement exclusion, seem likely to be vertical agreements for the supply of services: the Vertical Agreements Guideline does not consider how it applies to the supply of financial services and the E.C. Guidelines on Vertical Restraints is equally deficient.

The OFT accepts, however, that most provisions of a contract dealing with an interest in land will, in any event, be inappreciable even if outside the terms of the exclusion.

Where an agreement is only partly covered by the exclusion, and the Director has competition concerns about the object or effects of that agreement, he will have regard to the whole agreement (including that part of the agreement that falls within the land exclusion) in order to assess whether the Chapter I Prohibition has been infringed. He will not, however, be able to take any action against the excluded parts which benefit from the land exclusion without first withdrawing that exclusion. (Land Guideline, para. 3.2).

7.3.9 Withdrawal of the Exclusion

The Director has the power to remove the benefit of the exclusion for land agreements and examine an agreement under the Chapter I Prohibition. He can exercise this power in the same circumstances as applies to vertical agreements (see 7.2.7). The same anti-avoidance provision also apply. This prevents any new agreement in like terms between the same parties benefiting from the exclusion.

7.3.10 Exclusion in Practice

The OFT has attempted to elucidate the application of the land exclusion in its Land Guideline, which does not pick up closely on the language of the Land and Vertical Agreements Order. In consequence, it draws lines in places which seem more a matter of policy than of strict interpretation of the Order. Many of its more detailed observations seem to have lost sight of the facts that, as acknowledged at para. 3.1:

- most provisions in agreements relating to land that fall outside the land exclusion will be inappreciable, and
- some of the more commercially important provisions falling outside the land exclusion will benefit from the vertical agreements exclusion.

In the circumstances, a throwback to the formalistic complexities of an RTPA exemption is both unnecessary and confusing. A simpler and wider exclusion with acceptance that claw-back could deal with any abuse of the exclusion would have been of much greater assistance in saving burdens on business and administrative costs.

The Guideline will, nevertheless, give helpful guidance on the Director's policy and may influence the courts in the event of a dispute on interpretation. Two points are worth noting:

(1)   Paragraphs 2.6 to 2.9 emphasise that obligations are only intended to be covered by the exclusion if they benefit a party as a holder of an interest in land as opposed to in a trading capacity (or other (non-land) business capacity). A landlord whose only business is property investment/management is thus better off than one who also runs the primary retail business in a shopping centre or the primary manufacturing business on an industrial estate, who may be thought to take covenants for the protection of his business rather than for the purposes of managing his estate.

(2)   The OFT approach involves an element of "hair splitting" as appears in para. 2.9 in relation to insurance covenants in favour of an insurance company landlord. These covenants are said to benefit from the land exclusion if they allow the landlord to place the insurance (the tenant must insure *through* the landlord) but not if they require the tenant to insure *with* the landlord, even though the practical result may be the same. The formulation which the OFT states is not covered by the land exclusion would seem to benefit from the vertical agreements exclusion, although this is not made clear. Further, the courts will not necessarily want to inquire into business relationships in relation to covenants in usual form and may prefer simply to decide whether the covenant is of a type which does benefit a landlord as a holder of an interest in land, even if it also has other benefits for him.

7.3.11   Other United Kingdom Competition Scrutiny

The Exclusion Order does not provide an exclusion from the Chapter II Prohibition for land agreements. The Chapter II Prohibition will apply to conduct relating to land in the same way as it does to any other conduct. The FTA only applies to interests in land to a very limited extent, although this may be extended by statutory instrument (see Chapter 15, para. 15.5).

7.4   Mergers

7.4.1   Exclusions for Merger Agreements

To the extent that an agreement results in a merger which qualifies for investigation either under United Kingdom or E.C. legislation, it remains subject to the FTA or the E.C. Merger Regulation and is excluded from the two prohibitions (Sched. 1, Competition Act 1998). The exclusion extends to any provision directly related and necessary to the implementation of merger provisions.

Mergers which have a Community dimension are scrutinised by the European Commission under Council Regulation 4064/89 [1990] O.J. L257/13, as amended by Regulation 1310/97 [1997] O.J. L180/1 (together, the "EC Merger Regulation"). In the United Kingdom, mergers are subject to scrutiny under the FTA if they are above certain thresholds, broadly if either the value of the gross assets taken over exceeds £70 million or if the merged entity would supply or consume 25 per cent of the goods or services concerned. Water mergers are subject to a variant of the regime and newspaper mergers to a separate regime under the FTA.

Those mergers which are too small to qualify for investigation under the FTA are also excluded from the two prohibitions in order to avoid them being subject to the more stringent regime of the prohibitions.

The extent of this exclusion may be affected by changes to United Kingdom merger control law: see Chapter 1.

7.4.2   Definition of United Kingdom Merger

Schedule 1, para. 1 provides that the prohibition on anti-competitive agreements does not apply to agreements which result (or if carried out, would result) in any two enterprises ceasing to be distinct enterprises for the purposes of Part V of the FTA. Both qualifying and non-qualifying mergers are defined by reference to the FTA, section 65. This provides that an enterprise (*i.e.* the activities or parts of the activities of a business) shall be regarded as ceasing to be distinct from another enterprise, if either-

(a)   they are brought under common ownership or common control (whether or not the business to which either of them formerly belonged continues to be carried on under the same or different ownership or control), or

(b)   either of the enterprises ceases to be carried on at all and does so in consequence of any arrangements or transaction entered into to prevent competition between the enterprises.

There are three ways in which enterprises may be regarded as under common control — if they are:

(a)   enterprises of interconnected bodies corporate; or

(b)   enterprises carried on by two or more bodies corporate of which one and the same person or group of persons has control; or

(c)   an enterprise carried on by a body corporate and an enterprise carried on by a person or group of persons having control of that body corporate.

Sections 65(3) and (4) of the FTA define three levels at which control "may" be regarded as existing, namely where a person or a group of persons has:

(1)   the ability materially to influence the policy of another enterprise;

(2)   the ability to control the policy of another enterprise (de facto control); or

(3)   ownership of a controlling interest in another enterprise (legal control usually considered to arise with an equity shareholding of over 50 per cent).

For the purposes of the Competition Act the word "may" becomes "must" in sections 65(3) and 65(4) in order to remove any discretion which the Director might otherwise have to treat a particular transaction as a merger.

7.4.3   Water Mergers

Water mergers either fall into the regime described above or a variant regime under section 32 Water Industry Act 1991 with a different qualifying test (see *Competition*

Law and Practice Chapter 33 at 33.127). Either way they will involve enterprises ceasing to be distinct for the purposes of section 65 and benefit from this exclusion.

7.4.4   Newspaper Mergers

The prohibition of anti-competitive agreements does not apply in respect of any transfer which is a transfer of a newspaper or of newspaper assets for the purposes of section 57 FTA (Sched. 1, para. 2). Nor does it apply to any provision directly related and necessary to the implementation of the transfer.

7.4.5   Concentrations Subject to E.C. Control

Schedule 1, para. 6 provides that an agreement or conduct which gives rise to a concentration (as defined in the E.C. Merger Regulation) is excluded from the Chapter I Prohibition if the Regulation would give the European Commission exclusive jurisdiction. The definition of concentration includes full function joint ventures, not all of which will be United Kingdom mergers, as well as transactions in which a single party obtains decisive influence (E.C. Merger Regulation Article 3). The European Commission's exclusive jurisdiction provided for by the E.C. Merger Regulation, Article 21 depends upon the parties meeting certain turnover thresholds set out in Article 1 of the E.C. Merger Regulation, but does not arise where all parties have more than two-thirds of their Community turnover arising in a single Member State (*e.g.* in the United Kingdom). The E.C. Merger Regulation Article 6(1) gives the European Commission exclusive jurisdiction over restrictions directly related to and necessary for the implementation of a concentration within its jurisdiction.

7.4.6   Concentrations below E.C. Thresholds

Most concentrations below E.C. thresholds (or over which the United Kingdom can assert jurisdiction by way of exception, *e.g.* under Article 9) will be United Kingdom mergers. However, any transaction which is a concentration falling below the E.C. thresholds, but is not a merger in United Kingdom terms, could fall within the prohibition. Agreements in the nature of mergers most likely to be dealt with under the prohibition are joint ventures, which do not involve the acquisition of an enterprise from a parent or third party. However, many "greenfield" joint ventures do involve the acquisition of some business assets from a parent and there may be lively debate in such cases whether this is sufficient to constitute the acquisition of an enterprise and the extent to which the exclusion applies.

7.4.7   Ancillary Restrictions

The exclusion from the prohibition of anti-competitive agreements extends to any provision directly related and necessary to the implementation of a merger subject to United Kingdom merger control (Sched. 1, para. 1(2)) and to any similar provisions dealt with under the E.C. Merger Regulation. The Director has issued a guideline clarifying the types of restrictions which can properly be regarded as directly related and necessary (OFT Guideline *The Exclusion for Mergers and Ancillary Restraints*, OFT 416, September 1999, (the "Mergers Guideline")). The Mergers Guideline follows the Notice on restrictions ancillary to concentrations [1990] O.J. C203/5) issued by the European Commission (which is to be replaced by the Commission Notice on the Treatment of Ancillary Restraints under the Merger

Regulation, currently under review). By adopting for United Kingdom purposes the same language from the E.C. Merger Regulation and giving similar guidance, the intention of the Government and the OFT is that E.C. jurisprudence will apply. Examples of ancillary provisions (see Mergers Guideline, Part 4), drawing from E.C. decisions are:

- non-compete covenants on the vendor where there is a transfer of goodwill: a period of two years is likely to be the maximum where goodwill is transferred, rising to five years if both know-how and goodwill is involved;

- know-how, or intellectual property licences necessary for the running of the acquired business, where the vendor requires ownership of the rights in order to exploit them for activities other than those transferred;

- Some purchase and supply agreements of a transitional nature, where an acquired business was formerly part of an integrated group of companies and relied on another company in the group for raw materials or represented a guaranteed outlet for that company's product.

There may be other types of ancillary restrictions, depending on the circumstances of the particular case.

Issues relating to ancillary restrictions in United Kingdom mergers will be dealt with by the OFT's Mergers Branch in conjunction with the assessment of the merger itself.

7.4.8 Withdrawal of the Exclusion

Paragraph 4 of Sched. 1 provides that the Director may give direction for this exclusion from the Chapter I Prohibition not to apply to a particular agreement subject to United Kingdom merger control, if :

(a) he considers:
   (i) that the agreement will, if not excluded, infringe the Chapter I Prohibition; and
   (ii) that he is not likely to grant it an unconditional individual exemption; and
(b) the agreement is not a protected agreement (see below).

Procedure is the same as for the withdrawal of other exclusions (see 7.2.7).

7.4.9 Protected Agreements

Paragraph 5 of Sched. 1 sets out the four kinds of protected agreements:

(1) those which relate to a merger in connection with which the Secretary of State has announced his decision not to make a merger reference to the Competition Commission;

(2) those which relate to a merger where the Secretary of State has made such a reference and the Competition Commission has found that the agreement has, or would, give rise to a merger situation qualifying for investigation;

(3) an agreement which relates to a merger arising through the acquisition of a controlling interest (as opposed to the acquisition of material influence or the ability to control the policy of a company); and

(4)   an agreement relating to a water merger which has been referred to the Competition Commission and found to be a merger to which section 32 of the Water Industry Act 1991 applies.

None of the categories of protected agreement are mergers cleared by the European Commission under the Merger Regulation. However, the Merger Regulation, in Article 21(2), forbids action by national competition authorities on mergers subject to the Commission's jurisdiction except in very limited circumstances.

7.4.10   Agreements at Risk of Clawback

The merger agreements at risk from this "clawback provision" are therefore those giving rise to mergers falling within the United Kingdom merger control regime which:

(a)   do not involve the acquisition of outright control; and

(b)   have not been notified under the merger regime of the FTA and treated by the authorities as a merger falling within section 65 FTA.

7.4.11   Operation in Practice

Acquisitions of outright control (merger situations other than by virtue of subsections 65 (3) or 65(4)(b) FTA)

Acquisitions of outright control over a target business cannot be attacked under the prohibitions whether or not the transaction is a merger "qualifying" for investigation under the merger regime of the FTA. Indeed, even if the merger does qualify for investigation under the FTA but has not been examined under that Act within the relevant time limits, the Competition Act cannot apply.

Such acquisitions are excluded from the prohibitions of the Competition Act and can not be brought back into the scope of the Act by exercise of the Director's clawback powers. They are "protected agreements" for the purposes of para. 5 of Sched. 1. The only issue under the Competition Act for this type of merger is whether any agreements which are connected to the acquisition of control qualify as "ancillary".

Acquisitions of de facto *control/joint ventures of existing businesses/acquisition of material influence (merger situations under subsections 65(3) or 65(4)(b) FTA) which fall outside the E.C. Merger Regulation).*

The relevance of the Competition Act to this type of merger will depend on whether it has been examined by the United Kingdom Competition Authorities under the existing merger regime of the FTA or the Water Industry Act 1991.

If the merger is a qualifying merger under the FTA and has been examined under the FTA it will be excluded from the Competition Act with no possibility of being clawed back by the Director under the Competition Act where:

— it qualifies for investigation under the FTA; and
— it has been cleared by the Secretary of State (*i.e.* no reference to the Competition Commission) or has been referred to the Competition Commission and found to be a qualifying merger.
— The same applies to a Water merger which is referred to the Competition Commission and found to fall under the Water Industry Act 1991, section 32.

The situation is different where such a merger is not a "qualifying" one under the FTA or is "qualifying" but has not been examined under the FTA merger regime.

Under the current laws, many merger transactions are not notified for clearance under the merger regime of the FTA. Parties may decide that the transaction does not qualify or may believe that the transaction is a qualifying one but does not raise any serious competition concerns. Any risk is limited by the fact that the Secretary of State may only refer a merger to the Competition Commission within four months of either the date it was completed or the date when material facts about proposed arrangements were notified to the Director or the Secretary of State or made public (FTA s. 64(4)).

Under the Competition Act these types of mergers are excluded from the prohibitions but are subject to the risk of the Director clawing back the exclusion to examine the merger under the prohibitions (except to the extent that the merger gives one party outright control). There is no time limit on the exercise of the power of clawback. Take the example of the acquisition of a stake, which does not raise serious competition concerns when it is first formed. As such, the parties may well take the risk of an investigation under the FTA within a short time of the acquisition and the merger may not be submitted for a formal clearance under the FTA. However, the threat of clawback will always hang over the transaction. Therefore, if in later years, the joint venture developed a strong market position allied with that of the investing party, it could create greater competition concerns which might in turn entice the Director to exercise the power of clawback.

Where the parties to these types of qualifying mergers in the past have decided on balance not to seek a merger clearance, they will now have a stronger incentive to seek a merger clearance under the FTA, to avoid any risk of clawback and examination under the prohibitions in later years. Indeed, even where the merger does not qualify for investigation under the FTA, the parties may seek to engineer the transaction to make it a qualifying merger and seek a merger clearance given the risk of review in later years.

Mergers covered by the E.C. Merger Regulation

Mergers examined by the European Commission under the Merger Regulation generally cannot be examined by national competition authorities. In most cases where the Commission cedes jurisdiction in whole or in part to the United Kingdom authorities under Article 9 or the United Kingdom has concurrent rights for recognised public interest reasons under Article 22, the merger will have been examined under the FTA. There could be the odd case, *e.g.*, a joint venture to which the FTA merger regime does not apply, where the Competition Act could be used to allow examination of the transaction at national level where Article 9 of the E.C. Merger Regulation applies. As the Competition Act considers exclusively competition issues and Article 22 of the E.C. Merger Regulation is concerned with regulation for other purposes, such as security or plurality of the media, there seems little scope to use the Competition Act in conjunction with Article 22.

Coal and Steel Mergers

The exclusive jurisdiction of the European Commission over these product sectors includes merger control (see 7.6.7 below).

7.5   Exclusions for Agreements Regulated Under Other Legislation

7.5.1   Specific Exclusions

There are a number of special competition regimes, such as the Financial Services Act 1986 (to be replaced by the Financial Services and Markets Act 2000) in relation to the rules of self-regulatory bodies, exchanges and clearing houses. Agreements that are subject to legislation which scrutinises their anti-competitive effects are excluded from the two prohibitions in order to avoid duplication. The Competition Act 1998, Sched. 2 lists these categories of agreements, which include rules of certain bodies recognised under the Companies Acts and certain agreements relating to Channel 3 regulated under the Broadcasting Acts.

7.5.2   New Exclusions in Financial Services Regime

The New Financial Services and Markets Act 2000 ("FSA 2000"), which received royal assent on the of June 14, 2000 and is expected to come into force during the summer of 2001 introduces changes in this area. Section 311 replaces the exclusion from the Chapter I Prohibition previously in sections 125 and 127 of the Financial Services Act 1986 ("FSA 1986") (introduced by the Competition Act 1998, Sched. 2). The contents of the exclusion in section 311 covers similar matters to section 125 although the reference to self-regulating organisations has been replaced to reflect the fact that their functions will be taken over by the Financial Services Authority under the FSA 2000.

Section 311(7) goes rather further and excludes agreements which include a recognised body or person who is subject to the rules of a recognised body, to the extent to which the agreement consists of provisions the inclusion of which is required or encouraged by any of the body's regulatory provisions or practices. A recognised body is a clearing house or investment exchange which has been recognised by the Financial Services Authority and its "practices" are defined so as to be limited to its practices in its recognised capacity (s. 302 (1)). "Regulatory provisions" are also defined in section 302 (1).

The concept of recognised professional bodies in section 127 of the FSA 1986 is not carried forward into the FSA 2000.

In addition there is a new exclusion in FSA 2000 section 164 for agreements in which the parties consist of or include authorised persons or persons otherwise subject to the Authority's regulating provisions, to the extent which the agreement consists of provisions the inclusion of which is required or encouraged by any of the body's regulatory provisions or practices.

7.5.3   Approach to Regulated Utilities

The same approach has not been taken in respect of regulated utility regimes such as gas and electricity, where the Government has instead given concurrent powers to the individual sector regulators to apply the prohibition directly in their areas (see Chapter 4).

7.5.4   Agreements Covered by section 21(2) Restrictive Trade Practices Act 1976

The Chapter I Prohibition does not apply to an agreement in respect of which a direction under section 21 (2) of the RTPA was in force immediately before the coming into force of section 2 of the Competition Act 1998 (Sched. 3, para. 2) (a "s. 21(2) agreement"). This means that restrictive agreements which were previously thought to be of minor significance from a competition point of view will not automatically have to be re-examined under the new Act.

If a material variation is made to a section 21(2) agreement, the exclusion ceases to apply to the agreement at the time that the variation comes into force. The OFT has indicated that the Director will only regard a variation as material if it results in an appreciable adverse effect on competition (OFT Guideline *Transitional Arrangements*, OFT 406, March 1999, para. 4.16). It is not clear whether the addition of a new party subject to pre-existing restrictions is always material, but the OFT have suggested the addition of a significant competitor will be material.

The Director has the power to bring the exclusion to an end if he considers that the agreement falls foul of the Chapter I Prohibition and that, if the exclusion were removed, it would not be likely to qualify for an unconditional individual exemption.

7.6   General Exclusions

Sched. 3 contains (in addition to the s. 21(2) exclusion described at 7.5.4 above) a list of general exclusions from the Chapter I and/or Chapter II prohibitions.

7.6.1   Planning Obligations

The Chapter I Prohibition does not apply to an agreement to the extent to which it is a planning obligation for the purposes of sections 106 and 299A of the Town and Country Planning Act 1990, an agreement which is made under section 75 of the Town and Country Planning (Scotland) Act 1997 or an agreement which is made under article 40 of the Planning (Northern Ireland) Order 1991 (Sched. 3, para. 1). Such agreements are made by landowners with planning authorities and contain development-related obligations binding on the land which must be complied with in implementing the development.

In the House of Lords an attempt was made to widen the exclusion so that it covered agreements relating to land and this led to the exclusion for land agreements discussed at 7.3 above.

7.6.2   EEA Regulated Markets

The Chapter I prohibition does not apply to an agreement for the constitution of an EEA regulated market to the extent to which the agreement relates to any of the rules made, or guidance issued, by that market. Nor does it apply to a decision made by an EEA regulated market or to any practices of an EEA regulated market (Sched. 3, para. 3).

An "EEA regulated market" is a securities market which is listed by a European Economic Area country (*i.e.* a European Union Member State or Iceland, Liechtenstein or Norway) other than the United Kingdom, pursuant to Article 16 of Directive 93/22/EEC on investment services in the securities field and which operates without any requirement that a person dealing on the market should have a physical presence in the EEA country from which any trading facilities are provided or on any trading floor that the market may have.

7.6.3 Services of General Economic Interest

Neither the Chapter I Prohibition nor the Chapter II Prohibition applies to an undertaking entrusted with the operation of services of general economic interest or having the character of a revenue-producing monopoly in so far as the prohibition would obstruct the performance, in law or in fact, of the particular tasks assigned to that undertaking. This exclusion (Sched. 3, para. 4) paraphrases Article 86(2) (formerly Article 90(2)) of the E.C. Treaty.

Article 86(2) of the E.C. Treaty is addressed to undertakings entrusted with the operation of services of general economic interest or having the character of a revenue producing monopoly. It provides a qualified immunity from the E.C. competition rules. This provision applies equally to private undertakings, but only if they have been entrusted with the operation of services of general economic interest by an act of public authority. The exclusion is complex. It is necessary to establish that an undertaking has been "entrusted" with the operation of a service, that the service is of "general economic interest", that the application of the competition rules would obstruct the performance of the assigned tasks and that the granting of the exception would not effect the development of trade such as would be contrary to Community interests. The United Kingdom exclusion does not include the last element but, it could be a breach of the United Kingdom's Community Obligations to sanction an agreement which had such an effect on the development of trade. Uniform charging for letters was given as an example of a service that may qualify under this heading (*Hansard* (Standing Committee G) cols 86–100 (June 2, 1998)). Aspects of the activities of regulated utilities may qualify and this topic is covered in all the Guidelines issued by sectoral Regulators (see Chapter 12 at 12.4.2).

7.6.4 Compliance with Legal Requirements

The Chapter I Prohibition does not apply to an agreement or decision to the extent to which it is made in order to comply with a legal requirement; or a concerted practice which is followed in order to comply with such a requirement (debated at *Hansard* (Standing Committee G) col. 269–270 (June 9, 1998)). Legal requirement means a requirement imposed by or under any United Kingdom Act, by or under the E.C. Treaty or the EEA Agreement or imposed by or under the law in force in another Member State and having legal effect in the United Kingdom, Sched. 3, para. 5(3). It does not include legal obligations imposed by a court and there is therefore scope for conflict where the Regulator objects to such an obligation.

7.6.5 Avoidance of Conflict with International Obligations

The Secretary of State may by order exclude an agreement or behaviour from the Chapter I and II Prohibitions if he is satisfied that it would be appropriate to do so in order to avoid a conflict with an international obligation of the United Kingdom (Sched. 3, para. 6). Such an order may also provide that the prohibitions are to be deemed never to have applied in relation to the agreement.

An international arrangement relating to civil aviation and designated by an order made by the Secretary of State is to be treated as an international obligation for the purposes of this exclusion. This amendment was introduced during the House of Lords Report Stage. As previously drafted, the term "international obligation" only covered formal treaties. It was felt that this could be unduly narrow in the aviation sector. Inter-governmental agreements permitting flights between the United Kingdom and other countries are often not made as treaties. They may take the form of memoranda of understanding. In practice however such agreements are honoured as if they were treaties (*Hansard*, H.L., Vol. 585, No. 99, col. 973 (February 9, 1998)).

The United Nations Convention on a Code of Conduct for Liner Conferences (reproduced in [1979] O.J. L121/1) could be such an international obligation, but the existence of a parallel exemption laying down detailed rules for the application of Articles 81 and 82 of the Treaty to maritime transport which takes account of the Convention, should avoid any conflict even in the absence of a specific order from Council Regulation (EEC) No. 4056/86 [1986] O.J. L378/4). The relevant E.C. exemption has expired but is due to be replaced; see Chapter 8, at para. 8.4.4. No order has yet been made.

7.6.6 Public Policy

The Secretary of State can exclude an agreement or behaviour from the Chapter I and II Prohibitions if he is satisfied that there are exceptional and compelling reasons of public policy why the prohibitions ought not to apply (Sched. 3, para. 7). The exclusion can be retrospective. No order has yet been made.

7.6.7 Coal and Steel

The Chapter I and Chapter II Prohibitions do not apply to an agreement which relates to a coal or steel product to the extent to which the European Coal and Steel Community Treaty ("ECSC Treaty") gives the Commission exclusive jurisdiction in the matter (Sched. 3, para. 8). "Coal or steel product" means any product of a kind listed in Annex I to the Treaty establishing the European Coal and Steel Community. The ECSC Treaty contains its own equivalent of the prohibitions and a merger control regime. The ECSC Treaty expires in 2002, and is not expected to be extended. These products will then fall into the E.C. Treaty and national competition law will again be applicable. This exclusion is therefore of limited duration.

7.6.8 Agricultural Products

Certain agreements related to agricultural products are excluded (Sched. 3, para. 9). These include agreements which cover national market organisations; which are necessary for the attainment of the objectives of the Common Agricultural Policy, as set out in Article 39 of the E.C. Treaty; and agricultural co-operatives relating to the production, sale or use of joint facilities, where there is no obligation to charge identical prices. As is the case with exclusions for mergers and agreements under section 21(2) of the RTPA, the Director will have the power to clawback individual agreements to be considered under the prohibition. Such a clawback can be exercised only if the Director considers that the agreement is likely, or is intended, substantially and unjustifiably to prevent, restrict or distort competition in relation to an agricultural product. This is a high threshold, but one that will enable the Director to take action against agreements causing serious harm.

The exclusion of agricultural agreements was introduced at Report Stage in the House of Lords in response to representations made during the consultation. The exclusion is designed to ensure that agreements in the agricultural sector will be treated under the Act in a similar way as under E.C. competition law. This furthers the overall objective of seeking, so far as possible, consistency in the treatment of agreements under the E.C. and United Kingdom prohibition systems (*Hansard*, H.L., Vol. 585, No. 99, col. 974–975 (February 9, 1998)).

7.7   Professional Rules

7.7.1   Designated Rules

The Chapter I Prohibition does not apply to an agreement to the extent to which such an agreement constitutes a designated professional rule, imposes obligations arising from designated professional rules, or constitutes an agreement to act in accordance with such rules. "Designated" means designated by the Secretary of State. He must establish and maintain a list of designated professional rules. The list is to be established or altered by an order made by the Secretary of State. Any body regulating a professional service listed in Part II of Sched. 4 or the persons who provide, or wish to provide, that service may apply to the Secretary of State for rules of that body to be designated (Sched. 4, para. 3). If a rule is altered, the body concerned must notify the Secretary of State and the Director of the alteration as soon as is reasonably practicable (Sched. 4, para. 4).

7.7.2 Categories of Professional Services

Part II of Sched. 4 lists the following as professional services for the purpose of this exclusion:

Legal (the services of barristers, advocates or solicitors);
Medical (the provision of medical or surgical advice or attendance and the performance of surgical operations);
Dental (any services falling within the practice of dentistry within the meaning of the Dentists Act 1984);
Ophthalmic (the testing of sight);
Veterinary (any services which constitute veterinary surgery within the meaning of the Veterinary Surgeons Act 1966);
Nursing (the services of nurses);
Midwifery (the services of midwives);
Physiotherapy (the services of physiotherapists);
Chiropody (the services of chiropodists);
Architectural (the services of architects);
Accounting and auditing (the making or preparation of accounts or accounting records and the examination, verification and auditing of financial statements);
Insolvency (insolvency services within the meaning of section 428 of the Insolvency Act 1986);
Patent agency (the services of registered patent agents);
Parliamentary agency (the services of parliamentary agents entered in the register in either House of parliament as agents entitled to practise both in promoting and in opposing Bills);
Surveying (the services of surveyors of land, of quantity surveyors, of surveyors of buildings or other structures and of surveyors of ships);
Engineering (the services of persons practising or employed as consultants in the field of engineering);
Educational (the provision of education or training);
Religious (the services of ministers of religion).

This list is similar to the list of services excluded from "designated services" set out in Sched. 1 to the RTPA. However, the effect of the Competition Act exclusion is much narrower in that it only excludes the rules of the professions and certain directly related agreements. Under the RTPA any agreement between members of the relevant profession relating to the Sched. 1 professional services was outside the scope of the Act.

The list is arbitrary and many professional bodies complained that they were not on the list. There were a number of unsuccessful attempts during the Bill's progress through the House of Lords to alter the scope of this exclusion and to expand the range of excluded professional rules (*Hansard*, H.L., Vol. 585, No. 99, col. 976 (February 9, 1998)). The wording of section 75, although it gives the Secretary of State wide ranging powers to make supplementary amendments, is almost certainly not adequate to allow additions to the list and primary legislation would be required to make changes.

7.7.3 List of Designated Rules

The regulator of one of the listed professional services, or a body that wishes to regulate such a service, can apply to the Secretary of State for designation. The Secretary of State maintains a list of rules which have been notified to him and which he considers are professional rules. Alterations to designated rules have to be notified to both the Secretary of State and the Director. The Director is required to keep the list of designated rules under review, and to advise the Secretary of State if he feels that some or all of the rules in question should no longer be designated. An exclusion can be revoked by the Secretary of State on the receipt of such advice, but he must first consult any other Minister who has responsibilities for the particular professional service.

7.7.4 Practice

The authorities have stressed that designation is only needed if the rules fall within the prohibition (see, for example, OFT: *A Review of Competition Restrictions in the Professions*: consultation document, May 2000).

To date, no professional rules have been designated. There has been one request for designation by the Royal College of Veterinary Surgeons, on which the DTI expects to make an order soon. A number of professions have rules that may be thought to restrict competition: *e.g.* advertising limitations (which the OFT keeps under review). The Government has asked the OFT to carry out a review using its FTA powers. A consultation by the OFT, which was part of a review on possible restrictions on competition in the provision of professional services, closed on the June 30, 2000.

Chapter 8

Exemptions from the Chapter I Prohibition

8.1   Introduction
8.2   Individual Exemptions
8.3   Block Exemptions
8.4   Parallel Exemptions
8.5   Other Exemptions from the Chapter I Prohibition

8.1   Introduction

8.1.1   Effect of the Chapter I Prohibition

As discussed in Chapter 6, the Chapter I Prohibition prohibits agreements, decisions by associations of undertakings and concerted practices (which are referred to in this chapter as "agreements") which may affect trade within the United Kingdom and which have the object or effect of preventing, restricting or distorting competition within the United Kingdom, unless they are exempt (s. 2(1)) or excluded (s. 3). Agreements which are prohibited by the Chapter I Prohibition are void (s. 2(4)) and thus unenforceable. Parties to such agreements are also at risk of severe penalties for operating a prohibited agreement (see Chapter 10, para. 10.3.1).

8.1.2   Need for Exemption Process

The consequences of voidness are considered in Chapter 10, at 10.1. They may have the effect of rendering unlawful (in whole or in part) agreements which, although they may affect competition, nevertheless have corresponding and countervailing benefits to society and the economy, which outweigh any negative effects on competition. In order that restrictive agreements which have countervailing benefits may be lawfully performed without risk of financial penalty, it is necessary to have a procedure whereby such agreements can be exempted from the Chapter I Prohibition either on an individual basis or according to common characteristics. The process also provides protection against fines. The existence of exclusions (see Chapter 7 and the discussion at 8.1.6 below) lessens the need for exemptions by category, but does not remove it.

8.1.3   Exemptions from the Chapter I Prohibition

Under the provisions of the Competition Act 1998 agreements, if they fulfil certain criteria, qualify for exemption from the Chapter I Prohibition. Four types of exemptions are possible:

    (i)   *individual exemptions* (ss. 4 and 5)
           Individual exemptions reflect, in the Act, the system under Article 81(3) and Regulation 17/62 for granting exemptions to agreements which infringe Article 81(1), but which have countervailing benefits (see *Competition Law and Practice*, Chapter 3).

(ii) **block exemptions** (ss. 6 to 9)
Block exemptions reflect the system under Council Regulation 19/65 and Commission Regulations made thereunder whereby types of agreement which meet certain criteria are automatically exempt from Article 81(1).

(iii) **parallel exemptions** (s. 10)
Parallel exemptions have no counterpart in the text of Article 81, but are intended to ensure that agreements that are exempted from Article 81(1) by Article 81(3) are also exempted from the Chapter I Prohibition, in order to ensure consistency between the two systems in respect of an individual agreement or, in the case of block exemptions, the same types of agreements.

(iv) **exemptions for agreements subject to Article 84 E.C. (formerly Article 88 E.C.)** (s. 11).
Article 84 E.C. exemptions may be granted by the Secretary of State in cases where he exercises his residual powers under Articles 84 and 85 E.C. Treaty to enforce Article 81(1). These powers are provided by the E.C. Competition Law (Articles 88 and 89) Enforcement Regulations 1996 (S.I. 1996 No. 2199). These were used to enable consideration of the proposed "strategic alliance" between British Airways and American Airlines, which was subsequently abandoned. Use of these residual powers is likely to be rare, as there are few gaps in the E.C. Commission's powers to apply Article 81 (see further para. 8.5.1 below).

8.1.4 Decision on the Applicability of the Chapter I Prohibition

The Director also has powers to adopt a decision that the Chapter I Prohibition does not apply to an agreement. These powers (contained in ss 12, 14 and 16 of the Act) are somewhat similar to the powers of the E.C. Commission to grant "negative clearance" under Regulation 17/62 (a statement that an agreement does not infringe Article 81(1)), but the Director may also take a decision clarifying that a particular agreement is covered by a pre-existing exemption, such as a block or parallel exemption.

Chapter 9 deals further with the decision taking process (see para. 9.4).

8.1.5 Guidance from the Director

It is also possible to obtain guidance in confidence from the Director under sections 13 and 15. This may help parties to clarify whether their agreement falls within an existing exemption without courting publicity. If the Director concludes that an individual exemption would be needed, the parties will be in the same uncomfortable position as if they receive an administrative "comfort letter" from the E.C. Commission indicating that an Article 81(3) exemption is needed. It is common for the E.C. Commission to close its file in a case notified to it for an individual exemption after issuing such a letter. While this saves the Commission's resources, it leaves the parties at risk if there are disputed enforcement proceedings or later third party claims.

In the event of later dispute, a recipient of guidance that an individual exemption is needed will have to seek a formal decision, just as a recipient of an E.C. comfort letter indicating that an 81(3) exemption is needed will have to ask the E.C. Commission to re-open its file. Of course, if guidance indicates that changes are needed in order for an agreement to qualify for exemption or that an agreement is unexemptable, the parties will have to abandon or adjust their arrangements or face enforcement proceedings (see also 8.2.15 below).

As well as formal guidance under sections 13 and 15 which can only be given in relation to completed agreements, the Director may be prepared to give a non-binding, extra-statutory view upon agreements which are "informally" notified to him. As with extra-statutory confidential guidance in relation to proposed mergers, this may be of value when drawing up an agreement likely to fall within the prohibition. The OFT will, however, be very cautious in their use of this process, since at a later stage it may have to deal with a contested application for exemption, possibly with active third party complainants. The OFT's role as decision taker on the Chapter I Prohibition is much greater than the role of advising which mergers should be subject to detailed examination by the Competition Commission. The OFT must be able to approach any later complaint or application for a decision with an open mind. Chapter 9 deals further with the guidance process (see 9.3).

8.1.6   Distinction between an Exempted and an Excluded Agreement

The Act provides for a number of types of agreement to be excluded from the Chapter I Prohibition as discussed in Chapter 7, a technique little used in E.C. law. The Act also follows the E.C. legislative approach in providing for exemptions as described in this Chapter. It is worth considering the distinction between the two:

- An excluded agreement which has not been "clawed back" by the Director, is fully legally enforceable and there should be no risk of third party claims in respect of infringement of the Chapter I Prohibition: in other words, it carries a presumption of validity and legality under the laws of the jurisdictions within the United Kingdom (England and Wales, Scotland and Northern Ireland).

- An exempted agreement is one which has had to win the status of validity and legality, either by being drafted to fall within the terms of a relevant block exemption or parallel block exemption or by satisfying the Director (or in the case of a section 11 exemption, the Secretary of State) that it qualifies for an individual exemption. Where an individual exemption is needed, the agreement will carry the presumption of invalidity and risk of third party action until the exemption is granted (even if the exemption has full retrospective effect). Unless notified to the Director, it also carries the risk of fines, although these are unlikely if the agreement qualifies for exemption without any substantial changes.

An agreement which is excluded from the United Kingdom prohibition or which benefits from a United Kingdom exemption can, if it has an effect on trade between Member States, still infringe Article 81. Not all such agreements will benefit from an exemption under Article 81(3), although the majority should be eligible to do so. The alignment of the United Kingdom and E.C. approach to the application of competition law, as reinforced by section 60 (see Chapter 5) is important in reducing the risk of double jeopardy for agreements to which Article 81 could apply.

8.2   Individual Exemptions

8.2.1   The Director's Power to Grant Individual Exemptions

Section 4 of the Act gives to the Director a power to grant an individual exemption in respect of a particular agreement if:

(i)   it has been notified to him under section 14; and

(ii)   it is an agreement which satisfies the criteria for exemption under section 9.

An individual exemption is granted by the Director making a "decision", which must be reasoned and will be published. The procedure for making a notification for an individual exemption is dealt with in Chapter 9 at 9.2.

8.2.2   Immunity from Penalties

Agreements to which the Chapter I Prohibition applies and which have been notified under section 13 for guidance or section 14 for a decision are exempt from penalties. Penalties are examined in Chapter 10. This exemption covers the period between the date of notification and the date specified by the Director when the application is determined (s. 13(4)) and (s. 14(4)). This is plainly an incentive for undertakings to notify agreements which may be subject to the Chapter I Prohibition.

8.2.3   Grounds for Granting an Individual Exemption

Under section 4(1)(b) the Director may grant an individual exemption if the relevant agreement fulfils the criteria laid down in section 9 of the Act, which contains both "positive" and "negative" criteria. An agreement must comply with *all* criteria in order to be granted an individual exemption.

The "positive" criteria are set out in section 9(a) and they provide that an agreement which is subject to the Chapter I Prohibition may only be granted an individual exemption if it contributes to:

(i)   (a)   improving production or distribution (s. 9(a)(i)); or
      (b)   promoting technical or economic progress (s. 9(a)(ii)); and if it

(ii)   allows consumers a fair share of the resulting benefit.

An agreement which fulfils both these "positive" criteria will nevertheless not be capable of an individual exemption if it cannot fulfil the two "negative" criteria. The "negative" criteria are set out in section 9(b) and they provide that an agreement must not:

(i)   impose on the undertakings concerned restrictions which are not indispensable to the attainment of those objectives (*i.e.* the objectives represented by the "positive criteria") (s. 9(b)(i)); or

(ii)   afford the undertakings concerned the possibility of eliminating competition in respect of a substantial part of the products in question (s. 9(b)(ii)).

The requirements of section 9 reflect the language of Article 81(3) which is applied by the E.C. Commission when granting individual exemptions to agreements falling within Article 81(1).

8.2.4   Community Jurisprudence Concerning Individual Exemptions

There is an extensive volume of E.C. Commission decisions and ECJ and CFI jurisprudence devoted to the application of Article 81(3). For detailed discussion of this, see *Competition Law and Practice*, Chapter 3.

Under section 60, which concerns the "governing principles" (see Chapter 5), the Director must act (subject to limited exceptions) with a view to ensuring that the principles applied and the decisions reached by him in applying the Act are consistent with the principles laid down by the E.C. Treaty and the CFI/ECJ and any relevant decision of the CFI/ECJ in determining corresponding questions of Community law. The Director must also have regard to relevant statements and decisions of the Commission. These duties also apply, on appeal, to the Competition Commission and the courts. It is, therefore, helpful to summarise the approach of the E.C. Commission and the European courts in applying the four elements of Article 81(3) to a very wide range of agreements.

Community law requires that, for an exemption to be granted, it must be shown, on an objective basis, that the positive benefits to the public (and not to the parties) outweigh the negative effects on competition, *i.e.* that the agreement is, overall, pro-competitive. The Director's approach to the application of the criteria is discussed in part 4 of the OFT Guideline *The Chapter I Prohibition*, OFT 401, March 1999.

8.2.5   Contribution to Improving Production or Distribution, or to Promoting Technical or Economic Progress

It must be shown that benefits will flow from the notified agreement. Examples of improvements in production have included the development of new products which would not otherwise have been developed, improved product quality and better use of capacity. Improvements in distribution have included certain exclusive or selective distribution agreements and exclusive purchasing agreements, as well as franchise agreements. Technical progress has been held to encompass joint research and development and/or manufacture, whilst economic progress has included the exploitation of new intellectual property rights, the rationalisation of production and the pooling of specialist expertise in sectors such as insurance.

8.2.6   Allowing Consumers a Fair Share of the Resulting Benefit

A proper market analysis will often be needed to show that resulting benefits accrue to consumers and that they are not denied to some customers. "Resulting benefits" to consumers have included improved supply, the introduction of new or improved products and lower costs and prices. Whilst consumers need not be members of the public, but may be other undertakings who purchase goods or services from the parties to the notified agreement, it is likely that the Director will place emphasis upon benefits accruing to consumers who are members of the public. Both the Director and the Secretary of State take the view that the main purpose of competition legislation is to benefit consumers as regards price, quality and choice in the goods and services they are offered and have made this clear in public statements:

"I share the Secretary of State"s concern about consumer prices. Safeguarding the consumer interest is, and always has been, the OFT"s top priority". (Director, Press Release No.6/99, March 10, 1999); and

"My job is to protect consumers and to champion their interests. This is the fundamental intention of Parliament which underlies some twenty pieces of legislation accumulated over nearly thirty years and setting out my formal duties". (Director in a Speech given to the All-Party Parliamentary Group on Management, June 6, 2000).

8.2.7 Indispensability to Attainment of Objectives

It is an aid to understanding to disentangle the concept dealt with in section 9(b)(i) from the double negatives derived from Article 81(3). Restrictions on competition are only capable of exemption if they are indispensable to the attainment of the beneficial objectives of the agreement referred to in the positive conditions. This means that the agreement must adopt the least restrictive solution that achieves the benefits of the agreement or, more simply, that the restrictions must be no more than are necessary. While indispensability will be determined on a case-by-case basis, it is unlikely that the Director will ever regard restrictions such as price fixing between competitors, market sharing or minimum resale price maintenance as indispensable.

8.2.8 No Elimination of Competition in Respect of a Substantial Part of the Products in Question

The parties to the notified agreement must demonstrate that there are a number of alternative products or services to those covered by the agreement, and that these are provided by undertakings which compete with the parties in the same market. The alternative sources of supply must be sufficient to ensure effective competition. This is, again, very much a matter of fact and will depend upon an economic analysis of the relevant product and geographic markets: see OFT Guideline: *Market Definition*, OFT 403, March 1999 for the Director's approach to identifying the relevant market, further considered in Chapter 11 at 11.3.

8.2.9 Agreements which are Likely to benefit from an Individual Exemption

Based upon past experience under Article 81(1) and the RTPA, the following types of agreement are likely to benefit from an individual exemption:

(1) agreements which are not eligible for a block or parallel exemption for technical reasons, for example, by slightly exceeding a maximum permitted market share or involving more than the permitted number of parties. The exclusions for Land and Vertical Agreements may give rise to some similar "near misses" (see Chapter 7 at 7.2–7.3);

(2) common types of agreements for which there is presently no block exemption, for example, trade mark and copyright licences;

(3) joint venture agreements and agreements to create "strategic alliances" which are not excluded under the mergers exclusion (see Chapter 7 at 7.4), depending on the business and parties involved;

(4)   vertical agreements which contain some horizontal elements, *e.g.* possibly selective distribution agreements which have some restriction on sales between retailers; and

(5)   joint purchasing agreements and selling between small companies (for example, small retailers) who compete with large companies or who purchase from powerful sellers. Joint purchasing arrangements of agricultural co-operatives may also fall in this category: they are not specifically covered by the agricultural agreements exclusion discussed in Chapter 7, para. 7.6.8.

The OFT has stressed that it does not wish to receive technical or precautionary notifications. The Director has set his appreciability threshold at combined market share of 25 per cent (see Chapter 6, para. 6.7.4) which is well above the rule of thumb (5 per cent for horizontal agreements and 10 per cent for vertical agreements) set by the E.C. Commission. The Director also has power to give retrospective exemptions which should mean that parties are more likely to seek individual exemptions when issues arise, rather than at the time of entering into the agreement. As a result, at the time of writing, the public register maintained by the OFT contains particulars of only five notifications for a decision. The OFT say that only one notification for guidance has been received since the Act came into force. It is therefore too early to form any clear view on how the Director's exemption policy will develop.

8.2.10   Individual Exemptions may be Subject to Conditions or Obligations

An individual exemption may be granted subject to such conditions or obligations as the Director considers to be appropriate (s. 4(3)(a)). It may also be limited to a certain period of time (s. 4(3)(b)), which will be specified in the decision granting the exemption (s. 4(4)). This time period may commence with the date of the agreement or a later date, but is not tied to the date of notification.

It is likely, in the light of experience under Article 81, that individual exemptions will be for a limited period of time and will often be subject to conditions and obligations. Limiting the duration of an individual exemption enables the Director to review its appropriateness in the light of changing economic and market circumstances. The imposition of conditions or obligations enables the Director to grant an individual exemption in respect of an agreement but at the same time to limit or prevent any obviously anti-competitive effects that the exempted agreement may have, either by limiting the parties' activities or by requiring other action to be taken to make a market more competitive.

8.2.11 Difference Between Conditions and Obligations

It appears from sections 4 and 5 that conditions and obligations are different concepts and have different legal effects. However, both conditions and obligations are used by the E.C. Commission when granting individual exemptions under Article 81(3), and it has sometimes been difficult to draw a distinction between the two concepts. A condition is a requirement that must be satisfied by the parties if the exemption is to come into and remain in force: examples of conditions include requirements to delete certain offending provisions from the agreement or that certain manufacturing capacity be sold off or closed down within a certain period. Sometimes, conditions can be of an on-going nature, for example a requirement to maintain a particular regime for the dissemination of technical information to third parties (as the Commission imposed in the *British Interactive Broadcasting* case (No. IV/36.539, [1999] O.J. L312/1).

An obligation is an on-going requirement, owed to and enforceable by the Director, as to the parties' future conduct in relation to the exempted agreement: an example of an obligation would be a requirement to make periodic reports to the Director on the operation of the agreement or amendments to it.

Decisions of the Director granting individual exemptions will specify which requirements are conditions and which are obligations.

8.2.12 Different Consequences of Breaching a Condition or Obligation

The distinction between a condition and an obligation is most apparent in considering the consequences of breach.

If a party to an agreement breaches any *condition* of an individual exemption, the exemption will be automatically cancelled (s. 5(3)) and the benefits of the exemption will be lost. If a party fails to comply with an *obligation,* the Director may, by notice in writing take any of the steps mentioned in s. 5(1), *including* the cancellation of the exemption (s. 5(4)). These steps shall take effect from the date specified in the Director's written notice (s. 5(5)), and this may, if the Director suspects that a decision was based on incomplete, false or misleading information or if there has been failure to comply with an obligation, be earlier than the date of the Director's notice (s. 5(6)). As the consequences of breach of a condition differ from those for a breach of an obligation and result in automatic cancellation of the exemption, it will be important for the parties to ensure that provisions intended to be conditions are not framed in a way readily capable of minor breach.

8.2.13 Temporal Effect of an Individual Exemption

An individual exemption may be limited to a specified future period of time, or it may also be "backdated" so that it takes effect as from a date earlier than that on which it was granted (s. 4(5)). Such "back-dating" may, in principle, extend back to the date on which the exempted agreement came into force. This contrasts with the system which applied until recently under Article 81, where an exemption might be backdated only in limited circumstances, in particular when an agreement need not have been notified to the Commission, pursuant to Article 4(2) of Regulation 17/62, (see Regulation 17/62, Articles 4 and 6). This has now been changed by Council Regulation (E.C.) No. 1216/1999 [1999] O.J. L148/5, which gives the Commission the same flexibility to back-date exemptions as the Director has under the Competition Act 1998.

A party which has been granted an individual exemption for a limited period only may apply to the Director for the period to be extended (s. 4(6) and Director's Rules, r. 19).

8.2.14 Legal Effect of an Individual Exemption

The effect of the grant of an individual exemption is that the agreement does *not* infringe the Chapter I Prohibition: the consequences of infringement therefore do not apply to an exempted agreement. The Director may take no further action against an exempted agreement, unless he has reasonable grounds for believing that there has been a material change of circumstances since he gave his decision (s.16(2)(a)) or if he has a reasonable suspicion that the information on which he based his decision was incomplete, false or misleading in a material particular (s. 16(2)(b)).

An individual exemption also confers immunity from civil fines (s. 16(3)), unless:

(1)   one of the circumstances mentioned in section 16(2) applies (see above);
(2)   the Director considers that the agreement will infringe the Chapter I Prohibition; and
(3)   the Director gives written notice of the removal of immunity as from the date specified in the notice (s. 16(4)), which may, where a party has provided materially incomplete, misleading or false information, be earlier than the date on which the notice is given (s. 16(5)).

8.2.15   Cancellation or Variation of an Individual Exemption

The Director may cancel or vary an individual exemption if he has reasonable grounds for believing that there has been a material change in circumstances since the granting of the exemption (s. 5(1)). Variation of an exemption may take the form of either varying or removing any condition or obligation (s. 5(1)(b)) or the imposition of one or more additional conditions or obligations (s. 5(1)(c)). An agreement by the parties to amend an exempted agreement may amount to a material change in circumstances, as could a change in ownership. For example, if a shareholding in a joint venture were to be sold by a major established business to a new market entrant, some conditions and obligations might be relaxed or withdrawn.

The Director may also cancel or vary an individual exemption if he has a reasonable suspicion that the information upon which he based his exemption decision was incomplete, false or misleading in a material particular (s. 5(2)). If the exemption is cancelled, this may take effect earlier than the date of the Director's notice of cancellation (s. 5(5) and (6)).

The Director may act upon his own initiative or upon receipt of a complaint in varying or cancelling an exemption under section 5(1) or (2) (s. 5(7)). The circumstances in which an individual exemption may be varied or cancelled by the Director under section 5 are the same as for the removal of immunity under section 16 (see Chapter 9, para. 9.4.10).

The procedures which the Director will follow in cancelling or varying an individual exemption are set out in the Director's Rules which are set out in The Competition Act 1998 (Director's Rules) Order 2000 (S.I. 2000 No. 293) and are dealt with in Chapter 9 at 9.6.

8.2.16   Circumstances Where the Director Does Not Wish to Issue a Decision: the Use of Administrative Letters

The Director has moved away from his original intention to deal with a number of cases by administrative letter without giving a formal decision. This would have replicated practice of the European Commission, which concludes most applications informally, in a process which tends to encourage the use of competition law in any subsequent dispute between the parties, however threadbare the arguments used.

The E.C. Commission has embarked on a major review of the administration of Articles 81 and 82, (White Paper on *Modernisation of the Rules Implementing Articles 85 and 86 [now 81 and 82] of the E.C. Treaty*, Commission Programme No. 99/027, April 1999, [1999] O.J. C132/1 and draft Regulation published on

September 27, 2000). At the same time the United Kingdom authorities have put in place a process that encourages the taking of formal decisions and guidance where these are sought. The Director must return the applicant"s substantial fee and give reasons if he declines to give a decision or guidance. The Act also contains procedures to deal with undue delay. These matters are discussed further Chapter 9 at 9.3–9.4 and the E.C. Reforms in Chapter 17 at 17.7.

8.3   Block Exemptions

8.3.1   Introduction

It is possible that a large number of very similar agreements, containing very similar restrictions, may be subject to the Chapter I Prohibition. These agreements will often generally be pro-competitive and would be the types of agreements which would be granted either an individual exemption or favourable guidance if they were to be notified to the Director. Depending on the scope of other exemptions (particularly the ability of agreements to benefit from "parallel" E.C. block exemptions, discussed at 8.4 below) and exclusions, the volume of these agreements might cause severe administrative difficulties for the OFT, and delay and uncertainty for parties. Similar difficulties were identified at the Community level, which led to the introduction of a number of block exemptions which exempt specific types of agreements from Article 81(1) if the requirements of the relevant Regulation are complied with (see *Competition Law and Practice*, Chapter 3, paras 3.51 onwards). Sections 6 to 9 aim to replicate this system in English law.

8.3.2   Adoption of Block Exemptions

During the period between enactment and entry into force of the Act, the Secretary of State had the power to make block exemption orders (Sched. 13, para. 4), but did not utilise it. Section 6(1) lays down the procedure to be followed now the Act is in force. The Director may, after public consultation under section 9, recommend to the Secretary of State that an order be made specifying a category (or categories) of agreements that are likely to be agreements to which section 9 applies. The criteria to be applied in determining whether a category of agreements should benefit from a block exemption are the same as are to be applied by the Director in determining whether to grant an individual exemption under sections 4 and 14 (8.2.3 above). Before making his recommendation, the Director must publish details of it, allow for public consultation and consider any representations made to him (s. 8(1)). The Secretary of State may, following the Director's recommendation, make a block exemption order, either in the form recommended by the Director or with such modifications to it as are considered appropriate by the Secretary of State, taking into account the Director's comments on such modifications (s. 6(2)). The first draft proposed block exemption order covering public transport ticketing agreements is discussed at 8.3.9 below.

8.3.3   Revocation or Variation of a Block Exemption Order

A block exemption order may be revoked or varied by the Secretary of State upon the recommendation of the Director, following public consultation (s. 8(3) and (4)). The Secretary of State also has the power, under section 8(5), to revoke a block exemption order on his own initiative, following consultation with the Director.

8.3.4   Temporal Applicability of a Block Exemption

A block exemption order may provide for a block exemption to take effect from a date earlier than the date on which the order is made (s. 8(6)). Block exemptions made after the Act enters into force could, for example, be applied retrospectively to cover existing agreements for the period after the commencement of the Act. Block exemption orders may be applicable only for a specified period (s. 6(7)).

8.3.5   Legal Effect of a Block Exemption

An agreement which falls within a category of agreements specified in a block exemption order is exempt from the Chapter I Prohibition (s. 6(3)).

8.3.6   Obligations or Conditions in Block Exemptions

A block exemption may impose conditions or obligations subject to which it is to have effect (s. 6(5)). The difference between conditions and obligations is explained at 8.2.11 and 8.2.12 above. A block exemption order may provide that:

- breach of a condition has the effect of cancelling the block exemption in respect of an agreement (s. 6(6)(a)): cancellation has the effect that an agreement would no longer be exempt and would prima facie infringe the Chapter I Prohibition and need to be notified to the Director for individual exemption under section 14;

- if an obligation is not complied with, the Director may by written notice cancel the block exemption in respect of an agreement (s. 6(6)(b));

- if the Director considers that a particular agreement is not one to which section 9 applies, he may cancel the block exemption in respect of that agreement, (s. 6(6)(c)).

8.3.7   Block Exemptions: the Opposition Procedure

It is possible that a large number of agreements may not qualify for a block exemption for technical reasons, yet still fulfil the criteria for eligibility set out in section 9. Such agreements would normally need to be notified to the Director for an individual exemption, which would unnecessarily consume his resources. The Act therefore creates the possibility that a block exemption order may provide for an "opposition procedure" to apply in respect of agreements which do not qualify for the block exemption but which do satisfy specified criteria (s. 7(1)). Once notified to the Director, such agreements are to be treated as being entitled to the benefit of the block exemption, unless the Director gives notice of his opposition to the agreement being so treated within the notice period specified in the block exemption order (ss. 7(2) and 7(4)). Opposition by the Director automatically converts the notification into a notification under section 14 and an application for an individual exemption under section 14(3) (s. 7(3)). The opposition procedure was developed by the E.C. Commission, but the cumbersome internal processes of that body have meant that it has been of little practical benefit. It is to be hoped that the OFT would be more pragmatic in their approach if the process is introduced in block exemption orders made under the Competition Act.

8.3.8 Usefulness of Block Exemptions

Many block exemptions already exist at the Community level, and they will have effect under the Act as parallel exemptions (see 8.4 below). It is unlikely, therefore, that block exemptions made under the Act will cover the same fields as those adopted under E.C. law. The Director will have regard to existing E.C. block exemptions (which will lead to the grant of a parallel exemption under s. 10) in proposing block exemptions under the Act (*Hansard* (Standing Committee G), col. 335 (June 11, 1998)).

One sector where it had been anticipated that there would be a need for a block exemption was agriculture. Agriculture is subject to a special regime in Community law under the Common Agricultural Policy (the effect of which is that Article 81 does not apply to many agreements in the agricultural sector). Various agricultural agreements were exempted from the RTPA, the principal exemption being for agreements between members of agricultural and forestry associations and fisheries associations, including co-operatives (RTPA, s. 33) (see references in *Competition Law and Practice* at p. 269). It was anticipated that a block exemption order would be made covering agricultural co-operatives (White Paper, para. 4.2). Many agreements relating to the production of or trade in agricultural products are now, however excluded from the scope of the Chapter I Prohibition (see Chapter 7 at 7.6.8): this should ensure that agricultural products (as defined in Annex II to the E.C. Treaty) are treated in a similar fashion under the Chapter I Prohibition and under E.C. competition law.

One possible use of a block exemption order would be to set up an opposition procedure for agreements that almost, but not quite, meet the conditions for a parallel exemption. Since parallel exemptions will apply to agreements that are too small and national in character to justify examination by the E.C. Commission, this could be a valuable aid to greater legal certainty. The block exemption could cover agreements of types which have an opposition procedure at E.C. level, but possibly also other types of agreement for which such a process would be desirable, especially those subject to highly prescriptive and narrow E.C. block exemptions and those with difficult to define market share thresholds.

8.3.9 Proposed Block Exemption for Public Transport Ticketing Schemes

In July 2000 the OFT published a consultation paper with a series of questions and possible draft text for a block exemption for public transport ticket schemes (consultation period ended August 18, 2000). The proposal may cover agreements between operators of local and longer distance scheduled bus or coach services, and of scheduled services via trams, railway vehicles, light railway vehicles or ferries for the carriage of passengers. Local air services (*e.g.* to Scottish island communities) are outside the proposed category of services. The exemption, if adopted in accordance with the proposals, would cover ticketing around arrangements such as multi-operator travel cards (*e.g.* the zone cards for tube, train and bus services in and around London) through tickets using services of more than one operator (*e.g.* a combined train and ferry ticket from London to the Isle of Wight) and multi-operator individual tickets for routes covered by more than one operator (*e.g.* for trains of the three train operators presently operating between Penzance and Plymouth). Although international services are not specifically excluded, the block exemption would benefit principally agreements relating to services operating within the United Kingdom and not infringing Article 81. The proposal reflects the benefits to consumers from integrated ticketing schemes described in the Government consultation document. *"From Workhorse to Thoroughbred: A better role for bus travel"* (March 29, 1999) and contemplated in the Transport Bill before Parliament at the time of writing.

It is intended that ticketing schemes should only be exempt so long as they comply with certain conditions, which are very general in nature. There would, therefore, always be some doubt whether the conditions were complied with, and careless disclosure of information in the operation of a scheme could easily lose its parties the benefit of the block exemption. The proposed conditions are:

(1)   that the scheme should not have the object or effect of preventing any operator from participating in the scheme. This is not intended to prevent a scheme imposing reasonable financial and technical requirements and revenue sharing arrangements, but provisions which would be unreasonable are to be spelled out (*e.g.* unreasonable investment in on-board hardware for recording data required to administer the scheme);

(2)   that the scheme should not have the object or effect of limiting

● the frequency or time of any services (unless indispensable to the operation of the scheme), or

● the variety or number of routes on which any person provides services, or

● the price or availability of the fare structure relating to journeys confined to the services of a single operator, or

● the price or fare structure of individual components of a journey made with a through ticket.

(3)   that the scheme should not have the object or effect of facilitating the exchange of confidential information other than through the media of a third party in confidence dealing with prices, revenue and cost sharing, although the parties may agree methodology and collated data may be published to meet statutory requirements (see Chapter 6, para. 6.4.3).

As regard exchange of information, the parties will be guided by the Director's analysis of relevant E.C. case law in the OFT Guideline: *The Chapter I Prohibition*, OFT 401, March 1999, paras 3.21–3.28.

8.4   Parallel Exemptions

8.4.1   The Need for Consistency with Article 81

It is likely that many agreements which fall within the scope of the Chapter I Prohibition will also fall within the scope of Article 81, or would do so if they were to have an effect on inter-state trade. In order to ensure that the Chapter I Prohibition is not applied in a manner inconsistent with the application of Article 81, it is necessary to ensure that agreements which are exempted from Article 81(1) are also exempted from the Chapter I Prohibition. Uniform application will also reduce the regulatory burden on, and uncertainty for, businesses subject to both United Kingdom and E.C. competition law.

8.4.2   The Solution Chosen to Ensure Consistency with Article 81

Section 10 of the Act introduces the concept of "parallel exemptions". Agreements which are exempt from a "Community prohibition" are exempt from the Chapter

I Prohibition. Section 10(10) defines a "Community prohibition" as the prohibition contained in Article 81(1), in any corresponding provision replacing or derived from Article 81(1) or in any other Commission or Council Regulation specified by order by the Secretary of State. Section 10(11) extends the concept of a "Community prohibition" to Article 53(1) of the European Economic Area Agreement, as amended: thus, references to Article 81 include references to Article 53 EEA (see para. 8.4.13, below). However, the Director is given power to attach conditions or obligations to any parallel exemption or to cancel it, opening up opportunities for double regulation of the same agreement, as well as for variations on the theme of an E.C. block exemption (see 8.4.12 below).

8.4.3 Agreements Not Affecting Trade Between Member States

Section 10(2) provides that an agreement may benefit from a parallel exemption if it does not affect trade between Member States, but falls within the categories of agreement which would have been exempted from Article 81(1) by virtue of a Commission or Council Regulation had it had an effect on trade between Member States and thus been subject to Article 81(1).

8.4.4 Parallel Exemption by means of a Community Block Exemption

Agreements which are exempted from Article 81(1) by virtue of a Community block exemption benefit from a parallel exemption and are accordingly also exempt from the Chapter I Prohibition (s. 10(1)(a)). A number of Regulations have been adopted by the E.C. Commission using powers delegated to it by various Council Regulations, in order to give effect to Community block exemptions. Different criteria apply to eligibility for different block exemptions, although the Regulations usually contain a "white list" of permitted clauses and a "black list" of prohibited clauses. Some block exemption Regulations also contain a "grey list" of clauses which are neither *per se* permitted nor prohibited and in respect of which an "opposition procedure" applies. The new Vertical Agreements block exemption (see (4) below) represents a new and less prescriptive approach by the E.C. Commission but still contains a short "black list" and its application is limited by reference to market share and, in the case of agreements with actual and potential competitors, by the absence of reciprocity, level of competition and buyer's turnover (see comment at Chapter 7, para. 7.2.8 on the relationship of this block exemption with the United Kingdom exclusion for vertical agreements). Community block exemptions cover the following categories of agreement:

(1) bilateral exclusive distribution agreements (Regulation 1983/83, [1983] O.J. L173/1) expired on May 31, 2000 but with transitional application to December 31, 2001;

(2) bilateral exclusive purchasing agreements (Regulation 1984/83, [1983] O.J. L173/5) expired on May 31, 2000 but with transitional application to December 31, 2001;

(3) franchise agreements (Regulation 4087/88, [1988] O.J. L359/46) expired May 31, 2000 with transitional application to December 31, 2001;

(4) replacing (1), (2) and (3) above; vertical agreements (Regulation 2790/1999, [1999] O.J. L336/21) expiry May 31, 2010 with Commission Notice, Guidelines on Vertical Restraints, May 2000;

  (5)　selective distribution for motor vehicles and servicing agreements (Regulation 1475/95, [1995] O.J. 145/25) expiry September 30, 2002;

  (6)　specialisation agreements (Regulation 417/85, [1985] O.J. L53/1, as amended by Regulation 151/93, [1993] O.J. L21/8 and Regulation 2236/97, [1997] O.J. L306/12) expiry December 31, 2000. These are to be replaced by a block exemption for horizontal agreements (draft Commission Regulation together with a draft Guideline on the Applicability of Article 81 to Horizontal Co-operation, were published on April 27, 2000 ([2000] O.J. C118/3));

  (7)　research and development agreements (Regulation 418/85, [1985] O.J. L53/5, as amended by Regulation 151/93, [1993] O.J. L21/8 and Regulation 2236/97, [1997] O.J. L306/12) expiry December 31, 2000 to be replaced by the block exemption for horizontal agreements (see above);

  (8)　technology transfer agreements (patent and know-how licences) (Regulation 240/96, [1996] O.J. L31/2) expiry March 31, 2006;

  (9)　certain agreements in the insurance sector (Regulation 3932/92, [1992] O.J. L398/7) expiry March 31, 2003;

  (10)　certain agreements concerning air transport (Regulation 1617/93, [1993] O.J. L155/18, as amended by Regulation 1523/96, [1996] O.J. L190/11; and Regulation 1083/99, [1999] O.J. L131/27) expiry June 30, 2001; and

  (11)　liner shipping consortia agreements, decisions and concerted practices (Regulation 870/95, [1995] O.J. L89/7) expired on April 22, 2000. There are plans for a replacement. A draft Commission Preliminary Regulation was published on December 31, 1999 ([1999] O.J. C379/13); see also the Report on Commission Regulation 870/95 (January 28, 1999) available from the Commission.

Parallel block exemptions will be particularly useful for common types of horizontal agreement, such as specialisation and research and development agreements and for technology transfer agreements, since there are no relevant United Kingdom exclusions. Pure copyright and trademark licences are not, however, covered by any parallel exemption and are not excluded. These are the most widespread types of agreement involving a vertical relationship which may require individual exemption.

8.4.5　Parallel Exemption by Opposition Procedure

A number of Community block exemption Regulations (those concerning technology transfer, specialisation, research and development and franchise agreements) contain an opposition procedure. Agreements which do not satisfy all the requirements of the relevant block exemption may be notified to the E.C. Commission, and exemption will be granted automatically if the E.C. Commission does not oppose exemption within six months. Use of the opposition procedure has not been widespread, not least because the E.C. Commission frequently finds reasons for opposition (see *Competition Law and Practice*, para. 10.58). Section 10(1)(c) provides that an agreement which has been notified under an opposition procedure is entitled to a parallel exemption if the E.C. Commission has either not opposed exemption within the appropriate time for opposing it, or has withdrawn its opposition. An unresolved issue would appear to be the status of agreements which do not affect trade between Member States: they do not have to be notified to the E.C. Commission (as Article 81 does not apply) and there is no equivalent opposition procedure under the Act in such circumstances. Such agreements are not automatically exempt from Article 81(1), so a parallel exemption would seem not to be available in such a case. This could, presumably, be a suitable category for a domestic block exemption (see 8.3.8 above).

8.4.6 Parallel Exemption by Means of an Individual Exemption Granted under Article 81(3)

The E.C. Commission may grant, under Article 81(3), an individual exemption to an agreement which has been notified to it pursuant to Regulation 17/62 (see *Competition Law and Practice*, paras 3.01 to 3.50). The criteria for granting an individual exemption under Article 81(3) are essentially the same as the criteria set out in section 9 for granting an individual exemption under section 14 of the Act (see 8.2.3, above). Individual exemptions under Article 81(3) may only be granted by the E.C. Commission (Article 9(1) of Regulation 17/62) and only once an application has been made using Form A/B pursuant to Regulation 17/62 (*Distillers v. Commission* (Case 30/78) [1980] E.C.R. 2229, [1980] 3 C.M.L.R. 121). However, under proposed changes to the system of enforcing Article 81 (see Chapter 17 at 17.7) national authorities and courts will also be able to grant exemptions under Article 81(3).

8.4.7 Duration of Parallel Exemption

A parallel exemption takes effect from the date on which the exemption from the Community prohibition takes effect (*e.g.* the date specified in a E.C. Commission decision granting an individual exemption) or would have taken effect had the agreement in question affected trade between Member States and thus been entitled to the benefit of a block exemption (s. 10(4)(a)).

Section 10(4)(b)(i) provides that a parallel exemption ceases to have effect if the Community exemption ceases to have effect. Thus, a parallel exemption under section 10(1)(b) on the basis of an exemption granted under Article 81(3) which involves conditions (many individual exemptions and some block exemptions (*e.g.* Article 6(3)(b) Council Regulation (EEC) No. 3975/87 ([1987] O.J. L374/87) as amended by Council Regulation No. 2410/97 ([1992] O.J. L240/18) which lays down the procedure for the application of the rules on competition to undertakings in the air transport sector) have this feature) will be valid only provided that any conditions imposed by the E.C. Commission are complied with, as non-compliance with conditions renders the Community exemption void. If there has been a breach of an obligation, the parallel exemption will remain valid, so long as the E.C. Commission has not revoked the Community exemption under Article 8(3) of Regulation 17/62.

Section 10(5) permits the Director to cancel a parallel exemption in circumstances specified in his procedural rules (Director's Rules, r. 21). Breach of a condition imposed by the Director under section 10 (5)(a)–(c) will have the effect of cancelling the parallel exemption (s. 10(7)). The date of cancellation may be earlier than the date of the notice of cancellation (s. 10(6)).

8.4.8 Parallel Exemption by Virtue of Negative Clearance Granted by the E.C. Commission under Regulation 17/62

Agreements which benefit from negative clearance (*i.e.* a E.C. Commission decision that Article 81(1) does not apply to a notified agreement) made under Article

2 of Regulation 17/62) are entitled to a parallel exemption by virtue of section 10(9). This takes account of the fact that an agreement which did not infringe Article 81(1) could still have effects at the national level causing it to infringe the Chapter I Prohibition.

8.4.9   The Position of Comfort Letters and Parallel Exemptions

The E.C. Commission has been placed under an extreme administrative burden as an increasingly large number of agreements have been notified to it under Regulation 17/62 for negative clearance and/or individual exemption. It receives many times more notifications than its limited resources allow it to deal with. It has therefore adopted the procedure of issuing administrative "comfort letters" in the overwhelming majority of cases and concentrated its resources on cases with a real "Community interest". This policy was upheld by the CFI in *Automec (No.2)* (Case T–24/90) [1992] E.C.R. II–2223, [1992] 5 C.M.L.R. 431 and is further explained in the E.C. Commission's Notice on Co-operation between the Commission and the National Courts, ([1993] O.J. C39/6). A comfort letter has no legal status and is merely an administrative statement, with or without reasons, by the E.C. Commission that it does not intend to take any further action in respect of a notified agreement, either on the basis that it is not prohibited under Article 81(1) or that it is so prohibited, but would be exempted under Article 81(3), were the E.C. Commission to be minded to adopt a decision. In the latter case, there is little "comfort" to be derived from the letter, which may be better described as a "discomfort letter", since it confirms that the agreement is open to legal challenge but given no legal protection against such challenge. In some cases, where the Commission points to defects that would hinder the grant of an exemption but states that they are not sufficiently grave to merit the Commission's immediate attention, these are truly "discomfort letters".

Agreements benefiting from a comfort letter may be challenged in legal proceedings in the national courts, as Article 81(1) has direct effect. In some cases, the granting of a comfort letter is preceded by the publication in the *Official Journal* of an Article 19(3) notice, inviting public comments. A party which has been provided with a comfort letter is still at risk of a decision by the Director or the Competition Commission which declares unlawful an agreement which the E.C. Commission implicitly permits. The Commission's proposed substantial reform to the current system of enforcing Article 81 (see Chapter 17 at 17.7) will, if adopted, remove the obligation to notify agreements and therefore the need for the Commission to grant comfort letters, but will leave even more agreements exposed to uncertain treatment under both Article 81 and the Competition Act 1998, particularly if a dispute arises some years after the agreement was entered into.

8.4.10   The Director's Policy on E.C. Commission Comfort Letters

Comfort letters will be highly relevant in the application of the Chapter I Prohibition. The Act does not make any provision for informal action by the Director. The OFT Guideline, *The Chapter I Prohibition*, OFT 401, March 1999 paras 7.11 and 7.12 sets out the Director's intentions with respect to comfort letters issued by the E.C. Commission. As a general policy the Director will not depart from the E.C. Commission's assessment as set out in a comfort letter. In cases where the E.C. Commission issues a comfort letter because an agreement has no adverse effect on inter-state trade, the Director will have to review the agreement (for example, an agreement between United Kingdom bus operators) in order to ensure that it does not have any anti-competitive effects in the United Kingdom (*Hansard* (Standing Committee G) cols 342–344 (June 11, 1998)). Similarly, the Director would review an agreement which benefits from an E.C. comfort letter if it nevertheless raised particular concerns in relation to competition in the United Kingdom The Director has indicated that where he intends to depart from the E.C. Commission's assessment of an agreement benefiting from an E.C. comfort letter, he will normally expect to consult first with the E.C. Commission. In the case where the E.C. Commission has indicated that it would not be minded to issue an exemption under Article 81(3) (a true discomfort letter), the Director is likely to take the same approach as the E.C. Commission to the aspects of the agreement which have been identified as anti-competitive.

8.4.11 Legal Challenges to an Agreement Benefiting from an E.C. Comfort Letter

If an agreement which benefits from a E.C. Commission comfort letter is challenged in the United Kingdom courts under the Chapter I Prohibition, the Chapter I Guideline, para. 7.13 indicates that a notification may be made at this time and, if appropriate, the Director will grant an individual exemption with retroactive effect. Such cases will be given priority, which should be helpful in resolving the litigation speedily. Alternatively, agreements in respect of which favourable comfort letters have been issued by the E.C. Commission could be given the benefit of a block exemption under section 9, although this would mean that such agreements would receive somewhat less detailed competition scrutiny.

8.4.12 Parallel Exemptions May Be Subject to Conditions or Obligations

The Director may impose conditions or obligations subject to which a parallel exemption is to have effect (s. 10(5)). These conditions or obligations may be varied or removed by the Director who also has the power to add further conditions or obligations. It is plain that conditions or obligations imposed by the Director must comply with the requirement of E.C. law that national law does not prevent the proper application of E.C. competition law. They should therefore take account only of additional considerations arising only at the national level and not disturb the operation of the E.C. exemption at the Community level. The imposition of additional conditions and obligations should therefore be rare, but the existence of these powers opens up vistas of multiple regulation for individual agreements and further variations on the theme of Community block exemptions, all adding to the burden and complexity of competition law for business. The circumstances in which conditions and obligations may be imposed, varied or removed are set out in the Director's Rules, r. 21.

8.4.13 Parallel Exemptions and the European Economic Area

Article 53(1) of the European Economic Area Agreement is the mirror of Article 81(1) and applies to cases where trade is affected between the E.C. and the EFTA States (here meaning Iceland, Liechtenstein and Norway) or between the EFTA States. Article 53(1) is enforced in the same manner as Article 81(1), including by use of block exemptions, individual exemptions, negative clearance and comfort letters. In most cases, Article 53(1) is enforced by the E.C. Commission and in others, where an agreement primarily affects trade between the EFTA States, by the

EFTA Surveillance Authority (the "ESA"). Section 10(11) provides that parallel exemptions shall apply *mutatis mutandis* in relation to exemptions from the prohibition in Article 53(1), including individual exemptions granted by the ESA, subject to any modifications which the Secretary of State may by order prescribe.

8.5 Other Exemptions from the Chapter I Prohibition

8.5.1 Sectors Where the E.C. Commission Does Not Have Powers to Enforce Article 81(1)

In a limited number of sectors of the economy, the E.C. Commission does not have the competence to directly enforce Article 81(1), it not having been given the power to do so by a Council Regulation adopted under Article 83 (formerly Article 87). The principal sectors where this is the case are international air transport to airports outside of the European Union and international maritime tramp vessel services. Article 84 (ex 88) of the Treaty gives the Member States the competence to apply Article 81 (and Article 82) in such circumstances. In the United Kingdom, this power has been transposed into domestic law by the E.C. Competition Law (Articles 88 and 89) Enforcement Regulations 1996 (S.I. 1996 No. 2199). These powers were used to investigate the subsequently abandoned "strategic alliance" between British Airways and American Airlines. The Commission has residual powers under Article 85 (ex 89) to investigate suspected infringements of Article 81(1) in these sectors, but cannot enforce any decision that there has been an infringement: it can only authorise the Member State(s) concerned to take enforcement action.

8.5.2 Exemptions from the Chapter I Prohibition in Such Circumstances

Section 11(1) provides that the fact that a ruling may be given by virtue of Article 84 on the question of whether an agreement is prohibited by Article 81(1) does not prevent the agreement in question being subject to the Chapter I Prohibition. However, the Secretary of State may make regulations providing for an exemption (called a "section 11 exemption") to be granted in respect of such an agreement, in prescribed circumstances. A section 11 exemption is, in effect, an extension of the parallel exemption regime under section 10 to sectors where the E.C. Commission cannot directly apply Article 81. (*Hansard* (Standing Committee G) cols 356–364 (June 11, 1998)). Given the limited number of sectors where this is the case, s. 11 exemptions are likely to be very rare in practice. It seems possible, but very unlikely, that a section 11 exemption could be granted in respect of rulings made under Article 84 by competition authorities in other Member States, if such a ruling relates to an agreement having sufficient effects on competition in the United Kingdom.

Chapter 9

Procedure in Relation to Chapter I Prohibition

9.1   Introduction

9.1.1   Scope of this Chapter

This Chapter deals with notification for guidance or a decision in relation to the Chapter I Prohibition, with appropriate references to the provisions covering the Chapter II Prohibition (discussed in more detail in Chapter 13). It also deals with complaints, investigations and appeals under procedures common to both the Chapter I and the Chapter II Prohibitions.

This Chapter draws primarily on The Competition Act 1998 (Director's rules) Order 2000 (S.I. 2000 No. 293) ("Director's Rules") and on guidelines which have been published by the Office of Fair Trading. The guideline dealing with notification, *The Major Provisions*, OFT 400, March 1999 (the "Major Provisions Guideline") was produced prior to the finalisation of the Director's Rules and in its current form is not authoritative on procedural matters. As regards appeals, the rules are set out in sections 46 and 47 and The Competition Act 1998 (Notification of Excluded Agreements and Appealable Decisions) Regulations 2000 (S.I. 2000 No. 263)), which are heavily influenced by procedure in the European Court of First Instance.

9.1.2   No requirement to Notify

The Competition Act does not require parties to notify agreements or arrangements. Instead parties must consider whether the agreement is such that the Chapter I Prohibition is likely to be infringed. If the parties consider that they need to obtain an exemption or confirmation that the agreement is outside the relevant prohibition, details of the arrangements should be notified in accordance with the procedures discussed in this chapter.

9.1.3   Incentive to Notify

As the penalty for infringement of the Chapter I Prohibition is that the agreement is void, in whole or in part, and there is a risk of fines and third party claims for compensation and/or injunctions, it was expected that many parties would be keen to ensure that their agreement is either confirmed by the authorities to fall outside the prohibition, or granted an exemption. The main focus of the parliamentary debate relating to the provisions considered in this Chapter was on the transparency of the procedure and the availability of a certain outcome, such that United Kingdom businesses would not be prejudiced by the operation of the new regime.

The Regulators, however, have been concerned not to repeat the experience in other jurisdictions of a deluge of precautionary notifications. The scope in particular of The Competition Act 1998 (Land and Vertical Agreements Exclusion) Order 2000 (S.I. 2000 No. 310) and the exclusion from penalties of agreements of minor importance have cut down the volume of agreements that may need exemption. Other agreements, *e.g.* many technology agreements and research and development agreements benefit from a parallel exemption afforded to agreements covered by E.C. Commission block exemptions. Finally, there is the possibility of obtaining retrospective exemption if needed. These measures have been so successful in stemming the tide of notifications that only five notifications for decisions have been received to date (three of which are in the area of financial services). The message that notification should only be made in cases where there is real doubt about compliance with the Act has obviously been received. This is reinforced in the OFT booklet *Is notification necessary?* OFT 434, August 2000.

If, however, at any time the Director moves to impose penalties in relation to relatively minor unnotified infringements, a rapid change to precautionary notifications would occur.

9.1.4   Enforcement

The Director is given extensive powers of investigation, including the right to call for documents and to make "dawn raids". These are intended to ensure more effective action against agreements, particularly secret "market rigging" cartels.

9.1.5   Appeals

The consequence of the introduction of heavy financial penalties, as well as the ability to require termination of agreements, is the need for a full appellate process. This consists of a re-hearing by the Competition Commission and rights of appeal on law and level of penalty to the Court of Appeal (or equivalent courts in Scotland and Northern Ireland) and the House of Lords.

9.2   Notification Generally

9.2.1   Request for the Director to Examine Agreements

A party to an agreement may apply to the Director if he thinks that the agreement may infringe the Chapter I Prohibition on anti-competitive agreements. He may make:

(a)   an application for guidance (s. 13); or

(b)   an application for a decision (s. 14).

In the case of either application, no penalty may be imposed from the time notification is made unless the application results in an unfavourable guidance or decision, or the application is rejected. The benefit of this immunity can be removed in certain circumstances (see ss. 15(4) and 16(4)), and this with retrospective effect where the Director has a reasonable suspicion that he has acted on incomplete, false or misleading information (see ss. 15(5) and 16(5)). The OFT booklet *Is notification necessary?* OFT 434, August 2000, contains the OFT's guidance on when to notify displaying a helpful decision tree at p. 13 (reproduced below). The OFT will give informal guidance on whether a notification is necessary.

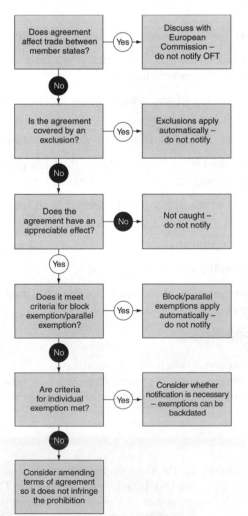

9.2.2   Procedure

Schedule 5 provides for the procedure to be followed by a person applying under Chapter I either for guidance or for a decision. This Schedule also sets out the procedure to be followed by the Director in considering the notifications. The procedure set out in the Schedule is not detailed and in the most part refers to further procedural rules made under section 51, which have taken shape as the Director's Rules.

9.2.3   Director's Rules

Authority is given to the Director under section 51 to propose, *inter alia,* such procedural rules as he considers necessary. Any rule made under this section must be approved by the Secretary of State before it comes into operation. The procedure for amending and revoking rules is set out at section 51. The basis on which the Director can regulate under section 51 is set out in Sched. 9, although it is clear, both from section 51(2) and the Director's Rules, that the Director is not limited to preparing rules based on the specific powers set out in Sched. 9. The Director's Rules provide for:

(a)   the form and manner in which an application for guidance or an application for a decision must be made;

(b)   the procedure to be followed in dealing with the application;

(c)   the documents and information which must be given to the Director in connection with the application;

(d)   the requirements for giving notice of the application to such other persons as may be specified;

(e)   the consequences of failing to notify other specified persons;

(f)   publicity in relation to applications for a decision and for such decisions, including the keeping of a public register;

(g)   the procedures which apply if the Director is to take further action after giving guidance or issuing a decision;

(h)   the disclosure of information provided by a third party;

(i)   procedure for withdrawal of exclusions;

(j)   procedures for variation of the length of the transitional period for agreements in existence prior to March 1, 2000;

(k)   third party appeals.

The procedure to be followed when the application is subject to the concurrent jurisdiction of the Director and a sector Regulator is covered in a separate order, The Competition Act 1998 (Concurrency) Regulations 2000 (S.I. 2000 No. 260).

9.2.4   Timetable

Schedule 9, para. 2(c) allows for the rules to be extended to lay down a timetable for dealing with applications, but this is not dealt with in the Director's Rules. As intended (despite extensive expressions of concern by industry who are adversely affected by uncertainty and delay) the timetable for dealing with applications will be drawn up only once the regime has been "bedded down" (*Hansard* (Standing Committee G) col. 381 (June 11, 1998)). Lord Haskell had previously said in the House of Lords: "until the system has bedded down and we have an idea of the volume of applications that may be made, we believe that it would not be right to tie the Director down to a fixed timetable" (*Hansard*, H.L., Vol. 583, No. 63, cols 349 and 350 (November 13, 1997)). So far the Director has not made known any internal administration timetables, although it was his intention that these should be in place from the outset (Speech given by Margaret Bloom, Director of Competition Policy, OFT on September 10, 1998, entitled *The OFT's Role in the New Regime*). Given the lack of early applications this is not troublesome, but would become so if not rectified when the numbers of applications build up. It is to be hoped that the United Kingdom regulators carry out their intention to avoid the unacceptable delays that characterised for many years the notification process under Article 81 and has, for some businesses, compromised the delivery of reasonable legal certainty. The E.C. Commission's habit of closing cases with a "comfort letter" often perpetuates legal uncertainty and may be a springboard for later litigation.

9.2.5 Making a Notification

Notification is to be made on Form N which forms Annex 1 of the Director's Rules and is also available separately from the Director and the sector Regulators. The procedure for determining an application will be mainly written and the Director does not consider it necessary to prescribe formal procedures in respect of oral representations (OFT Memorandum: *Competition Act 1998* para. 12; *proposed procedural rules under s. 51*). If the agreement or conduct is being or has been notified to the E.C. Commission under Article 82 a copy of the completed Form A/B and supporting documents is also required, together with any decision or comfort letter that may relate to the agreement or conduct. Any dispensation to comply with all of the information requirements in Form N should be discussed in advance with the OFT (the Major Provisions Guideline, para. 7.12 and Director's Rules, r. 4(3)).

The notifying party should send the OFT the original Form N together with two copies of it. Supporting documents such as relevant agreements and annexes, must be either originals or certified true copies (r. 3(3)) and must also be submitted with two extra copies. Where the market is subject to the concurrent jurisdiction of a sector Regulator, one further copy of the Form N for each of those Regulator(s) must be sent to the OFT together with the Form's annexes and copies of the relevant agreements (Director's Rules, r. 3(2)). The appropriate fee (see 9.2.8 below) must be paid at the time the Form N is submitted. Generally, an application will have effect on the date it is received by the Director, although applications received after 6pm on a working day shall be treated as having been received on the next working day (Director's Rules, r. 5(1) and r. 26(7)).

The party making an application must take all reasonable steps to notify all other parties to the agreement of whom he is aware that the application has been made and whether it is an application for guidance or for a decision (Sched. 5, para. 2 (2)). The Notice must be in writing and given within seven working days of receipt of acknowledgement if the application from the Director (Director's Rules, r. 7).

9.2.6 Effect of Making an Incomplete Notification

Where the Director finds that the Form N is incomplete he shall "without delay and in any event within one month from date on which that information was received and any fee payable in respect of the application has been paid. . ." give the applicant notice in writing of the information that is outstanding. The Director will also set a time limit for the provision of the outstanding information in writing. The application shall have effect on the date that the Director receives complete information and any fee payable in respect of the application (Director's Rules, r. 5(5)). If the Director has given notice that the information submitted as Form N is incomplete and has not received the outstanding information, the information submitted will be returned to the applicant and he will be informed that his application has not been made in accordance with rule 5. If, following notification, material changes in the facts communicated in the notification occur, the Director or the Regulator exercising prescribed functions must be informed without delay (Director's Rules, r. 4(4)) failing which the benefit of favourable guidance or a favourable decision may be removed (see 9.3.4 and 9.4.10 below).

9.2.7   Confidentiality

Where the applicant considers that any information in the application is confidential, he shall set out such information in a separate annex to the application headed "confidential information" and shall explain why it should be treated as such (Director's Rules, r. 4(2)). Information will be confidential where it is:

(a)   commercial information the disclosure of which would, or might, significantly harm the legitimate business interests of the undertaking to which it relates; or

(b)   information relating to the private affairs of an individual the disclosure of which would, or might, significantly harm his interests (Director's Rules, r. 30(1)(c)).

For further discussion of confidentiality in the context of proceedings regarding the prohibitions see 9.4.4 below.

9.2.8   Fees

The fees for applications are £5,000 for examining an agreement or considering conduct with view to giving guidance and £13,000 for examining an agreement or considering conduct with view to obtaining a decision (Director's Rules, r. 6(2) and Annex 2).

9.2.9   Advice and Information

The Director is under an obligation to explain how the Chapter I and Chapter II Prohibitions will operate through the publication of general advice and information about the application and enforcement of these prohibitions. Section 52(1) provides that:

As soon as is reasonably practicable after the passing of this Act, the Director must prepare and publish general advice and information about . . . . the application of the Chapter I Prohibition and the Chapter II Prohibition, and . . . . [their] enforcement.

The Director has issued a number of guidelines and will continue this process: see [p. l] for a list of current and draft guidelines at the date of going to press.

9.3   Guidance and its Effect

9.3.1   Application for Guidance

Under section 13(1) a party may notify the Director of an agreement and apply to him for guidance. Section 21(1) makes similar provision on notification of conduct for guidance in respect of the Chapter II Prohibition. Guidance is generally a confidential process and the outcome is known only to the parties to the agreement or conduct. The procedure is described in 9.2 above. The Director may (but is not obliged to) give the applicant guidance as to whether or not, in his view, the agreement is likely to infringe the prohibition.

In the event that a case is transferred to a sector Regulator after notification he will carry out all the functions of the Director described below.

If the Director (or sector Regulator to whom the case has been transferred) decides that the agreement is likely to infringe the prohibition, his guidance may indicate:

(a)   whether the agreement is likely to be exempt from the prohibition under —

  (i)   a block exemption;
  (ii)   a parallel exemption;
  (iii) a Section 11 exemption.

(b)   whether he would be likely to grant the agreement an individual exemption if asked to do so. (s. 13(3)).

Guidance will be given in writing, stating the facts on which the Director bases the guidance and his reasons for it (Director's Rules, r. 10(1)).

9.3.2   Effect of Guidance

If the Director determines the application under section 13 by giving favourable guidance (either that the Chapter I Prohibition does not apply or that an exemption is likely to apply or be given) :

(a)   he is to take no further action in respect of the agreement, subject to section 15(2)(a) to (d);

(b)   no penalty may be imposed in respect of the agreement (section 15(3)) subject to section 15(4).

There is therefore an immunity from penalties for those who have sought guidance, but in certain circumstances this immunity may be lost (see 9.3.4 below).

9.3.3   Refusal to Give Guidance

The Competition Act does not place the Director under an obligation to give guidance (ss. 13 and 21(2)). If the Director declines to give guidance, he must give written notice of that fact and return the fee in full (Director's Rules, r. 10 (2)). The Director may, perhaps, decline to give guidance when he believes notification of an agreement for an individual exemption decision is necessary, in which event the application would probably be resubmitted with a higher fee. As guidance is a confidential process, there may be occasions where the Director is reluctant to issue guidance without some consultation of interested parties. Again, in such cases, the Director is likely to steer the parties towards resubmission for a decision.

9.3.4   Further action

Under section 15(2), however, the Director may take further action in relation to an agreement on which he has given favourable guidance in the following circumstances:

(a)   He has reasonable grounds for believing that there has been a material change of circumstances since he gave his guidance;

(b)   He has a reasonable suspicion that the information on which he based his guidance was incomplete, false or misleading in a material particular;

(c)   If one of the parties to the agreement applies to him for a decision under s. 14 with respect to the agreement. (This may occur where the party needs to uphold the agreement in a civil dispute, either with another party to the agreement or a third party); or

(d)   A complaint about the agreement has been made to him by a person who is not a party to the agreement.

Section 23(2) makes similar provisions where guidance has been given that the Chapter II Prohibition does not apply, but does not allow the party concerned to re-open matters by applying for a decision (see Chapter 13, para. 13.3.2).

Rule 11 of the Director's Rules requires the Director to consult the person to whom the guidance was given if he proposes to take further action following guidance.

9.3.5   Imposition of a Penalty After Taking Further Action

Where the Director has issued favourable guidance, he cannot impose a penalty in respect of any infringement of the prohibition by that conduct (s. 15(3)). Under section 15(4) the benefit of immunity can be removed and the Director may impose a penalty if:

(1)   any of the circumstances in respect of which the Director may reconsider previous guidance occur (see para. 9.3.4 above);

(2)   the Director considers that it is likely that the agreement in question will infringe the Chapter I Prohibition; and

(3)   the Director gives notice in writing to the undertaking which originally applied for guidance that he is removing the immunity from penalty as from the date specified in the notice (s. 15(4)).

Similar provisions regarding Guidance on conduct in relation to the Chapter II Prohibition are contained in section 23(3) and (4) (see Chapter 13, para. 13.3.5).

The date from which the immunity is considered to be lost may be earlier than the date on which the notice is given if the Director has reasonable suspicion that information provided to him by a party to the agreement, on which he has based his guidance, was incomplete, false or misleading in a material particular (s. 15(5) and s. 23(5)). The parliamentary debate relating to the uncertainty caused by this power is discussed at 9.4.11 below.

Guidance is given in confidence to the notifying party and third parties are not consulted. As a result, guidance is necessarily less certain in its nature than a decision and is not legally binding, although where the Director has given favourable guidance he will only be able to re-open a case in the limited circumstances referred to above. After the Director has determined an application for guidance he must write to the applicant with his guidance, setting out the facts on which he bases the guidance and the reasons for it (Director's Rules, r. 10 (1)).

9.4 The Taking of a Decision and its Effects

9.4.1 Notification

Under section 14 (1), a party to an agreement may notify the Director of an agreement and apply to him for a decision. The outline procedure when applying for a decision mirrors that for notifications for guidance but involves publicity and additional steps. The common elements are described in 9.2 above. The Director may make a decision as to whether the prohibition has been infringed and, if it has not been infringed, whether that is because of the effect of an exclusion or because the agreement is exempt from the prohibition (s. 14(2)). A notification to the Director under section 14 may include a request for the agreement to be given an individual exemption if it does not otherwise fall outside the prohibition (s. 14 (3)).

Once a notification is made it may be dealt with by the Director or assigned to a sector Regulator, who thereafter has almost all the powers of the Director described below, but only the Director maintains the public register referred to in 9.4.2 below.

9.4.2 Publicity

The Director must arrange for an application for a decision to be published in the way he thinks most suitable for bringing it to the attention of those likely to be affected by it, unless he is satisfied that it would be sufficient for him to seek information from one or more particular persons other than the applicant (Sched. 5, para. 5(2)). The Director's Rules, r. 8 provides for details of applications for decisions (but not for guidance) to be entered on a public register maintained at the OFT and on the OFT's website. Notice of the outcome of the application, including any decision will be published in the same way. No formal procedure has been set out for the publishing of transfer from the OFT to a sector Regulator of a case after notification. The Director publishes a weekly gazette containing an update of new entries on the register and also often matters of interest to parties and practitioners. Cases of interest publicised in these ways are also likely to be mentioned in the press. Interested third parties may then express their views to the Director or, where a case is transferred to a sector Regulator, that Regulator.

The Director's Rules lay down a further express requirement for public consultation where the Director proposes to grant an exemption, whether or not subject to conditions or obligations (r. 12(1)(a)).

The Director may, but is not obliged to, consult the public when he proposes to take a decision that the Chapter I Prohibition is not infringed (r. 12(1)(b)). The same applies in relation to the decision that the Chapter II Prohibition has not been infringed (r. 12(2)) (see Chapter 13, para. 13.4.3).

Final decisions are published (Director's Rules, r. 15(1)(b)), as are directions under section 32, 33 or 35 (r. 17(3)). The Director must specifically consult any affected third party (ies). He may use the register to publicise his proposals and the Director's Rules (r. 30(4), r. 30(3)) require him to publish a notice stating his intended action and the reasons for it.

9.4.3   Communication with Parties and Interested Third Parties

Rule 14(1) of the Director's Rules requires the Director to give written notice stating the facts on which he relies, the matters to which he takes objection, his proposed action and the reasons for it in any case where he proposes to take a decision that the Chapter I Prohibition or the Chapter II Prohibition has been infringed or to grant an exemption from the Chapter I Prohibition subject to conditions or obligations. This notice must be given to:

— the applicant and, subject to rules 25 and 26, the persons whom the applicant has identified in the application as being the other parties to the agreement and any other person that the Director considers is a party to the agreement, or engaged in the conduct, (where application has been made);

— any person that the Director considers is a party to the agreement in question, or engaged in the conduct (where no application has been made).

Rule 25 lays down special rules for giving notice to associations of undertakings. Individual members are not entitled to notice unless they are individually an applicant for the decision.

Rule 26 deals with circumstances where it is not reasonably practicable for the Director to give written notice to all the persons mentioned in rule 14(1). In those circumstances he may publish the notice in his register, the London, Edinburgh and Belfast Gazettes, at least one national newspaper and one suitable trade journal (if any).

The notice must set out the matters to which the Director objects, the action he proposes and his reasons for it. The addressees of the notice may make written representations within a specified period (r. 14(7)) and must be given a reasonable opportunity to make oral representations (r. 14(8)). Each party, or his authorised representative, may inspect the documents on the Director's file relating to the proposed decision (subject to the Director's right to withhold any confidential or internal document under r. 14(6)).

The applicant and other parties he has identified must also be consulted in the case where the Director proposes to make a provisional decision (Director's Rules, r. 9, discussed at 9.4.7 below). The applicant and other persons he has identified will receive written notice, together with a statement of facts and the Director's reasons, and a statement of the period allowed for representations (r. 30(2) deals with consultation of particular persons). In cases where the Director proposes interim measures (see 9.5.3 below), he must allow the persons to whom he will give a direction under section 35 access to the file (r. 18(1)). The Act itself at section 35(3) provides that he must give written notice of the proposed interim measures direction, with reasons, to the proposed recipients and give them an opportunity to make representations. The Director has a heavy burden to be seen to act responsibly in cases where he is effectively prejudging his own decision and may cause substantial costs to those affected.

All decisions and directions must be notified to those affected with a statement of facts and reasons (Director's Rules, r. 15(1)(a), r. 17(1) and r. 17(2)). There are a number of other instances where the Director must consult parties (r. 16, further action after a decision; r. 20, cancellation of an individual exemption; r. 21, cancellation of a parallel exemption; r. 22 withdrawal of exclusions; r. 23, termination of a transitional period). Applications for extension of an individual exemption (r. 19) or of a transitional period (r. 24) follow procedures based on those for an initial application.

9.4.4   Confidentiality

Section 55 provides for the maintenance of confidentiality. Any information, relating to the affairs of an individual or business of an undertaking, which is received under the Act may not be disclosed without consent from specified parties. There are however several exceptions to this rule, set out at section 55(3). These include disclosure for the purpose of facilitating the performance by the Director or any of the sector Regulators of any of their functions under the Act, or the E.C. Commission's performance of any of its functions of E.C. competition law, disclosures to various United Kingdom Regulators for their regulatory purposes and disclosures in relation to criminal and civil proceedings in the United Kingdom In taking a decision whether to disclose confidential information, the Director (or other relevant authority or the Secretary of State) must have regard to the factors set out in section 56, which, in addition to business confidentiality, include the public interest and the extent to which such disclosure is necessary for the purpose for which it is proposed to be made.

The Director's Rules follow precisely the language of section 56 (3)(a) in defining what will be regarded as confidential, that is:

(i)   commercial information, the disclosure of which would, or might, significantly harm the legitimate business interests of the undertaking to which it relates;

(ii)   information relating to the private affairs of an individual, the disclosure of which would, or might, significantly harm his interests (Director's Rules s. 56(3)(a) and r. 30(1)(c)).

This differs from the language in sections 82(1) and 83(3A) Fair Trading Act ("FTA") providing for the exclusion of confidential information from reports of the Competition Commission in two material respects. First, the Competition Act test is objective (although this is qualified by various formulations (*e.g.* in r. 4(2) and r. 14(6)(a) and (b) which allow a measure of subjectivity in the designation of documents by the party concerned or the Director). Secondly, the FTA uses the formulation "seriously and prejudicially affect" rather than "significantly harm". The test of significant harm may be slightly lower, but the draftsman probably intended only to modernise.

There are a number of occasions in the course of proceedings relating to the prohibitions where this concept is relevant:

(1)   First, when applying for a decision, if the applicant considers that any information in the application is confidential, he shall set out such information

in a separate annex to the application headed "confidential information" and shall explain why it should be treated as such (Director's Rules, r. 4(2)). The same direction also applies to applications for guidance. Although these are normally confidential, it may be useful to separate such material, in case the application has to be converted into an application for a decision or the Director does wish to carry out some consultation before giving guidance. The rule is applied by reference to applications to extend an exemption (r. 19(4)) or a transitional period (r. 24(7));

(2)   Where the Director issues a written notice of his intention to take an adverse decision or to give an exemption subject to conditions or obligations he must allow all those who receive the notice a period within which to identify confidential matters (Director's Rules, r. 14(4)). This will help him when writing his formal decision which may be published and may also protect documents from disclosure to third parties (*e.g.* a complainant who is also a competitor);

(3)   When there are rights to inspect the file, the Director may withhold confidential documents (r. 14(6) and r. 18(2)). It is clear in E.C. procedure that documents which are excluded cannot found the basis of an adverse decision by the E.C. Commission, but it is not clear that the Director and sector Regulators are so bound. However, the effect of the European Convention on Human Rights would appear to require that the Director or relevant Regulator does disclose everything on which he wishes to rely. This has been recognised in talks given by OFT officials;

(4)   The Director will also withhold "internal documents" in the sense of rule 30(1)(f) in the circumstances mentioned in (5) above. These are documents produced within the OFT or the office of a sector Regulator, correspondence between them and correspondence between any of them and a government department or another competition authority, such as the E.C. Commission. There will be times when the Director will wish to disclose such material and he should do so if it contains statements from the E.C. Commission on his obligations under E.C. law, or where a government department is a customer or supplier of the party under investigation and provides evidence in the proceedings;

(5)   The Director's Rules, r. 27, gives protection for confidential information of complainants and other third parties from whom he obtains information. They are asked to place such material in a separate confidential annex when it is first provided and are entitled to written notice and a reasonable opportunity to make representations in any case where the Director proposes to disclose such material, where it is reasonably practicable for the Director to do this. This is the material that is likely to prove most difficult to deal with. On the one hand, the Director may need to use (and disclose) it to prove breach of the prohibition and, on the other hand, disclosure may identify the source, who may fear adverse consequences for his business. In these circumstances, the right to disclose in order to carry out the Director's functions would seem to prevail. It appears that the Director may go to some lengths to ensure that they key documents are produced under compulsion (*e.g.* in answer to a request under s. 25, which may be addressed to a class of people, including the source of the document).

9.4.5 Delay by the Director

It is intended that in due course any person aggrieved by the failure of the Director to determine an application for a decision in accordance with the specified procedure, may apply to the court. In England and Wales, the relevant court is the High Court, in Scotland it is the Court of Session and in Northern Ireland it is the High Court (s. 59).

Once section 59 is brought into force, if the court is satisfied that there has been undue delay on the part of the Director in determining the application, the court may give such directions to the Director as it considers appropriate for securing that the application is determined without unnecessary further delay (Sched. 5, para. 7).

The Opposition were keen to introduce a time limit within which the Director had to make his decision or give guidance on the basis that Sched. 5, para. 7 was insufficient comfort. The Government resisted the amendment, arguing that the Director's rules would include a timetable and that under Sched. 5, para. 7 parties would have the right to seek redress for undue delays as a "backstop" (*Hansard*, (Standing Committee G) col. 381 (June 11, 1998)). However, the timetable (at least in binding terms) has not been introduced and this "backstop" provision will not be brought into force until the notification procedure has "bedded down" (*Hansard*, H.L., Vol. 583, No. 63, col. 349 (November 13, 1997) and *Hansard* (Standing Committee G) col. 381 (June 11, 1998)). The Director intended to publish informal internal guidelines but has also not done so. Clearly the comfort of the "backstop" will depend on the meaning of the term "undue delay" which in the absence of a timetable, will be difficult to ascertain.

9.4.6 Decisions

Schedule 5 does not require the Director to actually determine applications for decisions — the provisions specify the procedure to be followed when the Director does determine applications, but also imply that the Director will not always come to a decision through the use of the term "if" in para. 6 of Sched. 5:

> "If the Director determines an application for a decision he must publish his decision, together with his reasons for making it, in such manner as may be specified."

The effect of this is twofold:

(1) the Act allows the Director to deal with applications through the use of an administrative letter, rather than through a decision; and

(2) there is a need for a procedure if the Director does not issue a decision.

The OFT has, however, confirmed, that despite this wording, it is not the Director's intention to make use of administrative letters, so most notifications will result in guidance or a decision. This is reinforced in that the Director's Rules, r. 15(2) provides that, if the Director exercises his discretion not to take a decision, he must notify the applicant and other parties to the agreement and repay the whole of the fee. This is a clear disincentive to the Director closing his file without taking a decision and is likely to be used only in cases where the application is wholly misconceived. It would not be a proper basis for removing immunity from penalties, for which a provisional decision taken after receiving representations would be the correct course (see 9.4.7 below).

When a decision is made this is required to be notified in writing without delay together with the facts on which the decision is based and the reasons for the same. This notice is given to the applicant and other persons who are party to the agreement or conduct, or, when no application has been made, to each person who the Director is aware is a party to the agreement or conduct (r. 15(1)(a)). The decision must also be published (Director's Rules, r. 15(1)(b)).

9.4.7   Provisional decisions

Schedule 5, para. 3 provides that, if after preliminary investigation of an application either for guidance or for a decision, the Director considers that it is likely that the agreement concerned will infringe the relevant prohibition (and it would not be appropriate to grant the agreement an individual exemption) he may make a provisional decision.

The procedure for making provisional decisions is set out in rule 9 of the Director's Rules. This requires the Director to consult the applicant where a provisional decision is proposed. The obligation to consult for the purposes of this Rule entails giving notice of the proposed action, the reasons for it and informing the applicant of his right to make written representations (r. 30(2)). The procedure for adopting provisional decisions should not be confused with that where an infringement decision is proposed, where it will be possible to meet with officials and elaborate points orally before the final decision is taken.

Provisional decisions can be expected to be taken only in clear and serious cases. The intention of the retrospective removal of immunity is to deter notifications simply designed to buy time for an arrangement which could never be approved.

The right for the party or parties to respond is essential with respect to Chapter I notifications given that, following a provisional decision, the period of immunity provided for in section 13(4), or section 14(4) as appropriate, is taken as having never applied. In other words if infringement is found in the final decision penalties can be assessed on the basis of performance right back to the date of the agreement.

The Opposition attempted to introduce a right to an oral hearing into the Act at Committee stage, but the amendment fell. The Government argued that the Director's Rules were the appropriate place for such a right to be considered. (*Hansard* (Standing Committee G) col. 381. (June 11, 1998)).

A provisional decision regarding either an application for guidance or an application for a decision does not, however, affect the final determination of the application (Sched. 5, para. 3(4)).

If the application is for a decision, a provisional decision does not disrupt the procedure under section 14 (see above). This may be regarded as sufficient to safeguard the rights of the defence, but it is to be noted that in rare cases where the E.C. Commission has used equivalent powers under Article 15 (6) of Council Regulation (EEC) 17/62, it has offered the parties an oral hearing (Article 7 of Council Regulation 17/62), not least, because in practice it is likely to result in the agreement or practice being brought to an end immediately, and, for practical purposes, the rights of the parties concerned are significantly affected. It may be better therefore for the Director to expedite the process for a final decision or take interim measures (see 9.5.3) to minimise delay, rather than rely on this process which, in itself, is likely to give rise to challenge.

9.4.8 Effects of a Decision that the Prohibition Is Infringed

An exemption decision is equated under the Act to a decision that the prohibition is not infringed. A decision finding an infringement which does not benefit from an exemption will remove immunity from financial penalties going forward and accompanying directions are likely to result in the agreement or practice being brought to an end or modified, unless an appeal tribunal of the Competition Commission suspends the direction (see 9.5 below). Where an agreement or practice has not been notified, or immunity has been withdrawn by provisional decision and the agreement or conduct has continued, heavy financial penalties may be imposed (see Chapter 10 at 10.3).

A third party may ask the Director to review a favourable decision (see 9.7), which may lead to an appeal process.

9.4.9 Effect of a Decision that the Prohibition Is Not Infringed

There are three consequences of the Director deciding under section 14 that an agreement or conduct does not infringe the relevant prohibition (whether because of its inherent properties or because it benefits from an exemption or exclusion):

(1)   the Director is to take no further action in respect of the agreement (s. 16(2) and s. 24(2)), except in limited circumstances;

(2)   no penalty may be imposed in respect of any infringement (s. 16(3) and s. 24(3));

(3)   any agreement covered by a favourable Chapter I decision is not void (under s. 2(4)) and can be enforced.

Just as with applications for guidance, there is an immunity from penalty which benefits the parties, although, as with the procedure relating to guidance, the benefit of immunity can be lost if further action is taken (see 9.4.11 below). In the case of an exemption decision, this will last for the period specified in the decision (s. 4(4) and (5)) but may be cancelled or varied in circumstances specified in section 5, including automatic cancellation on breach of a condition and optional cancellation on breach of an obligation).

9.4.10 Further Action

The Director can take further action only if:

"(a)   he has reasonable grounds for believing that there has been a material change of circumstance since he gave his decision; or

(b)   he has reasonable suspicion that the information on which he based his decision was incomplete, false or misleading in a material particular." (s. 16(2) and s. 24(2)).

These circumstances are more limited than in the case of guidance, reflecting the fact that a decision is taken only after public consultation, is itself published and is intended to produce legal certainty. The Director should, therefore, be reluctant to reopen the process, unless there are very serious grounds for doing so.

The Act does not spell out the interaction between sections 16 and 24 and any action which the Director might wish to take as a result of a request by a third party under section 47 that he review his decision. As the procedure under section 47 is described as an appeal, and must be carried out within a short time of the Director's decision, section 47 appears to be the over-riding provision. If that is the correct analysis, the Director can withdraw or vary a decision pursuant to section 47 without regard to the limitations set out in sections 16 and 24 and the grounds on which the Director may act under section 47 are restricted only by the terms of section 47 itself (see further 9.8 below). The limitations in sections 16 and 24 would apply thereafter to any varied decision of the Director resulting from an appeal under section 47. The situation would be the same if an appeal tribunal of the Competition Commission varied a decision of the Director.

9.4.11   Imposition of a Penalty After Taking Further Action

The Director may also remove the immunity from penalty given by section 16(3) and section 24(3) if:

(a)   he takes action in one of the circumstances set out above at 9.4.10;

(b)   he considers it likely that the agreement or conduct will infringe the relevant prohibition; and

(c)   he gives notice in writing to the party on whose application the decision was made, that he is removing the immunity as from the date specified in his notice.

The date on which cancellation of the immunity takes effect may be backdated if the reason for cancellation is that the information on which the Director based his decision, and which was provided to him by a party to the agreement, was incomplete, false or misleading in any material particular (s. 16(5)) or where there has been a failure to comply with an obligation, subject to which an exemption was granted.

An amendment to the Bill, to the effect that no penalties would become payable retrospectively, was proposed on the basis that retrospective liability did not aid certainty. The purpose of the penalty, namely to deter the provision of false, incomplete or misleading information, was considered more important and the text left unchanged. (*Hansard* (Standing Committee G) col. 326 (June 11, 1998)).

9.5   Enforcement and Interim Measures

9.5.1   Infringement of Chapter I or Chapter II Prohibition

Where a decision has been reached that there is an infringement of either the Chapter I or Chapter II Prohibition, the Director may give directions to such parties as he considers appropriate, requiring them to modify or terminate the agreement or conduct in question (ss. 32 and 33). The directions may, for example, be addressed to a parent company where the subsidiary is the party to the agreement but not the instigator of the infringement (para. 2.2, OFT Guideline, *Enforcement*, OFT 407, March 1999) (the "Enforcement Guideline"). The Director is required to give the parties his directions in writing (ss. 32(4) and 33(4)). The Director's Rules provide that the Director is also required to state the facts on which he bases the direction and his reasons for giving it (Director's Rules, r. 17(1)).

The directions will be published on the register that will be kept at the OFT and on the OFT's website.

Failure to comply with the directions without reasonable excuse authorises the Director to apply to the court for an order requiring the defaulter to make good the default or requiring the undertaking or its officers to carry out a direction relating to the management or administration of the undertaking as appropriate (s. 34(1)). Breach of a court order would be considered a contempt of court with the resulting sanction being a fine or imprisonment (Enforcement Guideline, para. 2.9 and the Major Provisions Guideline, para. 11.12).

9.5.2 Penalties

The Director has power to levy a penalty of up to 10 per cent of United Kingdom turnover of an undertaking which is party to the agreement or conduct which has been the subject of an infringement decision in the circumstances set out in section 36 (discussed in Chapter 10 at 10.3). The Director's Rules, r. 17(2) requires the Director to give written notice of the facts on which the penalty is based and the reasons for the penalty.

9.5.3 Interim Measures

Where the Director has not completed his investigation, he may impose interim directions under section 35 if (i) he has reasonable suspicion that there is an infringement of the Chapter I or Chapter II Prohibition and (ii) he considers it necessary to prevent serious irreparable damage to a particular person or category of persons or to protect the public interest by urgent action (s. 35(2)). Interim directions may be given by the Director of his own motion or following a request from a complainant seeking this relief, provided the two conditions mentioned above are satisfied (Enforcement Guideline, para. 3.7). The E.C. Commission has the power to impose interim measures (*Camera Care v. Commission* (Case C–792/79R) [1980] E.C.R. 119, [1980] 1 C.M.L.R. 334) which is not invoked very often due to the requirement that a prima facie case of an Article 81 or 82 infringement be established. Presumably the Director will find it easier to establish his suspicions for the purposes of exercising this power.

Generally, one would expect directions, so far as practicable, to be conservatory and to try to avoid practical prejudgement except in the clearest cases. Restrictive Trade Practices Acts 1976 and 1977 ("RTPA") precedent (against a much higher standard of proof) suggests that the Director is not obliged to give a cross undertaking in damages (*Institute of Independent Insurance Brokers* (1991) I.C.R. 822 at p. 830). The E.C. Commission has in some cases suggested that complainants should be prepared to give a cross-undertaking if they want interim measures which would clearly occasion the affected party financial loss and the complainant financial benefit, and it is not unreasonable to expect such a cross-undertaking. In such cases, however, the English courts would only grant an interim injunction in a private suit if on balance it was the more convenient course and there was a cross-undertaking in damages from a source able to meet any liability.

The term "reasonable suspicion" derives from the criminal law and indicates a fairly low standard of proof (*e.g.* in the law related to arrest (see *Archbold 2000*, Sweet & Maxwell, at 15.23 and *Blackstone's Criminal Practice 2000* at 1.8)). The concept of a cross-undertaking has no place in criminal law. It is to be hoped that it is not necessary to ascertain the position of a party affected by unlawful use of these powers, *e.g.* if interim measures were maintained in place after any suspicions were dispelled or if there was use of the powers without a proper basis for doing so, whether maliciously or otherwise, but civil liability might exist to compensate the affected party.

Before giving a direction, the Director must give written notice to the party or parties to whom he proposes to give the direction and give them an opportunity to make representations (s. 35(3)). The Director's notice must state the nature of the proposed direction as well as provide the reasoning behind it (s. 35(4)). Access to the file must be given (Director's Rules at r. 18, discussed at 9.4 above).

The Director has stated that he will allow the addressee of the notice the opportunity to make representations, in writing and orally at a meeting if requested (Enforcement Guideline, para. 3.10). There is no entrenched right to make oral representations such as is given by rule 14(8) of the *Director's Rules* to the recipient of a statement of objections prior to the final decision.

Any interim measures direction will be published on the register kept at the OFT and on the OFT's website and possibly in trade journals (Enforcement Guideline, para. 3.12).

As with directions given pursuant to sections 32 and 33, failure to comply without reasonable excuse may result in the Director seeking an order from the court to ensure compliance, breach of which would be punishable as a contempt of court.

Once the Director has reached a decision, he may replace any interim measures imposed by directions under sections 32 or 33, as appropriate (s. 35 (5)).

Interim measures directions may be appealed to the Competition Commission and the courts which may, as cases come before them, suggest refinements to the process to protect the rights of recipients of interim measures directions.

9.6   Other Procedures Related to Notification or Infringement Decision

9.6.1   Overview

The Director may take a number of decisions which are closely related to infringement or exemption decisions. The procedures are related to the principal procedures. They are:

- cancellation or variation of an individual exemption (s. 5(1) and r. 20);

- imposition of conditions or variations related to a parallel exemption, or their variation or cancellation of exemption (s. 10(5) and r. 21);

- withdrawal of exclusions (Sched. 1, para. 4, Sched. 3, paras 2 or 9 and r. 22);

- termination of transitional period (Sched. 13, para. 37 and r. 23);

- application for exclusion of transitional period (Sched. 13, para. 36 and r. 24);

- notification of excluded agreements (ss. 13 and 14 and the Competition Act 1998 (Notification of Excluded Agreements and Appealable Decisions) Regulations 2000 (S.I. 2000 No. 263) rules made under s. 12(3) and Sched. 13, para. 19(3) and Director's Rules, r. 29).

The Director's Rules apply with appropriate modifications, some of which are referred to in 9.4.3 and 9.4.4 above.

9.7 Complaints

9.7.1 Provision for Complaints

A party who believes that breach of the Chapter I or Chapter II Prohibition has occurred may complain to the Director.

One of the situations in which the Director may take further action following the giving of guidance is when a complaint about the agreement or conduct has been made by a person who is not party to the same (ss. 5(2)(d) and 23(2)(c)). No opportunity to take further action on this basis arises with respect to decisions because third parties are firstly, afforded an opportunity to comment on the agreement or conduct when the Director publishes details of the arrangement and again when he publishes his intention to take a favourable decision (see 9.4.2 and 9.4.3 above), and, secondly, have rights to seek review of a decision. Due to the confidential nature of guidance, the rights of potentially injured third parties are therefore addressed by the complaint procedure.

9.7.2 The Complaint

The Major Provisions Guideline confirms that there is no form to complete in order to make a complaint (see para. 8.2). Complainants will normally need to identify themselves and the reason for their complaint, explaining whether they are a competitor, customer or a consumer. The complaint should be detailed, with supporting correspondence or documents and information about the market involved. The OFT or one of the sector Regulators will normally be willing to discuss the situation before the written complaint is made.

The Guideline states that, to help the speedy handling of complaints, it is sometimes necessary for letters from complainants to be disclosed to the target of the complaint. This is clearly a sensitive issue so any complainant wishing to retain the confidentiality of the material sent should place it in a confidential annex. This action does not guarantee confidentiality (see discussion, Director's Rules, r. 27 at 9.4.4 above). The OFT has also published a booklet *Making a Complaint – a guide to making a complaint under the Competition Act 1998* (OFT 426).

When the Director decides to pursue a complaint, it may be necessary to divulge the source of the complaint because it must be able to specify the facts relied upon when proceeding to a decision. Ultimately, if the complainant cannot accept any risk of disclosure, the OFT may be unable to proceed. Therefore, in cases where the complainant is concerned that his business or career may suffer if he is identified, this must be explained to the OFT at the outset, so that it can consider ways in which his confidentiality can be protected. The OFT has given considerable thought to this issue, but any complainant must recognise that there is a risk of his being identified, even if he does not wish this.

9.7.3 The Director's Decision

The Major Provisions Guideline states that, if the complaint does not appear to reveal a breach of the Chapter I or Chapter II Prohibition, the Director must say as much as soon as possible and the matter will be closed (para. 8.3).

Where the Director considers that breach may have occurred, he may seek further information from the complainant and then take up the matter with the person complained about. The Director may exercise his powers of investigation (see 9.12 below) and only, when satisfied that there is a breach, will he proceed to a decision and directions in the usual way. If the investigation concludes that there has been no breach, the parties are informed and the matter closes.

9.7.4   Position of Dissatisfied Complainants

In *Automec Srl v. Commission* (Case T-24/90) [1992] E.C.R. II-2223, [1992] 5 C.M.L.R. 431, the CFI held that, where complaints are submitted to the Commission under Article 3 of Regulation 17, the Commission is not bound to give a decision on the alleged infringement, unless the subject matter of the complaint falls within its exclusive purview, or to conduct an investigation. This is for the reason that the Commission has the discretion to apply different degrees of priority to the cases referred to it. As the Act makes no provision for the procedure for complaints, the question arises as to whether complainants will be able to require the Director to take a decision or investigation. It may well be the case that the only course of action open to the complainant where there is no formal decision is an application for judicial review.

Where a complaint leads to a formal decision that there is no breach of the Chapter I or Chapter II Prohibition or (following notification) an exemption decision in respect of the Chapter I Prohibition then the complainant (if he has, or represents persons with, sufficient interest) would have the right of a third party to seek withdrawal or variation of the decision (see discussion at 9.8 below). This application may in turn give a right of appeal to the Competition Commission s. 47(6)). The short one month time limit for making application under section 47 (Director's Rules, r. 28(1)(a)) and the right to reject for insufficient reasoning, if there is nothing new in the arguments, suggests that the Director sees this as a mechanism by which complainants may gain the right to appeal to the Competition Commission when dissatisfied with his decision. Where a third party wishes to have a decision reopened at a later date, he will need to persuade the Director that there are reasonable grounds for believing that there has been a material change of circumstance (see 9.4.10 above).

9.8   Applications by Third Parties to the Director

9.8.1   Basis of Right of Application

Third parties with a "sufficient interest" in a published decision of the Director and persons representing such third parties are given the right to ask the Director to withdraw or vary his decision under section 47(1). The "sufficient interest" qualification test for third party appeals may be wider than the equivalent test "direct and individual concern" laid down in Article 230 (ex 173) E.C. Treaty and means that consumers and consumer-protection organisations may be able to contest the Director's decisions.

9.8.2   Extent of Right of Application

An application by a third party under section 47 may relate only to certain categories of decision of the Director:

a)   as to whether the Chapter I Prohibition has been infringed;

b)   as to whether the Chapter II Prohibition has been infringed;

c)   as to whether to grant an individual exemption;

d)   as to conditions or obligations attached to an individual exemption (whether to impose them or their terms);

e)   as to duration of an individual exemption;

f)   as to the cancellation of an individual exemption (s. 47(1) referring to s. 46(3)(a) to (f)).

The "as to" formulation would seem to allow an application by a third party against either a decision that there was no breach of a prohibition or a decision that there was a breach, or as to the absence or presence of conditions or obligations as well as their terms. A complainant may seek review of a favourable decision and a supporter such as a trade association, might seek review of an unfavourable decision or a condition or obligation which caused concern to the industry as a whole.

9.8.3   Application Procedure

The third party must first make a written application to the Director. Rule 28(1)(a) of the Director's Rules states that the application must be made within one month of the publication of the decision. It must state the applicant's reasons for believing he (or the persons he represents) has "sufficient interest" rule 28(2) and give his reasons for considering that the relevant decision should be withdrawn or varied section 47(2). The Director must respond:

(a)   by dealing with the application in accordance with the procedure set out in the Director's Rules (s. 47(5)) and rules 25 and 27 discussed below; or

(b)   by notifying the applicant that he has rejected the application on one of the following grounds set out in subsection 47(3) and (4):

(i)   because the third party lacks "sufficient interest" in the decision;
(ii)   in the case of a representative body claiming to represent persons who have sufficient interest, because the body does not represent such third parties;
(iii) because the persons represented lack sufficient interest;
(iv)   because the application does not show sufficient reason why the decision should be withdrawn or varied.

The Director's Rules provide that where the Director proposes to grant the third party application, he must consult the person to whom notice of the decision was given (Director's Rules, r. 28(6)). This person has the right to make written representations (Director's Rules, r. 30(b)). If the Director proceeds to grant the third party application, he must publish his decision and notify the third party and the person to whom the decision was originally given (Director's Rules, r. 28(7)).

The inter-relation between section 47 and sections 16 and 24 is discussed at 9.4.10 above.

9.8.4   Appeal from the Director's decision

A third party has the right to appeal to an appeal tribunal of the Competition Commission against the Director's decision rejecting his application. It is not clear that a third party has rights if his application is duly considered but ultimately fails or only partially succeeds. This is a lacuna arising from the failure of the Act (s. 47(5) and Sched. 9, para. 13) to spell out whether the procedure should include a right of appeal on matters of substance for the third party.

Further rights of appeal from a decision of the Competition Commission to the courts are the same as for affected parties.

9.8.5   Use of the Third Party Application Process

It is possible that the procedure for third party appeal could provide a basis for mis-chief-making, particularly where the decision has been taken after full public con-sultation during which the relevant third parties have an opportunity to put their case. However, the short time limit for challenge makes it unlikely that the Direc-tor will alter his decision, once made, on grounds already submitted to him in the process leading to the decision. It also shows that the process is likely to be most frequently used as a step to bringing an appeal to the Competition Commission, in reality, against the substance of the Director's decision. Whether the appeal tri-bunals of the Competition Commission and the courts will be prepared to deal with such an appeal as one on the substance of the matter, or merely consider whether the Director was right to find nothing new in the application, remains to be seen. The process does not exactly match any E.C. procedure or language from E.C. precedent. Therefore, the CFI and ECJ approach to third party applications for review of an E.C. Commission decision is not obviously of any relevance.

Another circumstance where the process may be used is to bring in an interested supporter of the recipient of an adverse decision (*e.g.* a trade association or another member of the same industry with similar agreements to those condemned) who will probably go on to support a substantive appeal by the affected party. The appeal process would also allow fine tuning *e.g.* where a particular condition or obli-gation attached to a decision has effects not anticipated by the Director when he formulated it. In this last case, the Director will have a useful opportunity to deal with the practical consequences of his decision where it causes problems for third parties.

There is, in the case of every application under section 47, some ability for a third party to cause delay and uncertainty while the Director satisfies himself there is no new matter which would cause him to change his decision, even if only by adding an additional condition or obligation, and it is possible that there could be a pro-longed period of uncertainty.

9.9   Powers of Investigation by the OFT

9.9.1   Director's Powers to Investigate

The Director has varying powers of investigation under the Act, which are deter-mined according to whether the investigation relates to a potential Chapter I or Chapter II infringement or is a result of a request from the E.C. Commission to conduct an investigation. The limited investigatory powers of the Director under the RTPA have been replaced by extensive powers of investigation under sections 25–31 of the Act. In addition, the Act strengthens the Director's powers to investi-gate complex and scale monopolies under the FTA to ensure that the Director's powers are comparable under the two Acts.

These powers and procedures are the subject of the OFT Guideline: *The Powers of Investigation*, OFT 404, March 1999 (the "Powers of Investigation Guideline"). The Director has prepared for use of these powers by recruitment and training initiatives which bring to the OFT the experience of the investigation branch of HM Customs and Excise, which has long enjoyed formidable powers of on the spot investigation. The OFT has also published a separate booklet which provides a brief guide to the powers of investigation, entitled: *Under Investigation – a guide to investigations under the Competition Act 1998* (OFT 427).

If the Director has reasonable grounds for suspecting that the prohibition on anti-competitive agreements, or against conduct which amounts to an abuse of a dominant position has been infringed, he has the power to conduct an investigation (s. 25). The information available (*e.g.* copies of secret agreements provided by a disaffected member of a cartel) and the judgement of the Director will determine whether there are reasonable grounds for suspicion (the Powers of Investigation Guideline, para. 2.1). The phrase "reasonable grounds for suspicion" is the standard criminal law formulation of the term "reasonable suspicion" discussed at 9.5.3 above. These powers are expected to be used most frequently following a complaint or where the Director has otherwise been alerted to a suspected infringement (Powers of Investigation Guideline, para. 2.2).

The Director has powers both to request information and to investigate at the premises of businesses, whether implicated in a possible infringement or merely third parties with relevant information. Some entry of private premises is also possible.

9.9.2 Powers When Conducting Investigations – Information Requests

Under section 26, the Director may require any person, by notice in writing, to produce to him a specified document or specified information which he considers relates to any matter relevant to the investigation. The Powers of Investigation Guideline emphasise that the Director can require any person, not just the parties to the agreement or conduct in question, to produce the information requested. Suppliers, customers and competitors of the parties may all be required to supply information by notice.

9.9.3 Procedure

The investigation powers available under section 26 are dependent on the service of written notice. This notice must state:

- the subject matter and purpose of the investigation;
- the nature of the offences created by the Act in the event of failure to comply; and
- the documents or information which are required, or categories of documents or information which are required.

The Powers of Investigation Guideline indicates that the notice will usually be sent by post or fax, and that where the addressee of the notice is an undertaking or association of undertakings, the person who is authorised to act on behalf of the undertaking or association of undertakings is the appropriate person to respond (para. 3.11).

9.9.4 Documents Which May Be Required

The notice may specify both:

(1)   the time and place at which any document is to be produced or information provided; and

(2)   the manner and form in which any document is to be produced or information provided (s. 26(5)).

A specified document or specified information is a document or information which is specified or described in the notice, or which falls into a category which is so specified or described. "Document" includes information recorded in any form (s. 59(1) such as computer records (*Hansard*, H.C., col. 392 (June 16, 1998)).

The reference to "specified information" was inserted into this section to ensure that information which might not have been compiled systematically but which is capable of being compiled — for example, from a sales director's knowledge or experience — will also be subject to the production obligation (*Hansard* (Select Committee G) at col. 392 (June 16, 1998)). The Competition Commission and its predecessor, the Monopolies and Mergers Commission, have used equivalent powers in the FTA (s. 44) to require the extensive creation of new documents, charts and analyses from underlying business records, specifying format and even the computer software to be used. The Director may take copies of any documents requested (s. 26(6)(a)(i)).

9.9.5 Power to Require Explanations

The Director's powers under section 26(6) extend to requiring the present and past officers and employees of a company (or other business) to provide an explanation of a document which is produced in answer to the request. An amendment, proposing that the company have the right to comment on the suitability of the officer questioned to answer the relevant questions, was proposed but not accepted for the reason that such a right would cause delay and that companies which suffered injustice as the result of the false testimony of its officers, would have the right to appeal (*Hansard* (Standing Committee G) cols 397–398 (June 16, 1998)). The Director's Rules have provided some comfort for those called upon to assist the Director in this way, as a person required by the Director to give such an explanation may be accompanied by a legal adviser (Director's Rules, r. 13(3)).

If the document is not produced, the Director can require further information on its whereabouts in as much as a person can be required to state, to the best of his knowledge and belief, where the document is (s. 26(6)(b)).

9.9.6 Confidentiality

Information produced to the Director following a notice which is considered to be confidential must be placed in a confidential annex and clearly marked as such. The Director must then consider whether he can disclose the information in accordance with one of the exceptions (referred to at 9.4.4 above).

9.9.7 Use of Powers

The use of the power to require production of documents may be the first stage in an inquiry but may be used at any time. Requests for information which have to be compiled may be used to gain statistical or analytical information to be included in a decision.

Request of third parties may be most useful for the Director when he wishes to see if other businesses in the same position as a complainant have similar information.

The right to require an explanation may well be used at a later stage to resolve ambiguities or to ensure that the document is not being misinterpreted or so that persons referred to can be identified.

9.10   Power to Enter Premises Without a Warrant

9.10.1   Power to Enter Premises Without a Warrant

Under section 27, any officer, authorised in writing by the Director, ("an investigating officer"), may enter any premises in connection with a section 25 investigation. Except in the cases identified below, the Director must give two working day's written notice to the occupier of the premises indicating the subject matter and the purpose of the investigation and the offences that may be committed in the event of a failure to comply (ss. 42 to 44). The occupier of the premises need not themselves be suspected of infringement.

The notice period is not necessary if:

(a)   the Director has a reasonable suspicion that the premises are or have been occupied by a party to the agreement under investigation or an undertaking whose conduct he is investigating; or

(b)   the investigating officer has taken all such steps as are reasonably practicable to give notice but has not been able to do so (s. 27(3)).

When the investigating officer exercises the power to enter without giving notice, he must produce evidence of his authorisation from the Director and a document which contains the same information as the notice would have (s. 27(4)).

9.10.2   Premises

In debate, the Government confirmed that, as well as business premises, domestic premises may be entered, but only if they are used in connection with an undertaking. The Minister regarded the idea of entering the home of a temporary or junior secretary, where this person worked from home, as "ludicrous" because the home had no connection with the business (*Hansard* (Standing Committee G) col. 421 (June 16, 1998)). The Powers of Investigation Guideline confirms that the OFT regards "premises" as including domestic premises only if the home is used in connection with the business or if business documents are kept there. It also confirms that "premises" includes any vehicle (para. 4.6). Certainly the two day notice period should apply to most domestic premises and privately owned vehicles (unless the notice period is not necessary for the reasons set out in 9.10.1 above).

9.10.3   Safeguards During Investigation

The Powers of Investigation Guideline states that the investigating officer will normally arrive at the premises during office hours (para. 4.9). OFT officials have stated on several occasions that they wish to find at the premises people who can help them with their inquiries. If they arrive out of business hours they will not get this help.

When the power to enter premises without notice was debated, there was great concern that the party occupying the premises have access to a legal adviser. The Director's Rules give the occupier the right to have his legal adviser present before the investigation continues, but only if he arrives within the period of "reasonable time" which is allowed for the adviser to arrive, after which the investigation may proceed without him (Director's Rules, r. 13(1)). "Reasonable time" means such period of time as the officer thinks reasonable in the circumstances (Director's Rules, r. 13(2)). The OFT has confirmed that it intends to follow the practice and policy of the E.C. Commission (as set out in the explanatory notes to Articles 14(2) and 14(3) of Regulation 17/62, under which investigations are conducted) whereby undertakings are given reasonable time to secure legal services only when the investigating official is confident that the documents will be safe in the interval (*Hansard* (Standing Committee G) col. 421 (June 16, 1998)). This is confirmed at paras 4.10 and 4.11 of the Powers of Investigation Guideline.

At para. 4.11 of this Guideline it is clear that the investigating officer may attach such conditions as he considers appropriate to the right to wait for the attendance of a legal adviser — for example he may require that cabinets be sealed, that e-mail be suspended and/or that he be permitted to occupy chosen offices. In addition, it is stated that if an undertaking has an in-house legal adviser, or has been given notice of the investigation, the investigating officer will not wait for the arrival of an external legal adviser (with expert knowledge and experience).

Businesses therefore need to be prepared to follow common sense procedures, such as ensuring that they keep a record of any questions and answers and an additional copy of all documents copied. They should, in any event, seek to ensure that expert advisers are on site as quickly as practicable and to have guidance at the telephone in the meantime.

9.10.4   Powers of the Investigating Officer

The investigating officer has the following powers under section 27(5). He may:

(a)   take with him such equipment as appears to him to be necessary (for example, portable computer equipment);

(b)   require any person on the premises —
   (i)   to produce any document which he considers relates to any matter relevant to the investigation; and
   (ii) if the document is produced, to provide such explanation of it as the officer may require;

(c)   require any person to state to the best of his knowledge and belief where any such document is to be found;

(d)   take copies of, or extracts from, any document which is produced;

(e)   require any information which is held in a computer and is accessible from the premises and which the investigating officer considers relates to any matter relevant to the investigation, to be produced in a form:
   (i)   in which it can be taken away, and
   (ii) in which it is visible and legible.

The reference in (b)(ii) above to the officer's power to require an explanation of a document is subject to the right of the person not to incriminate themselves (see 9.12.3 below). The powers of the investigating officer set out above are also subject to the rules on privileged communications (see 9.12.1 below).

9.11 Power to Enter Premises Under a Warranty

9.11.1 Issue of Warrant

Under section 28, a High Court Judge may issue a warrant in three circumstances:

(a) there are reasonable grounds for suspecting that there are on any premises documents required under sections 26 and 27 which have not been produced as required;

(b) there are reasonable grounds for suspecting that:

   (i) there are on any premises documents which the Director has power under section 26 to require to be produced; and

   (ii) if the documents were required to be produced, they would not be produced but would be concealed, removed, tampered with or destroyed; or

(c) in exercising his powers under section 27 the investigating officer has attempted to enter premises but has been unable to do so and there are reasonable grounds for suspecting that there are on the premises documents which could have been required under section 27 (s. 28 (1)).

The warrant authorises a named officer of the Director and any of his officers whom he has named in writing to exercise the powers granted under the Act. It seems that where the Director relies on section 28(1)(b) in seeking a warrant, he must identify the documents with some particularity. If the Judge is satisfied that it is reasonable to suspect that there are also on the premises other documents relating to the investigation concerned, the warrant will extend to those other documents (s. 28 (3)). Every warrant must indicate the subject matter and purpose of the investigation and the nature of the offences committed if a person fails to comply (s. 29(1)). The warrant continues in force for one month from the date of issue (s. 28 (6)).

The Director must have used one of his other investigatory powers first before applying for a warrant, unless the application is based on the grounds set out in section 28(1)(b). The OFT have indicated that they will always be prepared to apply for a warrant at short notice if faced with obstruction when visiting premises without a warrant. The OFT may use a warrant where there is an obvious mismatch between documents supplied in answer to a written notice and those the OFT has obtained from other sources, but this will be a case by case decision.

9.11.2 Powers of the Named Officers

Under section 28(2), a named officer and any other officers who the Director has authorised in writing to accompany the named officer, shall have the following powers under the warrant which may be exercised only on production of the warrant:

(a)   to enter the premises specified in the warrant, using such force as is reasonably necessary for the purpose (the officer cannot use force against a person): there is also a duty to leave the premises as effectively secured as the officer found them, unless the occupier is present (s. 28(5)). The OFT has said that a locksmith rather than a sledgehammer is their preferred method of overcoming resistance or the absence of the occupier.

(b)   to search the premises and take copies of, or extracts from, any document appearing to be of a kind in respect of which the warrant was issued. The officers may only exercise their powers (search, copy, extract etc.) in relation to categories of documents which are the subject of the warrant and no others (*Hansard* (Standing Committee G) col. 422 (June 16, 1998));

(c)   to take possession of any documents appearing to be of the relevant kind if such action appears to be necessary for preserving documents of that kind or preventing interference with them or if it is not reasonably practicable to copy them on the premises: original documents may be retained for up to three months (ss. 28(2)(c) and 28(7));

(d)   to take any other steps which appear to be necessary for the purpose of preserving the documents or preventing interference with them;

(e)   to require any person to provide an explanation of any document appearing to be of the relevant kind or to state to the best of his knowledge and belief, where it may be found;

(f)   to require any information which is held in a computer and is accessible from the premises and which the named officer considers relates to any matter relevant to the investigation, to be produced in a form in which it can be taken away and in which it is visible and legible;

(g)   Any person entering premises by virtue of a warrant under this section may take with him such equipment as appears to be necessary (s. 28(4)), *e.g.* for reading material held on computer.

The reason for which the warrant was granted will determine the category of documents that the named officer can take possession of or copy.

Grounds for Warrant	Category of document
Warrant is granted after the addressee of a notice has failed to produce documents required	Documents which were required to be produced and not produced
Warrant is granted because there is reasonable ground for suspecting that there are documents at the premises which the investigating officer has power to require under s. 26 but that if they were so required they would be tampered with	Documents which the named officer had power to require to be produced under s.26 and, if it is reasonable to suspect that there are any, other documents relating to the investigation
Warrant is granted after the investigating officer has failed to enter the premises.	Documents which the investigating officer considers relate any matter relevant to the investigation.

It is evident that sections 28(2)(c) and 28(7) could be used as an instrument of oppression, since the removal of a large number of key documents (including computer discs) for up to three months could bring a business to a grinding halt. The courts must be vigilant to ensure that this procedure is not abused.

9.11.3 Presence of Legal Advisers

The person whose premises are entered has the right to request the attendance of his legal adviser, (Director's Rules, r. 13(1)). The named officer's duties in this respect are as set out in 9.11.2 above.

9.12 Dealing With the Investigation

9.12.1 Privileged communications

Under section 30, a person is not required to produce or disclose any privileged communications. A privileged communication is defined as a communication, (a) between a professional legal adviser and his client, or (b) made in connection with, or in contemplation of, legal proceedings and for the purposes of those proceedings, which, in proceedings in the High Court, would be protected from disclosure on grounds of legal professional privilege. In Scotland, references to the High Court are to be made as references to the Court of Session and references to legal professional privilege to be read as references to confidentiality of communications. Communications to and from in-house lawyers which would attract privilege in civil proceedings will be treated as privileged for the purposes of investigations under the Act, in contrast with the position under E.C. law (see 9.14.4 below).

When the Director is conducting an investigation relating to Article 81 or 82 at the request of the E.C. Commission(see 9.14 below), the named officer will have the powers of an official authorised by the E.C. Commission and the category of documents which are regarded as privileged will be the narrower category in accordance with European jurisprudence meaning that, for example, correspondence between a client and an in-house legal adviser will not be privileged.

In any investigation, where there is any uncertainty about the status of documents, it should be possible to agree procedures with the investigating officers which preserve the rights of the affected party while detailed consideration is given to the issue.

9.12.2 Confidentiality

Persons who are investigated have the right to request that documents and information produced during the visit be treated as confidential. The Powers of Investigation Guideline suggests that, where possible, the occupier of the premises should, following a site visit, identify any information or copy documents considered to be confidential (para. 6.6). The Director then has the final say as to whether the documents are to be disclosed, in the usual way.

9.12.3 Right of Silence

The position under E.C. law is set out in the case *Orkem v. Commission* (Case 374/87) [1989] E.C.R. 3283, [1991] 4 C.M.L.R. 502, which provides that the Commission may not compel an undertaking to provide it with answers which might involve an admission on its part of an infringement which it is incumbent on the

Commission to prove. So in practice under the Act, the person cannot be required to give explanations as to the document where these explanations amount to self incrimination (*Hansard* (Standing Committee G) col. 401 (June 16, 1998)). It is not entirely clear that this protects an individual employee or director where it is only the company which is exposed to a penalty. The OFT has not yet issued any guidance on its approach to the question of whether an individual director or employee can take advantage of privilege against self incrimination where the undertaking rather than the individual is subject of a notice to give an explanation of a document or to supply information and the subject of an infringement investigation. The European Convention of Human Rights has however been used to protect against self incrimination in these circumstances (see *Saunders v. United Kingdom* [1996] 23 E.H.R.R. 313 and 9.19).

If an individual would be admitting to a criminal offence (*e.g.* the destruction of documents) after he was aware that the inspectors had arrived, then his right to silence is in danger of being interpreted as the further offence of failing to produce documents or obstructing the enquiry (see 9.13). Will the court accept that he has a "reasonable excuse" for refusing to state where a document is to be found?

9.12.4   Decisions Following an Investigation

Under section 31, the Director, if he proposes to make a decision that the prohibition has been infringed as the result of an investigation, must give notice to the person or persons likely to be affected by the proposed decision and give that person (or those persons) an opportunity to make representations before making the decision. This requirement is subsumed in the general rule to this effect in the Director's Rules, r. 14, discussed at 9.4.4 above.

9.13   Criminal Offences in Relation to Sections 26 to 28

9.13.1   Specific Documents

Under section 42, it is a criminal offence to fail to comply with the requirements to produce a specified document or specified information (s. 26), or to fail to assist with the provision and explanation of documentation (including information held in a computer) or to state where it is during "dawn raids" (ss. 27 and 28). Section 42 provides a defence if the person required to produce a document proves that either (i) he did not possess the document nor was it under his control, or (ii) that it was not reasonably practicable for him to comply with the requirement.

There will also be a defence if the person can prove that he had a reasonable excuse for failing to comply with a requirement:

(a)   to provide information;

(b)   to provide an explanation of a document; or

(c)   to state where a document is to be found (s. 42(3)).

In addition, there is a defence as of right under section 41(4). This is triggered when an investigating officer acts *ultra vires* or fails to produce evidence of authorisation upon request when demanding specific documents or specific information (under s. 26) when entering premises without a warrant (under s. 27).

It is also an offence intentionally to obstruct an officer acting in the exercise of his powers when entering premises without a warrant (under s. 27) or when conducting dawn raids (under s. 28) (ss. 42(5) and (7)).

9.13.2   Punishments

Persons guilty of failure to comply with the requirements made of them by the officer under sections 26, 27 or 28, or who obstruct an officer acting in the exercise of his powers under section 27 are liable on summary conviction or on indictment to a fine (s. 42 (6)), whilst persons who intentionally obstruct an officer in the exercise of his powers under a warrant issued under section 28 ("dawn raids") are liable to a fine on summary conviction, or a fine and/or up to two years imprisonment on indictment (s. 42(7)). See the table below for a summary.

Offence	Statutory Defence	Sanction	
		On summary Conviction	On conviction on indictment
Failure to comply with a requirement to produce document, or information (s. 42 (1))	Proof that: — the document required was not in the person's possession or control, and — it is not reasonably practicable to comply (s. 42(2))	Fine (not exceeding the statutory maximum)	Unlimited fine
Failure to provide an explanation of the documents/ information, or state where they may be found (s. 42(1))	Proof that there is a reasonable excuse for failing to comply	Fine (not exceeding the statutory maximum)	Unlimited fine
Failure to comply with a requirement imposed during an investigation following notice (s. 42(1))	The person imposing the requirement has failed to act in accordance with the Act (s. 42(4))	Fine (not exceeding the statutory maximum)	Unlimited fine
Intentionally obstructing an officer acting in the exercise of his powers to investigate premises without a warrant (s. 42(5))	—	Fine (not exceeding the statutory maximum)	Unlimited fine

Offence	Statutory Defence	Sanction	
		On summary Conviction	On conviction on indictment
Intentionally obstructing an officer acting in the exercise of his powers to investigate premises without a warrant (s. 42(5))	—	Fine (not exceeding the statutory maximum)	Unlimited fine
Intentionally obstructing an officer acting in the exercise of his powers to investigate premises with a warrant (s. 42(7))	—	Fine (not exceeding the statutory maximum)	Imprisonment for a term up to two years or an unlimited fine or both.
Destruction or falsification of documents (intentionally or recklessly) required to be produced (s. 43(1))	—	Fine (not exceeding the statutory maximum)	Imprisonment for a term up to two years or an unlimited fine or both.
Provision of false or misleading information (s. 44 (1))	—	Fine (not exceeding he statutory maximum)	Imprisonment for a term up to two years or an unlimited fine or both.

9.13.3   Destruction of Documents

It is also an offence to dispose of or destroy (either with intent or recklessly), falsify, or conceal documents in the event of dawn raids or requests for specific documents (s. 43(1)). Delegation of the destruction, disposal, falsification or concealment to another also constitutes an offence (s. 43(1) (b)). Offenders under section 43(1) may be liable to a fine on summary conviction or to a fine and/or up to two years imprisonment on indictment.

9.13.4   Provision of Information

Section 44 builds on the preceding section by addressing the offences which relate to the provision of information (as opposed to documentation), either to the Director himself or to a third party whom he knows will subsequently pass the information to the Director. Knowledge or recklessness as to the provision of false or misleading information in a material particular constitutes an offence (s. 44(1)), although in the event of the information being given to a third party, the provider

must have knowledge that the information is to be used for the purposes of informing the Director (s. 44(2)): this could perhaps arise where the responsible people
within a company deliberately give false or misleading information to their lawyer
to pass on to the OFT in answer to an enquiry. The offender is liable to a fine on
summary conviction and a fine and/or up to two years imprisonment on conviction
or indictment.

9.13.5   Liability of Officers of a Company

The Powers of Investigation Guideline states that the officer as well as the body corporate is guilty of any of the offences described above if the offence that is committed by the body corporate is proved to have been committed with the consent or
connivance of an officer or attributable to his neglect (para. 7.4). For these purposes, an "officer" means a director, manager or secretary of the company or a
person purporting to act in such a capacity.

9.13.6   Severity of Penalties

These offences go far beyond the relatively minor financial penalties which may be
imposed on undertakings under Regulation 17 for information offences. Many
think they go too far and may lead to what will appear to be personal vendettas in
which individuals taken by surprise are prosecuted. Companies have a heavy burden to prepare staff to deal with a visit which may carry such serious consequences
if an individual is thought by the investigators to be concealing relevant material or
being less than frank.

9.14   Investigation Powers in E.C. Commission Investigations

9.14.1   Director's Powers to Investigate

The Act grants the Director new powers of investigation for use when the E.C.
Commission has requested assistance in carrying out an investigation in connection
with Articles 81 or 82 (ss. 61 to 64).

The Director's staff may be assisting the E.C. Commission (s. 62) or carrying out
the investigation at the E.C. Commission's request (s. 63).

9.14.2   Powers to Enter Premises

The Director must apply for a warrant to enter premises in whichever capacity he
is acting.

In either case a High Court Judge may issue a warrant, if satisfied that the investigation is being, or is likely to be, obstructed (ss. 62(1) and 63(1)).

There is an obstruction if:

- the E.C. Commission official, or authorised officer, has attempted to enter
  premises but (despite having produced his authorisation) been unable to do
  so and there are reasonable grounds for suspecting that there are books or
  records on the premises which the E.C. Commission official, or authorised
  officer, has power to examine (ss. 62(2) and 63(2)); or

- there are reasonable grounds for suspecting that there are at the premises
  books or records which the E.C. Commission official, or authorised officer,

has requested be produced and which have not been produced (ss. 62(3) and 63(3)).

There is likely to be an obstruction if:

- the E.C. Commission official, or authorised officer, is authorised to require the production of books or records which are reasonably suspected to be at the premises and there are also reasonable grounds for suspecting that, if the E.C. Commission official, or authorised officer, exercised his power, they would not be produced but would be concealed, removed, tampered with or destroyed (ss. 62(4) and 63(4)).

For the purposes of this investigative power the term "premises" comprises any premises, land or means of transport which an E.C. Commission official has or would have power to enter, which would probably not include domestic premises or privately owned vehicles. There are proposals to widen the E.C. Commission's powers as part of the reform of Regulation 17/62 discussed in Chapter 17 at 17.7.

Warrants issued under sections 62 or 63 must state the subject matter and purpose of the investigation and the offences which a person will commit if he intentionally obstructs any person exercising powers under the warrant (s. 64). The warrant continues in force for a period of one month from the date of issue (s. 62(8) and s. 63(8)).

9.14.3   Scope of Powers under the Warrant

The powers granted to the authorised officers and any named official of the E.C. Commission are broadly similar to those granted in the context of an investigation of a Chapter I or Chapter II infringement, namely the power to enter the premises specified, search for books and records which the officer or E.C. Commission official has power to examine, using such force as is reasonably necessary for the purpose. The warrant authorises the officer and his team to take any equipment which appears to be necessary.

There is no reference in the Act to the right of the occupant of the premises to request the attendance of his legal adviser. However, it is the practice and policy of the E.C. Commission to permit the occupant reasonable time to secure legal services subject to the investigating officer being confident that the books and records will be safe in the interval (Regulation 17/62) *Dow Benelux v. E.C. Commission* (Case 85/87) [1989] E.C.R. 3137, [1991] 4 C.M.L.R. 410, *Dow Chemical Iberica v. E.C. Commission* (Joined Cases 97–99/87) [1989] E.C.R. 3156, (1991) 4 C.M.L.R., *Hoechst v. E.C. Commission* (Case 46/87 227/88) [1989] E.C.R. 2859, [1991] 4 C.M.L.R. 410).

9.14.4   Privileged Communications

The category of documents recognised as being privileged is narrower in the context of an investigation conducted under sections 62 to 65 than it is in a Chapter I or Chapter II investigation. In accordance with the decision of the European Court of Justice in *AM & S Europe Ltd v. Commission*, (Case 155/79) [1982] E.C.R. 1575, [1982] 2 C.M.L.R. 264 at para. 3 only correspondence between a client and legal adviser, entitled to practice in a Member State which either:

- follows the initiation of proceedings by the E.C. Commission and concerns the defence of the client; or

- existed prior to the E.C. Commission's proceedings were initiated but "has a relationship" with the subject matter of those proceedings, will be privileged.

Correspondence with an in-house legal adviser will not therefore be privileged, nor will correspondence with any lawyer not directly related to the subject matter of the investigation.

During an on-the-spot investigation under sections 62 or 63 of the Act, the occupier may claim legal privilege for documents, putting his case to the E.C. Commission. If the E.C. Commission rejects the claim, the documents must be handed over. The occupant may challenge this decision before the Court of First Instance (Powers of Investigation Guideline, para. 10.8). In practice such documents are often provided to the E.C. Commission pursuant to an agreed procedure, whereby the documents remain sealed and therefore not available to the E.C. Commission unless the court rules that they are not subject to privilege. This overrides the risk of fines and prevents documents being destroyed. This enables claims of privilege to be resolved without the need for litigation where the party and the E.C. Commission each have a proper opportunity to consider their respective positions and put their position to the other.

9.14.5   Criminal Offences

A person will be guilty of an offence if he intentionally obstructs any person in the exercise of his powers under sections 62 or 63 (s. 65(1)). The sanction is a fine of up to the statutory maximum on summary conviction, and on indictment an unlimited fine and/or a maximum of two years' imprisonment.

9.15   Investigations Under the Fair Trading Act 1973

9.15.1   Director's Powers of Investigation

Although much of the previous competition law regime has been replaced by the Act, the complex monopoly and scale monopoly provisions of the FTA have been retained. In procedural terms though, the Director has been accorded new powers under the Act which allow him similar powers of investigation to those available under Chapter I and Chapter II investigations, in respect of any business which may be a scale monopoly supplying or acquiring over a quarter of the goods or services of any description in the United Kingdom or a part thereof, or which may form part of a complex monopoly (as defined in FTA s. 11 (1)) (see Chapter 15 for further discussion).

These new powers enable the Director to:

(a)   require the production of specified documents, estimates, forecasts, returns and other information from certain producers, suppliers and customers;

(b)   enter business premises without notice and require the production of relevant documents and the provision of an explanation of the documents produced.

As with investigations of Chapter I or Chapter II infringements, the person occupying the premises has the right to request the attendance of a legal adviser on the same basis.

9.15.2 Criminal Offences

The amendments to the FTA include the creation of the following criminal offences:

(a)   refusing or wilfully neglecting to comply with a requirement to produce documents or other information;

(b)   wilfully interfering with documents;

(c)   intentionally obstructing the Director in the exercise of his powers.

The sanction for the offence of obstruction following conviction on indictment is an unlimited fine; the sanction for the other offences following conviction on indictment is an unlimited fine and/or imprisonment for a maximum of two years.

9.16   Appeals to the Competition Commission

9.16.1   Overview

The Act provides for appeals to an appeal tribunal of the Competition Commission from three categories of persons:

(1)   any party to an agreement in respect of which the Director has made a decision (s. 46(1));

(2)   any person in respect of whose conduct the Director has made a decision (s. 46(2)); and

(3)   third parties who have had certain applications to the Director for review of a decision rejected (s. 47, discussed at 9.8 above).

In addition, procedural rules may provide for the joinder in an appeal of persons not party to proceedings before the Director (Sched. 8, para. 14).

The appeal tribunal processes are laid down in Schedule 8 and in the Competition *Commission Appeal Tribunal Rules 2000* (S.I. 2000 No. 261) (the "Appeal Rules") and further guidance is given in the Competition Commission's *Guide to Appeals*, June 2000 (the "Appeal Guide").

9.16.2   Appeals by Parties to Agreement or Conduct

An appeal by a party to an agreement the subject of a Chapter I decision or a party to conduct the subject of a Chapter II decision is possible on the substance of the Director's decisions as well as on the level of penalties imposed.

For the purposes of section 46, parties may appeal against the following Director's decisions:

(a)   as to whether the Chapter I Prohibition has been infringed;

(b) as to whether the Chapter II Prohibition has been infringed;

(c) as to whether to grant an individual exemption;

(d) in respect of an individual exemption —
   (i) as to whether to impose any condition or obligation;
   (ii) where such a condition or obligation has been imposed, the period of date fixed in relation to such condition or obligation;
   (iii) as to the period of any exemption;
   (iv) as to the date from which the exemption runs.

(e) as to whether to extend the period of an individual exemption or the period or any such extension;

(f) cancelling an exemption;

(g) as to the imposition of any penalty or the amount of any such penalty;

(h) to withdraw or vary any of the decisions in paragraphs (a) to (f) following an application to the Director by a third party;

(i) a direction given under section 32 (agreements), section 33 (conduct) or section 35 (interim measures).

In addition, the Competition Act 1998 (*Notification of Excluded Agreements and Appealable Decisions*) Regulations 2000 (S.I. 2000 No. 263) adds two further categories of appealable decision:

(1) a decision of the Director imposing conditions or obligations subject to which a parallel exemption is to have effect, or varying or removing any such conditions or obligations;

(2) a decision of the Director, in relation to an agreement which is notifiable by virtue of Regulation 5 of the Regulations, that the Chapter I Prohibition would be infringed if it applied to the agreements. This covers agreements notified in anticipation of the expiry of a transitional period or because the Director is considering withdrawing the benefit of an exclusion.

This means that, even if a decision is favourable, an appeal may be made on some individual findings in the decision.

It should be noted that, other than an appeal against a decision as to the imposition or amount of any penalty, the making of an appeal will not in itself suspend the effect of the decision appealed. An application for interim measures under the Appeal Rules, r. 32, may result in an order suspending a disputed decision in whole or in part or varying conditions or obligations pending determination of the appeal (see 9.16.14).

9.16.3 Appeals by Third Parties

Third parties may challenge the Director's decisions on items (a) to (f) initially by application to the Director but may appeal from his decision to the Competition Commission (s. 47(6)) if he rejects an application on the grounds of lack of sufficient interest or sufficient reasons.

9.16.4   The Appeal Tribunal's Powers

Appeals to the CFI and ECJ from the E.C. Commission are in the nature of judicial review of the procedural and legal basis of the E.C. Commission's decision, with a power to vary penalties. In contrast, an appeal to an appeal tribunal of the Competition Commission is on the merits (Sched. 8, para. 3(1)) and the appeal tribunal may substitute its decision for that of the Director, for example, in the grant of an exemption, and may set aside any of the Director's findings of fact (Sched. 8, para. 3(4)), even if it upholds his decision.

An appeal tribunal may substitute its own decision for that of the Director by changing the level of a penalty; by altering, granting or cancelling an individual exemption; or making any other decisions which the Director himself is empowered to make (Sched. 8, para. 3(2)). These decisions take effect and may be enforced as if made by the Director (Sched. 8, para. 3(3)).

The Major Provisions Guideline, para. 14.5, states that it is not the role of the appeal tribunal to carry out investigation work. In the event of substantial new evidence emerging on appeal, the appeal tribunal may therefore remit the matter to the Director for further investigation (Sched. 8, para. 3(2)(a)). Unless the appeal is rejected on procedural grounds (*e.g.* as out of time), the appeal tribunal may confirm or reverse the Director's decision.

9.16.5   Confidentiality

The decision of an appeal tribunal must be published (Sched. 8, para. 4).

The Competition Commission may receive confidential information during the course of its investigation, as a "designated person" (as defined in Sched. 11). It is bound by the rules in sections 55 and 56 with regard to confidential information and material received from, or to be disclosed to, interveners (Appeal Rules, r. 14(8)) and has the same duties as the Director when considering whether to disclose confidential information in published decisions (see 9.4.4 above).

Appeal Tribunals are directed to consider holding hearings in private where dealing with confidential information to which sections 55 and 56 applies (Sched. 8, para. 9(1)(a) reflected in the Appeal Rules, r. 23). Applications for confidentiality by appellants and the respondent should be made in the application or within 14 days thereafter (r. 6(8) of the Appeal Rules which is applied to the defence by r. 12(6)). The Appeal Guide suggests that interveners should make their position clear within 14 days after the application to intervene, as the principal parties will be heard on the application before it is admitted or rejected (Appeal Guide, para. 6.3). Chapter 6 of the Appeal Guide contains a convenient summary of the appeal tribunal's approach to confidentiality — it emphasises concern about commercially sensitive information but warns against over-wide applications (para. 6.7).

9.16.6   Rules as to the Appeals Process

Section 48 of the Act confers power on the Secretary of State to make rules relating to appeals and appeal tribunals following consultation with the President of the Competition Commission Appeal Tribunals and other appropriate persons. Schedule 8, Part II makes further reference to the Secretary of State's rule-making power, but, as with rules made under section 51, the power is not limited by the terms of the relevant schedule. The Secretary of State has enacted the Appeal Rules. Apart from dealing with the management and constitution of the Appeal tribunals, and providing for representation by lawyers with rights of audience before a court in the United Kingdom and (at the discretion of the tribunal) other persons (Part I), the Appeal Rules cover:

- Commencing proceedings (Part II);

- Response to the application (Part III);

- Intervention by parties with sufficient interest consolidation and location of proceedings (Part IV);

- Preparation for deciding the Application, including pre-hearing review and directions (Part V);

- The hearing (Part VI);

- The Decision of the Tribunal (Part VII);

- Appeals (Part VIII);

- References to the European Court (Part IX);

- Interim orders and measures (Part X);

- Supplementary matters (Part XI).

The Appeal Rules are heavily influenced by the procedures of the European Court of First Instance of which the first President of the Appeal Tribunals, Sir Christopher Bellamy Q.C., was a distinguished member. They are also influenced by High Court procedure and are based on the same general philosophy as the new rules of civil procedure introduced by the 1998 Woolf reform: dealing with cases justly, ensuring that the parties are on an equal footing, that expense is saved and that appeals are dealt with expeditiously and fairly (Appeal Guide, para. 2.1). The Appeal Guide provides useful assistance in the interpretation of the Rules.

The general principles of the Rules as explained in Chapter 2 of the Appeal Guide are:

- Early disclosure in writing;

- Active case management;

- Strict timetables, with the aim of completing straightforward cases in under six months;

- Effective fact finding procedures, including oral cross-examination where necessary;

- Short and structured oral hearings.

9.16.7 Starting an Appeal

Appeals must be made to the Registrar of the Competition Commission Appeals Tribunal within two months of the date on which the applicant was notified of the disputed decision, but this time limit may be extended in exceptional circumstances (Appeal Rule, r. 6). According to the Appeal Guide (para. 4.9) service by fax or e-mail is not allowed and must be made by hand or first class post (although r. 34(1)(d) allows the Tribunal to authorise these additional means in the future).

Although service via a document exchange is permitted by rule 34(1)(c), the Appeal Guide reveals that the Competition Commission has no document exchange address.

If time expires on a day which is not a business day, it is extended to the next business day (r. 35, which also deals with the calculation of periods). Service takes effect on the day of delivery by hand, unless after 5 p.m. and on the second day after dispatch by first class post (r. 34(2)). The Appeal Guide, para. 4.13, gives useful examples of the operation of these rules in practice and para. 4.15 emphasises the value of liaison with the registry during preparation of the appeal.

The application must be fully reasoned (r. 6(5)) and accompanied so far as practicable, by all documents (including witness statements) relied upon (r. 6(6)). The lack of transparency and comparative informality of the Director's processes, as well as its investigatory rather than adversarial nature, sits ill with these requirements. It is far from certain that the applicant will have all this material to hand when the Director takes his decision, and it may be extremely difficult to create it in the time available. The requirement for annexation of all documents relied upon is likely to lead to unnecessary expense (since an original and seven copies must be supplied), in order to avoid the risk of procedural shut-out from use of marginally relevant documents, the importance of which may be unclear until issues are joined. The Appeal Guide on this point is not of much assistance:

- it emphasises the need for full reasoning (paras 5.4–5.6 and 5.10–5.11) and identification of contested facts (para. 5.9);

- it assumes a high standard of procedural formality in the Director's proceedings (*e.g.* the existence of witness statements) for which the Director's Rules make no provision (paras 5.21–5.22) and of precision in the Director's decision (paras 5.20, 8.2);

- it emphasises that "Documents of only peripheral relevance to the case should not be annexed" (para. 5.19) but warns that the tribunal may exclude from consideration material which could reasonably have been included with the application, but which was not (para. 5.24). The second statement is hardly an encouragement to economy in the provision of documents at a time when the ways in which the Director or Regulator will wish to add support to his decision are not known and where his reasoning or factual basis may not be clearly spelled out in his decision.

The Appeal Tribunal will have to be astute to ensure that procedural laxity and lack of clarity in decision taking by the Director or a Regulator do not operate to the prejudice of the applicant in the operation of its own rules. The emphasis on the need for a complete application ab initio is also likely to encourage appellants to include procedural matters in their appeals, such as reliance on matters in the decision which were not included in the statement of objections or incompleteness of access to file, and attacks on the sufficiency of decisions (*e.g.* as to reasoning or statement of the materials relied upon).

CFI proceedings show how the E.C. Commission frequently shifts ground from the arguments put forward in its decisions, and the Director and sector Regulators may be expected to do likewise (see the criticism of the Director General of Electricity Supply for shifting reasoning in judicial review proceedings: *London Electric-*

ity v. DGES (judgement of Harrison J, May 15, 2000 reported in *The Times*, June 13, 2000).

The appeal tribunal's powers to give directions regarding applications which are materially incomplete, unduly prolix or lacking in clarity (r. 7) may be worked over-time on account of its rules for the initiation of proceedings which require immediate production of material often better produced once issues are joined.

Applications may be struck out if they disclose no valid ground of appeal, are brought by a vexatious litigant, are materially defective and the defect has not been remedied, or where the applicant has failed to comply with a direction (r. 8). Applications may be amended with the permission of the tribunal (r. 9), but an additional ground may be added only if:

(a)   the new ground is based on matters of law or fact which have come to light since the appeal was made;

(b)   it was not practicable to include the ground in the application; or

(c)   the circumstances are exceptional.

The Appeal Guide, para. 11.1, helpfully explains that the rules on amendment are not so restrictive as would be the case in High Court litigation "Thus it will not normally be necessary to apply formally to "amend", simply to put in different words in the written submissions made in support of a ground of appeal which already figures in the application". A party wishing to raise a new ground of appeal or to develop an existing ground of appeal in a manner which could not reasonably be foreseen should seek directions from the tribunal as soon as possible.

Until the degree of access to material held by the Director is clearly established, this rule seems also likely to be invoked frequently. It will also be needed where the Director or Regulator raises new matters in his response. The Appeal Guide (para. 8.3) seems to encourage the Director to take his time to produce all relevant documents on which he relies, by suggesting that agreement of working bundles may be substituted for the application of rule 12(4) which requires the respondent (who will always be the Director or a sectoral Regulator) to annex documents in a similar way (see 9.16.9 below).

Appeals may be withdrawn only with the permission of the tribunal or, in early stages, the President (r. 10). Acknowledgement of the appeal is sent by the Registrar to the applicant and a copy is sent to the respondent (the Director or a sector Regulator (r. 11)). A summary is published (r. 13).

9.16.8   Procedure for Response

The Response must be given within six weeks or such further time as the tribunal may allow (r. 12). It must be reasoned and again have documents and witness statements annexed and be supplied with seven extra copies. Although there is some laxity in the approach to the production of documents, the Appeal Guide (para. 8.4) emphasises the importance of early production by the respondent of witness statements and, in particular, expert evidence. Although the Rules appear favourable to the respondent, applicants should have confidence that the appeal tribunal will ensure a fair balance in the operation of the Appeal Rules in relation to the Defence. Provisions for curing defects, striking out and amendment are adapted from those applying to the application (r. 12). It is notable that the respondent

Director or Regulator is treated more generously in terms of extension of time than the applicant who is the true defendant, possibly facing very severe business disruption or economic loss and damage to reputation. The respondent also has the procedural advantage of making submissions at the first case conference *before* he has to present his defence (r. 17(3)(e), Appeal Guide paras 7.5 and 8.5).

9.16.9   Addition of Parties

Parties with sufficient interest may be added (r. 14) on reasoned application within one month of publication of the summary of the application. It is only if an application is admitted that the tribunal will lay down a timetable for the provision of a statement of intervention (to which apply rules adapted from those for appeals). The Appeal Guide encourages interveners to come forward as early as possible (para. 9.31), but to consider first whether they have a sufficient interest and, even if they do, whether one of the main parties will adequately protect their interests (para. 9.4). Interveners are again likely to have longer to prepare than the appellant although their role is ancillary and full pleadings may not be needed.

The tribunal is also bound to protect (Appeal Guide, para. 9.9) confidential information to the like extent as the Director is under sections 55 and 56 of the Act, whether in relation to disclosure to the intervener or the applicant (r. 14(8)). If this resulted in the applicant being denied relevant information, there would be doubt about compliance with the Human Rights Act 1998 (see 9.18). It is unfortunate that, when confidential information has been excluded from the Director's statement of objections and decision, it may be introduced again by an intervener, with the risk of the appeal tribunal being influenced by matters not fairly disclosed to the appellant. There is a heavy burden on the tribunal to prevent this situation arising.

9.16.10   Consolidation and Location

Where there are several appeals from the same decision or involving the same or similar issues, they may be consolidated by the tribunal after hearing representations from the affected parties (r. 15). In deciding on the place of proceedings, the tribunal has regard primarily not to the convenience of the parties, but to their principal place of business and the place where an agreement or conduct had effect (r. 16(2)). However, it shall give directions with regard to the just, expeditious and economical conduct of proceedings (r. 16(3)). Thus, if national or international companies with head offices dotted around the home counties are party to a cartel in north-east England, it is something of a toss up whether proceedings will take place there, or in London, which will almost certainly be more convenient and cheaper for the tribunal, the parties and their advisers. It depends how much weight the tribunal will attach to the interests of interveners based in the regions. It seems likely that where effects are primarily in Scotland or Northern Ireland, with their distinct legal systems, proceedings are more likely to be assigned to Edinburgh or Belfast than to English regions in cases where a location in England is involved. Wales does not have a separate legal system, but, with its devolved administration and potential use of the Welsh language, location of proceedings in Wales is more likely where Wales or some part of it is the affected area. The Appeal Guide does not deal with this issue.

9.16.11   Directions and The Hearing

There are detailed rules for case management conferences and directions including the hearing of witnesses, discovery and the instruction of experts (r. 17), and
specifically for a pre-hearing review (r. 18) designed to ensure the efficient conduct
of proceedings and, where appropriate, facilitate their settlement, as well as to lay
down timetables, including that for an oral hearing (r. 19) and to determine evi-
dential matters (r. 20 and r. 21). The first case management conference will generally be within four weeks of the appeal being lodged and prior to service of the
defence. The sanctions for failure to comply with directions may involve being
debarred from further involvement in the proceedings without the permission of the
tribunal (r. 22). About two weeks prior to the hearing, the tribunal will normally
send the parties a report for the hearing (r. 19(d)) summarising the factual context
and the principal submissions. This will be available to the public (more detail is
given in the Appeal Guide, para. 12.4).

Case conferences will normally be in private and may be held in a different place
from the hearing, if this is more convenient (Appeal Guide, para. 7.7). Hearings will
take place in public, except when considering information that the tribunal is satisfied
is confidential (r. 23). Court of First Instance procedure will be followed and the hearing structured in accordance with a timetable (r. 19). This will normally allow the principal parties up to 45 minutes for a formal address, followed by questions from the
Court and then concluding remarks, with adaption in cases involving oral evidence
(Appeal Guide, paras 12.5, 12.7 and 12.8). Procedure at the hearing is controlled by
the President or Chairman of the Tribunal and is to be as informal as is appropriate
given the objectives of clarifying the issues and just handling of the process (r. 24).

The Appeal Guide, Chapter 7, deals with the steps following the lodging of an
appeal and Chapter 10 with Directions for the hearing. There is a particular
emphasis on restricting expert evidence to that reasonably required to resolve the
proceedings (paras 10.4–10.5) following Part 35, Civil Procedure Rules 1998 (S.I.
1998 No. 3132 L.17). This is particularly important as decisions, particularly on
the Chapter II Prohibition, may be fundamentally based on the analysis of expert
economists on market definition or the economic effect of conduct (see also Appeal
Guide, para. 2.7, on agreement between experts).

9.16.12   The Decisions

Decisions will be delivered in public (r. 25) and also published on the Competition
Commission's website and commercially. There will be arrangements made, in consultation with the parties, to ensure that the published version does not contain
confidential information (Appeal Guide, Chapter 13).

If proceedings are discontinued by consent with an order that may have a significant effect on competition, the tribunal will carry out public consultation before
approving the order (r. 28, paras (4) to (9)).

9.16.13   Financial Matters

The tribunal may provide for the award of costs (r. 26) so that one party may have
to pay costs of one or more other parties. Parties may also be ordered to pay costs
incurred by the tribunal (*e.g.* if it engages its own expert). Where a penalty has been
suspended on appeal, the tribunal may order payment of interest at the rates which
might be set by the courts (r. 27).

9.16.14   Interim Orders and Measures

The tribunal may by interim order grant any remedy which it could grant in its final decision (r. 32(1)). This is a general power, but the tribunal is directed to consider particularly the necessity to act urgently to prevent serious irreparable damage to a particular person or category of person, or to protect the public interest. It is to consider all the circumstances, including urgency, the effects on the party seeking interim relief if the order is not made and on competition if it is made. Typical orders would suspend the effect of a disputed decision in whole or in part or vary conditions or obligations attached to an exemption. A reasoned application must be submitted and decisions will normally be made after hearing the other parties to the proceedings (or if the application pre-dates an appeal, the Director or sector Regulator who took the decision). In cases of extreme urgency, the tribunal may act in advance of a written request or without receiving submissions from other parties.

9.16.15   Supplementary Rules

Rule 33 allows the President or tribunal Chairman to act alone as regards decisions under a number of the rules. Rule 34 deals with service of documents including place and time of service (see 9.16.8 above) which apply in all cases where documents have to be served. Rule 35 deals with the calculation of time limits. Rule 36 deals with the management of irregularities and rule 37 gives the tribunal a general power to regulate its procedure subject to the Rules and for the issuing of practice directions by the President.

9.16.16   Appeals Against Appeal Tribunal Decisions

The applicant, the Director or sector Regulator party to the tribunal proceedings and (probably) a third party who has been admitted as an intervener by the appeal tribunal may, with permission of the tribunal given under Rules 29 and 30, or of the appellate court, appeal against the decisions of the appeal tribunal on points of law and penalty levels (s. 49(1) and (2) — findings of fact on which an Appeal Tribunal has relied are therefore not subject to appeal). The appeal is made to the Court of Appeal in England and Wales and Northern Ireland and the Court of Session in Scotland. The Secretary of State may make rules relating to such appeals (s. 49 (3)), but has not done so.

Practice Direction 52 of the Court of Appeal for England and Wales, para. 21.10, deals with appeals from the Competition Commission Appeal Tribunals. Notice of Appeal must be lodged with the Court of Appeal within 14 days of the determination of the application for leave by the tribunal (whether at the hearing at which the decision is given or in writing). If no application is made to the tribunal for leave, notice must be lodged within 14 days after the end of the period within the appellant could have made a written application for leave. The initiation of the process is the same where leave to appeal is given and where (either because the appeal tribunal refused leave or no application was made to it) the appellant seeks permission to appeal from the Court of Appeal. Thereafter procedure will follow that laid down for appeals which is outside the scope of this book.

At the present time Northern Ireland has not made any rules but the author understands they will normally follow a similar procedure to that adopted in English practice direction.

In Scotland the appeal is made to the Inner House of the Court of Session in the normal way under Parts I, II, III and VIII of Chapter 41 of the Rules of the Court of Session which set out the procedure for appeals under statute.

9.17 Judicial Review

9.17.1 Appeals to Courts

On matters where an appeal may be made to the appeal tribunal of the Competition Commission, this procedure must be followed and the Courts would not entertain actions under the judicial review process. The involvement of the courts will only arise where an appeal lies from a decision of the appeal tribunal (see 9.16.16 above).

9.17.2 Scope for Judicial Review

As administrative bodies, the Director and the appeal tribunal (despite its quasi-judicial function) may be subject to judicial review. Normally judicial review will not lie to the extent that there is an express right of appeal, but the rights of appeal from the Director, for example, do not cover procedural irregularity affecting the course of a continuing investigation and do not extend to third parties, except in limited circumstances. Thus there may be room for judicial review during the course of proceedings before the Director or an appeal tribunal or on their termination adverse to the interests of a third party.

One obvious area for judicial review would be the misuse of powers in relation to "dawn raids" and another would be disputes on disclosure of confidential material. It can be expected that the Competition Commission appeal tribunal will take account of procedural matters when hearing appeals from decisions of the Director, but this may (particularly on the matters referred to above) be too late to remedy any injustice. The courts' willingness to hear review cases will, however, be affected by the extent to which the appeal tribunal can effectively deal with any issue.

9.17.3 Grounds for Judicial Review

The principal grounds upon which an administrative action is subject to control by judicial review are (i) illegality (on the basis that the decision-maker must correctly understand the law that regulates his decision-making power and must give effect to it); (ii) irrationality (on the basis that "a conclusion is so unreasonable that no reasonable authority could ever have come to it"); or (iii) procedural impropriety (*e.g.* on breach of the principle of natural justice of *audi alteram partem*).

9.17.4 Rejected Complaints and Third Party Applications

Where the Director fails to take action on a complaint or rejects it without taking a decision capable of review and appeal under section 47, then the complainant or other third party has no right of appeal to the Competition Commission. In such a case he may be able to seek judicial review, with a view to having the complaint examined fully or reconsidered.

9.18 References to the European Court

Because issues arising under the Competition Act are subject to the governing principles rules in section 60 (discussed in Chapter 5) which require consistency with

E.C. law, the tribunal rules, rule 31, provide for the possibility of a reference to the ECJ in order to resolve any ambiguity in the relevant principle of E.C. law. Proceedings are stayed pending resolution of any such appeal. The ECJ has indicated that it will accept such cases (*Bernd Giloy v. Hauptzollant Frankfurt am Main-Ost* (Case C–130/95) [1997] E.C.R. I–4291). The ECJ also guided a national court on a question of national law based on Article 82, although it was not clear that Article 82 itself had been infringed in *Oscar Bronner GmbH & Co. KG v. Mediaprint Zeitungs-und Zeitschriftenverlang GmbH & Co. KG* ((Case No. C-7/97) [1998] E.C.R. I–7791; [1999] 4 C.M.L.R. 112).

9.19   Effects of the Human Rights Act 1998

The Human Rights Act 1998 ("HRA") in force from October 1 2000 incorporates many of the substantive rights set out in the European Convention of Human Rights (1949) ("the Convention"), making it possible to rely on those rights in United Kingdom courts. Section 2 of the HRA indicates that United Kingdom courts or tribunals must also take Convention case law, reports and decisions into consideration when determining a question in connection with a Convention right.

Section 6 of the HRA provides that it is "unlawful for a public authority to act in a way that is incompatible with a Convention Right". "Public authority", as defined in section 6(3) ". . . any person whose functions are . . . of a public nature", includes government departments (*Hansard*, H.L., Vol. 583, No. 65, col. 475 (November 18, 1997)). The Director is clearly a government department and the Competition Commission and the sectoral Regulators are within the Convention's definition of "Public Authority".

Those who have been directly or indirectly affected by an act which fails to comply with section 6 can rely upon the HRA: as a cause of action in legal proceedings against a public authority; as a criminal or civil defence; as a new ground for judicial review; as a ground for striking down a local authority's action; to claim "such relief, remedies or other orders as a court considers just and appropriate"; and to obtain a declaration of incompatibility.

The right to a fair hearing (Article 6 of the Convention) and the right to respect private and family life (Article 8) are the Convention rights most likely to be used to curb the Director's, the OFT's and the sector Regulators' powers.

The right to a fair hearing has been used in the past by both individuals and companies who have been compelled to answer questions during investigations and subsequently subjected to penalties (*Saunders v. United Kingdom* (1996) 23 E.H.R.R. 313), and by undertakings who have challenged decisions made by the E.C. Commission against them (*Transocean Marine Paint Association v. Commission*, (Case 17/74) [1974] E.C.R. 1063; [1974] 2 C.M.L.R. 459). Article 6 has also been used to protect the right to remain silent and not incriminate oneself (*Funke v. France*, (1993) 16 E.H.R.R. 297). This Article could also be used against the Director and sector Regulators when investigated parties are not given access to documents or information used as a basis for the Director's or sector Regulator's decisions for reasons of confidentiality (see discussion at 9.16.9).

Prisoners and journalists have invoked the right to respect private and family life against state bodies who have seized private documents and information without consent (*Malone v. United Kingdom* (1984) (1985) 7 E.H.R.R. 14 and *Golder v. United Kingdom* (1979–80) 1 E.H.R.R. 524) and in *Niemetz v. Germany* (1992) 16 E.H.R.R. 97, it was stated that "There appears, furthermore to be no reason of principle why this understanding of the notion of "private life" should be taken to exclude activities of a professional or business nature . . .".

The rights contained in the HRA will almost certainly be used as grounds for judicial review against the Director's and sector Regulators' decisions and for appeals from appeal tribunals' decisions to the Court of Appeal.

Chapter 10

Consequences of Infringing the Chapter I Prohibition

10.1   As Between the Parties to an Agreement
10.2   Liability to Third Parties
10.3   Fines
10.4   Directions to Terminate
10.5   Interim Measures
10.6   Criminal Offences in Course of an Investigation

10.1   As Between the Parties to an Agreement

10.1.1   Principle of Voidness

Any provision in an agreement which causes the agreement to infringe the prohibition of anti-competitive agreements is void (s. 2(4)) unless the agreement benefits from an exemption or exclusion.

10.1.2   Interpretation

The effect of section 60(2) is that this provision must be interpreted in a manner which is consistent with the case law of Article 81(2). This would mean that in accordance with the principles set out in *La Technique Minière v. Machinenbau Ulm GmbH* (Case 56/65) [1966] E.C.R. 235, [1966] C.M.L.R. 357,ECJ only "those elements of an agreement" which infringe the prohibition are void. It has been established that, where an entire clause infringes Article 81 it will be struck out. However, the E.C. case law requires national courts to apply their domestic law in deciding how far an agreement survives the application of Article 81(2).

It is probably correct to assume that the courts are free to apply English, Northern Irish or Scottish law in the same way as if Article 81(2) applied rather than the prohibition and without regard to the express words of section 2(4), which could be read as declaring the whole agreement void. In equivalent Republic of Ireland legislation the position was clarified (s. 4(7) Competition Act 1991) and it is unfortunate that the United Kingdom Government have declined to give similar clarification.

Courts will be bound by findings of fact by the Director when identifying provisions that infringe the prohibitions (see 10.2.7 below).

10.1.3   English Law on Severance

Under English law it has been established by the Court of Appeal in *Chemidus Wavin Ltd v. Société pour la Transformation et L''Exploitation des Résines* [1978] 3 C.M.L.R. 514 (CA) that where an entire clause infringes Article 81 it will be struck out. Buckley LJ said:

"where in a contract there are certain clauses which are annulled by reason of their being in contravention of Article 85(1) [now Article 81(1)] one must look at the contract with those clauses struck out and see what the effect of that is in the light of the domestic law which governs the particular contract . . . It seems to me that, in applying Article 85 to an English contract, one may well have to consider whether, after the excisions required by the Article of the Treaty have been made from the contract, the contract would be said to fail for lack of consideration or on any other grounds, or whether the contract would be so changed in its character as not to be the sort of contract the parties intended to enter into at all."

It is also clear from the judgment given by Goff L.J. in that case that an independent promise supported by consideration and wholly unaffected by the invalidity of other provisions in the agreement will be enforceable even though the promisor has made other promises, supported by the same consideration, which are void, and has included the valid and invalid promises in one document.

This case has been followed in a number of cases arising in relation to Article 81. *Inntrepreneur v. Mason* at first instance and approved by the Court of Appeal [1993] 45 E.G. 130, provides a good example of its application and relates it to the restraint of trade cases arising under English law.

10.1.4   Other Approaches

Difficulties arise where valid obligations are contained alongside invalid obligations in the same clause or where the implementation of a clause entails the performance of acts, some of which infringe and some of which do not. It is possible that the "blue pencil" doctrine of severance contained in some restraint of trade cases may apply, at least in relation to certain types of obligation, *e.g.* non-compete clauses in the sale of a business (*Goldsoll v. Goldman* [1914] 2 Ch 603, *Marshall v. NM Financial Management Limited* [1997] 1 W.L.R. 1527).

Another possible approach is that clauses in breach of the prohibition are "void" only in so far as they infringe the prohibition, but remain enforceable to the extent that obligations imposed under them are not in breach of the competition rules. This approach would not require any words to be struck out but a possible objection is that it could require words to be added; the clause would be applied as if the words "except to the extent prohibited by section 2" were to be implied. Another way of looking at this approach is to say that the only part of the agreement which is "void" under section 2 (4) is the right to enforce a valid clause in a manner which infringes the competition rules. It seems clear, however, that a final order for performance *inter partes* of a term of an agreement in breach of Article 81 (and consequently s. 2) would not be made by a court.

10.1.5   Is There Any Right for One Party to Seek Damages from Another?

Whether there are any circumstances in which a party to an agreement in breach of Article 81 can be liable to the other party in damages arising from that breach of Article 81 (in circumstances where there is no breach of Article 82) is presently before the European Court of Justice: reference in *Inntrepreneur Pub Co v. Langton and another* [2000] 08 E.G. 169. As a matter of English law, the courts have answered this question in the negative and this will be the position as regards both Article 81 and the Chapter I Prohibition unless there is some overriding requirement of E.C. law to provide a remedy. It is unclear whether any such requirement will be accepted as a "question in relation to competition"

for the purposes of creating private rights in any of the United Kingdom jurisdictions (see 10.2.4–10.2.6 below).

10.2   Liability to Third Parties

10.2.1   Principle

The principles and case law which apply to questions arising under Part I of the
Competition Act 1998 must not be inconsistent with the principles and case law
under Articles 81 and 82 of the E.C. Treaty (s. 60(2)). The sort of "question" to
which section 60(2) applies may be limited by the purposive section 60(1) which
talks of "questions arising under this Part [of the Act] in relation to competition".
The better view is that section 60(2) should not be interpreted restrictively, in particular with regard to any provision in Part I of the Act or subsidiary legislation
made under it, which is modelled on E.C. law. A particular difficulty regarding the
rights of third parties is that Part I has no mention of third party rights for breach
of the prohibitions (save for the right to ask the Director to reconsider a decision
under s. 47). The issues for the courts in deciding whether there are any private civil
rights for breach of the prohibitions and, if so, what those rights are, are discussed
further at 10.2.4 below.

10.2.2   Breach of Article 81 or Article 82

The basis for a private right of action in the United Kingdom for a breach of
Articles 81 or 82 is somewhat uncertain. It may be derived purely from the
Community obligation to provide an effective remedy under national law or from
this obligation read as a requirement to provide a remedy equivalent to that under
national law — for which the closest analogy has been the cause of action for breach
of statutory duty created by section 35 RTPA (now repealed). The case law under
Articles 81 and 82 suggests that there should be a right to damages for affected
third parties as well as a right to injunctive relief (see *Garden Cottage Foods v. Milk
Marketing Board* [1984] A.C. 130). At the interlocutory stage the usual principles
in respect of interlocutory injunctions apply (see *American Cyanamid v. Ethicon*
[1975] A.C. 396).

It is not clear how the Community principle (which is one of Community law)
can be used to create a cause of action for third parties in relation to the prohibitions (see 10.2.4–10.2.6 below).

10.2.3   Process

The prohibitions against anti-competitive agreements and abuse of a dominant
position raise issues which can usually only be dealt with at a full trial after discovery. For this reason pleadings based on either of these prohibitions cannot easily be
struck out and the party affected suffers the expense and difficulty of dealing with
a full trial on what may often be a tenuous argument. Even in cases where there is
some substance to competition defences, the process of determining the rights of
the parties and the principles to be applied can be extremely protracted: for example, the various cases involving *Inntrepreneur* form a series that started in 1992 and
is still ongoing (see the references at 10.1.3 and 10.1.5).

Questions of restitution on the break-up of an illegal joint venture and the exact
rights of affected third parties have not been fully worked out under Articles 81 and
82.

10.2.4 What are Third Party Rights Under the Prohibition — Summary

It will require considerable ingenuity on the part of the courts to establish private rights for breach of the Chapter I Prohibition. Clearly a void provision cannot be enforced and the whole agreement may be affected (see 10.1.2 and 10.1.3 above). Whether there is a right of third parties to claim damages is not clarified by the Competition Act. In relation to the application of Articles 81 and 82 of the E.C. Treaty, the ECJ has made it clear that procedural conditions should not be less favourable than those relating to similar actions of a domestic nature. However, as yet, the English courts have to reach a clear decision on the full extent of remedies for breach of Articles 81 or 82. Lord Diplock's approach in *Garden Cottage Foods* (see 10.2.2 above), which equates breach of Articles 81 or 82 of the E.C. Treaty with breach of statutory duty, has general approval, but does not appear to provide a basis for reaching the same conclusion in relation to the Competition Act 1998. The use of section 60 (by a process of "double renvoir") simply takes us back to basic principles under national law. This is because the courts will have to take account of the express requirement in section 60(6)(b) that the decisions of the European Court, with which the United Kingdom courts are to ensure there is no inconsistency (s. 60(2)), include any decision as to the civil liability of an undertaking for harm caused by its infringement of Community law.

10.2.5 Interpretation Issues

There are interpretational difficulties under the Competition Act itself and in relation to the ECJ decisions in deriving a private cause of action in respect of breach of the prohibitions from European jurisprudence:

- Part I does not create any private rights itself and therefore the question of whether there is such a right may not be a question arising under Part I, but under the general law. Further, the question is procedural and not "in relation to competition", if the use of those words in section 60(1) has any limiting effect on the scope of section 60(2);

- Assuming that the courts take a broad view which overcomes these objections, the relevant ECJ cases deal with the constitutional question of the status of Article 81(1) and Article 82 as directly effective Treaty provisions, which are different in kind from the provisions of a United Kingdom statute and do not necessarily give rise to the same consequences (see the discussion in *Competition Law and Practice*, paras 27.08–27.17);

- Finally, the ECJ refers the question of remedies back to national courts (leading to a double *renvoi* to the extent that the United Kingdom courts look at ECJ decisions): for a discussion of *renvoi* see Dicey and Morris, *Conflict of Laws* 13th ed. para. 4–019 and Cook, *Logical and Legal Bases of the Conflict of Laws*, p. 239 (1942)).

In *Rewe v. Hauptzollant Kiel* (Case 158/80), [1981] E.C.R. 1805, [1982] 1 C.M.L.R. 449, the ECJ stated that the Treaty "was not intended to create new remedies in the national courts to ensure the observance of Community law other than those already laid down by national law. On the other hand ... it must be possible for every type of action provided by national law to be available for the purpose of ensuring observance of Community provisions having direct effect, and the same conditions regarding admissibility and procedure as would apply were it a question of ensuring observance of national law"

Although the ECJ cases tell us how to approach remedies for rights which arise in relation to directly effective Treaty provisions which, at least, require the same remedies as for breach of equivalent national law and, at most, the full range of national civil remedies, including damages, they do not tell us anything about the approach to be taken on private remedies for breach of any United Kingdom statute (other than the European Communities Act 1972 to the extent it is itself, from the United Kingdom perspective, the source of Community obligations).

The range of procedures and remedies available between private parties for breach of a United Kingdom statute varies considerably and is determined from a consideration of the individual statute in order to determine legislative intention. In *Cutler v. Wandsworth Stadium Limited*, [1949] A.C. 398, [1949] 1 All E.R. 544, HL a statute found to be intended to benefit the public attending greyhound races gave no private right of action at all (either for an injunction or in damages) to a bookmaker directly affected by its contravention; the purpose of the statute and the criminal penalties that it imposed were considered to exclude a private remedy.

It is possible that breach of a prohibition may constitute in some circumstances an economic tort (*e.g.* a cartel could constitute a conspiracy to interfere with trade by unlawful means). However, the other elements of the tort would have to be present: see *Clerk & Lindsell on Torts*, Sweet & Maxwell, 17th ed. (1995) at 23.80.83 and Fourth Cumulative Supplement (1999) and the cases there cited. The best view to be derived from the cases is that:

- Where the unlawful means alleged constitutes the breach of a statute, then the statute must be construed to identify whether it falls into one of the classes on which a private cause of action can be founded: *Lonrho v. Shell (No.2)* [1982] A.C. 173 (see particularly Lord Diplock at 183G, 185 and 186A–C);

- Statutes give rise to a private right, either where they impose an obligation or prohibition for the benefit of a particular class, or where they create a public right and the particular claimant has suffered special damage peculiar to himself from the interference with the public right;

- The primary purpose of a conspiracy to use unlawful means may be to further or protect legitimate interests (*e.g.* development of a profitable business) but there appears to still be a need to have some intention to injure the claimant, possibly to prevent a multiplicity of actions (*Lonrho v. Fayed* [1992] A.C. 448).

This area of law is ripe for review and also for clarification as to the circumstances in which remedies are limited and when they include a right to claim damages.

Because of the uncertainty, where Parliament wishes to ensure that there is a private remedy, it will normally be specifically provided for in the statute: as in RTPA section 35(2). Certainly, the United Kingdom courts in considering the question of private rights, should have regard to the United Kingdom's financial penalty regime, which is much more severe than that of the E.C. Although this regime was created under section 36 (in Part I of the Act), the penalty regime appears to be recognised as procedural and not constrained by section 60 or by the E.C. model.

A good opportunity has been missed in which Parliament could have clarified the position both under Articles 81 and 82 and under the Chapter I and Chapter II Prohibitions. In the absence of any legislation on the point the courts may be prepared to take notice of *Hansard* in accordance with the principles established in *Pepper v. Hart* [1993] A.C. 593 in determining that there is a private right of action for damages and/or injunctive relief. During the Act's drafting Lord Haskel stated on behalf of the Government:

> ". . . our clear intention in framing this Bill is that third parties may seek injunctions or damages in the courts if they have been adversely affected by the action of undertakings in breach of prohibitions. This is an important element of the regime. There is no need to make explicit provision in the Bill to achieve that result. Third party rights of action under the domestic regime are to be the same as those under Articles 85 and 86." (*Hansard*, H.L., Vol. 583, No. 69, col. 955–956 (November 25, 1997))

10.2.6 Conclusion on Private Rights

It is arguable, that the Act raises no ambiguity which would entitle the courts to refer to *Hansard*. It simply fails to create third party private rights under normal principles of statutory interpretation which are not displaced on this point by s. 60 itself or by European cases, which deal only with the nature of rights created by directly effective Treaty provisions and, in any event, refer the issue of appropriate remedies back to national law.

The *Wandsworth* line of reasoning would not derive private rights from an Act with a comprehensive public enforcement and penalty regime of considerable severity. It is more likely, however, that the courts will find a way to permit third parties a private right for damages and injunctions.

10.2.7 Use of Decisions of the Director and Regulators

There are a number of ways in which third parties may be assisted in any actions they have the right to bring:

(1) Under section 58 final findings of fact by the Director are binding on the parties unless the court directs otherwise, or the Director has decided to take further action in relation to a matter on which he has made a decision in accordance with section 16 (2) (in respect of Chapter I infringements) or section 24 (2) (in respect of Chapter II infringements). Findings will have the status of binding findings, if the time for bringing an appeal in respect of the finding has expired without an appeal being brought or the decision of an appeal tribunal of the Competition Commission has confirmed the finding. The Act does not deal specifically with the case where an appeal tribunal takes a decision which involves new and additional finding of facts, but as the appeals tribunal are entitled to take any decision the Director could have made and its decisions may be enforced in the same manner (Sched. 8, Part 1, para. 3(3)) its findings of fact should be held to be equally binding.

(2) The ability of the Director to disclose material to third parties about a breach is subject to certain safeguards (s. 55). Section 55(3)(b), however, allows disclosure to be "made with a view to the institution of, or

otherwise for the purposes of, civil proceedings brought under or in connection with this Part [Part I]". In context, this may be a reference to proceedings by the Director (*e.g.* to enforce directions) but it may be interpreted to cover disclosure in answer to a discovery order or subpoena in private litigation alleging breach of one or both of the prohibitions. Section 56 expressly requires the Director to exclude sensitive material so far as practicable.

10.3   Fines

10.3.1   Principle

Where the Director has determined that an agreement infringes the prohibition against anti-competitive agreements, he may impose financial penalties on a party to the agreement up to 10 per cent of the party's group turnover (s. 36). He may improve the penalties if he is satisfied that the infringement was committed intentionally or negligently and he is not satisfied that the party acted on a reasonable assumption that it enjoyed immunity by virtue of being a small or medium sized enterprise (see 10.3.8 below). The section leaves the extent of the turnover to be taken into account to be defined by statutory instrument. The Competition Act 1998 (Determination of Turnover for Penalties) Order 2000 (S.I. 2000 No. 309) (the "Penalties Order") provides that the maximum penalty may be calculated by reference to the United Kingdom turnover of the undertaking for up to the three business years preceding the date on which the infringement ended for the purposes of the infringement decision (see 10.3.5 below for the calculation of fines, including in cases where the infringement lasted less than three years). The restriction to United Kingdom turnover is in accord with Government indications as the legislation went through Parliament, but the three year period (which could raise the maximum fine to over 30 per cent of the last year's turnover where turnover is declining) goes beyond any indications at the time and departs from the E.C. precedent. Thinking at both Government and OFT level has been influenced by research of different competition regimes, including those of the European Community and the United States.

It is clear that the highest fines for breach of the Chapter I Prohibition are highly likely to be for participation in secret cartels. The E.C. Commission has imposed some very high fines for this activity (*e.g.* 70 million Euros on ABB for participation in the Pipes cartel: *Pre-Insulated Pipes Cartel* (Case IV/35.691/E-4), [1999] O.J. L024/1 (see Chapter 6, para. 6.8.3). The current record fine under Articles 81 and 82 is on Volkswagen at 90 million Euros (reduced from 104 million Euros on appeal), for operation of a selective distribution system to keep up prices and limit trade between Member States (*VW/Audi* (Case IV/35.733–VW), [1998] O.J. L124/60).

10.3.2   Nature of Penalties

The financial penalties are intended to be civil rather than criminal in nature but it is likely that the procedures adopted for their imposition should be of the same standard as those used in criminal cases in order to comply with the requirements of the Human Rights Act 1998 and the ECHR (see *Société Stenuit v. France*, (1992) 14 E.C.H.R. 509). The English Courts have adopted a similar approach to the classification of penalties imposed under Articles 81 and 82 in the context of privilege against self-incrimination (see judgment of the Court of Appeal and speech of Lord Wilberforce in *Re Westinghouse Electric Corporation Uranium Contract Litigation MDL Docket* 235 [1978] A.C. 547).

10.3.3 Requirement of Intention or Negligence

Under section 36(3) the Director may impose a penalty on an undertaking only if he is satisfied that its infringement has been committed intentionally or negligently. This language follows Council Regulation (EEC) 17/62, Article 15(6). Under E.C. law to establish intention or negligence it is not necessary for there to have been action by, or even knowledge on the part of, the partners or principal managers of the undertaking concerned. E.C. case law establishes that it is enough for there to have been an action by a person who is authorised to act on behalf of the undertaking *Musique Diffusion Francaise SA v. Commission* (Case C–100–103/80), [1983] E.C.R. 1825, [1983] 3 C.M.L.R. 221. This approach will be followed by the Courts if section 60(2) requires them to do so (see discussion at 10.2.5). The Director may have regard to previous Restrictive Practices Court orders and undertakings in lieu in determining whether an infringement of the Chapter I Prohibitions by anti-competitive activities was committed negligently or intentionally (The OFT Guideline, *Enforcement*, OFT 407, March 1999, para. 4.4 (the "Enforcement Guideline"). Parties will not be able to rely on the fact that the Act is new against a finding of intention or negligence (para. 4.5).

Intention

The Enforcement Guideline, para. 4.6 indicates that the following factors will be considered in determining whether an infringement is committed intentionally:

(i)   whether the agreement or conduct has as its object the restriction of competition;

(ii)   whether the undertaking in question is aware that its actions will be, or are reasonably likely to be, restrictive of competition but still wants, or is prepared, to carry them out; or

(iii)   that the undertaking could not have been unaware that its agreement or conduct had as its object the restriction of competition, even if it did not know that it would infringe the Chapter I or Chapter II Prohibitions.

Ignorance or a mistake of law cannot be used to counter a finding of intentional infringement. The Director will have regard to internal documents prepared by an undertaking to determine whether there is intention. If parties deliberately conceal an agreement or practice this will be strong evidence of intention (Enforcement Guideline, paras 4.7–4.8).

Negligence

The Director will probably find that there has been a negligent infringement of the Chapter I or Chapter II Prohibitions where an undertaking knew or ought to have known that its actions would result in an infringement (*United Brands Co and United Brands Continental BV v. Commission*, (Case C-27/76), [1978] E.C.R. 207, paras 298–301, [1978] 1 C.M.L.R. 429). An undertaking cannot rely on the fact that particular conduct has not been previously found to breach the prohibition to escape a finding of negligence (Enforcement Guideline, para. 4.9–4.10).

Involuntary infringement

If an undertaking has participated in an infringement under pressure, the Director has indicated that it can still have acted intentionally or negligently, although in certain circumstances penalty may be reduced *cf. Re Tipp-ex* [1987] O.J. L222/1, [1989] 4 C.M.L.R. 425 (Enforcement Guideline, para. 4.11, The Director's Guidance on Penalties, para. 7.3). Only acts or omissions entirely beyond the control of the undertaking would escape liability for a fine under E.C. law: *Re Deutsche Philips,* [1973] O.J. L293/40, [1973] C.M.L.R. D241. The Director can be expected to take the same approach.

10.3.4 Tax Position

The Inland Revenue has indicated that penalties will not be deductible in calculating trading profits for tax purposes. This is because civil or criminal penalties imposed by or under the authority of, an Act of Parliament are not deductible, but are "losses not connected with or arising out of the trade" and so not deductible by virtue of section 74(1)(e) of the Income and Corporation Taxes Act 1988 (*Commissioners of Inland Revenue v. Alexander Von Glehn & Co Ltd,* [1920] 2 K.B. 553).

10.3.5 Guidance on Level of Penalty

Section 38 requires the Director to publish guidance as to the appropriate amount of any penalty to be imposed for a breach of either the Chapter I or Chapter II Prohibition. He must have regard to this guidance in determining the level of a penalty in any particular case. He may, at any time, alter the guidance but if he does so, he must publish the guidance as altered. No guidance may be published without the approval of the Secretary of State. If the Director is preparing or altering guidance he is under a duty to consult those persons he considers appropriate. If the Director is preparing or altering guidance in connection with a matter where a Regulator has concurrent jurisdiction with him, he must consult the Regulator.

The Director General of Fair Trading's Guidance as to the *Appropriate Amount of a Penalty,* OFT 423 (the "Director's Guidance on Penalties") was published in final form in February 2000. The aims of the penalties policy as set out at para. 2.1 of the Guidance are stated to be to impose financial penalties on infringing undertakings which reflect the seriousness of the infringement and to deter undertakings from engaging in activities which infringe the Act. The deterrent effect is aimed not only at the undertakings subject to the decision, but also at other undertakings which might be considering activities contrary to the Chapter I and II Prohibitions.

The Director's Guidance on Penalties being approved by the Secretary of State and developed in tandem with the Penalties Order, is more authoritative than the earlier Enforcement Guideline and the Director is bound to take account of the Guidance where they differ on the same subject matter.

The five step calculation method for setting financial penalties is set out at paragraph 3.1 of the Director's Guidance on Penalties: -

Step 1 – calculation of the starting point

The starting point for the calculation of any penalty is to apply a rate of up to 10 per cent to the relevant turnover (*i.e.* turnover in relevant product and geographic market — this is not limited to the United Kingdom if the geographic market is wider). The actual percentage rate applied will depend on the seriousness of the infringement and will be set for each undertaking. Seriousness will be judged in all cases by reference to a number of factors, including the nature of the product, the structure of the market, the market share(s) of the undertaking(s) involved in the infringement, entry conditions and the effect on competitors and third parties. The damage to consumers will also be important, whether it is caused directly or indirectly.

The Director has stated in his Guidance on Penalties (para. 4.2) that cartel activities such as price fixing or market sharing, and abuses of dominant position likely to have a serious effect on competition, such as predatory pricing, will be viewed as among the most serious infringements. In these cases the starting point will be at or near 10 per cent of the relevant turnover for each infringing undertaking.

Step 2 – adjustment for duration

This adjustment can be up to 100 per cent for each year or part year of the infringement.

Step 3 – adjustment for other factors

This adjustment has been inserted to ensure that the policy objectives of setting penalties (see para. 2.1 of the Director's Guidance on Penalties) are met. At this point, the Director may take into account the gains made from the infringement in the relevant product and geographic markets and, possibly, elsewhere. The underlying aim appears to be to allow an appropriate uplift so that effective penalties can be imposed on large undertakings even where the infringement in question only took place in a small relevant market and to deter similar conduct by that undertaking or by others. Major bus companies and national chains operating from local premises (shops, public houses) seem particularly at risk from this step.

Step 4 – adjustment for aggravating and mitigating factors

The factors are similar to those taken into account by the E.C. Commission in its Guidelines on the method of setting fines imposed pursuant to Article 15(2) of Regulation No.17 and Article 65(5) of the ECSC Treaty ([1998] O.J. 98/C9/03) and are set out at para. 7.2 and 7.3 of the Director's Guidance on penalties:
Aggravating factors include:

- role of the undertaking as a leader in, or an instigator of, the infringement;

- involvement of directors or senior management;

- retaliatory measures taken against other undertakings aimed at ensuring the continuation of the infringement;

- continuing the infringement after the start of the investigation;

- repeated infringements by the same undertaking or other undertakings in the same group.

Mitigating factors include:

- role of the undertaking, for example, where the undertaking is acting under severe duress or pressure;

- genuine uncertainty as to whether the agreement or conduct constituted an infringement;

- adequate steps having been taken with a view to ensuring compliance with the Act (see the Office of Fair Trading's booklet *How your business can achieve compliance – A guide to achieving compliance with the Competition Act 1998* (OFT 424, August 1999) and the Director's Guidance on Penalties which provides for more information on compliance issues);

- infringements which are committed negligently rather than intentionally;

- co-operation which enables the enforcement process to be concluded more effectively and/or speedily than would otherwise be the case, over and above that expected of any undertaking.

Step 5 – adjustment if the maximum penalty is exceeded

The maximum penalty is set by section 36(8) and further limited by The Penalties Order to 10 per cent of applicable turnover which is capped in two ways:

(1)   First by reference to the maximum period for which turnover is to be calculated (the shorter of a period equal to the length of the infringement and three years, but taking account of applicable turnover for the last three complete business years (Article 2); and

(2)   Second, by the definition of turnover, which is limited to turnover generated in the United Kingdom , that is "amounts derived by the undertaking from the sale of products and the provision of services falling within the undertaking's ordinary activities to undertakings or consumers in the United Kingdom after deduction of sales rebates, value added tax and other taxes directly related to turnover". Aid granted by a public body (*e.g.* a government grant) directly linked to and reflected in the price of goods or services will be counted as turnover (Penalties Order, Sched. para. 8). Special rules for calculating turnover for credit institutions, financial institutions and insurance undertakings are set out in the Schedule at paras 5 and 6.

Paragraph 4 provides for the turnover of an association of undertakings to be the aggregate of the turnover of its members. This would seem capable in practice, of more than doubling the fine, where an association has led an infringement but members are also individually implicated. There is no requirement to adjust for this double jeopardy. Account must be taken of any fine imposed by the European Commission or by a court or body in another Member State in respect of the same agreement or conduct (s. 38(9)). It is not at all clear how this adjustment will be made, either by arithmetical reduction by exclusion of turnover in the other fining jurisdiction from the starting point, or some other proportional reduction.

10.3.6   Compliance Programmes

One of the factors in determining whether there are any mitigating circumstances the Director will take into account is the existence of a compliance policy which has been actively implemented.

The booklet *How your business can achieve compliance — A guide to achieving compliance with the Competition Act 1998* (OFT 424, August 1999) sets out four features any compliance programme must have to be effective:

(1)   Support of senior management;

(2)   Appropriate policy and procedures;

(3)   Training; and

(4)   Evaluation.

The support given by senior management should be visible, active and regularly reinforced. Any such policy must consist of an overall commitment to comply with the Act and should place a duty on all employees and directors to comply with the policy, enforceable by disciplinary action. Employees should have mechanisms for seeking advice on the application of the act to particular activities and to report suspected infringements. Training should be given on an on-going basis and the effectiveness of the whole scheme regularly evaluated. Policies that fall short in any of these respects are unlikely to be given the same weight as mitigating factors. The Director is looking for programmes that create a culture of compliance and punish non-compliant behaviour.

10.3.7   Whistleblowers

The Director originally announced an intention to follow a policy similar to that of the E.C. Commission (Enforcement Guideline, para. 4.39). The Director's thinking has moved on and the E.C. Commission's policy is now of little more than comparative interest.

The E.C. Commission's Notice on *The non-imposition or reduction of fines in cartel cases* [1996] O.J. C207/4, sets out the conditions which an undertaking cooperating with the E.C. Commission during investigation of a secret cartel must meet to benefit from an exemption from or reduction of fines.

The policy actually adopted in the Director's Guidance on Penalties has, however, been heavily influenced by the United States' Department of Justice's corporate leniency policy. This policy with its clarity and certainty of entry to the leniency programme (*i.e.* at the point the undertaking comes forward, rather than the date of the decision) has been extremely effective. The Department of Justice has had on average two whistleblowing businesses coming forward each month, whereas whistleblowing is quite rare under the E.C. regime, because the E.C. Commission gives no certainty of benefit until it reaches its final decision (although the E.C. Commission recognises that the existence of its policy will raise legitimate expectation of leniency).

In common with other policies, the Director's policy relates only to cartel practices, *i.e.* agreements, decisions by associations of undertakings or concerted practices involving price fixing, bid rigging (collusive tendering), the establishment of output restrictions or quotas and/or market sharing or market dividing practices (footnotes 6 and 13), based on the OECD definition of "hard core cartels"). At para. 9.2 the Director states that it is the secret nature of such cartels and the interests of the United Kingdom economy, customers and consumers which justify the policy and outweigh the policy objective of penalising infringing parties in these cases.

The Director's policy (like that of the Department of Justice) gives total immunity for the first to come forward before an investigation has commenced (Director's Guidance on Penalties, para. 9.3.2). The Director also has discretion to give total immunity for the first to come forward after an investigation has started, but before the Director has given written notice of his intention to take an infringement decision (para. 9.3.4), if no undertaking has come forward earlier. Undertakings who are the first must comply strictly with conditions as to co-operation and future behaviour set out at para. 9.3.2, and cannot benefit if they were the ring leader of a cartel or forced others to participate.

The E.C. policy is much less lenient, particularly where its investigation has started, where the maximum reduction would be 50–75 per cent, even for the first to come forward.

The Director's policy allows a reduction of up to 50 per cent for others who come forward after the first, and before he has given written notice of his intention to take an infringement decision (para. 9.4.1). Again, there are conditions as to co-operation and future behaviour. In addition, if any undertaking involved in an investigation of a cartel comes forward with evidence of a second cartel, this will provide an additional reduction in penalty in relation to the first cartel (as well as benefiting them in relation to the second cartel) (para. 9.6).

Undertakings seeking favourable treatment must come forward and ask for it (para. 9.5) and the Director will endeavour to protect the identity of whistleblowing undertakings (para. 9.7). This may not always be possible, since other parties are entitled to see evidence relied on by the Director as the basis of his decision (see Chapter 9, para. 9.7.2).

Reductions under the leniency policy are applied after the penalty has been calculated for the whistleblowing enterprise in accordance with the five step process described above (para. 8.2). Co-operation by parties not granted favourable treatment, or in cases where the policy does not apply (agreements not in the nature of secret cartels and the Chapter II Prohibition) will be taken account of at step four in the five step process. Co-operation in these circumstances — *e.g.* in relation to a long running infringement — might not reduce the penalty below the maximum.

Draft leniency letters for full and partial leniency have been published by the OFT (May 2000). These set out the obligation on parties entering the leniency programme in a form intended to be legally binding.

10.3.8   Small and Medium Size Enterprises ("SMEs")

Parties to a "small agreement" are immune from penalties (s. 39) under certain circumstances although the Director can remove this immunity (see 10.3.9). This is intended to ensure that SMEs are not unduly burdened by the operation of the prohibition against anti-competitive agreements. This is only an immunity from fines, however, and the Director may take action to halt an infringement. The position of third parties is the same as in relation to breaches of the prohibition by larger businesses.

A "small agreement" is defined in section 39 as an agreement which meets the following conditions:

- The parties fall below certain thresholds based on their turnover or market share; and

- The agreement is not a price fixing agreement.

In accordance with Government indications (*Hansard*, H.L., col. 434 (November 17, 1997)) the threshold has been set based purely on turnover and is at the lower end of the Government's stated range of £20 million to £50 million. The Competition Act 1998 (Small Agreements and Conduct of Minor Significance) Regulations 2000 (S.I. 2000 No. 262) Article 3 defines the category of "small agreements" as "all agreements between undertakings, the combined applicable turnover of which for the business year ending in the calendar year preceding one during which the infringement occurred does not exceed £20 million", The Regulations provide for calculation of turnover on a similar basis to that used to ascertain the maximum penalty (Step 5, see 10.3.5 above) except that worldwide turnover is taken into account.

A price fixing agreement is defined for this purpose as an agreement which has as its object or effect, or one of its objects or effects, to restrict the freedom of a party to the agreement to determine the price to be charged (otherwise than as between that party and another party to the agreement) for the product, service or other matter to which the agreement relates (s. 39(9)).

The legislation does not address specifically how "small agreements", which cease to be exempt because of changes in the combined turnover of parties, will be dealt with. It is therefore important at the time of any acquisition of a company or business by a large company for it to identify any agreements for which immunity will be lost and take any necessary steps to protect the on-going position (*e.g.* by amendment or filing under Chapter I).

An undertaking would be immune from fines if the Director is satisfied that the undertaking acted on the reasonable assumption that the rules on SMEs gave it immunity (s. 36(4)).

10.3.9   Withdrawal of Immunity from Small Agreement

The Director may withdraw immunity if, following an investigation, or preliminary investigation (s. 39(4)) he considers that the small agreement is likely to infringe the prohibition against anti-competitive agreements.

If the Director decides to withdraw immunity he must give an affected party written notice of that decision. A decision to withdraw immunity takes effect on such date as is specified in the decision of the Director and the withdrawal date must be a date after the date on which the decision is made. In determining the withdrawal date the Director may take into account the amount of time which the parties are likely to require in order to secure that there is no infringement of the Chapter I Prohibition with respect to the agreement.

10.3.10   Agreements Notified to the European Commission

Where an agreement has been notified to the European Commission for the purpose of seeking an exemption under Article 81 of the E.C. Treaty the Director may not penalise a party for a breach of the Chapter I Prohibition (s. 41). This immunity should cover any infringement occurring after the date of notification and before the European Commission determines the matter by a formal decision or informal comfort letter. Notifying an agreement to the European Commission does not, however, prevent the Director from investigating the agreement (s. 41(4)) and taking other enforcement measures.

Where the E.C. Commission grants an individual exemption for an agreement, that agreement will be granted an automatic exemption from the Chapter I Prohibition by virtue of a parallel exemption under section 10. Although the Director cannot withdraw an Article 81 exemption (except under the Vertical Agreements Block Exemption Commission Regulation (E.C.) No. 2790/1999, [1999] O.J. L336/21, Article 7), he can terminate a parallel exemption (Procedural Rules, r. 21).

If the E.C. Commission withdraws the benefit of provisional immunity from penalties on the grounds that, after a preliminary examination, it is of the opinion that Article 81(1) of the E.C. Treaty applies and the application of Article 81(3) is not justified (Article 15(6) of Commission Regulation (EEC) No. 17/62), then immunity from penalties for a breach of the Chapter I Prohibition ceases to apply as from the date of withdrawal.

10.3.11   Agreements Notified to the OFT

Once an agreement is notified to the Director for guidance or a decision, it will have a provisional immunity from fines in respect of any infringement occurring in the period between the date of notification and the date specified in a notice given in writing to the applicant by the Director on determination of the application (s. 13 and s. 14). The date specified in the notice cannot precede the date on which the notice is given.

An application for early guidance made before March 1, 2000 has the same effect as an application for guidance made after that date and provides the applicant with immunity from penalties from the date the Act came into force.

10.3.12   Provisional Decision

If after the preliminary investigation of an application for guidance or a decision the Director decides that it is likely that the agreement would infringe the Chapter I Prohibition and that it would not be appropriate to grant the agreement an individual exemption he may make a preliminary decision to that effect (Sched. 5, para. 3). If he makes such a preliminary decision an applicant will lose the immunity from penalties normally applicable from the date of notification of the agreement. The retrospective loss of immunity is intended to discourage notification of any agreements that obviously infringe and have no hope of exemption, simply to enable the agreement to be carried on without fear of penalty. Notification does not give protection from penalties for conduct in breach of the Chapter II Prohibition.

10.3.13   Immunity after Decision or Guidance

Where the Director has made a decision that an agreement does not infringe the Chapter I Prohibition or is exempt from the Chapter I Prohibition or given guidance that an agreement is unlikely to infringe the Chapter I Prohibition then, except in limited circumstances, no penalty can be imposed (s. 15 and s. 16). There is a similar immunity from penalty in respect of the Chapter II Prohibition after the Director has given guidance that the conduct is unlikely to infringe the Chapter II Prohibition or has made a decision that the conduct has not infringed it (see Chapter 14, para. 14.2.4). This immunity from penalties in respect of the Chapter I and Chapter II Prohibitions can be removed by the Director if:

(i)   he has reasonable grounds for believing that there has been a material change of circumstances since he gave guidance or a decision;

(ii)   he has a reasonable suspicion that the information on which he based his guidance or decision was incomplete, false or misleading in a material particular; or

(iii)   in the case of guidance the matter is reopened when one of the parties to an agreement applies to him for a decision or a complaint is received from a third party.

Where the Director has a reasonable suspicion that information on which he based his guidance or decision provided to him by a party to the agreement was incomplete, false or misleading in a material particular, the date specified in the notice may be earlier than the date on which the notice is given.

10.3.14 Who Has to Pay?

In Chapter I proceedings the Director can require any undertaking which is party to an infringing agreement to pay a penalty. In accordance with section 60, the Director will follow E.C. law on the meaning of the term "undertaking". Consequently any natural or legal person carrying on commercial or economic activities, whatsoever its legal status, is an undertaking (*Höfner and Elser v. Macroton* (Case C-41/90), [1991] E.C.R. 1979, [1993] 4 C.M.L.R. 306). A parent and subsidiary company are regarded as one undertaking as long as the subsidiary has no economic independence. In determining liability for payment of a penalty, the Director will have regard to the responsibility of the parent and subsidiary for the infringement. Where a penalty is imposed on both parent and subsidiary it may be imposed jointly and severally (see Chapter 6, para. 6.3.2 for a fuller discussion of the concept of an undertaking).

Where an infringing undertaking is taken over by a company a penalty can be imposed on that company, since it may have benefited from the infringement *The Sugar cartel: Suiker Unie v. Commission* (Cases C-40-48, 50, 54-56, 111, 113-114 [1975] E.C.R. 1663, [1976] 1 C.M.L.R. 295). Moreover where an undertaking changes its legal identity this will not prevent it or its component parts from being penalised. The Director will as far as possible try to establish which body is responsible for an infringement (*cf*. the E.C. approach in *Welded Steel Mesh*, O.J. L260/1, [1991] 4 C.M.L.R. 13). Consequently where an infringing undertaking is transferred from one undertaking to another, the transferor will not necessarily escape penalty. If the original undertaking has ceased to exist by the time a penalty is imposed, the successor undertaking may be penalised.

If a trade association has infringed the Chapter I Prohibitions, then it, its members or both may be penalised.

10.3.15 Appeals

An undertaking can bring an appeal to an appeal tribunal of the Competition Commission in relation to both the decision to impose a penalty and the decision as to the amount of the penalty. Third parties cannot appeal a decision on penalties (s. 47(1) in relation to s. 46(3)). An appeal must be brought within two months of the date on which the Director's decision was notified to the appellant. (The Competition Commission Appeal Tribunal Rules 2000 (S.I. 2000 No. 261), Rule 6(2)).

Where an appeal has been made to the appeal tribunal in respect of the imposition or amount of a penalty, the penalty will be suspended until the appeal is determined. The infringement decision will still have effect. The appeal tribunal can impose, revoke or vary the amount of a penalty (Sched. 8, para. 3).

Further appeals may be made to appellate courts on points of law (s. 49). Those courts' own procedures would determine whether there was a stay on any penalty confirmed or set by the Competition Commission.

The Competition Commission Rules, r. 27 provides that interest may be awarded to be payable as from the date of appeal (or later) on any penalty which the Competition Commission confirms, varies or imposes. It will form part of the penalty and be recoverable in the same way.

10.3.16 Payment and Enforcement of Penalty Decision

When imposing a penalty the Director must serve a written notice on the undertaking required to pay the penalty, specifying the date before which the penalty must be paid. The date for payment must not be before the deadline for bringing an appeal against the notice.

Where an undertaking has not paid a penalty by the due date and it has brought no appeal against the penalty notice within the time permitted or such an appeal has been made and determined, the Director can bring proceedings to recover the required amount as a civil debt (s. 37).

Section 36 contemplates payment of a penalty in a single lump sum, but the Director would have discretion to agree payment by instalments rather than take proceedings if he considered this an appropriate course. The court could order payment by instalments and provide for interest in the same way as in any civil debt action (Civil Procedure Rules, r. 40.11).

10.4 Directions to Terminate

10.4.1 Principle

Where the Director has made a decision that an agreement infringes the prohibition against anti-competitive agreements, he is entitled to give directions to such person or persons as he considers appropriate to bring the infringement to an end (s. 32). He is not limited to giving directions to the infringing parties. He can for example, address them to parent companies where the infringing party is a subsidiary of that parent. A direction, which must be given in writing, may require an undertaking to modify or terminate the agreement or conduct in question. In addition directions may require infringing parties to inform third parties that an infringement has come to an end and to report regularly to the Director on issues such as the price charged. They will be published on the register held at the OFT and on the Internet.

Where the Director makes an infringement decision he has indicated (Enforcement Guideline, para. 2.4) that directions are likely to form part of the decision where the directions and decision are addressed to the same person(s).

10.4.2 Appeals

Directions can be appealed to an appeal tribunal of the Competition Commission (s. 46(3)), although this will not suspend the effect of a direction. The appeal tribunal may issue an interim order suspending the effect of the direction (Competition Commission Rules, r. 32).

10.4.3 Enforcement

Where a person fails to comply with the Director's written direction, the Director may apply to the court for an order compelling the person to rectify his default within a specified time (s. 34). If the Director makes such an application, the court may order that costs be borne by the person in default or any officer of the undertaking who is responsible for the default.

If the direction relates to something to be done in the management or administration of the undertaking, the order can require the undertaking or its officers to comply with it. A breach of a court order may be punishable as a contempt of court, the sanction for which may be a fine or imprisonment.

10.4.4 Breach of an Exemption Condition or Obligation

Where a party to an agreement, which is subject to an individual exemption, breaches any condition of the exemption, the exemption will be automatically cancelled. If a party fails to comply with an obligation the Director may cancel the exemption, vary or remove any condition or obligation and impose one or more additional conditions or obligations (see Chapter 8, paras 8.2.11 and 8.2.12).

10.5 Interim Measures

10.5.1 Principle

In order to cut short any harm before the Director can take a decision, the Director may under section 35, pending completion of his investigation, impose interim measures on an undertaking where:

(i) he has a reasonable suspicion that there has been an infringement of the prohibition against anti-competitive agreements (or the Chapter II Prohibition); and

(ii) he considers it necessary as a matter of urgency to act in order to:

— prevent serious irreparable damage to a particular person or category of persons; or

— to protect the public interest.

10.5.2 Reasonable Suspicion

The Enforcement Guideline para. 3.4 indicates that information which may constitute reasonable suspicion will include:

— Copies of secret agreements provided by disaffected members of a cartel;

— Statements from employees or ex-employees; and

— Complaints providing evidence of an infringement.

10.5.3 Serious Irreparable Damage

It may be necessary to act urgently to prevent serious irreparable harm to third parties where, for example, a small competitor is being forced out of business or is suffering a significant competitive disadvantage. Damage to a business which was the victim of a collective boycott justified one of the rare instances of interim action under the RTPA (*Re Institute of Independent Insurance Brokers* [1991] I.C.R. 822). The Director could be expected to use these powers in similar circumstances.

10.5.4 Protection of the Public Interest

The Director may also take interim measures when he considers that it is necessary to act in order to "protect the public interest". This is on the face of it wider in scope than the equivalent requirement laid down by the ECJ that there must be "a serious risk of irreparable harm to the public interest" (*Camera Care v. Commission*

(Case C–729/79R), [1980] E.C.R. 119, [1980] 1 C.M.L.R. 334). In the United Kingdom context this language could allow wide ranging considerations to be taken into account. It is, however, difficult to see why the Director would wish to act when there was no serious damage to any person or category of persons, and this limb seems likely to see little independent use: perhaps in the case of a blatant abuse by industry leaders where affected third parties would be adequately compensated by damages and would therefore not suffer irreparable harm. The example given by the Director is damage to an industry as a whole (Enforcement Guideline, para. 3.6), but the sort of circumstances he has in mind are not clear. Perhaps this limb could be relied on in a case when consumers would suffer damage indirectly which would be individually trivial but in its totality significantly damaging to their interests, or to the local or national economy.

The Director can issue such interim measures as he believes appropriate. These might include issuing measures requiring the person concerned to suspend or modify the operation of the agreement in question. Once an interim measures direction has been issued it will last as long as the Director has a reasonable suspicion that there has been an infringement of the Chapter I or Chapter II Prohibition and until his investigation is complete. There is no requirement, as there is under E.C. law, that any measures ordered must be temporary and conservatory and not exceed what is necessary in a given situation. However, if the Director makes interim orders of greater effect, it seems likely that the appellate process will, in due course, result in his adopting an approach which recognises these principles. Whether this will be in consequence of their recognition as "higher principles" to which section 60 applies, or because the appeal tribunal's or the court's own procedures will instinctively lead them to require a conservatory approach by the Director in relation to measures taken before a full examination of the facts. The interim measures directions will be published on a register maintained by the OFT and on the Internet. The Director may also publish the interim measures directions in an appropriate trade journal.

10.5.5 Appeals

A decision to impose interim measures will be appealable to an appeal tribunal of the Competition Commission (s. 46). The making of an appeal does not suspend the effect the decision to which the appeal relates, but the Competition Commission itself may give interim relief which could suspend or vary the Director's decision to impose interim measures (Competition Commission Rules, r. 32).

10.5.6 Enforcement

An interim measures direction can be enforced by the Director in the same way as a direction to terminate (see 10.4.3 above).

10.5.7 Future Rights

There is concern that once an interim measures decision has been taken by the Director there will be delay in reaching a formal decision. It is, however, intended that parties will be able to apply to the court for an order that there is no undue delay by the Director in determining applications for decisions (Sched. 6, para. 7). The Government has indicated that this right will not become available until such time after the Act comes into force, when the system has "bedded down".

10.6   Criminal Offences in Course of an Investigation

10.6.1   Range of Offences

The Act at sections 42, 43, 44 and 65 creates various offences which may arise if the investigatory process (or an investigation carried out by or on behalf of the E.C. Commission) is obstructed in a variety of ways, such as destruction of documents, giving of false or misleading information, or failure to answer certain questions. These offences are directly related to the investigatory powers of the Director and are described at Chapter 9, para. 9.8.1. Section 67 deals with similar offences relating to the new investigative regime under the Fair Trading Act 1973 established by section 66 and related to suspected monopoly situations.

10.6.2   Application to Individuals

These criminal offences can be committed by individuals that are not undertakings, such as directors, employees or agents of undertakings at whose premises an investigation is being carried out or to whom questions are addressed in the course of an investigation. In the case of an investigation at private premises, occupants not engaged in the business at all could be implicated (*e.g.* if they obstructed authorised entry). Undertakings may be liable, *e.g.* for a decision by a board of directors to deny entry or destroy documents.

10.6.3   Level of Penalties

On summary conviction a fine of up to the statutory maximum (currently £5,000, s. 32(9) Magistrate's Court Act 1980) may be imposed and on conviction on indictment an unlimited fine may be imposed. Individuals may be imprisoned for up to two years, even if also fined, except in the cases to which section 42(6) or section 67(7) apply.

Chapter 11

Prohibition of Abuse of Dominant Position

11.1   Outline of the Prohibition
11.2   Interpretation of the Chapter II Prohibition
11.3   The Relevant Market
11.4   Dominance
11.5   Abuse of a Dominant Position
11.6   Effects on Trade within the United Kingdom
11.7   Limited Immunities
11.8   Notification
11.9   Consequences of Infringement

11.1   Outline of the Prohibition

11.1.1   Introduction

Section 18 of the Competition Act 1998 prohibits anti-competitive behaviour by dominant undertakings. It is closely based on Article 82 (formerly Article 86) of the E.C. Treaty.

The aim of the provision is to control the conduct of undertakings which are monopolists or are otherwise unconstrained by competition in a market and as a result are able, for example, to increase prices or restrict choice to the detriment of consumers. It is not directed at preventing undertakings achieving or legitimately maintaining a dominant position but rather preventing the adverse effects arising from the abusive exploitation of the market power arising from that dominant position.

Like the Chapter I Prohibition on anti-competitive agreements, the prohibition is effects based, or judged by results. However, unlike the Chapter I Prohibition (which relates to agreements and similar forms of joint conduct), this provision can apply to the conduct of a single dominant undertaking as well as that of several undertakings which are jointly dominant. Abuse of a dominant position is prohibited if it affects trade within the United Kingdom

Section 17 of the Competition Act 1998 repeals sections 2–10 of the Competition Act 1980 which had previously dealt with the control of anti-competitive practices.

11.1.2   The Prohibition

Section 18(1) of the Competition Act 1998 states that:

> ". . . any conduct on the part of one or more undertakings which amounts to the abuse of a dominant position in a market is prohibited if it may affect trade within the United Kingdom."

It is known in the Act as the "Chapter II Prohibition" (s. 18(4)). To contravene the prohibition an undertaking must be dominant and abuse that dominance.

Limited exclusions are provided by sections 19 (see Chapter 12).

Section 18(2) sets out a non-exhaustive list of types of conduct which may constitute an abuse of a dominant position (this list also mirrors Article 82 (formerly Article (86)).

These are as follows:

(a)   directly or indirectly imposing unfair purchase or selling prices or other unfair trading conditions;

(b)   limiting production, markets or technical development to the prejudice of consumers;

(c)   applying dissimilar conditions to equivalent transactions with other trading parties, thereby placing them at a competitive disadvantage; and

(d)   making the conclusion of contracts subject to acceptance by the other parties of supplementary obligations which, by their nature or according to their commercial usage, have no connection with the subject of the contracts.

11.1.3   Differences from Article 82

The principal difference between the Chapter II Prohibition and Article 82 is that Article 82 prohibits the abuse of a dominant position:

(1)   within the common market or a substantial part of it;

(2)   which affects trade between the Member States.

By contrast the Chapter II Prohibition applies to conduct which affects trade within the United Kingdom

Section 18(3) defines "dominant position" as being a dominant position within the United Kingdom (being England, Wales, Scotland and subsidiary islands but not the Isle of Man or the Channel Islands, and Northern Ireland). The United Kingdom is also defined to include any part of the United Kingdom As a result, the existence of dominance and the effects of the abuse of dominance are to be assessed by reference either to the United Kingdom as a whole or any part of the United Kingdom The Chapter II Prohibition may therefore apply to conduct which may not be prohibited by Article 82 since it may relate to a small geographical area within the United Kingdom This is discussed in para. 11.3.4 below. Conversely, the Chapter II Prohibition will not apply where dominance arises or abuse has effects entirely outside the United Kingdom (see Chapter 6, para. 6.6.3); Article 82 may apply in such circumstances.

However, where conduct by an undertaking dominant within the United Kingdom (or a part of it) affects the pattern of exports from the United Kingdom, it may be considered to affect trade within the United Kingdom *e.g.* in cases where a dominant shipping line manipulates berthing slots to the disadvantage of a competitor (*cf. B & I Line Plc v. Sealink Harbours Ltd* (Case IV/34.174)[1992] 5 C.M.L.R. 255) following the line of cases considering exports from the Community to third countries (*e.g. Transocean Marine Paint Association v. Commission,* (Case C–17/74) [1974] E.C.R. 1063; [1974] 2 C.M.L.R. 459 based on Article 81).

11.1.4   Exclusions

Section 19 of the Act provides for certain exclusions from the Chapter II Prohibition which are discussed in more detail in Chapter 12. The Act also provides for limited immunities discussed in 11.7 below. Unlike the Chapter I Prohibition there are no exemptions from the Chapter II Prohibition, in the same way as there are no exemptions from Article 82.

11.2   Interpretation of the Chapter II Prohibition

11.2.1   Interpretation Consistent with Community Law

It is intended that the Chapter II Prohibition will be interpreted in a way which is consistent with the interpretation of Article 82 (see Chapter 5). In drafting the legislation, it was therefore important that its wording closely follow Article 82.

11.2.2 Undertakings

The European Court has held that Article 82 should, where it uses the same language, be interpreted in the same way as Article 81. "Undertaking" for the purposes of the Chapter II Prohibition will be defined in the same way as Article 81. That is as a single economic entity regardless of legal structure (see Chapter 6 at 6.3).

The Chapter II Prohibition also applies to the Crown (s. 73). Given the wording of the Chapter II Prohibition this will only arise where the Crown is pursuing a commercial activity in respect of which it can properly be regarded as an "undertaking". There are a number of Government departments that have such functions: *e.g.* Ordnance Survey, the National Mapping Agency of Great Britain, forms part of the Department of Transport, Environment and the Regions and is established as a separate trading unit required to operate profitably. It produces and sells a wide range of maps and books (The Ordnance Survey Trading Fund Order 1999 (S.I. 1999 No. 965) made under The Government Trade Funds Act 1973 as supplemented by The Government Trade Act 1990). This type of Government activity is likely to be regarded as the activity of an undertaking. Factual considerations should determine whether any of the varied economic activities of the Crown, which is a single legal person, constitute a separate undertaking for the purposes of the prohibitions.

11.2.3   Dominance

In *United Brands v. Commission* (Case 27/76) [1978] E.C.R. 207, [1978] 1 C.M.L.R. 429, ECJ, at para. 65 the ECJ held that the dominant position referred to in Article 82:

> "relates to a position of economic strength enjoyed by an undertaking which enables it to prevent effective competition being maintained on the relevant market by giving it the power to behave to an appreciable extent independently of its competitors, customers and ultimately of its consumers".

This passage is quoted in the OFT Guideline, *The Chapter II Prohibition* OFT 402, March 1999 (the "Chapter II Guideline") at para. 3.10.

The existence of dominance must be assessed by reference to the operation of competitive forces in a market. It is therefore important to define the relevant market as a step in ascertaining whether dominance exists.

The definition of the market is discussed in 11.3 below. In 11.4 dominance is considered in more detail.

11.2.4   Abuse of Dominance

The list of possible abuses of dominance in section 18(2) of the Act is not exhaustive. Abuse is discussed in more detail in 11.5 below.

11.3   The Relevant Market

11.3.1   Introduction

Market definition involves the economic analysis of a range of facts. The E.C. Commission's Notice on Market Definition ([1997] O.J. C372/03) (the "EC Market Definition Notice") states that market definition is a tool to identify the boundaries of competition between firms and thereby identify the competitive constraints faced by undertakings in that market. It enables competitors to be identified and market shares to be calculated. Since market definition is a step in assessing dominance, the wider the market is defined, the less likely that dominance will be found to exist. A market will be defined principally by reference to a product and the geographical area in which that product is bought and sold. The OFT in its Guideline, *Market Definition*, OFT 403, March 1999 (the "OFT Market Definition Guideline") para. 1.3 adopts the same approach to market definition as the Commission Notice. The Guideline points out that market definition is not mechanical but rather a step in the process of assessing whether an undertaking has market power. This is important since the process of precise market definition may be hampered by the lack of evidence in many cases.

Since market definition depends entirely on the particular facts and circumstances at a particular time, findings as to market definition in previous cases can at best only serve as a useful guide. In *The Coca-Cola Company v. Commission (*Cases T–125/97 and T–127/97) [2000] All E.R. (E.C.) 460 at para. 82, the CFI made this clear, saying:

> "Moreover, in the course of any decision applying Article [82] of the Treaty the Commission must define the relevant market again and make a fresh analysis of the conditions of competition which will not necessarily be based on the same considerations as those underlying the previous finding of a dominant position".

11.3.2   Product Market

E.C. Regulations dealing with Articles 81 and 82 and the regulation of mergers define relevant product markets as follows:

> "A relevant product market comprises all those products and/or services which are regarded as interchangeable or substitutable by the consumer, by reason of the products' characteristics, their prices and their intended use". (Section 6 of Form A/B with respect to Regulation (EEC) No. 17/62 and section 6 of Form CO with respect to Regulation (EEC) 4064/89).

Consistently with this definition, the E.C. Market Definition Notice and the OFT

Market Definition Guideline both adopt a similar approach to product market definition. Both focus primarily on identifying those products which, from the perspective of the customer, are substitutable (the demand side) and which are thereby in the same product market. Another factor considered is supply-side substitution. This arises where suppliers not present in a market can, in response to price increases in that market, fairly easily and rapidly produce goods or services which are substitutable from the perspective of the customer for goods or services in that market.

The factors taken account of in determining the relevant product market are discussed below together with the evidence which may need to be considered in each instance.

(1) **Demand Substitution**

In *Hoffman-La Roche v. Commission* (Case 85/76) [1979] E.C.R. 461 [1979] 3 C.M.L.R. 211, the ECJ stated that for goods to be in the same market, there must be a sufficient degree of interchangeability between those goods insofar as the use of those goods is concerned. In that case, the ECJ held that different types of vitamins were in separate markets since for some consumers they were not substitutes for one another. However, substitutes need not be identical products at similar prices. Substitution may take place where products, although different in nature, perform the same function, or where large differences in price simply reflect differences in quality.

(2) **Cross Elasticity of Demand**

The more readily consumers will switch from product A to product B in the face of increases in the price or the reduced availability, of product A (*i.e.* the more elastic the demand) the more likely that these products form part of the same market. For example, in *Eurofix Ltd v. Hilti AG* (E.C. Commission Decision 88/138) [1988] O.J. L65/19, [1989] 4 C.M.L.R. 677 and *Hilti AG v. Commission* (C-53/92 P) [1994] E.C.R. I–677, [1994] 4 C.M.L.R. 614, the E.C. Commission found that nails for Hilti nail guns formed a separate market and did not form part of a market for fixing systems. This was due to the different characteristics of nail gun systems and a low elasticity of demand for nail gun fixings. Nail gun fixings, which were used in a nail gun system, were a minor cost compared with total construction costs, so that consumers were likely to continue to pay for the benefits of the nail gun system in the face of significant price increases.

In the E.C. Market Definition Notice, the E.C. Commission postulates a test for market definition. That is, starting with the products of the undertaking in question, whether consumers would switch to readily available substitute products in response to a hypothetical small (5 per cent to 10 per cent) but permanent price increase of the product in question. If substitution would be enough to make the price increase unprofitable because of a resulting loss of sales, additional substitute products are included in the relevant market until, it is possible to make small but permanent increases in prices profitably. The same approach is adopted in the OFT Market Definition Guideline, para. 3.2 and it is similar to that used by the United States Department of Justice. The OFT Market Definition Guideline, para. 3.5 also notes that although the situation may vary from case to case, generally if substitution takes longer than one year, such substitute products would not be included in the same market.

A difficulty with the test is that it pre-supposes that the price to which the 5 per cent to 10 per cent increase is applied is the competitive price. It will often be difficult to ascertain the competitive price and current prices may not be truly competitive if there is a dominant undertaking in the market. In this regard, the OFT Market Definition Guideline, paras 3.2 & 3.6 notes that market definition cannot be undertaken in isolation but only in conjunction with other evidence useful in assessing dominance (this is discussed in 11.4 below). The OFT also makes it clear that it will treat the 5 per cent to 10 per cent test as a rough guide rather than a rule (Market Definition Guideline, para. 3.2).

The OFT Market Definition Guideline also states that relevant evidence on demand substitution will include the following: interviews with competitors and customers as to how they would react to a hypothetical price rise; details of the costs of switching between products (the higher the cost, the less likely a customer will switch); any other obstacles to switching; information as to customer preferences; historical data as to the effect of price changes on customer demand and evidence of price elasticities.

(3) **Supply-side Substitutability**
Substitution can take place by suppliers, if one supplier can easily convert its production to manufacture products (or re-arrange resources to provide services) which are substitutable from the consumer's point of view. As the E.C. Market Definition Notice states, suppliers must be able to switch production to the relevant products and market them in the short term (the OFT Market Definition Guideline at para. 3.15 uses one year as a rule of thumb) without significant additional costs or risks (in production, distribution or marketing) in response to a small, but permanent change in the price of the relevant products. In effect, such suppliers represent potential competitors which operate as a constraint on the existing suppliers within the market. Existing suppliers are limited in their ability to increase prices since, if they do so, new suppliers would enter the market and through competition reduce price. In *Nederlandsche Banden Industrie Michelin NV v. Commission* (Case 322/81) [1983] E.C.R. 3461, [1985] 1 C.M.L.R. 282, the ECJ found that the producers of tyres for heavy vehicles and for cars were not in the same market, as there were significant differences in production techniques and considerable investment was required to convert production.
According to the OFT Market Definition Guideline, paras 3.20–3.21, analysis of supply side substitution will require identification of potential suppliers and evidence from these potential suppliers of the technical feasibility of substitution (given a 5 per cent to 10 per cent price increase), the cost and time required for substitution, spare capacity as well as the views of consumers.

The Guideline also points out that it is the supply-side substitutable products which are added to the market definition, not the supplier. So in calculating market shares supply side substitutes need to be added. Where there is difficulty in estimating the volume of supply side substitutes (which will be common) then supply-side substitutes will not be assessed for the purposes of calculating market share, but can be treated as potential entrants to the market that constrain existing competitors. This will be relevant to determining whether an undertaking is dominant.

(4)   **Other Factors**
The E.C. Commission and E.C. Courts have often looked at other factors such as price and physical characteristics in order to determine the product market. For example, in the *Michelin* Case (Above, para. 11.3.2(3)), the ECJ considered the market for retread tyres for lorries and buses was a distinct market from new tyres although they serve the same purpose. Re-treads were considerably cheaper, but were considered to be less safe and not acceptable by a number of transport undertakings.

The OFT Market Definition Guidelines also suggest that time might either be a further aspect of the product or a further dimension of the market to be considered. Time is relevant in defining the market where customers cannot substitute consumption between time periods. The Guideline gives the example of peak and off peak rail tickets. Time is also relevant where a suppliers capacity may vary according to time, for example, the seasonal nature of fresh fruit supply.

The E.C. Commission has on occasion distinguished product markets by their intended use. So that in *Hoffman-La Roche* (Above, para. 11.3.2(1)) a market for vitamins for pharmaceutical use was distinguished from a market for technological use as preservatives. The ECJ has tended to take a wider view and in *Europemballage and Continental Can v. Commission* (Case 6/72) [1973] E.C.R. 215, [1973] C.M.L.R. 199, the ECJ rejected the E.C. Commission's finding of separate markets for light metal containers for preserved meat and fish and found there was a more general market for light metal containers.

It should be noted that the E.C. Market Definition Notice now makes clear that product characteristics and intended use are insufficient to define the product dimension of a market. However, they may be useful as a first step to limit the field of investigation as to what may be substitutable products.

Finally, in analysing the market, it may also be useful to identify the functional level at which the product in operation is being supplied, for example, whether the goods or services are being supplied at a wholesale level (to distributors, wholesalers or retailers for resale) or on a retail level for sale to end customers. These different levels in many cases will constitute separate markets, even though some purchasers at a lower level in the distribution chain may have the ability to change their purchasing to a higher level in the distribution chain in response to higher prices.

(5)   **Potential Competition**
Potential competition that might, for example, arise from imports also operates as a competitive constraint. However, the E.C. Market Definition Notice states that this will not be taken into account in defining markets, but rather the potential for imports will be considered as part of the assessment of the state of competition in the market.

11.3.3 Geographic Market

The geographical limits of the market enable the identification of potential competitors for the supply of products and services in question. E.C. Regulations define relevant geographic markets as follows:

"The relevant geographic market comprises the area in which the undertakings concerned are involved in the supply and demand of products or services, in which the conditions of competition are sufficiently homogeneous and which can be distinguished from neighbouring geographic areas because the conditions of competition are appreciably different in these areas". (Section 6 of Form A/B with respect to Regulation (EEC) No. 17/62 and section 6 of Form CO with respect to regulation (EEC) 4064/89).

The ECJ has defined the geographic market more simply as the area in which "the objective conditions of competition applying to the product[s] in question [are] the same for all traders". (*United Brands v. Commission* (Case 27/76) [1978] E.C.R. 207, [1978] 1 C.M.L.R. 429).

The test for determining the geographic limits of the market is essentially the same as for product definition. The E.C. Market Definition Notice postulates a similar test. That is, assuming the existence of a hypothetical monopolist in the region under consideration, would that monopolist be able to profitably increase prices by 5 per cent to 10 per cent. If the hypothetical monopolist is unable to do so since suppliers from adjoining geographic regions will supply into the region under consideration, the geographic market is widened until the hypothetical monopolist is able to increase prices profitably. The OFT Market Definition Guideline, para. 4.3 takes the same approach. As with the product market, both demand and supply side considerations will be relevant.

Geographic markets will in effect be defined by reference to the ease with which customers can obtain alternative goods or services from suppliers in other areas on reasonable terms. The OFT Market Definition Guideline, paras 4.3–4.10, indicate that evidence of the mobility of consumers, the value of the product, distribution/transport costs and the existence and extent of any barriers to imports will be relevant in defining the geographic market.

As a result, for easily transported commodity products such as wheat or oil, the market may be international. Constraints on the mobility or interchangeability of goods and services such as transportation costs, language, local laws and regulations, cultural preferences or the need for a physical presence may result in a narrower geographic market.

11.3.4 Market Within the United Kingdom

The Chapter II Prohibition applies where the abuse of dominance affects trade within the United Kingdom (or any part of it) (s. 18(1)). Dominance must also exist within the United Kingdom (or any part of it) (s. 18(3)).

As a result, whilst a relevant market for the purposes of the Prohibition may be regional, national or international, some part of it must be in at least a part of the United Kingdom Geographic market definition will therefore be important in the context of the application of the Act.

The Chapter II Prohibition is wider than Article 82 (formerly Article 86) in its application to markets within the United Kingdom (including local or regional markets). The Chapter II Prohibition is specifically intended to prevent abuse of dominance in respect of markets which are, at least in part, located in part of the United Kingdom

Examples of local or regional markets might be the provision of public transport within a small town, (for example, regulated bus franchises) or the provision of goods or services in geographically isolated areas where transportation costs exclude suppliers from outside the area participating in the market. A region's unique cultural preferences (for example, for certain types of food not produced outside the region) may also give rise to a regional market. Where it is not economic to establish competing local infrastructure, there may be a separate market for the services provided by that infrastructure, for example, a local port facility or sports stadium. Businesses in which the premises used in their trade are integral to their business are likely to be regarded for many purposes as operating in the series of local or regional markets, *e.g.* operators of public houses and undertakers. This approach is found in a number of FTA monopoly investigations: *e.g. Funerals* (1989), *Beer* (1989) Cm. 65.

By contrast Article 82 requires the holding of a dominant position "within the common market or a substantial part of it". The reference to a substantial part of the common market is not a simple geographic requirement, but rather one based upon the economic importance of the area. The Commission and the ECJ have therefore considered purely national markets under Article 82. However, it is more problematic under Article 82 whether a local or regional market can amount to a substantial part of the common market and this will depend upon its economic importance. Regions of a major country, such as Germany are more likely to pass the test *Re Sugar Cartel: Suiker Unie v. Commission* (Cases 40–48, 50, 54–56, 111, 113–114) [1975] E.C.R. 1663, [1976] 1 C.M.L.R. 295. Very limited markets directly related to interstate trade have been considered substantial *e.g.* the London (Heathrow)—Dublin flight route: *British Midland v. Aer Lingus* [1992] O.J. L96/34, [1993] 4 C.M.L.R. 596. In the merger case, *Nestlé/Perrier* ((Commission Decision 92/553) (Case No. IV/M190) [1992] O.J. L356/1, [1993] 4 C.M.L.R. M17 [1992] E.C.M.R. B100) the market did not follow national boundaries but radiated around major centres of supply.

The purpose of the Article 82 requirement is to ensure the market in question has a sufficient Community dimension to justify being subject to Article 82. There is no such check under the Competition Act 1998 (for further discussion see Chapter 6, at para. 6.6.2). There is clearly an intention that the United Kingdom authorities should be able to examine local markets. The protection for smaller businesses is an immunity from fines (see Chapter 6, para. 6.7.5) not from the prohibition itself.

11.4   Dominance

11.4.1   Within the United Kingdom

As discussed above, for the Chapter II Prohibition to apply, dominance must exist within the United Kingdom (or a part of it) (s. 18(3)). The E.C. Commission and ECJ have developed a considerable jurisprudence on the issue of dominance in connection with Article 82. Section 60 of the Act requires insofar as possible, consistency with the interpretation of Article 82.

11.4.2   Assessment of Dominance

The OFT has stated in its Chapter II Guideline that the essence of dominance is "the power to behave independently of competitive pressures". Dominance will be manifest where, for example, an undertaking is able to charge higher prices than it could if it faced effective competition.

The OFT has also issued a Guideline to the *Assessment of Market Power* (OFT 415, March 1999) (the "Market Power Guideline"). The existence of market power will suggest that an undertaking is dominant.

In assessing dominance the Director will consider whether and to what extent an undertaking will face effective constraints on its ability to raise prices above competitive levels, which will include: existing competitors (having regard to their strength), potential competitors (having regard to any barriers to entry) and other factors such as the countervailing "buyer power" of customers.

In assessing the strength of existing competitors it will be relevant to look at market shares of market participants over time, their size and economic strength.

The effectiveness of the competitive constraint offered by potential competitors or new entrants will largely depend on an analysis of the existence and extent of barriers to entry.

Finally, the conduct of an undertaking will itself be evidence of dominance to the extent that it may have been able to charge excessive prices, generate excessive profits or otherwise act in a way which would not be possible in a market where there was effective competition. These issues are discussed below.

   (1)   **Market Shares**

   Generally, persistently high market shares will suggest market power. An undertaking with a persistently high market share is likely to be an unavoidable trading partner that even discontented customers must deal with. At the same time, persistently high market shares suggest an inability on the part of competitors to develop rapidly to limit the dominant undertaking's freedom of action. A high market share may also suggest that the undertaking will have considerable resources to enable it to act independently of its competitors. (See *United Brands* and *Hoffman La Roche* above at paras 11.2.3 and 11.3.2(1)).

   As the Market Power Guideline states at para. 4.2, high market shares in this context may either be high in absolute terms or high relative to those of competitors.

   Very large market shares, for example in excess of 75 per cent have been considered by the ECJ as giving rise to a presumption of dominance. The OFT refers in Chapter II Guideline para. 3.13 and its Market Power Guideline para. 2.11 to the decision of the ECJ in *AKZO Chemie BV v. Commission* (Case 62/86) [1991] I-E.C.R. 3359, [1993] 5 C.M.L.R. 215 which states that dominance may be presumed where the market share persistently exceeds 50 per cent in the absence of evidence to the contrary. Market shares for example, in excess of 40 per cent together with other factors may be an indicator of dominance. The Guidelines also note that the Director considers it unlikely that an undertaking will be individually dominant if its market share is below 40 per cent absent other relevant factors (such as the weak position of competitors in the market).

It is also important to analyse the market share of all market participants over time — this will assist in identifying whether the high market shares of a particular undertaking are in fact evidence of dominance. For example, if an undertaking's market share is steadily falling (although still high) then this may suggest that, although market share is still large, the undertaking concerned cannot act independently of its competitors: *Elf Aquitaine — Thyssen/Minol* (Case No. IV M235) [1992] O.J. C232/14, [1992] 5 C.M.L.R. 203, [1993] E.C.M.R. B109 and *Courtaulds/SNIA* (Case IV/M113) [1991] O.J. C333/16; [1992] 4 C.M.L.R. 349; [1991] E.C.M.R. B23. Changing market shares and new entry will suggest a competitive market.

In assessing market shares the OFT is likely to seek evidence from market research, trade or consumer associations, participants in the market and their customers and suppliers. The Market Power Guideline para. 4.4 contains greater detail on the approach to the calculation of market share and in particular when to measure share by value or volume and by reference to production or sales and the treatment of exchange rates, production for internal use and imports, etc.

It will be apparent from the discussion of market definition above that this will involve complex and difficult issues. The Market Power Guideline para. 4.7 indicates that the Director will consider market share data in the light of all possible market definitions. If the conclusion is the same regardless of market definition, for example, a low market share, in circumstances where the precise market definition does not affect the assessment of actual and potential competition, then it may not be necessary to finally determine which market definition should be used. By contrast if market shares and therefore the assessment of market power varies according to market definition then the Director will seek more information on market definition. This may include market share data on alternative market definitions together with submissions as to why one definition should be preferred.

Ultimately, market share will be an important tool of analysis but may not be determinative.

(2) **Overall Size and Strength**
Although an undertaking may have a relatively low market share in a particular market, its overall size and strength may enable it to act independently of its competitors in that market (see for example, *Michelin*, at para. 11.3.2(3) above, where Michelin had a low market share in the Netherlands but its international size gave it an advantage in terms of research and investment as well as product range). It follows that although dominance must exist in the United Kingdom or part of the United Kingdom, the ultimate source of that dominance may be in markets outside the United Kingdom or may be derived from overall strength in the national market in a region where most competitors are local businesses.

(3) **Barriers to Entry**
These are defined in the Market Power Guideline para. 5.2 as costs which must be borne by a new entrant to a market that do not need to be borne by an existing participant. Barriers to entry can reduce scope

for competition as existing participants may be able to increase prices. That said, the Director would not regard efficiency based cost advantages as a barrier to entry. Some barriers, such as scarcity of suitable sites for which planning permission could be obtained, are only indirectly related to cost. Some regulatory barriers raise an absolute barrier (not cost related), for some potential competitors, *e.g.* the requirement that Community companies running airlines must at all times be effectively controlled (either owned directly or through majority ownership) by Member States and/or nationals of Member States (Council Regulation of July 23, 1992 on Licensing of Air Carriers, reg. 2407/92, O.J. L240/1).

The OFT in the Chapter II Guideline (para. 315) and the Market Power Guideline (para. 5.3) identify three types of barrier to entry; absolute advantages, strategic advantages and exclusionary behaviour;

Absolute advantages are those which reflect unequal access to important assets or rights necessary to participate in a market. This may include intellectual property rights, statutory/regulatory controls or the limitation of access to essential facilities, which preclude or limit entry into the market. Essential facilities are defined as assets or facilities to which access is indispensable to compete as a market and where duplication is impossible (these are discussed below).

Strategic advantages can include the advantages which an undertaking enjoys from being first in the market. Existing market participants have a strategic advantage over a new entrant who must incur sunk costs to enter the market and cannot recover if it has to exit. They can also include economies of scale which new entrants will not possess.

Exclusionary behaviour (or the likelihood of it occurring) on the part of an existing market participant discourages new entry. Examples of exclusionary behaviour include predatory pricing, refusal to supply or vertical arrangements tying up essential parts of the supply chain, all of which are discussed below (see 11.5). A participant with a reputation for aggressive market behaviour may deter entry more effectively.

The greater the barriers to entry, the more likely a finding of dominance.

The history of actual entry and exits from the market will be useful in considering whether barriers exist. Lack of entry may be evidence of high barriers to entry. Also as the Market Power Guideline para. 5.8 points out the rate of innovation will be important. The greater the innovation, the more likely existing barriers to entry will not survive. Similarly, the growth of the market is relevant. The greater the growth the more likely entry will be. The Market Power Guideline, para. 5.25 also states that the Director may ask potential entrants as well as market participants about entry barriers, for example, for estimates as to sunk costs, costs of entry, etc.

(4) **The Extent of the Threat of Import Competition**
The more significant actual or potential import competition, the more likely there will be no finding of dominance.

(5) **Government Regulation**
Regulation may constrain the behaviour of undertakings particularly, for

example, by regulated utilities. Generally this will not change the assessment of dominance, but may limit the ability to exercise market power abusively.

(6) **Buyer Power**
Any market power of a supplier may be constrained by buyers on the other side of the market. Thus, whilst an undertaking may be able to set prices above the competitive level, this could be prevented by buyer power. Buyer power arises where the supplier is more dependent on the buyer than the buyer is on any one supplier. It requires the buyer to have good information about alternative sources of supply and to be able to switch suppliers or indeed start its own production at minimal cost.

(7) **Conduct of the Undertaking in the Market Place**
Evidence of dominance may in fact be the observed ability of the undertaking to carry out abusive conduct since an undertaking which was not dominant would be unable to sustain such conduct. In effect, it demonstrates independence from a competitive constraint. It is of course important to distinguish this sort of conduct from normal competitive market behaviour which may appear similar. For example, it may be difficult to distinguish vigorous price competition from predatory pricing (discussed in more detail at 11.5.3 (1) below). Conduct must therefore be assessed by reference to the structure of competition in the market over time, having regard to, for example, the history of price and profitability of undertakings in the market, product differentiation, after sales service, vertical integration, excess capacity, customer awareness and inertia. The Market Power Guideline, para. 6.3 suggests that such conduct may be evidenced by an undertaking consistently increasing prices in excess of costs or persistently generating excessive profits (*i.e.* a higher rate of return than could be earned from investing elsewhere having regard to the risks incurred by investing in that particular company: see Chapter II Guideline, para. 4.8). Of course, high profits may be due to innovation and excessive profits can be the result of efficiency in production methods. Care must be taken to measure profits over a suitable time-scale and to ensure that price increases are considered in the context of product development.

11.4.3   Joint Dominance

Like Article 82, the Chapter II Prohibition provides that conduct by one or more undertakings may amount to an abuse of dominant position. By implication, it follows that a dominant position may be held jointly by one or more undertakings. The application of joint dominance in the context of Article 82 has to date been limited there but are several important decisions related to E.C. Mergers.

It is generally not necessary to rely upon joint dominance where the conduct involves legal entities within a corporate group since the concept of "undertaking" refers to the economic entity or the group as a whole (including all the constituent legal entities). In *Commercial Solvents v. European Commission* (Case 6/74 and 7/74) [1974] E.C.R. 223, [1974] 1 C.M.L.R. 309, the U.S. parent company controlled world supplies of aminobutonal. The case concerned the refusal by the Italian subsidiary to supply the complainant. The U.S. parent company was held to be legally answerable for the refusal to supply. However, joint dominance may have application to entities within the same corporate group where they are not considered to operate as a single economic entity.

Joint dominance may arise from anti-competitive arrangements, for example, through trade associations or cartels. However, these arrangements can be more easily dealt with under the Chapter I Prohibition and/or Article 81. It is arguably easier to demonstrate the existence of an agreement and its effect in distorting trade than having to establish the existence of both dominance and its abuse. However, such agreements would not be eligible for an exemption if they give rise to or maintain a position of dominance (*Tetra Pak I (BTG Licence)* (E.C. Commission Decision 88/501) [1988] O.J. L272/27, [1990] 4 C.M.L.R. 47).

Most importantly, joint dominance may arise where there is tacit anti-competitive parallel behaviour or tacit collusion. Such situations, it is suggested, can arise in oligopolistic markets where the structure of the market is such that parallel or tacitly collusive behaviour (such as one participant following the other's prices rises) becomes a more rational strategy than competition. That is to say that the market structure makes such collusion feasible and maintainable (see *Gencor Ltd v. Commission* (Case T–102/96) [1999] ALL E.R. (E.C.) 289, [1999] 4 C.M.L.R. 971, CFI and *Airtours/First Choice* (Case IV/M1524) [2000] O.J. L093/1). Since there is no agreement or concerted practice, neither the Chapter I Prohibition or Article 81 would apply.

The CFI in *Societa Italiano Vetro SpA v. Commission* (Cases T–89/89) [1992] II E.C.R. 1403, [1992] 5 C.M.L.R. 302 (the Flat Glass case) recognised the principle of joint dominance :

> "There is nothing, in principle, to prevent two or more independent economic entities from being, on a specific market, united by such economic links that, by virtue of that fact, together they hold a dominant position *vis-à-vis* the other operators on the same market".

"Economic links" may fall short of agreements or concerted practices which would be caught by Article 81. The decision of the CFI in *Gencor* makes clear that although such economic links could be structural, such as joint technology agreements or licenses which give rise to a lead over their competitors, they may also arise from a relationship of interdependence which can exist between participants in an oligopolistic market. They are in a position to anticipate each other's behaviour and are therefore likely to align their conduct in a way to maximise joint profits by restricting production and increasing prices. At the same time each is aware that an attempt to increase market share by cutting prices will lead to an identical reaction by the other so that it would not gain market share and will suffer as a result of a price cut. In short, the circumstances must exist both to facilitate and maintain parallel behaviour. Thus for example, it may be relevant if:

(1) the undertakings together have high market shares and similar cost structures;

(2) the product in question is homogenous with transparent pricing;

(3) the market is characterised by barriers or disincentives to entry (such as stagnant demand, mature technology and limited capacity).

The OFT's Chapter II Guideline, para. 3.21 also notes that "economic links" may be structural or they may be factors which facilitate undertakings adopting the same conduct on the market.

Finally, joint dominance may arise where the market is characterised by a series of suppliers who are unable to compete and who thereby become monopolists of a market segment with positions individually too small to amount to individual dominance. As a result, conduct by one amounts to an exercise of collective power. The Commission took this approach in *BP v. Commission,* [1977] O.J. L119/1, [1977] 2 C.M.L.R. D1, (Case 77/77) [1978] E.C.R. 1513, [1978] 3 C.M.L.R. 174. In that case the oil crisis led to petrol rationing so that normally competitive petrol resellers were no longer in a position to compete.

11.4.4   Dominant Purchasers

Joint dominance, like single firm dominance is not limited to suppliers.

In *National Association of Licensed Opencast Operators v. British Coal Corporation* [1993] 4 C.M.L.R. 615 the Commission described the only two purchasers in the United Kingdom of coal for power generation as being jointly dominant. No basis is given for such a finding. However, both were state owned at the time and the regulatory requirements in which they operated left no room for independent conduct by either of them. It will be interesting to see whether and in what circumstances the OFT builds upon MMC or Competition Commission findings of a complex monopoly to identify industries and companies who enjoy joint dominance. This may be relatively easy where industries are concentrated in the hands of a few players, but less so in other cases. There are important differences in the tests in the two pieces of legislation and complex monopoly behaviour may affect only one aspect of an industry which is generally competitive.

11.5   Abuse of a Dominant Position

11.5.1   Effect in the United Kingdom

Section 18 of the Competition Act provides that both the dominant position and the effect of the abuse of that position must occur in the United Kingdom, or a part of it. This limits the territorial scope of the Chapter II Prohibition. As discussed above, (see para. 11.3.4 above), the Chapter II Prohibition will apply to abuse which arises from dominance in local or regional markets within the United Kingdom which are too small for Article 82 to apply. Where abusive conduct is carried out by an undertaking operating throughout the United Kingdom, it may be exposed to action both under the Chapter II Prohibition and if it affects trade between Member States, Article 82. Proposals discussed in Chapter 17 at 17.7 would result in only Article 82 applying where there is an effect on trade between Member States, but would lave parties exposed to multiple penalties for breach imposed by the competition authorities of the affected Member States.

An undertaking that is dominant in a market in the United Kingdom which abuses that dominance elsewhere in Europe will not contravene the Chapter II Prohibition but may contravene Article 82.

11.5.2   Abuse Generally

It is important to remember that the Chapter II Prohibition is directed towards the abuse of a dominant position rather than the existence of dominance itself.

The examples contained in Section 18(2) of the Competition Act are not exhaustive. The ECJ held in *Continental Can* (above, para. 11.3.2(4)) that an abuse can arise where an undertaking in a dominant position strengthens that dominance in a way which substantially hinders competition. However, the mere use of economic power which results from dominance is not an abuse. The undertaking must act in a way which is different from that which would occur in a competitive market. In *Hoffman-La Roche* (Above, para. 11.3.2(1)), the ECJ stated that:

> "The concept of abuse is an objective concept relating to the behaviour of an undertaking in a dominant position which is such as to influence the structure of a market where, as a result of the very presence of the undertaking in question, the degree of competition is weakened and which through recourse to methods different from those which condition normal competition in products and services on the basis of the transactions of commercial operators, has the effect of hindering the maintenance of the degree of competition still existing in the market or the growth of that competition".

In the same case, the ECJ rejected the argument that the abusive conduct must only be possible by reason of dominance. As a result, dominant undertakings may be required to be more constrained in their conduct than smaller competitors which are not dominant.

The OFT's Chapter II Guideline makes clear that where there is an objective and legitimate justification to conduct it will not be abusive even if its effect is to restrict competition. So that, for example, a refusal to supply on credit because a customer is a poor credit risk is unlikely to be abusive. However, such conduct must be proportionate to the legitimate objective.

Whilst the test of abuse is objective, evidence of an undertaking's intent to harm competitors or restrict competition will be influential in the finding of abuse (see *ECS/AKZO* [1985] O.J. L374/1, [1986] 3 C.M.L.R. 273 on appeal *AKZO Chemie BV v. Commission* (Above, para. 11.4.2(1); *Tetra Pak II* [1992] O.J. L72/1, [1992] 4 C.M.L.R. 551 on appeal *Tetra Pak International SA v. Commission* (Case T–83/91), [1994] E.C.R. II–755, CFI). Evidence as to the intentions or motives of an undertaking will be relevant where a legitimate commercial justification is claimed for the conduct (see the OFT Chapter II Guideline, para. 4.26 *et seq.*). Evidence of intention will be particularly significant in determining whether a pricing strategy is predatory, aimed at driving out or preventing the entry of a competitor, as opposed to simply increasing sales to increase profit.

It is interesting to note that the Chapter II Prohibition differs from Article 82 in that it refers to "any conduct which amounts to an abuse" whereas Article 82 only refers to "abuse".

This raises the question as to how a Court might interpret "any conduct". One possibility is that a Court may require some positive action to amount to an abuse. The failure to act may not be enough. As a result a refusal to supply may not amount to a breach of the Chapter II Prohibition, even though it has been accepted that this will amount to a breach of Article 82. In the House of Commons debate on June 4, 1998 the Government made clear that it intended that a failure to act (such as a failure to adopt innovations) could amount to an abuse under the Chapter II Prohibition (*Hansard* (Standing Committee G) cols 223–226 (June 4, 1998)).

11.5.3   Types of Abuse

Abuses fall into two broad categories. The first may be described as exploitative, that is taking benefits not available to other competitors in the market, for example, by high or discriminatory prices. The second are exclusionary abuses, that is shutting out competitors or restricting competition by behaviour such as predatory pricing, vertical restraints or the refusal to supply existing or potential competitors; in effect, reinforcing dominance and damaging competition itself. The OFT has published a Guideline *The Assessment of Individual Agreements and Conduct*, OFT 414, September 1999 (the "Individual Agreements and Conduct Guideline") which deals with types of abuse and the evidence which the Director will consider. This overlaps with the Chapter II Guideline, section 4.

Examples of abuse include the following:

(1) **Unfair Pricing & Trading Conditions**
     Excessive Prices Section 18(2)(a) of the Competition Act identifies the imposition of unfair prices or other unfair trading conditions as possibly an abuse. This will include unfairly high prices by a dominant seller or unfairly low prices paid by a dominant buyer either of which may result in above normal profits. That is to say, prices which are persistently excessive (or low, in the case of dominant buyers), either by reference to prices which would otherwise prevail in a competitive market or by reference to the economic value of the product supplied, and are thereby exploitative. For example, in *General Motors Continental NV v. Commission* (Case 26/75) [1975] E.C.R. 1367, [1976] 1 C.M.L.R. 95, the ECJ upheld the Commission"s finding that charging excessive fees for certification of car imports constituted an abuse. That said, the OFT recognises that high prices may be a result of normal market mechanisms (for example as a reward for innovation) which stimulate either innovation or new entry and with which the Director would be loath to interfere (see the Chapter II Guideline para. 4.9 and the Individual Agreements and Conduct Guideline paras 2.9–2.11).

     The OFT in these Guidelines suggests that evidence of excessive pricing may be found in an analysis of the costs of a product or a comparison with the price of competing products. Another test is whether the undertaking is consistently making significantly excessive profits in the market under examination having regard to the cost of capital for the particular risks involved, particularly where there has been no new entry or innovation.

     Predatory Prices Conversely, unfair pricing can also include unfairly low or predatory pricing. This is a form of exclusionary abuse directed at eliminating a competitor or preventing a new competitor entering the market so as to protect or strengthen a position of dominance which can be exploited at a later time. Although consumers benefit from low prices, predatory pricing is objectionable since in the long run weakened competition may lead to higher prices, less choice or lower quality products.

     The difficulty in the case of unfairly high or low pricing is to establish as a matter of evidence that this is taking place particularly as low prices will be a feature of legitimate competition. In the *Tetra Pak II* case (at para. 11.5.2 above), the ECJ found (applying its decision in the *AKZO* case (at para. 11.4.2(1) above)) that predation should be presumed where prices are below the average variable cost of production. Pricing at this level is unlikely to be rational (since losses are incurred on each additional item sold) but may be justified for example, if it is loss leading (where the purpose is to increase sales of complementary products and thereby profits). Where prices are above average variable costs, but below total average costs, there will be predatory conduct if it can be demonstrated that the purpose is to eliminate a competitor (see also *Compagnie Maritime Belge Transports SA & Others v. E.C. Commission* (Case T–24–26, 28/93), [1996] E.C.R. II–1201, [1997] 4 C.M.L.R. 273). In this instance the OFT Guidelines state that the Director may consider other evidence on costs. If prices were above average variable costs but below average long run avoidable costs, then this may be evidence of predation. Long run avoidable costs are both fixed and variable costs which could be avoided if the undertaking were to cease the activity in question. They would not include sunk costs (unless incurred as part of the alleged predatory strategy) or common costs attributable to a range of activities. Pricing below long run avoidable costs would suggest predation, as the undertaking would incur smaller losses by ceasing the business entirely. Where prices are above average cost, then there will be no evidence of predation.

The OFT has also indicated in the guidelines that the following evidence of intention may be relevant. Incremental losses may suggest predation; for example, excessive discounting which although it increases sales reduces overall profit or increases losses. The targeting of price cutting to respond to a new entrant or limiting it to the area in which a new entrant is operating would also suggest predation. Finally, a predatory intention can be gleaned from documentary evidence.

As mentioned above, predation is necessarily a short term tactic with the objective of recouping the costs later through higher prices which are possible due to weakened competition. The guidelines make clear that the Director does not consider (following the *AKZO* and *Tetra Pak II* cases, at para. 11.5.2 above) that it is necessary to demonstrate the feasibility of recouping losses in order to establish predation.

In the debate on the issue of the application of the Act to predatory pricing on May 11, 1998 in the House of Commons, the Secretary of State emphasised that the *AKZO* and *Tetra Pak II* decisions would apply under the Act (*Hansard*, H.C., Vol. 312, No. 169, col. 28 (May 11, 1998)). Parliament ultimately rejected an amendment specifically directed at prohibiting predatory pricing of newspapers.

Cross Subsidy A cross-subsidy may also be an abuse where an undertaking finances low pricing of a product in a market from the profits of another market in which it holds a dominant position.

Other Trading Conditions Since competition is not limited to price but extends to the quality of goods and services as well as other trading conditions, abuse can occur through the imposition of unfair conditions or predatory behaviour in relation to such conditions: *e.g.* a patent owner taking ownership of any intellectual property developments by a licensee without compensation could be exploitative (this is blacklisted in the E.C. Technology Transfer Block Exemption (Regulation 240/96/E.C, [1996] O.J. L31/2). The grant of unusually generous warranties could be part of a strategy to prevent market entry by raising the costs of entry for a new competitor.

(2) **Limitation of Production, Markets or Technical Development**
Section 18(2)(b) of the Act identifies limitation of production, markets or technical development to the prejudice of consumers as another

possible form of abuse. This may involve exploitation of a dominant position by limiting output in order to increase prices and profitability and it can extend to refusing to supply potential competitors. Abuse can also include limitation of the range of goods supplied or stifling of innovation and development (inertia can be enough).

Refusal to supply is an example of an exclusionary abuse. Whilst a dominant undertaking is not obliged to deal with all customers or suppliers, a refusal to deal without an objective legitimate commercial justification is likely to be abusive. It need not be a refusal; delay or a lower quality of service may be enough. For example, a vertically integrated manufacturer of raw materials was held to have abused its dominant position in the market for the supply of those raw materials by refusing to supply existing customers, in order to gain access for itself to the downstream product market (see *Commercial Solvents* at 11.4.3 above).

By contrast, a refusal to supply for credit or capacity reasons or as the result of the legitimate exercise of an intellectual property right will not constitute an abuse. The legitimate exploitation of intellectual property rights is to be dealt with more fully in the OFT Guideline: *Intellectual Property Rights* which is unlikely to be available before this book goes to press.

The Chapter II Guideline para. 4.49 and Individual Agreements and Conduct Guideline, paras 7.1 & 7.5 also note that refusal to allow access to essential facilities may be an abuse. An essential facility is one where access to it is essential to compete in the market and duplication of the facility is impossible or extremely difficult owing to physical, geographical legal or public policy constraints. Facilities such as ports, bus stations, utility distribution networks and telecommunications networks may be essential facilities, but it is a matter of fact in each case: *Oscar Bronner v. Mediaprint and Others* (Case C–7/97) [1998] E.C.R. I–7791, in which the ECJ took a narrower view of what would constitute an essential facility than did the Advocate General, to whose opinion the Guidelines refer. The Director would expect competitors to have access to essential facilities subject to capacity at economically efficient prices. The refusal to give access where capacity is not assigned to an existing or planned use is likely to be an abuse. In certain circumstances the refusal to create capacity may be an abuse. It is to be noted, however, that the Commission decisions requiring capacity to be made available to competitors by new businesses have both been overturned: Eurotunnel (*Société Nationale des Chemins de Fer Français and British Railways Board v. Commission* (Cases T–79/95 and T–80/95), [1996] O.J. C370/11, [1996] E.C.R. II–1491, [1997] 4 C.M.L.R. 334, CFI) and European Night Services (*European Night Services v. Commission*, (Cases T–374, 375, 384, 388/94) [1998] 5 C.M.L.R. 718).

(3)   **Discrimination**
Section 18(2)(c) provides that applying dissimilar conditions to equivalent transactions may amount to an abuse. Discriminatory pricing between different customers which does not reflect differences in the costs of supplying those customers may be abusive where it results in excessive prices or less competition (see for example *United Brands* above

11.2.3). This may involve increasing prices to customers who have fewer alternative sources of supply (*i.e.* there is less competition) and/or reducing prices to customers for whom there is greater competition. This is a form of exploitative abuse. However, the effects of price discrimination need to be considered on a case-by-case basis. The Chapter II Guideline para. 4.15 and the Individual Agreements and Conduct Guideline para. 3.7 note that discrimination may be justified where fixed costs are high and marginal costs are low, as in utility or telecommunications industries. Without price discrimination it would be difficult to recover fixed costs. Price discrimination in such industries will tend to lead to a higher level of output and is not likely to be abusive.

(4) Supplementary Obligations

Section 18(2)(d) identifies the imposition of supplementary conditions on customers, which are unrelated to the transaction, as another form of abuse. Vertical restraints, such as selective or exclusive distribution (particularly when creating a strong exclusive network) or bundling of products which cannot be bought separately may amount to an abuse if in particular cases they lead to a reduction in competition, although more often they will enhance competition. Vertical restraints other than resale price maintenance are excluded from the application of the Chapter I Prohibition (see Chapter 7, at 7.2). However, this will not apply to the Chapter II Prohibition and vertical restraints imposed by dominant undertakings may still be prohibited. They can be abusive since they may foreclose the market or at least dampen competition. It may be difficult for new suppliers or purchasers to enter a market due to the existing contractual links between market participants – it may be harder or more expensive to gain access to customers or suppliers. For example, in *Hoffmann La-Roche* (above, 11.3.2(1)) a discount was offered if the customers purchased all or nearly all of their requirements from the supplier, in effect tying them exclusively to their supplier. Rebates are generally justifiable and not abusive if they are genuinely based on the cost savings related to larger or regular orders, for example, discounts for quantity purchases reflect the lower cost of producing or supplying in bulk.

Vertical agreements can produce benefits which outweigh any anticompetitive effects. For example, they may enable suppliers to achieve economies in distribution or enable retailers to offer pre or post sales services. Examples of possibly abusive vertical restraints given in the Chapter II Guidelines include, in addition to the examples mentioned above, resale price maintenance, exclusive purchasing, minimum quantity obligations and non-linear pricing (*e.g.* where there is a separate franchise fee, unrelated to the supply of goods or services, or where a retailer requires a supplier to pay a "slotting fee" to have its goods stocked or to contribute to various capital spending projects for the retailer's business).

(5) Tacit Collusion

The Chapter II Guideline para. 4.13 notes that where undertakings are jointly dominant, tacit collusion may amount to an abuse. Tacit collusion is unlikely to be caught by the Chapter I Prohibition as a concerted practice. Tacit collusion might be characterised by uniform price movements where prices were excessive or opportunities for price competition were

ignored. However, similar prices for similar products may be the result of
competition so that tacit collusion will be difficult to detect (*Re Woodpulp
cartel; A Ahlstrohm Oy v. Commission* (Cases 89, 104, 114, 116–117,
125–129/85) [1993] I E.C.R. 99, [1993] 4 C.M.L.R. 407).

11.6   Effects on Trade Within the United Kingdom

11.6.1   Actual or Potential Effects

The Chapter II Prohibition will apply where the result of the abuse of dominance
is an effect on trade within the United Kingdom or part of it.

It is not necessary to show an actual effect on trade. A potential effect may be
predicted. However, under Articles 81 and 82, the Commission and the ECJ
require that there be an appreciable effect on trade. This is discussed more fully in
Chapter 6 at 6.7.

11.6.2   Trade

The wording of the Chapter II Prohibition differs from Article 82 in that it refers
to affecting trade within the United Kingdom This is an adaptation of the words of
Article 82 which refers to conduct which may effect trade between Member States.
However, since the Chapter II Prohibition is intended to apply to regional and local
markets in a part of the United Kingdom it does not depend upon the existence of
a market with a "United Kingdom dimension" in the way that Article 82 requires
a Community dimension in assessing the effects of the abuse. Further, an abuse of
a dominant position will necessarily affect trade within the market in question and
therefore trade within the United Kingdom or a part of it. It is therefore uncertain
as to whether the words "affect trade within the United Kingdom" will carry an
additional meaning and impose an additional requirement. It has been suggested
that the reference to "trade" was intended to limit the application of the Chapter II
Prohibition to commercial activities. However, the reference in the prohibition to a
market might well have achieved this in any event.

In the House of Commons Committee Debate on June 2, 1998, (*Hansard*, H.C.,
Vol. 313, No. 178, cols 87–100 (June 2, 1998)) the Minister for Competition and
Consumer Affairs stated that "trade" meant that the prohibition must involve
matters concerning trade which contemplates a wide range of economic activity.

11.7   Limited Immunities

11.7.1   Introduction

The Competition Act provides for limited immunity conduct of minor significance
section 40.

11.7.2   Scope of the Immunity

In the case of conduct of minor significance, the penalties provided in section 36 of
the Act for infringement of Chapter II Prohibition will not apply unless the Director withdraws that immunity. Other consequences of such conduct will still apply,
such as possible third party actions.

The immunity will only be withdrawn if after having investigated the conduct, the
Director determines that the agreement or the conduct is likely to infringe the Chapter

II Prohibition (s. 40 (4)). The Government is concerned to ensure small firms dominant in small markets do not abuse their position. The Director will therefore investigate and consider conduct of minor significance where appropriate.

The decision to withdraw the immunity takes effect on the date specified in the decision notified to the parties. The withdrawal date must be after the date on which the decision is made (s. 4(5)–(7)). In determining the withdrawal date, the Director must have regard to the time that the parties are likely to require to ensure that no further infringement of the Chapter II Prohibition occurs (s. 40 (2)).

11.7.3   Conduct of Minor Significance

Conduct of minor significance is defined in the Competition Act 1998 (Small Agreements and Conduct of Minor Significance) Regulations 2000 (S.I. 2000 No. 262) as all conduct by an undertaking which in the business year ending in the calendar year preceding one during which the infringement occurred, had an applicable turnover not exceeding £50 million. Applicable turnover is the turnover for the undertaking arising from the sale of products and provision of services falling within the undertaking's ordinary activities after deduction of sales rebates, VAT and other turnover taxes, but special rules apply to credit and financial institutions and insurance undertakings. "Undertaking" has the same meaning as in E.C. law and therefore denotes an economic rather than a legal entity. In most circumstances, therefore, the turnover of the entire group of companies (for Companies Act purposes) to which the business belongs will be the applicable turnover, although some groups comprise more than one undertaking (see, for example, *Metro SB – Grossmarkte GmbH & Co KG v. Commission* (Case 75/84) [1986] E.C.R. 3021, [1987] 1 C.M.L.R. 118). In some cases the turnover of other companies under the control of an individual could be relevant. (See Chapter 6 at 6.3 for a more detailed discussion).

This is a matter of concern for a large business purchasing a business which has benefited from this immunity, but which appears to have a strong position in a local or niche market. The purchaser will need to examine past practices and ensure that any questionable conduct is changed in order to avoid the risk of fines.

11.8   Notification

Where a person considers that their conduct may constitute a breach of the Chapter II Prohibition they may notify the conduct to the Director for consideration either seeking:

(1)   confidential guidance as to whether the conduct is likely to infringe the Chapter II Prohibition (ss. 20 and 21); or

(2)   a decision as to whether the conduct falls within the prohibition (ss. 20 and 23).

Unlike the position relating to the Chapter I Prohibition, it is not possible for the Director to grant an exemption for conduct which infringes the Chapter II Prohibition or for the Secretary of State to make block exemption orders.

There will be circumstances where an agreement excluded or exempted from the application of the Chapter I Prohibition may contravene the Chapter II Prohibition, for example, a vertical agreement with foreclosing effects to which a dominant undertaking is party, is likely to be excluded. Under the Act such an agreement could be subject to attack for breach of the Chapter II Prohibition. In the Chapter II Guideline, para. 2.7 it is stated that the position under the Chapter II Prohibition will depend upon the type of exemption:

- If the agreement has an individual exemption granted by the Director it cannot be looked at again. The same position applies if the agreement benefits from a parallel exemption because it has an individual exemption under Article 81(3) (formerly Article 85(3)). The Act only provides for an exemption from only the Chapter I Prohibition in these circumstances (s. 4 and 10) so the Guideline represents a statement of the policy of the Director, presumably on the basis that in considering an individual exemption any abusive effects will have to be taken into account by the E.C. Commission. A third party might be able to attack such an agreement under the Chapter II Prohibition in court, even if it had been exempted from the Chapter I Prohibition and the Director was not prepared to take any steps under the Chapter II Prohibition (see Chapter 10, para. 10.2.5 for a discussion of the position of third parties).

- Agreements which fall in the category excluded from the Chapter I Prohibition only, or which are exempt from the Chapter I Prohibition by reason of a block exemption under the Act (or a parallel exemption by reason of a European block exemption) could still be in breach of the Chapter II Prohibition.

The notification process is dealt with in more detail in Chapter 13.

11.9   Consequences of Infringement

A number of possible consequences flow from the infringement of the Chapter II Prohibition, including:

(1)   The imposition of fines by the Director.

(2)   The imposition of interim measures by the Director to stop the conduct allegedly in breach of the Chapter II Prohibition, in order to protect third parties or the public interest pending the completion of the Director's investigations.

(3)   A stop order by the Director (which may be enforced by a Court) to end the abusive conduct.

(4)   Third party actions for interlocutory injunctions and/or final injunctions.

(5)   Third party actions for damages.

These are all considered in more detail in Chapter 14.

Chapter 12

Exclusions from the Prohibition of Abuse of a Dominant Position

12.1   Introduction

The Competition Act 1998 only provides for a very limited number of exclusions from the prohibition against an abuse of a dominant position (the "Chapter II Prohibition"). These are created by section 19(1) of the Act. The Chapter II Prohibition will not apply in the case of mergers and concentrations (set out in detail in Sched. 1 to the Act), and in a series of general exclusions (set out in Sched. 3 to the Act).

Under section 19(2) the Secretary of State may at any time, by order, amend Sched. 1 by adding, amending or removing any case.

The new Financial Services and Markets Act 2000 will also exclude certain practices of recognised bodies and persons regulated by the Financial Services Authority from the Chapter II Prohibition. These exclusions are part of the replacement of provisions in the Competition Act 1998 Sched. 2, which did not, in their original form, give any exclusion from the Chapter II prohibition.

Schedule 3 sets out some general exclusions from the Chapter II Prohibition. The Secretary of State may also make further exclusions in particular circumstances.

It should be noted that the Chapter II Prohibition contains fewer exclusions than the prohibition on anti-competitive agreements and that, unlike the Chapter I Prohibition, there is no system of obtaining exemptions.

12.2   Mergers

A merger leading to a dominant position is not itself subject to the Chapter II Prohibition which is directed at the *abuse* of that dominant position. However, any subsequent abuse of that dominance would be caught.

Mergers will continue to be subject to either the Fair Trading Act 1973 (United Kingdom) ("FTA") or the E.C. Merger Regulation.

The Competition Act does not reform existing merger control legislation in the United Kingdom Those mergers which are too small to qualify for investigation under the FTA are also excluded from the two prohibitions in order to avoid them being subject to the more stringent prohibitions. For a more detailed commentary on the effect of the Competition Act on United Kingdom mergers, see Chapter 7 at 7.4. The main difference in respect of the Chapter II Prohibition is that the withdrawal of the exclusion as described in Chapter 7, para. 7.4.8 does not extend to the Chapter II Prohibition.

The exclusion from the Chapter II Prohibition extends to any provision directly related and necessary to the implementation of a merger (para. 2(1)(b) of Sched. 1). As originally drafted, the Bill did not provide for an express provision to this effect but an amendment was introduced at the House of Lords stage in order to exclude ancillary restrictions from the Chapter II Prohibition (*Hansard*, H.L., Vol. 583, No. 63, col. 330 (November 13, 1997) and Vol. 585, No. 99, col. 957 (February 9, 1998)).

Mergers which have a Community dimension are scrutinised by the E.C. Commission under the Council Regulation on the control of concentrations between undertakings 4064/89, [1990] O.J. L257/13 as amended by Council Regulation 1310/97, [1997] O.J. L180/1.

12.3   Practices of Recognised Bodies and Regulated Persons Under the Financial Services and Markets Act 2000

12.3.1   New Exclusions

The Financial Services and Markets Act 2000 ("FSA 2000"), which received royal assent on June 14, 2000 and is expected to come into force during the summer of 2001 introduces new exclusions from the Chapter II Prohibition.

12.3.2   Conduct of Regulated Bodies

The FSA 2000 section 164(3) provides an exclusion for the conduct of authorised persons (defined in FSA 2000, s. 31) and the conduct of any person who is otherwise subject to the Financial Services Authority's regulating provisions to the extent to which the conduct is encouraged by any of the Authority's regulatory provisions.

12.3.3   Practices and Conduct of Regulated Bodies

Section 312 gives an exclusion from the Chapter II prohibition for (a) the practices of a recognised body; (b) the adoption or enforcement of such a body's regulatory provisions; and (c) any conduct which is engaged in by such a body or by a person who is subject to the rules of such a body to the extent to which it is encouraged or required by the regulatory provisions of the body.

A recognised body is a clearing house or investment exchange which has been recognised by the Financial Services Authority. Its "practices" are defined so as to be limited to its practices in its recognised capacity (s. 302 (1)). "Regulatory provisions" are also defined in section 302 (1).

12.4   General Exclusions

12.4.1   General Exclusions

Several of the exclusions set out in Sched. 3 to the Act give an exclusion only from the Chapter I Prohibition. Those that apply to the Chapter II Prohibition are described below. All of these also apply to the Chapter I Prohibition.

12.4.2   Services of General Economic Interest

The Chapter II Prohibition will not apply to an undertaking which is entrusted with the operation of services of general economic interest or having the character of a revenue producing monopoly in so far as the prohibition would obstruct the performance in law or in fact of the particular tasks assigned to that undertaking (para. 4, Sched. 3). This exclusion paraphrases Article 86(2) (formerly Article 90(2)) of the E.C. Treaty. It is a complex exclusion and requires proof that an undertaking has been "entrusted" with the operation of a service, that the service is of "general economic interest", and that the application of the competition rules would obstruct the performance of the assigned tasks (Commission Decision (91/50/EEC) *British Telecommunications*, [1982] O.J. L360/36, [1983] 1 C.M.L.R. 457). The additional condition that recognition of the exception would not affect the development of trade contrary to Community interests does not form part of the United Kingdom test but the United Kingdom has a Community obligation not to take any measure which would have such an effect derived from Article 10 of the E.C. Treaty. Some activities of the regulated utilities, the Royal Mail and other bodies are given a public service mission (such as the BBC) may benefit from this exclusion. One of the few cases where the E.C. Commission has specifically acknowledged that Article 86(2) applies, relates to the BBC's establishment of its News 24 Channel. This should, presumably, transfer directly into the application of the exclusion (Commission Press Release, September 29 1999 IP/99/706).

The Guidelines issued in final form or draft by some of the Regulators with concurrent powers jointly with the OFT deal with this exclusion. They indicate an intention, following E.C. precedent, to apply the exclusion sparingly: only if there is a clear conflict between the ability of the utility to perform a specific task which it has a duty to perform and the application of the prohibitions (see for example, OFT Guideline: *Competition Act 1998 Application in the Water and Sewerage Sectors*, OFT 422, February 2000, para. 3.14).

The Guideline states that the exclusion will not apply unless the undertaking has an obligation to carry out the task: mere approval is not enough. The exclusion is, however, wider than the "legal requirement" obligation (see 12.4.3 below) and will apply where an undertaking has discretion as to how it sets about carrying out its tasks and is therefore not simply following a mandatory process. This is exemplified at E.C. level in the BBC case referred to above.

OFGEM emphasises that it will examine whether there are alternative non-restrictive ways of performing the task at an acceptable cost and will not apply the exclusion where this is the case (formal consultation Draft Guideline, *Competition Act 1998 Application to the Energy Sectors*, OFT 428, May 2000, para. 3.37).

12.4.3 Compliance with Legal Requirements

The Chapter II Prohibition does not apply to conduct to the extent to which it is engaged in order to comply with a legal requirement (para. 5(2), Sched. 3). Legal requirement means a requirement imposed by or under any United Kingdom Act, by or under the Treaty of Rome or the EEA Agreement or imposed by or under the law in force in another Member State and having legal effect in the United Kingdom (Sched. 3, para. 5(3)). It does not include legal obligations imposed by a court and there is therefore scope for conflict where the Regulator objects to such an obligation. Parties may be ordered to engage in conduct or enter into agreements by statute. Compliance with directions given by the Rail Regulator under section 17 of the Railways Act 1993 is an example of conduct which may benefit from the exclusion (formal consultation draft Guideline *The Competition Act 1998 Application to Railways Services*, OFT 430, February 2000, para. 1.9).

12.4.4   Avoidance of Conflict with International Obligations

The Secretary of State may, by order, provide that the Chapter II Prohibition will
not apply, in order to avoid a conflict with an international obligation of the United
Kingdom (para. 6, Sched. 3). International obligations expressly include international civil aviation arrangements which are designated by order of the Secretary of
State (para. 6(b), Sched. 3). This is because such arrangements are made by informal means, which may not be otherwise recognised by the courts and the Regulators as obligations binding on the United Kingdom

12.4.5   Public Policy

The Secretary of State, if satisfied that there are exceptional and compelling reasons
of public policy, may provide that the Chapter II Prohibition does not apply in particular circumstances (para. 7(4), Sched. 3). Such an order may have retrospective
effect (para. 7(5), Sched. 3)).

12.4.6   Coal and Steel

The Chapter II Prohibition does not apply to conduct which relates to a coal or
steel product to the extent to which the ECSC Treaty gives the E.C. Commission
exclusive jurisdiction in the matter (para. 8, Sched. 3). This exclusion will fall away
when the ECSC Treaty expires in 2002 (see Chapter 7, para. 7.6.7).

Chapter 13

Procedure in Relation to Chapter II Prohibition

13.1   Overview
13.2   Notifications Generally
13.3   Guidance and its Effect
13.4   The Taking of a Decision and its Effect
13.5   Procedures Common to Chapter I and Chapter II Prohibitions

Note: *It should be noted that the guidance on procedure contained in Part 7 of the OFT Guideline:* The Major Provisions, *(OFT 400), March 2000 has been overtaken by the final version of The Director's Rules. The OFT have confirmed that the guideline will be reviewed in due course but say there are no immediate plans to do so.*

13.1   Overview

This Chapter deals with the way in which cases relating to the Chapter II Prohibition are handled. It draws on Guidelines, which have been published by the OFT and makes references to The Competition Act 1998 (Director's Rules) Order 2000 (S.I. 2000 No. 293) (the "Director's Rules") as appropriate. Much of the procedure before the Director is the same as for Chapter I cases and cross reference is made where appropriate to Chapter 9. That chapter may also contain greater detail on the notification process described in this chapter. Where there are no material differences in procedure this chapter simply cross refers to the relevant part of chapter 9.

13.1.1   Notification

Any person who thinks that their conduct may be an abuse of a dominant position which infringes the Chapter II Prohibition may apply to the Director for the conduct to be considered by him (s. 20). There is no statutory requirement to notify conduct to the Director and it is for the person or persons concerned to determine whether a notification is appropriate. Notification may be made for guidance (s. 21) or a decision (s. 22). It is likely that the formal notification process's principal use in relation to the Chapter II Prohibition will be defensive (in response to a complaint), supplementary to the notification of an agreement by a business recently held to be dominant or at the request of a Regulator in order that he can clarify what is acceptable. The equivalent notification process for a negative clearance in relation to Article 82 (formerly Article 86) E.C. Treaty has been little used: see *Competition Law and Practice* at 23.03.

13.1.2   Investigations

Under section 25(b), the Director has the power to conduct an investigation into conduct where there are reasonable grounds for suspecting that the Chapter II Prohibition has been infringed. The procedure is the same as in respect of the

Chapter I Prohibition, which is dealt with in Chapter 9, paras 9.9–9.12. He may also assist in investigations by the E.C. Commission in relation to Article 82 (see Chapter 9, at 9.14).

13.1.3   Complaints and Third Party Proceedings

Third parties may complain to the Director or to the relevant Regulator where they believe that there has been a breach of the Chapter II Prohibition. The consequences of such a complaint are the possibility of an investigation and civil proceedings brought directly by the complainant(s). Under section 47 third parties may ask the Director to vary or withdraw a decision (*e.g.* a decision that the Chapter II Prohibition does not apply) Again, there are no material differences in procedure between the position of third parties with respect to either the Chapter I or Chapter II Prohibition (see further Chapter 9, at 9.7 and 9.8 and Chapter 10 at 10.2).

13.2   Notifications Generally

13.2.1   Types of Notification

An application may take the form of either a notification for confidential guidance as to whether the notified conduct is *likely* to infringe the Chapter II Prohibition, or a notification for a decision as to whether the notified conduct *does* fall within the prohibition in Chapter II (ss 21–22).

In contrast to the procedure under Chapter I, the Director may not grant an exemption for conduct which infringes the Chapter II Prohibition.

The following parts of this section 13.2 are self contained, but the procedure is essentially the same as for notification in relation to the Chapter I process. Chapter 9 may contain additional detail.

13.2.2   Rules on Notification

Schedule 6 deals with the procedure for notification in relation to the Chapter II Prohibition. In addition, Schedule 9 sets out the matters which the rules that govern procedure may cover, but these provisions do not limit the Director's ability to make rules under section 51 (*Hansard*, (Standing Committee G) col. 501 (June 18, 1998)).

Applications for guidance or a decision must be made in accordance with the rules which the Director makes under section 51 (Sched. 6, para. 2(1)) which have taken shape as the Director's Rules (see 13.1 supra for reference). The detailed rules on the form of application, content, fees and the maintaining of a register of applications for decisions at the OFT and on its website are set out in Rules 1–8.

The notifying party must take all reasonable steps to notify all of the other parties to the conduct of whom he is aware that the application has been made and whether it is an application for guidance or a decision (Sched. 6, para. 2(2)). Rule 7 of the Director's Rules requires that notice must be given in writing within seven working days from the date when the applicant receives acknowledgement of receipt of his application from the Director.

13.2.3   Making a Notification

The notifying party should send the OFT the original Form N together with two copies of it. Form N is in the nature of an information request and the information required can be provided in any form, including by cross reference to other documents, such as a Form A/B submitted to the E.C. Commission. Supporting documents such as relevant agreements and annexes, must be either originals or certified true copies (r. 3(3)) and must also be submitted with two extra copies. Where the market is subject to the concurrent jurisdiction of a sector Regulator, one further copy of the Form N for each of those Regulator(s) must be sent to the OFT together with the Form's annexes and copies of the relevant agreements (r. 3(2)). The appropriate fee (see 13.2.6 below) must be paid at the time the Form N is submitted. Generally, an application will have effect on the date it is received by the Director, although applications received after 6pm on a working day will be treated as having been received on the next working day (r. 5(1), 26(7) Director's Rules).

If the conduct is being or has been notified to the E.C. Commission under Article 82 a copy of the completed Form A/B and supporting documents is required, together with any decision or comfort letter that may relate to the conduct. Any dispensation to comply with all of the information requirements in Form N should be discussed in advance with the OFT or the relevant sector Regulator (The OFT Guideline, *The Major Provisions of the Act*, OFT 409, March 1999 (the "Major Provisions Guideline") para. 7.12 and r. 4(2), Director's Rules). A dispensation will only be allowed in limited circumstances where the Director considers that such information or documents are not necessary for the examination of the case (r. 4(3), Director's Rules).

The procedure for determining an application will, largely, be written and the Director does not consider it necessary to prescribe formal procedures in respect of oral representations. However, in cases where an infringement decision is proposed, Rule 14(8) of the Director's Rules provides that the relevant party may make oral representations on the reasoned notice issued by the Director under Rule 14(3). The Director's reasoned notice will state the facts on which he relies, the matters to which he has taken objection and his proposed action. If requested, the Director must give the party(ies) an opportunity to inspect the Director's file relating to a proposed infringement decision, although this will not include access to any information which is confidential (as defined in r. 30(1)(c) or to the Director's internal documents (r. 14(5) and 14(6)).

13.2.4 Effect of Making an Incomplete Notification

The Director has one month following receipt of a notification and payment of the application fee to inform the applicant that the application is incomplete (r. 5(3), Director's Rules) failing which it appears the notification will be deemed to have become effective on the date it was received by the Director.

Where the Director finds that the Form N is incomplete he shall inform the applicant and set a time limit in writing for the applicant to provide the outstanding information. The application shall have effect on the date that the Director receives the complete information and any fee payable in respect of the application (r. 5(3), (4), (5) Director's Rules). If the Director has given notice that the information submitted as Form N is incomplete and not received the outstanding information, the information submitted will be returned to the applicant and he will be informed that his application has not been made in accordance with Director's Rules, r. 5(6).

13.2.5 Confidentiality

Section 55 provides for the maintenance of confidentiality. Any information relating to the affairs of an individual or business of an undertaking, which is received under the Act, may not be disclosed without consent from specified parties. There are, however, several exceptions to this rule, set out at section 55(3), including amongst others, disclosure for the purpose of facilitating the E.C. Commission's performance of any of its functions of Community competition law, disclosures to various United Kingdom Regulators for their regulatory purposes and disclosures in relation to criminal proceedings in the United Kingdom.

Where the applicant considers that any information in the application is confidential, he shall set out such information in a separate annex to the application headed "confidential information" and shall explain why it should be treated as such (r. 4(2), Director's Rules). Information will be confidential where it is:

(i)   commercial information, the disclosure of which would, or might, significantly harm the legitimate business interests of the undertaking to which it relates; or

(ii)   information relating to the private affairs of an individual, the disclosure of which would, or might, significantly harm his interests (r. 30(1)(c), Director's Rules).

This differs in two material respects from the language in sections 82(1) and 83(3A) Fair Trading Act 1973 ("FTA") providing for the exclusion of confidential information from reports of the Competition Commission. First, the test is objective (although this is qualified by various formulations (*e.g.* in r. 4(2), 14(6)(a) and (b)) which allow a measure of subjectivity in the designation of documents by the party concerned or the Director). Secondly, the FTA uses the formulation 'seriously and prejudicially affect" rather than 'significantly harm". The test of significant harm may be slightly lower, but the draftsman probably intended only to modernise.

13.2.6   Fees

The Director's Rules set out the fees for applications, which are £5,000 for examining an agreement or considering conduct with view to giving guidance and £13,000 for the consideration of conduct with view to obtaining a decision (r. 6 (2), (3) which refer to Annex 2).

13.2.7   Timetable for Dealing with Applications

There has been considerable industry concern that the OFT will follow the habit of the E.C. Commission and respond very slowly to notifications and rarely with an answer which has any legal effect, so creating a wider level of uncertainty for business.

In debate in the Standing Committee in the House of Commons, Mr McCartney said that "the rules are to cover a timetable, once the regime has bedded down" (*Hansard*, (Standing Committee G) col. 381 (June 11, 1998)). Lord Haskell had previously said in the House of Lords: "until the system has bedded down and we have an idea of the volume of applications that may be made, we believe that it would not be right to tie the Director down to a fixed timetable" (*Hansard*, H.L., Vol. 583, No. 63, col. 349 (November 13,1997)). At the time when draft Director's Rules were published, the Director said that he intended to set down non-binding administrative timetables for dealing with applications as soon as the prohibitions come into force. There is, however, nothing in the Director's Rules as adopted and there are, as yet, no administrative guidelines, despite the pressure from industry for clear timetables. This is not of concern while only a handful of agreements have been notified.

13.2.8 No Immunity from Penalties

Notifications made in respect of the Chapter II Prohibition do not carry the provisional immunity from financial penalties which follows from notifications in respect of the Chapter I Prohibition. Immunity will normally follow from favourable guidance or a favourable decision (see 13.3.4 and 13.4.7 and 8 below).

13.3 Guidance and its effect

13.3.1 Procedure on Notification

Where guidance is sought, the applicant must notify the Director of the conduct to be considered and apply to him for guidance (s. 21(1)). The Director may give the applicant guidance as to whether he considers that the notified conduct is *likely* to infringe the Chapter II Prohibition, although the Competition Act does not place him under any obligation to do so (s. 21(2)). If the Director declines to give guidance he must give written notice of that fact and return the fee in full (r. 10(2) Director's Rules).

13.3.2 Action to be taken by the Director

In considering a notification for guidance, the Director will determine whether it is likely that the conduct which has been notified to him infringes the Chapter II Prohibition. Guidance is given in confidence to the notifying party and third parties are not consulted. As a result, guidance is necessarily less certain in its nature than a decision and is not legally binding. Where, however, the Director has found that conduct is unlikely to infringe the Chapter II Prohibition, he will only be able to re-open a case in limited circumstances (see para. 13.4.7 below). After the Director has determined an application for guidance he must write to the applicant with his guidance, setting out the facts on which he bases the guidance and the reasons for it (r. 10(1), Director's Rules).

13.3.3 Notified Conduct Likely to Infringe the Chapter II Prohibition

Following a preliminary investigation, where the Director considers that it is likely that the notified conduct will infringe the Chapter II Prohibition, he has a number of courses open to him. He could decline to give guidance and/or invite the person(s) concerned to upgrade their application to one for a decision, so that he could carry out public consultation. In a case where he wished to ensure that the conduct was brought to an end rapidly, he could go on to make a provisional decision in respect of that conduct. The effect of making a provisional decision is considered at paragraph 13.4.5 below (Sched. 6, para. 3(1)). In many cases, however, an informal expression of concern may be sufficient for the conduct to be modified, so that the Director can go on to give favourable guidance, or stopped altogether.

13.3.4 Notified Conduct Unlikely to Infringe the Chapter II Prohibition

Where the Director issues guidance that conduct which has been notified to him is unlikely to infringe the Chapter II Prohibition, he can take no further action with respect to that conduct unless:

(1)   the Director has reasonable grounds for believing that there has been a
       material change of circumstance since he issued his guidance;
(2)   the Director has a reasonable suspicion that the information on which his
       guidance was based was incomplete, false or misleading in a material par-
       ticular; or
(3)   a complaint has been lodged with the Director in respect of the conduct
       (s. 23(1), (2)).

In these circumstances, the Director can take further action in respect of the
notified conduct and may lift the general immunity from penalty which applies to
conduct which he originally considered was unlikely to infringe the Chapter II Prohibition (see para. 13.3.5 below). In that case, the Director must first consult the
person to whom he has given guidance (r. 11, Director's Rules).

In the Standing Committee of the House of Commons, Mr McCartney confirmed that the test of reasonable suspicion is sufficient to ensure the Director will
be able to investigate complaints effectively if he has a reasonable suspicion or
grounds for doing so. If representations made in the consultation process allay the
Director's suspicion, he could take no further action. Where he feels that there is
still reasonable suspicion, he may move forward (e.g. to a provisional decision) on
notice to the party(ies) concerned in the conduct (Hansard, (Standing Committee
G) col. 375 (June 11, 1998)).

13.3.5   Imposition of Penalties

Where the Director has issued guidance that conduct which has been notified to
him is unlikely to infringe the Chapter II Prohibition, he cannot impose a penalty
in respect of any infringement of the prohibition by that conduct (s. 23(3)). This
immunity may be removed by the Director where:

(1)   any of the circumstances in respect of which the Director may reconsider
       previous guidance under Part I occurs (see para. 13.3.4 above);
(2)   the Director considers that it is likely that the conduct in question will
       infringe the Chapter II Prohibition; and
(3)   the Director gives notice in writing to the undertaking which originally
       applied for guidance that he is removing the immunity from penalty as
       from the date specified in the notice (s. 23(4)).

Generally, the lifting of immunity may not operate retrospectively. However,
the Director may lift the immunity from a date earlier than that on which the
notice is given where he has a reasonable suspicion that the information on which
he based his guidance, and which was provided to him by the undertaking engaging in the conduct, was incomplete, false or misleading in any material particular
(s. 23(5)).

13.4   The Taking of a Decision and its Effect

13.4.1   Procedure on Notification

The outline procedure when applying for a decision mirrors that for notifications
for guidance but involves publicity and additional steps. The applicant must notify
the Director of the conduct which is to be considered and apply to him for a deci-

sion as to whether such conduct *does* infringe the Chapter II Prohibition (s. 22(1)). The Director cannot grant an exemption for conduct which does infringe the Chapter II Prohibition.

13.4.2 Publication of an Application for a Decision

The Director is under a general duty to arrange for applications for a decision (but not applications for guidance) to be published in the manner which he considers to be most suitable so as to bring them to the attention of those who are likely to be affected by them (Sched. 6, para. 5(2)). This is done by making an entry on a public register available for inspection at the OFT on business days between 10.00a.m. and 4.30p.m. and on the OFT's website (r. 8, Director's Rules). The register contains a summary of the nature and objectives of the conduct notified and, once available, the outcome of the application. In addition, the Director publishes a weekly gazette containing summaries of notifications for decisions and the results of the notifications (The Major Provisions Guideline, para. 7.5).

13.4.3 The Director's Decision

The Director may make a decision as to whether the Chapter II Prohibition has been infringed. Where the Director's decision is that the notified conduct does not infringe the prohibition in Chapter II, he may state whether that is as a result of the conduct falling within one of the exclusions to the Chapter II Prohibition, which are considered in Chapter 12 (s. 22(2)).

In coming to a decision, the Director must follow such procedure as may be specified (Sched. 6, para. 5(1)). Rule 12(2) of the Director's Rules gives him the right, but not the obligation to carry out public consultation where the Director proposes to make a decision that the Chapter II Prohibition has been infringed.

The Director is under a duty to take into account representations which are made to him by persons other than the applicant (Sched. 6, para. 5(3)). However, the Director does not need to publish such applications where he is satisfied that, in coming to a decision, it will be sufficient for him to seek information from one or more particular persons other than the applicant (Sched. 6, para. 5(2)). This gives rise to the risk that the Director will consult too narrowly when considering an application for a decision but may be welcomed by parties who are concerned about confidentiality.

13.4.4 Action to be taken by the Director

In respect of an application for a decision, the Director will consider whether the notified conduct does in fact infringe the prohibition set down in Chapter II. The findings of fact which the Director makes in the course of determining such an application will be binding on the parties where:

(i) the time for bringing an appeal has expired without the undertakings whose conduct is alleged to have infringed the prohibition bringing an appeal; or

(ii) on appeal, an appeal tribunal has confirmed the Director's findings.

The findings will not, however, be binding where the court directs otherwise or where the Director takes further action in respect of the conduct under section 24(2) (see para. 13.4.7 below).

13.4.5   Adoption of a Provisional Decision

Where, following a preliminary investigation on an application for guidance or a decision, the Director considers that the notified conduct is likely to infringe the Chapter II Prohibition, he may make a provisional decision to that effect (Sched. 6, para. 3(1)). The Director must notify the applicant in writing of his provisional conclusion, setting out the facts on which he bases his conclusion and the reasons for it (Sched. 6, para. 3(2) and r. 9, Director's Rules).

A provisional decision has been described as a form of written 'statement of objections" in which the Director will set out the reasons for contemplating such a decision and invite a written response. Before a final decision is taken, it will usually be possible for parties to meet with officials of the OFT to elaborate on written representations which they have made already (The Major Provisions Guideline, para. 7.8).

A provisional decision does not affect the Director's final determination of the application (Sched. 6, para. 3(4)). The Director is not bound by it (see also Chapter 9 at 9.4).

13.4.6   Interim Measures

Where the Director has not completed his investigation, he may impose interim directions under section 35 of his own motion or following a request from a complainant seeking this relief, provided that he may also take interim measures he has reasonable suspicion that there is an infringement of the Chapter I or Chapter II Prohibition. If he considers it necessary to prevent serious irreparable damage to a particular person or category of persons, or to protect the public interest by urgent action (s. 35(2) and Enforcement Guideline, para. 3.7) (see also Chapter 9, para. 9.5.3).

13.4.7   Notified Conduct Does Not Infringe the Chapter II Prohibition

Where the Director makes a decision that the notified conduct does not infringe the Chapter II Prohibition, he can take no further action in respect of that conduct unless:

(1)   he has reasonable grounds for believing that there has been a material change of circumstance since he gave his decision; or
(2)   he has a reasonable suspicion that the information on which he based his decision was incomplete, false or misleading in a material particular (s. 24(2)).

In these circumstances, the Director may lift the general immunity from penalty which attaches to conduct which is the subject of a decision that it does not infringe the Chapter II Prohibition. Unlike guidance, the Director cannot re-open a decision simply because a complaint is made by a third party.

13.4.8   Imposition of Penalties

Where the Director has previously found that conduct which has been notified to him for a decision does not infringe the Chapter II Prohibition, he may not impose any penalty under Part I in respect of an infringement of the prohibition by that conduct (s. 24(3)). This immunity may be removed by the Director where:

(1)   circumstances arise which allow the Director to re-open a previous deci-
      sion which found that the conduct did not infringe the Chapter II Prohi-
      bition (see para. 13.4.7 above);
(2)   the Director considers it likely that the conduct in question will infringe
      the prohibition in Chapter II; and
(3)   the Director gives notice in writing to the undertaking which originally
      applied for a decision that he is removing the immunity from the date
      specified in the notice (s. 24(4)).

Generally, the lifting of immunity may not operate retrospectively. However, the
Director may lift the immunity from a date prior to that on which the notice is given
where he has a reasonable suspicion that information on which he based his decision, and which was provided to him by an undertaking engaging in the conduct in
question, was incomplete, false or misleading in a material particular (s. 24(5)) (see
13.3.4 above).

13.4.9   Publication of Decisions

The Director must publish the decisions which he makes and the reasons on which
they are based (Sched. 6, para. 6 and r. 15(b), Director's Rules). Publication is
intended to be made by way of the public register which will be held at the OFT
and will be accessible on the OFT's Internet website and through the Director's
weekly gazette (the Major Provisions Guideline, para. 7.5).

13.4.10   Undue Delay in Reaching a Decision

In the House of Lords, Lord Haskell indicated that the provisions in the Act "to
ensure that there is no undue delay in decisions made by the Director . . . .are
expected to be brought into force once the system has bedded down" (*Hansard*,
H.L., Vol. 583, No. 63, col. 349 (November 13, 1997)) (see para. 13.2.7). These
provisions (in s. 59) have not yet been brought into force. Once section 59 comes
into force, any person who is aggrieved by the Director's failure to determine an
application for a decision in accordance with the specified procedure will be able to
apply to the Court for relief. In England and Wales, the relevant Court is the High
Court; in Scotland, it is the Court of Session; and in Northern Ireland, it is the
High Court. Where the court is satisfied that there has been undue delay on the
part of the Director in determining the application, it will be able to give such directions to the Director as it considers appropriate in order to secure the determination of the application without any further unnecessary delay (Sched. 6, para. 7).

13.5   Procedures Common to Chapter I and Chapter II Prohibitions

13.5.1   Rights of Third Parties

The rights of third parties to complain, to request changes to the Director's decision and in relation to judicial review are dealt with in Chapter 9 at 9.7, 9.8 and
9.17.

13.5.2   Investigations

Investigations are dealt with in Chapter 9, at 9.9 to 9.13.

13.5.3   Appeal Against Decisions

Any person in respect of whose conduct the Director has made a decision as to whether the Chapter II Prohibition is infringed may appeal against the decision to the Competition Commission (s. 46). The procedure to be followed in launching an appeal and the effect of an appeal on the decision in question are dealt with at Chapter 9, para. 9.16.

Chapter 14

Consequences of Infringing the Chapter II Prohibition

14.1 Liability to Third Parties
14.2 Fines
14.3 Directions to Terminate
14.4 Interim Measures
14.5 Enforcement Against Director

14.1 Liability to Third Parties

14.1.1 Principle

The basis for a private right of action in the United Kingdom for a breach of Article 81 and 82 is somewhat uncertain and the basis in relation to the prohibitions is more so. The Act does not clarify the position, although Government policy is that civil liability for breach of the domestic prohibitions is to be the same as for a breach of Articles 81 and 82. It is likely that the United Kingdom courts will strive to establish a private right of action for damages and injunction for a private party affected by a breach of the Chapter II Prohibition. The issues that the courts will have to consider are discussed fully in Chapter 10, paras 10.2.4–10.2.6.

In many respects the same issues arise in relation to enforcement of the Chapter II Prohibition. This chapter refers, where appropriate, to more detailed discussion in Chapter 10.

14.2 Fines

14.2.1 Principle

Where an undertaking infringes the prohibition against abuse of a dominant position, the Director may fine the offending party up to a maximum of 10 per cent of turnover (s. 36(2)).

14.2.2 Level of Penalty

Financial penalties may be imposed up to a maximum limit set by The Competition Act 1998 (Determination of Turnover for Penalties) Order 2000 (S.I. 2000 No. 309). The maximum is 10 per cent of United Kingdom turnover for a period equal to the duration of the infringement (but capped at 10 per cent of United Kingdom turnover in the last three complete financial years and further reduced if the infringement was of shorter duration) (see Chapter 10, para. 10.3.5). The Director's *Guidance as to the Appropriate Amount of a Penalty*, OFT 423, March 2000 (the "Director's Guidance on Penalties") issued pursuant to section 38(1) explains the Director's approach to assessing a penalty. This is explained in more detail in Chapter 10, para. 10.3.5. The leniency policy explained in the Director's

Guidance on Penalties has no application in cases of breach of the Chapter II Prohibition.

There are no special rules on penalties relevant only to the Chapter II Prohibition. Before imposing a penalty the Director must be satisfied that the infringement has been committed intentionally or negligently by the undertaking (see also Chapter 10, para. 10.3.4) and that it did not act on the reasonable assumption that the conduct had immunity under section 40 as conduct of minor significance (see 14.2.3 below). Penalties will not be tax deductible (see Chapter 10, para. 10.3.1). None of these heads allow any discount from the fine in relation to deliberate conduct, but the Director can be expected to use his discretion where the conduct he condemns is of a type which has not previously been condemned as a breach of either Article 82 or the Chapter II Prohibition, particularly if it is similar to the behaviour of smaller competitors and the undertaking has been fully co-operative in bringing the conduct to an end. On the other hand, until recently the highest fines under the E.C. regime have been for breach of Article 82. The current record fine on *Volkswagen - Audi* ([1998] O.J. L124/60–108 of 102 million Euros reduced to 90 million Euros on appeal is for the operation of a network of agreements by a single large company in breach of Article 81. It displaces the longstanding record, which was for breach of Article 82, *Tetra Pak II* (Case C92/63), [1992] O.J. L72/1; [1992] 4 C.M.L.R. 551.

14.2.3   Small and Medium Sized Enterprises ("SMEs")

A person whose conduct is "conduct of a minor significance" is immune from fines (s. 40). This is intended to protect SMEs and ensure that they are not unduly burdened by the operation of the prohibition. In order to determine whether conduct is of minor significance a turnover threshold has been set by The Competition Act 1998 (Small Agreements and Conduct of Minor Significance) Regulations 2000 (S.I. 2000 No 262) Article 4. This provides that conduct will be of minor significance if the applicable turnover of the undertaking does not exceed £50 million in the business year ending in the calendar year preceding that in which the infringement occurred. The applicable turnover is calculated in accordance with the Schedule and is worldwide turnover for the group of companies that comprises the undertakings. In the case of an association, the turnover of all member undertakings is aggregated. The adoption of a turnover threshold follows Government indications in Committee *(Hansard,* H.L., Vol. 583, No. 64, col. 434 (November 17, 1997)) and is at the higher end of the range of £20 million to £50 million stated at that time.

As with the similar provisions relating to the prohibition of anti-competitive agreements (see Chapter 10, para. 10.3.1) it is intended that this will only provide immunity against fines and not against action by the Director to halt infringements of the prohibition or against third party actions. A business will also be immune from fines if the Director is satisfied that the business acted on the reasonable assumption that the rules on SMEs gave it immunity (s. 36(5)).

As with small agreements the Director may withdraw immunity from conduct of minor significance if he considers it likely that the conduct infringes the prohibition (see Chapter 10, para. 10.3.9 for further discussion). If immunity is withdrawn the Director must give the business concerned notice that he intends to remove immunity on a date after the date on which the decision is made. In determining the date of withdrawal of immunity the Director must take into account the amount of time the affected business will need to ensure there is no further infringement.

14.2.4 Immunity after a Decision or Guidance

A notification under the Chapter II Prohibition does not provide provisional immunity from penalties and consequently a provisional decision of the Director that a conduct infringes Chapter II does not result in the loss of immunity.

However subject to the removal of immunity from penalties for favourable guidance or a favourable decision under certain circumstances (see Chapter 10, para. 10.3.9) a penalty cannot be imposed for an infringement of the Chapter II Prohibition where the Director has given guidance that the conduct is unlikely to infringe the prohibition (s. 23) or has made a decision that the conduct does not infringe it (s. 24).

14.2.5 Rights of appeal

Where the Director has made a decision to fine a business for a breach of the prohibition against abuse of a dominant position, there is a right of appeal (see Chapter 10, para. 10.3.15 for a detailed discussion). An appeal will suspend the obligation to pay the fine but the Competition Commission may vary the penalty or add interest.

14.2.6 Payment and Enforcement

Notice of a penalty must be in writing and specify the date by which a penalty must be paid (for further details see Chapter 10, para. 10.3.9). Where an undertaking has not paid the penalty by the due date and it has brought no appeal against the penalty notice within the time permitted or the appeal has been made and determined) the Director can bring proceedings to recover the required amount as a civil debt (s. 37).

Under the Chapter II Prohibition, the Director may require either the undertaking concerned to pay a penalty or, where joint dominance has been established and more than one undertaking has infringed the prohibition, each undertaking may be required by the Director to pay a penalty. A more detailed discussion of enforcement of penalty decisions is set out in Chapter 10, para. 10.3.16.

14.3   Directions to Terminate

14.3.1   Principle

The Director has the power, where he has made a decision that conduct infringes the Chapter II Prohibition, to give directions to such persons or person as he considers appropriate to bring the infringement to an end (s. 33). This would include directions requiring the person concerned to terminate or modify his conduct.

14.3.2   Enforcement Action

Where a person fails, without reasonable excuse, to comply with a section 33 direction to terminate or modify his conduct, the Director may apply to the court for an order compelling the person to rectify his default within a specified time (s. 34). The court order may provide for the costs to be borne by the person in default or any officer of an undertaking who is responsible for the default. Breach of the order would be punishable as a contempt of court, the sanction for which may be a fine or imprisonment. For a more detailed discussion of directions to terminate see Chapter 10, paras 10.4.1–10.4.3.

14.4   Interim Measures

14.4.1   Principle

During the Director's investigation of a possible breach of the prohibition of abuse of a dominant position he may exercise his power under section 35 to take interim measures to stop or control the behaviour in question until his investigation is completed where :

(i)   he has a reasonable suspicion that the Chapter II Prohibition has been infringed; and

(ii)   it is necessary to act in order to
— prevent serious irreparable damage to third parties; or
— to protect the public interest.

For a further discussion of the Director's powers to impose interim measures see Chapter 10, paras 10.5.1 and 10.5.2.

14.4.2   Appeals

A decision to impose interim measure will be appealable to a tribunal of the Competition Commission (s. 46(3)), although the making of such an appeal will not suspend the effect of the interim measures decision.

14.4.3   Enforcement

An interim measures direction can be enforced by the Director in the same way as a direction to terminate can (see Chapter 10, para. 10.4.3).

14.5   Enforcement Against Director

14.5.1   Failure to Take a Decision

The Government has indicated that at some stage after the Act has come into force it is intended that parties should have the right to apply to the court for an order that the Director does not delay an application for a decision (Sched. 6, para. 7).

14.5.2   Other Procedural Irregularities

Some procedural irregularities may be capable of judicial review (see Chapter 9 at 9.17) as the rights of appeal given by section 46 are limited in extent. Such rights may be available to third parties with sufficient interest as well as undertakings under investigation.

Chapter 15

Retention of the Existing Monopoly Investigation Regime

15.1 Introduction
15.2 Complex Monopolies under the FTA
15.3 Scale Monopolies under the FTA
15.4 Remedies
15.5 Changes to FTA
15.6 Enforcement
15.7 Interrelationship between the Monopoly Provisions of the FTA and the Prohibitions

15.1 Introduction

15.1.1 Parallel Systems to Control Dominance

In the Government's Consultation Paper of August 1997 (the "Consultation Paper"), the emphasis was largely on the shift to prohibitive approaches to anti-competitive behaviour. In line with this, the investigative approach contained in sections 2–10 of the Competition Act 1980 was repealed by the Competition Act 1998. The existing investigative system contained in the monopoly provisions of the Fair Trading Act 1973 ("FTA"), has not, however, been replaced, but has been modified to run in parallel with the prohibitions.

15.1.2 Rationale — Complex Monopolies

The Consultation Paper made it clear that the Government did not consider that regulation of market power could successfully be dealt with solely by a prohibitive approach. Where a single company is involved, a prohibition of abuse of dominant position would, for most purposes, be effective. However, where there was no evidence of anti-competitive agreements, which could be dealt with under the prohibition of such agreements, the prohibitive approach was not thought to be flexible enough to deal with anti-competitive parallel behaviour between a number of parties (Consultation Paper, p. 21). During the Bill's Committee Stage in the Lords, Lord Simon for the Government emphasised the value of the wide-ranging and impartial investigations, which can be carried out by the Monopolies and Mergers Commission ("MMC") (now replaced by the Competition Commission, see 15.1.6 below) under the FTA. The Government was keen to retain the wide range of remedies available under the FTA which, because of their potential strength, should only be available under Parliamentary scrutiny (*Hansard*, H.L., Vol. 583, No. 63 col. 300 (November 13, 1997)).

The OFT's Guidelines under the Competition Act 1998 echo this (see OFT Guideline, *The Major Provisions*, OFT 400, March 1999, Part 13) stating that the existing provisions of the FTA and the provisions of the Act are not intended to be used in parallel. Suspected breaches of the Act are normally to be investigated under the Act, not the FTA. The complex monopoly provisions of the FTA will be used to deal with behaviour outside the scope of the prohibitions, such as non-collusive parallel conduct.

Since the Act was passed, developments in E.C. jurisprudence in relation to joint dominance establish that the concept is clearly recognised by the ECJ and employed by the E.C. Commission: *France, Société Commerciale des Potasses et de L'Azote (SCPA) and another v. Commission (Kali und Salz)* (Joined Cases C–68/94 and C–30/95) [1998] O.J. C209/2, [1998] E.C.R. I–1375, [1998] 4 C.M.L.R. 829); *Airtours/First Choice,* IV/M1524 [2000] O.J. L093/1. Although these cases are under the Merger Regulation, they show the possibility of using Article 82 (and the Chapter II Prohibition) to address abusive conduct carried out in parallel by a small number of undertakings enjoying joint dominance. The joint dominance doctrine is, however, not apt to deal with parallel practices by large numbers of businesses, such as have been tackled under the complex monopoly doctrine, for example, over a hundred complex monopolists in *Residential Mortgage Valuations* (1994) Cm. 2542 and an indefinite (but very large) number of retailers in *Contact Lens Solutions* (1993) Cm. 2242. There are real difficulties in establishing which (if any) undertakings enjoy joint dominance in industries where smaller competitors have the same business structure and trading practices as the market leaders, and deciding whether industry-wide business practices can be abusive for some but not others. The complex monopoly regime, on the other hand, can be a powerful tool to change business practices throughout an industry, affecting both large and small businesses. For example, the supply of beer (Loan Ties, Licensed Premises and Wholesale Prices) Order 1989 (S.I. 1989 No. 2258) affected practices of both small and large brewery businesses following the complex monopoly report: *Beer* (1989) Cm. 691.

15.1.3   Rationale — Scale Monopolies

The Government considered that if there is a likelihood of abusive behaviour by a dominant player in a particular market in the future, after an individual abuse has been dealt with under the prohibition, it may be appropriate to tackle the problem of dominance by using a structural approach. It stated that the scale monopoly provisions of the FTA would be retained to deal with the situation where the prohibition alone would not be a sufficient deterrent to prevent future abuse (Consultation Paper, pp. 21–22).

The scale monopoly provisions of the FTA can be used to take structural measures to reduce market power and prevent future abuses. These measures cannot be readily imposed under the prohibitive approach. Lord Simon emphasised in the Lords that the Government saw the retention of this regime as a reserve to fill any gaps between the new prohibitions. However, the scale monopoly provisions could also still have value in the case of utilities (*Hansard*, H.L., Vol. 583, No. 63, cols 301–302 (November 13, 1997)).

The OFT Guideline, *The Major Provisions*, OFT 400, March 1999 explains that, except in relation to regulated utilities, the scale monopoly provisions of the FTA should only be used where a prior infringement of the prohibitions has been found and the Director believes further abuse by the same party is a real likelihood (see 15.3.3 below).

15.1.4   Application of the Existing Regime to Regulated Utilities

The Guidelines make it clear that the scale monopoly provisions will still be available for use as the primary form of regulation for regulated utilities without a prior infringement of the prohibitions under the Act. This approach has been adopted because of the special conditions surrounding the regulated utilities and the difficulty of establishing competition in those sectors (see Chapter 4, paras 4.5.1). It is notable that a scale monopoly reference coupled with a licence reference was a prelude to the restructuring of gas supply in the United Kingdom (*Gas:* (1993) Cm. 2314, Cm. 2316, Cm. 2317; *British Gas Plc (Licence modification reference)* (1993) Cm. 2315).

15.1.5 Effect of Policy

How far the monopolies provisions of the FTA will continue to be used remains to be seen. Certainly, one major complex monopoly reference has been made since the Competition Act 1998 came into force: *Banks* (March 20, 2000) an inquiry into the provision of banking services by clearing banks to small and medium sized firms in the United Kingdom (Press Release P/2000/194). There is no doubt, however, that with both investigative and prohibition regimes, British business is subject to more competition regulation than exists in other comparable jurisdictions and that this will create significant costs for business. (See further Chapter 17 at 17.7 for the possible impact of proposed E.C. reforms).

15.1.6 Changes to the Monopolies and Mergers Commission

The investigative functions previously carried out by the MMC are now carried out by the Competition Commission. The previous MMC members form the nucleus of the Competition Commission (see Chapter 3, para. 3.4.1. *et seq*).

15.2 Complex Monopolies Under the FTA

15.2.1 Definition

A complex monopoly exists in relation to the supply of goods or services where at least one quarter of all the goods or services of a particular description supplied in the United Kingdom or any part of the United Kingdom are supplied by or to (or, in the case of services, for) members of the same group. The "group" is not a group of companies, but a number of unrelated businesses who produce or supply goods or services of the same description. The persons constituting the group must fulfil the condition that, whether voluntarily, or not, and whether by agreement, or not, they so conduct their respective affairs as in any way to prevent, restrict, or distort competition (FTA, ss. 6(2) and 7(2)).

The determination of whether one quarter of any particular description of goods or services may be supplied by or to members of such a group is made initially by the Director, on any grounds he thinks 'suitable" (see FTA, s. 10(6)). This test is not an economic approach but does give the Director a simple jurisdictional test to apply. While the Director is not bound to approach the task using the economic tools of market definition he is likely in most cases to follow the approach set out in the OFT Guideline, *Market Definition*, OFT 403, March 1999.

15.2.2 Outline of Procedure

The Director may use enhanced investigative powers introduced into the FTA by the Competition Act 1998 to determine whether a complex monopoly situation exists (see para. 15.5.2). If the Director believes that a complex monopoly situation exists, he can make a reference to the Competition Commission under FTA section 50 to investigate and report on the existence and effect on the public interest of the monopoly situation, or the effect on the public interest of specific practices which appear to him to be anti-competitive. The Competition Commission will report on these matters and submit a report to the Secretary of State with its conclusions of the effects on the public interest of the practices investigated. It will also report on the desirability of taking particular action to remedy or prevent any practices in the monopoly situation which are adverse to the public interest. The Secretary of State, advised by the Director, can make orders or accept undertakings to remedy such adverse effects. The Secretary of State may also make references under FTA section 51 and may veto references by the Director (FTA, s. 50(6)).

In addition, the Secretary of State, advised by the Director, has powers to accept undertakings in lieu of a reference to the Competition Commission (FTA, ss. 56 A–G introduced by the Deregulation and Contracting Out Act 1994). The use of undertakings is unlikely in the case of a complex monopoly, unless it has a very small number of participants (see *Competition Law and Practice*, Chapter 20, for a more detailed account).

15.2.3 Public Interest

When considering the public interest, the Competition Commission (or in relation to proposed undertakings in lieu, the Director) will take into account all matters which it considers relevant and will have regard to separate factors set out in FTA section 84, namely the desirability:

"(1) of maintaining and promoting effective competition between persons supplying goods and services in the United Kingdom;

(2) of promoting the interests of consumers, purchasers, and other users of goods and services in the United Kingdom in respect of the prices charged by them and in respect of their quality and the variety of goods and services supplied;

(3) of promoting, through competition, the reduction of costs and the development and use of new techniques and products, and of facilitating the entry of new competitors into existing markets;

(4) of maintaining and promoting the balanced distribution of industry and employment in the United Kingdom; and

(5) of maintaining and promoting competitive activity in markets outside the United Kingdom on the part of producers of goods, and of suppliers of goods and services in the United Kingdom."

It can be seen that the maintenance of competition is not the exclusive object of the public interest tests. In practice though, most monopoly inquiries concentrate on the effects on competition: see *Competition Law and Practice*, Chapter 20 at 20.41 *et seq.*

15.2.4   Findings of the Commission

The Competition Commission may find that there is no harm to the public interest. In this situation, no action can be taken under the FTA to deal with the members of the group involved in the alleged complex monopoly. Negotiations between the Director and the parties involved may in fact lead to changes in the way they behave. The Director may keep the situation "under review" and repeat references within a relatively short space of time are not uncommon (*e.g.* the three references *Tampons* (1980) Cm. 8049, *Tampons* (1985) Cm. 9470 and *Tampons* (1986) Cm. 9705; the two references *New Motor Cars* (1992) Cm. 1808 and *New Motor Cars* (2000) Cm. 4660) are the best recent examples).

Alternatively, the Competition Commission can find that there is harm to the public interest and make recommendations on appropriate remedies. In this case, the Secretary of State has wide powers to remedy the situation. These are dealt with below at 15.4.

15.3   Scale Monopolies Under the FTA

15.3.1   Definition

A scale monopoly exists in the supply of goods or services where at least one quarter of all the goods or services are supplied by or to one and the same entity or interconnected bodies corporate (FTA, ss. 6(1)(a) and (b) and 7(1)(a) and (b)). Companies are treated as "interconnected" if one is a subsidiary of the other or of a common parent within the meaning of section 736 of the Companies Act 1985.

15.3.2   Making a Scale Monopoly Reference — Policy Change

The Government stated in the Consultation Paper that use of scale monopoly investigations should be limited to situations where there "has already been proven abuse under the prohibition, and the Director believes there is a real prospect of future different abuses by the same firm" (Consultation Paper, p. 22). The Commission should only be asked to investigate in these circumstances. This policy intention is broadly reflected in the Guidelines. It does not apply to regulated utilities (see Chapter 4, para. 4.5.1). The detailed approach suggested by Lord Simon has not been spelled out. In Committee, Lord Simon stated that before a reference to the Commission was framed, the Director might have to make a wide examination of the case and determine what activities were covered by the prohibitions. These activities would then be excluded from the reference; they would be dealt with using the prohibitions (*Hansard,* H.L., Vol. 583, No. 63, cols 263–264 (November 13, 1997)).

It was originally thought that the Secretary of State would give a direction to the Director to consider making a scale monopoly reference only in the circumstances where abuse has been proven under the prohibition and future abuse was apprehended, or in relation to a business which is a regulated utility. This could be done under the powers which the Secretary of State has under FTA section 12(2)(c). It appears, however, that it is being dealt with more informally simply as a policy of the Director which both he and the Secretary of State are free to over-ride on a case-by-case basis. If the Director makes a reference against the wishes of the Secretary of State then the Secretary of State may use his powers under section 50(6) to block the reference.

This leaves a considerable degree of uncertainty as to what approach will in fact be adopted, with the constant threat that scale monopoly investigations could become used more frequently in future as a result of a change of political climate. When considered in the light of the prohibitive approach, this additional level of scrutiny may be considered to be over-regulation and potentially an unnecessary burden on industry.

15.3.3   Scale Monopoly Investigations

Scale monopolies can be investigated by the Director and referred to the Commission by the Director or Secretary of State in the same way as complex monopolies. The same public interest test applies and the Competition Commission may make findings in the same way and of the same nature (see 15.2.2 to 15.2.4 above).

15.4   Remedies

15.4.1   Process

Where the Competition Commission finds that a scale or complex monopoly situation operates in a way adverse to the public interest, it will identify the matters which give rise to concern and recommend possible remedies (FTA, s. 54(3)). The Secretary of State may follow their suggestions or consider other remedies with the advice of the Director. Remedies may be dealt with by undertakings to the Secretary of State, negotiated by the Director (FTA, s. 88) or by orders (FTA, s. 56). Compliance with undertakings and orders is policed by the Director and he will advise the Secretary of State on possible relaxation, release or revocation if the situation warrants it.

15.4.2   Behavioural Remedies

Orders may be made under FTA section 56 and Sched. 8, Part 1, *inter alia*:

(1)   to require termination of an agreement or place limits on the extent to which it can be lawfully performed;

(2)   to declare it unlawful to refuse supply to specified individuals;

(3)   to declare it unlawful to discriminate between any persons in the prices charged for goods or services or any other specified practice which could amount to such discrimination;

(4)   to declare it unlawful to give preference in the supply of goods or services to any person or to procure others to do such things;

(5)   to require any person to provide information on the prices charged and the quantities of goods sold and the areas in which the goods or services were supplied;

(6)   to regulate prices; and

(7)   to prevent notification of prices to other parties.

The Secretary of State can only introduce price regulation where the Competition Commission has specified that the prices charged for goods or services of the relevant description operate, or may be expected to operate contrary, to the public interest. These powers will remain unchanged under the new regime (see *Competition Law and Practice* Chapter 28 for a more detailed account).

15.4.3   Structural Remedies

The Secretary of State also has powers in FTA, Schedule 8, Part 2, to order divestment of property and to order businesses to be broken up and sold or groups of companies to be divided. He can also order companies to be formed or wound up and property divided between them. These powers (which require an order approved by affirmative resolution of both Houses of Parliament) are, however, rarely used. The powers were used in response to the MMC's report *Beer* (1989) Cm. 651. The Supply of Beer (Tied Estate) Order 1989 (S.I. 1989 No. 2390) required brewers holding over 2,000 licensed premises on November 1, 1992 to release the tenants of a certain proportion of them from exclusive purchasing obligations or to dispose of either their brewing interests or all their licensed premises in excess of a total of 2,000.

As such orders have a flavour of expropriation of property, their use has to be considered carefully against the requirements of the European Convention of Human Rights (Article 1 of the First Protocol). The effect of the Human Rights Act 1998, is to incorporate the European Convention on Human Rights into English law. It took effect on October 2, 2000 (The Human Rights Act 1998 (Commencement No. 2) Order 2000 (S.I. 2000 No. 1851)). Orders will, therefore, have now to be made, read and given effect to in a way which is compatible with the Convention. The courts will have the power to review orders and may declare them incompatible with the Convention. However, such a declaration will not affect the validity or enforceability of the order, although clearly it will be persuasive and such an order would be likely to be repealed.

15.4.4 Undertakings and Assurances

Undertakings to the Secretary of State may arise either in lieu of a monopoly reference (FTA, ss. 56A–56G, introduced by the Deregulation and Contracting Out Act 1994) or following a reference instead of an order under section 56 (FTA, s. 88). Remedies by way of undertaking are negotiated against the backdrop of Sched. 8, but can cover other matters not precisely on all fours with anything in Sched. 8. The Director publishes the undertakings given to the Secretary of State. In addition, the Director has an extra statutory practice of accepting assurances in lieu of a monopoly reference and these will also be published, in some cases with a report of his extra statutory assessment of the monopoly situation: *e.g., British Sky Broadcasting* (position in the Wholesale Pay TV Market,) December 1996, and informal undertakings (OFT Press Release, July 1996) and the current OFT review of BSkyB's position in the Wholesale Pay TV market and the appropriateness of undertakings given in July 1996 (OFT Press Release, March 1, 2000).

These possibilities continue to exist, although it seems unlikely that they will be used simply to avoid the trouble of a formal (and appealable) decision under the Competition Act 1998. More likely, they will be used as a fishing expedition where no clear breach of the prohibitions has been identified so adding to the burdens on business and, to some extent, circumventing the safeguards afforded in the Competition Act procedures (see also 15.5.2 and 15.5.6 below).

15.5 Changes to FTA

15.5.1 Land Agreements

The amendments to the FTA described below are largely procedural, but the Competition Act 1998 section 68 amends FTA section 137 to allow the Secretary of State to bring within the definition of services for the purposes of both the monopolies and the merger provisions of the FTA "any activity specified in the order which consists in, or in making arrangements in connection with, permitting the use of land". Any such activity may also be removed from the ambit of the definition of services by order. There are consequential powers to amend or repeal any of paras (c), (d), (e) or (g) of FTA section 137(3), which currently deal with aspects of the use of land, for example in relation to bus stops (FTA, s. 137(3)(d)).

This change will enable a more comprehensive approach to land agreements to be put in place and greater flexibility in the application of the FTA. It is, perhaps, only reasonable that land agreements, which are to benefit from a fairly comprehensive exclusion from the Chapter I Prohibition should be able to be fully regulated under the FTA. To date, however, no orders have been made under section 68. Any such change would extend to the mergers jurisdiction as well as the monopolies jurisdiction.

15.5.2   The Director's and Sector Regulator's Powers of Investigation

The Director is given new powers by section 66 of the Competition Act 1998, amending FTA section 44 to gather information to decide whether to make a monopoly reference or whether to propose that the Secretary of State accept undertakings from the parties to a suspected monopoly under FTA section 56A (see FTA ss. 44(1) and 44(1A) as amended). These powers are broadly similar to those given to the Director under Chapter 3 of the Act in relation to investigations under the Chapter I and Chapter II Prohibitions, although they do not provide for the power to obtain a warrant to enter premises. The premises which may be entered are also limited to business premises.

It would be unfortunate if the availability of these powers (which are a hangover from draft legislation prepared before the inclusion of the Chapter II Prohibition) encouraged use of the monopoly provisions of the FTA simply as a "fishing expedition" in relation to businesses with large market shares, when there was no evidence of abuse. It would nullify Government assurances that the monopoly jurisdiction would be reserved for use in tackling structural matters and (except in the case of utilities) would not be used for single company (scale monopoly) investigations unless breach of the Chapter II Prohibition was already established and behavioural remedies were not adequate.

Any of the utility Regulators with power to make monopoly references will use the same new investigatory powers under the FTA as the Director and will be able to use them in the same way as the Director where relevant to their sector.

15.5.3   Requests for Information

The Director, instead of being able to require companies to furnish him with information, can now require any producer, supplier of or customer for goods or services in the United Kingdom to provide him with any specified documents or any documents falling within a specified category (FTA, s. 44(2)). The request must be made in writing (s. 44(4)), must specify or otherwise describe the documents required and extends to those documents which are in the custody or control of that person and are "relevant" (s. 44(2)(a)). Furthermore, the Director may require anyone who is carrying on a business in the United Kingdom to give him specified estimates, forecasts, returns or other information at the time and in the form and manner specified by him (s. 44(2)(b)). This considerably strengthens the Director's powers in relation to both scale and complex monopoly references. Section 45, which previously provided lesser powers in relation to possible complex monopolies is repealed (Competition Act 1998, Sched. 14).

Where documents are to be produced, the Director may copy the documents or extracts of them (FTA, s. 44(5)). He can require the person notified to produce the documents and require any person who is a present or past officer of that entity, or any one who has been an employee of that entity at any time, to provide explanations of the documents. If a document is not produced, the notified person can be required to state where it is to the best of his knowledge and belief.

15.5.4 "Relevant" Documents

Parties can only be required to produce relevant documents. Relevance is defined in FTA, section 44(8). A "relevant" document is one that is relevant to the decision to be made whether to make a reference to the Competition Commission under the monopoly provisions of the FTA, or to take undertakings in lieu of such reference, but only if the document is requested for the purpose of assisting the Director in taking this decision. Documents include information recorded in any form and where it is not legible, it must be produced in a legible form if this is possible.

15.5.5 Power to Enter Premises

This power is backed up by a power inserted in FTA, section 44(2)(c) to enter any premises used for the business purposes of a producer or supplier of or customer for goods and services in the United Kingdom and require any person on those premises to produce any documents on the premises which are in his custody or control and which are "relevant". The Director can insist that such persons to give such explanation of the documents as he may require.

15.5.6 Procedural Safeguards

Evidence of authorisation must be produced before any person is obliged to comply with any of these requests (FTA, s. 44(7)). Furthermore, no person will be compelled to produce any document which he could not be compelled to produce in civil proceedings before the High Court or, in Scotland, the Court of Session (FTA, s. 44(6)). Similarly, no person will be compelled to give such information as he would not be compelled to give in evidence in such proceedings. The definition of "relevant" appears to provide in itself a procedural safeguard as the document will not be relevant unless the Director's use of the powers is genuinely to assist him in taking a decision on a monopoly reference or the scope of undertakings in lieu. It will be for the courts to decide whether he can use these powers as a "fishing expedition" to find evidence of abusive conduct or anti-competitive agreements caught by the prohibitions and at what stage he must assert his powers under the Act (ss. 25–26) to pursue an investigation.

The Human Rights Act 1998, will also provide an additional layer of safeguards. This Act, in section 6 makes it unlawful for a public authority to act in a manner which is incompatible with a Convention Right unless the effect of primary legislation is that the authority could not have acted differently, or if the primary legislation cannot be read in such a way as to be compatible with the Convention, the authority was acting in such a way as to give effect to, or enforce the provisions of, that legislation.

15.5.7 Differences from Investigative Powers under the Prohibition

The powers given to the Director in the conduct of monopolies inquiries are now very similar to those which will be available to the Director when investigating breach of the prohibitions. The Director will not, however, have the power to obtain a warrant and enter premises, by force if necessary, to ensure that he obtains all the information requested in relation to a potential monopoly inquiry.

15.5.8   Powers of the Competition Commission

The Competition Commission's powers as a reporting body are largely unchanged from those of the MMC. The Competition Commission is constituted by the Competition Act 1998 section 45 and Sched. 7. Obligations in relation to interested parties in FTA section 81 have been repealed. This topic is now dealt with in Sched. 7, para. 19(2) which gives discretion to the group of the Competition Commission hearing each case. The Competition Commission retains the power to compel witnesses to attend, give evidence and produce specified documents which may be required to be created for the purpose of the inquiry. Most of the Competition Commission's fact gathering will, however, continue to be done through the less formal use of questionnaires to interested parties, a practice which the MMC developed in reliance on the existence of its powers to compel evidence (see *Competition Law and Practice*, Chapter 24 for a more detailed account).

15.6   Enforcement

15.6.1   Offences

FTA section 46 is amended by the Competition Act section 67 so that it will be an offence to refuse or wilfully neglect to comply with the requirements in FTA section 44(2). This offence will be punishable on summary conviction either by a fine, or if convicted on indictment, by a fine, or (for an individual) a term of imprisonment not exceeding two years, or both.

It will also be an offence punishable by a fine under FTA section 46(7) to obstruct intentionally the Director in excising his powers of investigation under FTA section 44. Under section 46(8) it will be an offence to suppress or destroy any document which has been required to be produced under section 44, punishable on summary conviction by a fine, or on conviction on indictment, by a fine or a term of imprisonment of up to two years, or both.

15.6.2   Defences

It will be a defence under FTA section 46(5) to the offence of failing to produce the required document, to prove that the document was not in a party's possession or control and that it was not reasonably practicable for him to comply with the requirement. Similarly, it is a defence in respect of a failure to provide an explanation of a document, or failure to state where a document can be found, that the person had a reasonable excuse for failing to do so.

15.7   Interrelationship Between the Monopoly Provisions of the FTA and the Prohibitions

15.7.1   Complex Monopolies

FTA powers to investigate complex monopolies may be a first step by the Director, taken without any evidence of a prohibited agreement or prohibited behaviour. If his own inquiries show evidence of breach of one of the prohibitions, he may proceed under the Competition Act instead of making a reference. If evidence of breach emerges after the Competition Commission investigation has started then the parties are exposed to investigation under both regimes, unless the monopoly reference is amended so as to limit its scope or is discontinued. A complex monopoly investigation may provoke third parties to launch litigation against the businesses involved, if the investigation reveals either a prohibited agreement or conduct which might amount to abuse of a jointly held dominant position. These dangers are undoubtedly greater now that there are both national and European prohibitions. The primary purpose of using the complex monopoly jurisdiction, however, will be to deal with fairly concentrated industries where there is no evidence of prohibited agreements, but where similar patterns of behaviour may have damaging effects on competition.

Examples of a complex monopoly reference, where it looks as if many of the investigated parties would have infringed neither prohibition, are the *Brown Goods* and *White Goods* references (1997) Cm. 3675 and Cm. 3676, which led to a ban on recommended resale prices for certain categories of electrical goods, by all suppliers, large and small.

15.7.2   Scale Monopolies

The implication of the Government's thinking as set out in the Consultation paper and by Lord Simon in the Lords, as well as the OFT's Guidelines, is that (except for regulated utilities) the Chapter II Prohibition will be the first provision that will be used and that it will be used to tackle individual abuses. The scale monopoly provisions should only be used later to tackle the structural problems of dominance: *e.g.* by ordering divestiture of part of a business or a long term regulatory regime. For the risks of a departure from this process, see 15.5.2 and 15.5.6 above.

If a finding of abuse has already been made under the Chapter II Prohibition, any potential third party litigation is already likely to have been provoked and an adverse finding by the Competition Commission under the scale monopoly provisions is unlikely to give new opportunities to third parties. If, however, the scale monopoly provisions were used first, then any adverse finding could provoke third party litigation and a further investigation by the Director in relation to the Chapter II Prohibition.

Chapter 16

Transitional Arrangements

16.1   Introduction

The transition from existing competition legislation to the new Act is dealt with in Sched. 13 to the Act. The transitional arrangements were intended to allow businesses reasonable time to modify agreements and practices to comply with the new regime under the Act, and to reduce the regulatory burden by providing longer periods for agreements which had been filed under the previous legislation, or which fell into categories exempted from, or falling outside, that legislation. Following the Competition Act 1998 coming into force, the main purposes of looking at the transitional provisions is to ascertain whether an existing agreement benefits from the transitional arrangements, when any applicable transitional arrangements come to an end and whether enforcement of an agreement is still affected by a failure to file under the Restrictive Trade Practices Act 1976 ("RTPA").

16.2   Transition from the Restrictive Trade Practices Act 1976 and Resale Prices Act 1976

The RTPA and the Resale Prices Act 1976 (the "RPA") were repealed on March 1, 2000 when the Chapter I Prohibition came into force ("the starting date"). The starting date was over 16 months after the date of enactment of the Act on November 9, 1998 ("the enactment date"). The application of the RTPA and RPA to an agreement is determined by reference to whether the agreement was entered into before the enactment date or in the period between the enactment date, and the starting date ("the interim period"). Since the RTPA and RPA were repealed on the starting date, some agreements subject to those Acts are now subject to the Chapter I Prohibition, but many still benefit from the transitional arrangements and are not yet subject to the Chapter I Prohibition. The operation of the transitional arrangements of the RTPA in relation to agreements made before the date of enactment and during the interim period is illustrated in Charts 16.1 and 16.2 respectively and explained more fully below.

16.2.1 Agreements Made Prior to the Enactment Date

Agreements made before the enactment date continued to be subject to the provisions of the RTPA. Consequently particulars of any agreement entered into before that date which was registrable under the RTPA should have been furnished to the Director within the time limits for notification set out in RTPA, Sched. 2. In most instances an agreement, or a variation to it, should have been furnished within three months of its execution. This applies even if an agreement was entered into within three months before the enactment date and if the deadline for furnishing particulars of the agreement was after the enactment date.

Where a registrable, non-notifiable agreement was entered into before the enactment date any registrable variation to that agreement prior to the starting date should have been filed in accordance with RTPA, section 24 and section 27 and the Registration of Restrictive Trading Agreements Regulations 1984, Reg. 5. Not all variations were registrable, in particular variations that did not affect or add to the restrictions, and in assessing any old agreement which has been varied during the interim period with an unregistered variation it will be necessary to assess whether it was registrable.

16.2.2 Agreements Made in the Interim Period

Non-notifiable agreements

Even if it was a registrable agreement an agreement, entered into during the interim period was a non-notifiable agreement for the purposes of the RTPA if it was not, and never had been, a price fixing agreement.

A price fixing agreement is defined in RTPA, section 27A(3) (introduced by the Restrictive Trade Practices (Non-notifiable Agreements) (E.C. Block Exemptions) Order 1996 (S.I. 1996 No. 349) as an agreement to which the RTPA applies by virtue of one or more restrictions being accepted as to:

—   the prices to be charged, quoted or paid for goods supplied, offered or acquired, or for the application of any process of manufacture to goods (RTPA, s. 6(1)(a));

—   the prices to be recommended or suggested as the prices to be charged or quoted in respect of the resale of goods supplied (RTPA, s. 6(1)(b));

—   the charges to be made, quoted or paid for designated services supplied, offered or obtained (RTPA, s. 11(2)(a)),

A price fixing agreement will also encompass an agreement combining one or more information provisions in respect of the prices charged, quoted or paid or to be charged, quoted or paid for goods which have been or are to be supplied, offered or acquired or for the application of any prices of manufacture to goods (RTPA, s. 7(1)(a)).

It is likely that "most favoured nation" clauses which refer specifically to price will give rise to a price restriction. A "most favoured nation" clause is one which requires a better price (or other contractual terms) offered to a third party to be substituted for the contract price (or equivalent term). If such terms are offered by a supplier/licensor they may have the effect of keeping prices down (approved in Article 2(10) of the technology transfer agreements block exemption, Regulation 240/96/E.C.) and may be regarded as benign in competition terms. When accepted by a distributor, the effect may be the opposite. If an agreement that contains such a term was not filed, then the provision may be void, even if the agreement would benefit from the vertical agreements exclusion (See Chapter 7 at 7.2). A most favoured nation clause which only refers to terms and conditions may also be a price restriction on the basis that price is a term of a contract, even if not expressly mentioned. An agreement predating the starting date which continues a most favoured nation clause may have been a notifiable price fixing agreement if another party accepted a registrable restriction.

The aim of designating certain agreements as non-notifiable was to help companies to prepare for the new Act. The Director had the right under RTPA section 26 to call in non-notifiable agreements if he believed them to be anti-competitive. He also reserved a discretion to institute Restrictive Practices Court proceedings (Sched. 13 para. 6(a)) and in urgent cases to obtain an interim order to restrain an anti-competitive agreement under RTPA section 3. None of these powers were used.

Notifiable Agreements

Where an agreement was notifiable (*e.g.* a price fixing agreement or a registrable variation of an agreement already on the register) the rules laid down in the RTPA on the time limits for filing and related conditions continued to apply. The Director had a discretion to institute Restrictive Practices Court Proceedings but had no need to take any action under RTPA section 21 (Sched. 13, para. (6)(b)). Notifiable agreements entered into after the enactment date could not therefore benefit from a full exclusion from the Competition Act 1998 (see para. 16.4.5 below and Chapter 7, para. 7.5.3).

Registrable Agreements with a Deadline for Furnishing Particulars Expiring after the Starting Date

Where the deadline for furnishing particulars of an agreement or variation was on or after the starting date, special rules applied. The rules affect notifiable agreements made in the three months before the starting date, and notifiable variations made in those three months (price fixing agreements and interim period variations to agreements entered into before the enactment date). The rules are set out below:

(i) Parties were not under a duty to furnish particulars and they will not be subject to any penalty for failure to do so as long as they did not give effect to any restrictions contrary to RTPA section 27ZA before the starting date. Where parties choose not to furnish particulars of an agreement or variation to it, they cannot benefit from any transitional period (Sched. 13, para. 20 (2)) and the agreement or variation can be scrutinised under the new regime as from the starting date.

(ii) Where parties chose to furnish particulars they had to do so before the starting date. Such agreements qualify for a one year transitional period (Sched. 13, para. 25(3)). Again this benefit would be lost if the parties had given effect to the restrictions before furnishing particulars to the agreement.

16.3 Early Guidance on the Chapter I Prohibition

16.3.1 Principle

Where an agreement was made during the interim period parties were to make an application to the Director for early guidance as to whether the agreement would infringe the Chapter I Prohibition when the Chapter I Prohibition came into force and, if so whether exemption would be likely (Sched. 13, para. 7). This process was sparingly used (17 applications according to the OFT). As the process was confidential, it is difficult to assess how worthwhile it was for those who used it. In other cases, parties' more informal contacts with the OFT may have proved useful in helping them to draft their agreements and decide whether to notify it for a ruling on the application of the Chapter I Prohibition or an exemption. Such contacts had no effect on the ability of the Director in relation to the agreements involved.

16.3.2   The Effect of Early Guidance

Early guidance will have the same effect as full guidance given after the starting date under section 15: it will be binding on the Director in the same way as under the full guidance system and will provide parties with immunity from penalties to the same extent as under section 15. Where the Director is still considering an application for early guidance at the starting date, the application will be treated as if it had been made under the full guidance system under section 13. In this case parties will benefit from provisional immunity from penalties until the application is determined by the Director. For a discussion of the guidance process and its effects see Chapter 9 at 9.3.

16.4   The Transitional Periods

16.4.1   When Does the Chapter I Prohibition Start to Apply?

Where an agreement is made before the starting date there are a number of rules which determine when, or if, the Chapter I Prohibition applies:

(i) The general rule is that an agreement of the type not described in sub-paragraphs (ii)–(ix) below, particulars of which have been furnished to the Director under the RTPA or which fell outside the RTPA, will benefit from a one year transitional period of exclusion from the Chapter I Prohibition (Sched. 13, para. 19);

(ii) An agreement which benefits from a direction under RTPA section 21(2) before the starting date is excluded from the Chapter I Prohibition for its duration (Sched. 3, para. 2(1)) described at Chapter 7, para. 7.5.3 and 16.4.5 below. This exclusion can be lost in certain circumstances (see 16.4.5 below);

(iii) To the extent that an agreement is found not to be contrary to the public interest by the RPC it will receive a five year transitional period (Sched. 13, para. 23(1)). Agreements in this category are very few in number: the agreements between the Football Association, Premier League and BSkyB and the BBC fall into this category following the RPC decision in July 1999. The case referred to at (iv) below relates to both the RTPA and the RPA.

(iv) To the extent that an agreement which contains provisions relating to the resale price maintenance of goods falls within an exemption order under RPA section 14 it will receive a five year transitional period (Sched. 13, para. 24(1)). At the time of writing the RPC is considering whether (in proceedings issued in January 2000) the current exemption for resale price maintenance of over the counter ("OTC") medicine is contrary to the public interest. Depending on the outcome, the agreement will either have a five year transitional period or none (Sched. 13, para. 20(4));

(v)   There will be a five year transitional period for certain agreements which have been reviewed under the Financial Services Act 1986 or the Broadcasting Act 1990 (Sched. 13, para. 26) (see 16.4.2 below);

(vi)   Certain utilities agreements exempted from RTPA will receive a five year transitional period from the starting date (see 16.4.3 below);

(vii) An agreement does not benefit from a transitional period to the extent to which before the starting date it is void or subject to any restraining order under the RTPA, or a person has unlawfully given effect to a restriction prior to furnishing particulars in breach of RTPA section 27ZA (*Hansard*, H.C., col. 4767 (July 8, 1998)). Similarly an agreement will receive no transitional period to the extent to which it is unlawful or void under the RPA (Sched. 13, para. 20(1) and 20(2));

(viii) Notifiable agreements and variations where the deadline for notification is after the starting date, and which are not notified by the starting date, receive no transitional period (Sched. 13, para. 20(3));

(ix)   Except in the case of certain utilities agreements (see 16.4.3 below) agreements made after the starting date cannot benefit from a transitional period.

16.4.2   Schedule 13, para. 26, Special Cases

There is a five year transitional period in the special case of certain agreements which have been subject to scrutiny under the Financial Services Act 1986 or the Broadcasting Act 1990.

Schedule 13, para. 26(1)(a) provides that this is the case for an agreement in respect of which a direction under section 127(2) of the Financial Services Act 1986 (which sets out the terms of restrictions of recognised professional bodies which may enable the Secretary of State to require the Director not to make an application to the Restrictive Practices Court) is in force immediately before the starting date.

Schedule 13, para. 26(1)(b) provides that this is the case for an agreement in respect of which a direction under section 194A(3) of the Broadcasting Act, (which relates to the appointment of a single body as the news provider for Channel 3) is in force immediately before the starting date.

16.4.3   Utilities Agreements

Special transitional period rules apply to agreements relating to electricity, gas and railways (Sched. 13, paras 27–34). Under these special rules agreements exempt from the RTPA are excluded from the Chapter I Prohibition for a period of five years from the starting date.

Energy Agreements

Agreements in the electricity and gas sector benefiting from this include:

(i) agreements to which before the starting date the RTPA did not apply by virtue of section 100 Electricity Act 1989 or section 62 Gas Act 1986 or orders made thereunder. These benefit from a five year transitional period from the starting date;

(ii) agreements made during the five year transitional period commencing on the starting date which would not have qualified for a section 100 order if the RTPA had not been repealed, and agreements (made before or after the starting date) which are varied to become agreements of that type during the five year transitional period. These agreements have a transitional period from the date the agreement or variation is made to the end of the five year transitional period;

(iii) agreements of a type specified in a transitional order issued by the Secretary of State. These will benefit from a transitional period commencing on the date specified in the Secretary of State's order and continuing until the end of the five year transitional period commencing on the starting date. No such order has been made, but one could be made at any point during the five year transition.

If an agreement is varied so that it is no longer one to which the RTPA would have applied at all it will lose the benefit of a transitional period.

Railways Agreements

In the railways sector there are two classes of agreement which benefit from a transitional period:

(i) agreements to which before the starting date the RTPA did not apply by virtue of section 131 Railways Act 1993 and directions made thereunder. These benefit from a five year transitional period commencing from the starting date;

(ii) agreements (made before or after the starting date) to the extent to which they are required or approved under the Railways Act 1993 in that transitional period. These benefit from a five year transitional period deemed to have commenced on the starting date.

Where an agreement as described in (i) is varied during the five year transitional period, it is treated in the same way as an agreement of the type described in (ii). It should be noted that the RTPA is disapplied to an agreement under section 131 only if *all* of the provisions in the agreement are required or approved. Individual provisions in agreements of the type described in (ii) can benefit from transitional periods (to the extent to which they are required or approved — see para. 16.4.4 for a further discussion of "to the extent to which").

16.4.4 When does the Transitional Period Start?

The transitional period will begin on the starting date (Sched. 13, para. 19(1)) except in the case of:

(i)   certain utilities agreements (see 16.4.3 above); and

(ii) agreements subject to Restrictive Practices Court Proceedings which continue after the starting date (see 16.7.2). In this case the transitional period available will begin at the conclusion of the continuing proceedings (see Sched. 13, paras 21–22). Therefore if an agreement is found not to be contrary to the public interest following RPC continuing proceedings it would receive a five year transitional period from the ending of those proceedings (Sched. 13, para. 23(3)). On the other hand if as a result of continuing RPC proceedings an agreement is found to be contrary to the public interest then there would be no applicable transitional period and the Chapter I Prohibition would apply immediately from the ending of those proceedings. See *Re OTC* (see para. 16.4.1 above) for the only agreement to which these provisions in practice will apply.

The Chapter I Prohibition will not apply "to the extent to which" a transitional period is available (Sched. 13, para. 19(2)). In relation to some transitional periods, the transitional exclusion applies "to the extent to which" an agreement meets the relevant criteria (see 16.4.1 and 16.4.3 above). Consequently the transitional period may in some instances apply only to certain parts of an agreement and not to others. As a result transitional periods of differing lengths may apply to different parts in the same agreement. For example in the case of an agreement subject to a requirement to furnish particulars under the RTPA entered into before the enactment date which was not duly furnished, the relevant restrictions will be void and have no transitional period. The remaining parts of the agreement however, may have a benefit from a transitional period, as would subsequent variations unless notifiable. Where this is the case, the Director may scrutinise the entire agreement (and not just the non excluded parts) to determine whether there has been a breach of Chapter I Prohibition (Sched. 13, para. 1(5)). If the Director determines that such an agreement does in fact infringe the Chapter I Prohibition then the provisions to which the transitional exclusion applies will not be prohibited or be subject to the consequence of infringement unless they can be and have been "clawed back".

16.4.5   Agreement Cleared under Section 21(2) RTPA

Agreements which immediately before the starting date benefit from a direction under section 21(2) of the RTPA are excluded from the Chapter I Prohibition for their duration (Sched. 3, para. 2(1)). This exclusion will only be available to agreements entered into before the enactment date, as section 21(2) directions will not be available for any agreement made on or after the enactment date (Sched. 13, para. 6(b)). Furthermore the Director retains the right, to "*claw back*" this exclusion (Sched. 3, para. 2(3)).

If variations after the starting date to an agreement benefiting from section 21(2) directions are duly furnished and the Secretary of State has not withdrawn the section 21(2) directions then the agreement as varied will benefit from the exclusion. This will apply whether the variations are made before the enactment date or during the interim period. If a "material" variation is made to an agreement benefiting from a section 21(2) direction then the exclusion ceases to apply from the date the variation comes into force (Sched. 3, para. 2(2)). The Director has indicated (OFT Guideline, *Transitional Arrangements*, OFT 406. March 1999 (the "Transitional Arrangements" Guideline), para. 4.16 that variations will only be "material" if they result in an appreciable effect on competition within the meaning of the Chapter I Prohibition. Minor adjustments to parties trading relationships such as changes in delivery dates, mode of transportation, credit terms or manner of payment would not normally be caught by the test. However variations such as converting any joint marketing area into partitioned markets, or the addition of a significant competitor as a party to an agreement, would normally be considered material if the effect on competition were likely to be appreciable.

16.5   Transitional Procedures

16.5.1   Extension of Transitional Period

The Director can either on his own initiative or on an application by a party extend transitional periods on one occasion (Sched. 13, para. 36). He can extend the one year transitional periods by not more than twelve months and any other transitional period by not more than six months. In applying for an extension a party must make its application not less than three months before the end of the transitional period. It must ensure that the application is in writing and includes the agreement and other relevant information as required under rule 24 of the Director's Rules.

Under rule 24 (4) the Director must give the applicant written notice of his decision not less than one month before the date of expiry of the transitional period. This will allow the parties, if an extension is refused, to apply for guidance or a decision under Chapter I if necessary. The procedure in rule 24 does not exactly follow that described in the Transitional Arrangements Guideline, para. 5.3, which pre-dates the Director's Rules and in particular does not clarify the position if the Director does not take a decision within the time laid down in rule 24 (4).

The Director has indicated (para 5.4) that he will grant extensions where:

(i)   it appears that the agreement may infringe the Chapter I Prohibition, if it were not for the transitional period, but not seriously infringe it; and

(ii)   there are good reasons for making an extension – for example, the agreement is being re-negotiated, the agreement is due to expire shortly after the end of the unextended transitional period, or the parties have a legitimate need for more time to prepare a notification.

Where an agreement seriously infringes Chapter I and is unlikely to be granted an exemption, or will only be granted an exemption subject to conditions, the Director has stated that he will not grant an extension.

16.5.2   Termination of a Transitional Period

Principle

Subject to certain exceptions (see below) the Director may by written direction terminate the transitional period (Sched. 13, para. 37–39(1)):

(i)   if he considers that the agreement would, but for the transitional period or a relevant exclusion, infringe the Chapter I Prohibition and he would not be likely to grant it an unconditional individual exemption. A relevant exclusion is defined as an exclusion relating to mergers (Sched. 1, para.

1), section 21(2) agreements (Sched. 3, para. 2) and certain agricultural agreements (Sched. 3, para. 9); or

(ii)   if a person fails (without reasonable excuse) within seven working days to provide information sought by the Director to enable the Director to determine whether to give a direction terminating the transitional period for that agreement (Sched. 13, para. 38 (1)–(2) and r. 23 of the Director's Rules).

The Director has no power under the Act itself to terminate the transitional period or require a party to give him information in respect of any agreement which is excluded from the Chapter I Prohibition, except if it is excluded by virtue of it being a merger (Sched. 1, para. 1), benefiting from section 21(2) directions (Sched. 3, para. 2) or being an agricultural agreement (Sched. 3, para. 9). The Order creating exclusions for Vertical Agreements and Land Agreements gives the Director similar powers (see Chapter 7, para. 7.1.2 and 16.5.5 below).

16.5.3   Procedure

A copy of the direction must be given to each of the parties concerned and the Secretary of State not less than 28 days before the date on which the direction is to have effect. Both the Director and the Secretary of State may revoke the direction prior to it taking effect. If the direction is revoked the Director can only give a further direction terminating the transitional period in respect of the same agreement if he is satisfied that there has been a material change of circumstances since the revocation. Of course, even if parties have been given notice of the termination of a transitional period they can still make an application for an individual exemption (see 16.6), but they will be under pressure to amend the agreement to remove seriously offending provisions first.

16.5.4   Resale Price Maintenance Agreements

In relation to agreements consisting of provisions on resale price maintenance of goods which fall within the scope of an exemption order under section 14 of the RPA the Director has no power to give a direction terminating the transitional period or to require information in connection with the agreement. (Sched. 13, para. 39).

16.5.5   Termination of a section 21(2) Exclusion

Where an agreement benefits from a direction under RTPA section 21(2) it is normally excluded for its whole life, not just a transitional period. The Director does, however, have equivalent powers to gather information and terminate the exclusion (Sched. 3, paras 2(4)–(6) discussed in Chapter 7).

16.6   Application for Guidance or a Decision

Parties to agreements which benefit from the transitional period are able under section 13 to apply to the Director for guidance during the transitional period as to whether the Chapter I Prohibition will be infringed once the transitional period ends and, if so, whether exemption is likely (subject to Regulations made by the Secretary of State under Sched. 13, para. 19). Where the transitional period for an agreement has been terminated a party may notify the agreement for a decision, including a request for individual exemption (s. 14). The OFT's Transitional Arrangements Guideline para. 5.13 indicates that application should not be necessary unless there is an appreciable effect on competition, which is unlikely if the parties' share of the relevant market is less than 25 per cent (OFT Guideline, *The Major Provisions*, OFT 400, March 1999, para. 3.5). When notifying an agreement the parties should indicate in the Form N the duration of any transitional period which they believe applies to the agreement.

16.7   Restrictive Practices Court Orders and Proceedings

16.7.1   Restrictive Practices Court Order

The following orders will cease to have effect on the starting date:

(i)   Restraining orders under RTPA section 2(2) and section 35(3) (and undertakings in lieu of these orders);

(ii)   Orders relating to agreements important to the national economy under RTPA section 29(1);

(iii)   Orders relating to agreements holding down prices under RTPA section 30(1);

(iv)   Orders relating to agreements of agricultural and forestry associations and fisheries associations under RTPA section 33(4);

(v)   Orders for an examination on oath under RTPA section 37(1);

(vi)   Compliance orders under RPA section 25(2) (see Sched. 13, para. 9).

An approval in force immediately before the starting date under RTPA section 32 ceases to have effect on that date.

It is not clear that informal assurances, which are commonly given in lieu of orders under the RPA (see *Competition Law and Practice*, Chapter 17.03) would automatically fall away. They are in the nature of agreements and may remain in force, although the Court would have a discretion whether to enforce in the light of the release of orders under the underlying legislation. In any event the prior existence of an order of assurance would form relevant background for dealing with any similar agreement under the Chapter I Prohibition.

Orders existing before the starting date will remain important:

(i)   Breach of an order before the starting date will be a contempt of court and the Director may take action to remedy this. The Director's right of action will not lapse at the starting date;

(ii)   Parties to a private action for breach of statutory duty brought after the starting date will be able to rely, under RTPA section 35(7) on issues of fact and law determined in proceedings brought by the Director for a section 35(3) order (Sched. 13, para. 13(1)).

Interim orders under RTPA section 3 could have continued to apply after the starting date in certain circumstances but in the event there are none.

16.7.2   Proceedings before the Restrictive Practices Court

Where proceedings before the Restrictive Practices Court were not determined before the starting date there are detailed provisions regarding their continued application.

Proceedings which Cease

Proceedings under a number of provisions under the RTPA and RPA including those for restraining orders under RTPA section 2(2) and section 35(3) cease to have effect on the starting date (Sched. 13, para. 8).

Proceedings which Remain Ongoing

Certain proceedings where the application (including any appeal made) is made but not determined by the starting date may continue past the starting date to their conclusion (Sched. 13, paras 11–12 and 14–17). An application is not determined until any appeal is disposed of or withdrawn or until the period in which the relevant party may appeal has expired (Sched. 13, para. 15(3)).

Certain but (not all) undetermined applications are defined as "continuing proceedings". These include proceedings under:

(i)   RTPA section 1(3) in which the Director has applied for declaration as to whether or not restrictions or information provisions are contrary to the public interest;

(ii)   RTPA section 4 application to RPC to review a previous decision;

(iii) RPA section 16 applications for a class of goods to be exempted by an order under section 14;

(iv)   RPA section 17 applications for the Restrictive Practices Court to review its previous exemption decisions.

Continuing proceedings can continue until their conclusion and the Chapter I Prohibition will not apply to an agreement subject to continuing proceedings (Sched. 13, para. 14(1–2)). If after continuing proceedings the agreement benefits from a transitional period this will start from the completion of the continuing proceedings (see 16.4.4 above).

Different rules apply to applications under RTPA section 3 for interim orders and applications under RTPA section 26 for a declaration of the court as to the registrability or notifiability of an agreement and for rectification of the register. There were, however, no such applications left undetermined at the starting date.

16.7.3   Private Actions/Void Agreements

Even though RTPA section 35 and RPA section 25 are repealed by the Act, their provisions continue to apply in respect of a person who before the starting date has a right to bring civil proceedings in respect of an agreement but only if that right relates to any period before the starting date or, where there are continuing proceedings, the determination of the proceedings (Sched. 13, para. 13).

The repeal of the RTPA and RPA is not intended to validate those provisions made void by the Acts prior to their repeal, Transitional Arrangements Guideline para. 6.9. However, the language of Sched. 13, para. 13 could be interpreted as limiting the right of the courts to take into account any effects of section 35 after the starting date.

16.8   The RTPA Register

The Director has a duty to maintain the RTPA register after the starting date although the category of agreements which need to be added to it will be significantly reduced. They will include particulars of notifiable agreements furnished but not entered on the register before the starting date, agreements which are the subject of continuing proceedings which are not determined until after the starting date and agreements in relation to which the court gives directions after the starting date on the applicability of the RTPA prior to the starting date (Sched. 13, para. 10(2)–(4)). The Director has indicated in the Transitional Arrangements Guideline, paras 7.1 and 7.2 that he will continue to allow parties seeking to discover the effect of the RTPA on an agreement to have access to the register. He has also indicated that for an initial period after the starting date the register will continue to be open to inspection by the general public to the extent permitted prior to the starting date. After this, when the level of requests for access to the register no longer justifies the costs involved, regulations reducing access to the register will probably be made (Sched. 13, para. 10(5)).

16.9   Transition from the Fair Trading Act 1973 and the Competition Act 1980

16.9.1   The Fair Trading Act 1973

The Monopolies and Mergers Commission ("MMC") has been replaced by the Competition Commission (s. 45) which assumes all the former functions of the MMC, as well as appellate functions under the Competition Act 1998. This was effected by the Competition Act 1998 (Competition Commission) Transitional, Consequential and Supplemental Provisions Order 1999 (S.I. 1999 No.506) on April 1, 1999.

Investigations by the Competition Commission under a number of pieces of legislation, including the Fair Trading Act 1973, which continued at the starting date, were permitted to take account of certain matters, which prior to the starting date would have been considered under the RTPA (Sched. 13, para. 40)).

Following a monopoly or mergers reference any remedial order made by the Secretary of State which, by virtue of Sched. 8, para. 3 Fair Trading Act 1973, has no effect in relation to matters covered by the RTPA will one year after the starting date have that limitation removed and be applicable as if the limiting provision never had effect (Sched. 13, para. 41). This will apply to all agreements covered by the RTPA, including agreements benefiting from section 21(2) directions.

Applications by the Director under Part III of the Fair Trading Act 1973 against traders who have persisted in a course of conduct that is detrimental to the interest of or unfair to consumers will in future be handled by the High Court (or its equivalent in Scotland and Northern Ireland) (Sched. 12, para. 1). There were no applications affected by the transitional pending proceedings at the starting date with the Restrictive Practices Court (Sched. 13, para. 42).

16.9.2   The Competition Act 1980

By virtue of section 17, the provisions of the Competition Act 1980 dealing with anti-competitive practices were repealed on the starting date. The Competition Act 1998 will not however, affect the provisions of the 1980 Act section 11, which give the Secretary of State the ability to make a Competition Commission reference in respect of the efficiency and costs, the services provided by and the possible abuse of a monopoly situation by public bodies and certain other bodies.

Any undertaking accepted by the Director under section 4 or section 9 Competition Act 1980 ceased to have effect on the starting date except where the undertaking related to an agreement, which on the starting date was the subject of continuing proceedings (Sched. 13, para. 43).

Any on-going investigations by the Director and the Competition Commission under the provisions of the Competition Act 1980 dealing with anti-competitive practices ceased on the starting date. There were, however, no proceedings which were affected by the repeal of the principal provisions of the Competition Act 1980.

16.10   Transitional Arrangements for the Chapter II Prohibition

There are no transitional provisions in relation to the prohibition of the abuse of the dominant position and the Chapter II Prohibition will apply immediately from the starting date.

16.11   Concurrency

The transitional arrangements make provision for agreements relating to electricity, gas and the railways (see also 16.4.3 above). The sector Regulators (who include the water Regulator and the telecommunications Regulator in addition to those of electricity, gas and railways) may exercise a number of functions under the transitional arrangements concurrently with the Director (in relation to sectoral matters) (Sched. 13, para. 35). References to the Director in Sched. 13 in matters where he has concurrent jurisdiction with a sector Regulator are to be read as including references to the sector Regulators (Sched. 13, para. 1(4)). The sector Regulators will have concurrent powers in:

(i)   providing advice and information about the transitional arrangements (see 16.4.3 above);

(ii)   giving early guidance (only the Director can issue directions on the procedure for early guidance but before doing so he must consult with the relevant sector Regulators in relation to matters where they have concurrent jurisdiction (Sched. 13, para. 35(3));

(iii) extending and terminating the transitional periods (see 16.5 above).

Chart 16.1

AGREEMENTS MADE BEFORE DATE OF ENACTMENT

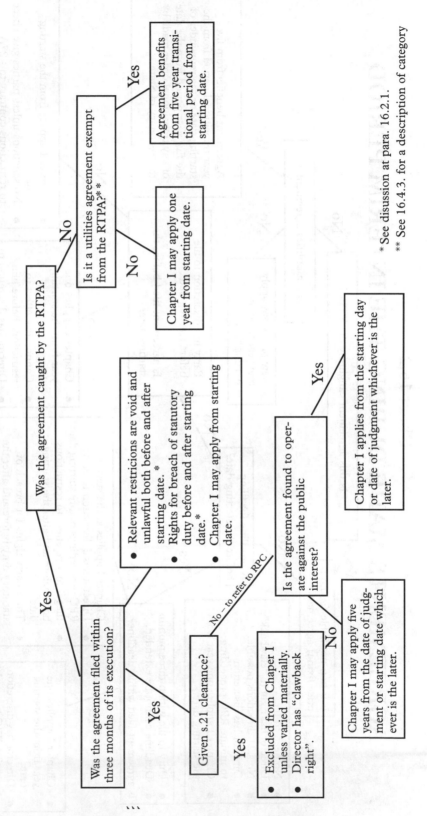

Was the agreement caught by the RTPA?

Yes / **No**

Was the agreement filed within three months of its execution?

Is it a utilities agreement exempt from the RTPA?**

Yes

Agreement benefits from five year transitional period from starting date.

No

Chapter I may apply one year from starting date.

Yes

- Relevant restricions are void and unlawful both before and after starting date.*
- Rights for breach of statutory duty before and after starting date.*
- Chapter I may apply from starting date.

No – to refer to RPC

Given s.21 clearance?

Yes

- Excluded from Chaper I unless varied materially.
- Director has "clawback right".

No

Is the agreement found to operate against the public interest?

Yes

Chapter I applies from the starting day or date of judgment whichever is the later.

No

Chapter I may apply five years from the date of judgment or starting date which ever is the later.

* See disussion at para. 16.2.1.

** See 16.4.3. for a description of category

Chart 16.2

AGREEMENTS MADE DURING THE INTERIM PERIOD

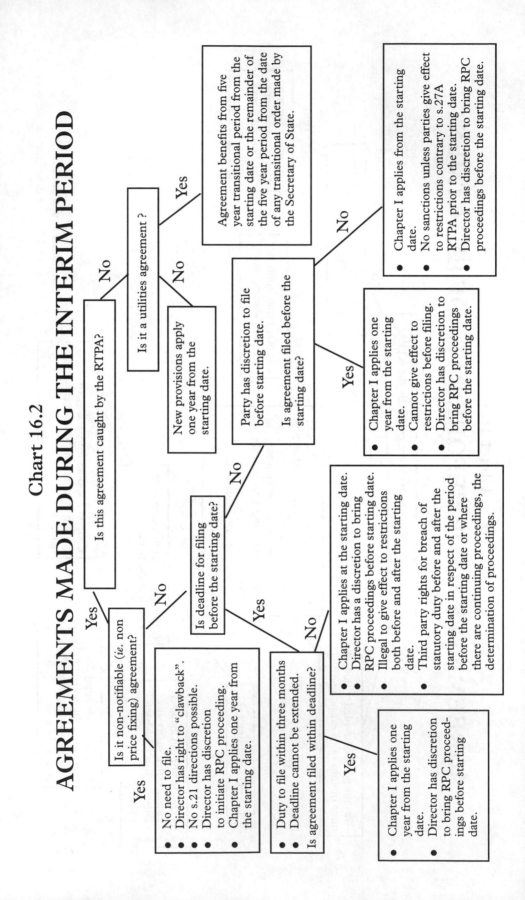

Chapter 17

Reform Provisions

17.1 Structural Reform of OFT

Having just put in place a major reform of United Kingdom competition law, the Government is considering structural reform of the OFT (and other regulators) to replace the office of the Director with a Commission composed of several persons (none full time) (DTI Press Release P/2000/337, May 18, 2000). This proposal has been much criticised as potentially removing clarity of decision making, reducing efficiency and compromising independence from Government. Nevertheless, the Government itends to proceed with the reform and is consulting on the proposed structure and on the transparency of its procedures (DTI Press Release P/2000/639, September 21, 2000 (consultation closes January 26, 2001)).

17.2 Reform of Energy Regulation

The combined energy regulatory body being introduced by the Utilities Act 2000, s. 1 takes the form of a body corporate, the Gas and Electricity Markets Authority ("GEMA"). This new Authority is likely to be in place by December 2000 and will assume the powers of the Directors General in relation to the Competition Act 1998.

17.3 Reforms in the Transport Bill

17.3.1 Concurrent Powers for the Civil Aviation Authority ("CAA")

Part I, Chapter V of the Transport Bill currently before Parliament gives the CAA concurrent powers with the Director under the Competition Act 1998 and the monopoly provisions of the Fair Trading Act 1973 ("FTA") in matters which relate to the supply of air traffic services. Air traffic services are defined in Clause 97 and are the services, which comprise what is commonly called air traffic control. In relation to the exercise of powers under the FTA, specific regulatory matters are to be taken into account. These regulatory functions are set out in Clause 87 and are very close to the regulatory duties set out in Clause 2 which will apply when the CAA carried out licensing functions under Chapter I of Part I. The CAA is, therefore, to carry out a balancing act between issues of, for example, safety, economy or environmental objectives and the promotion of competition.

17.3.2 Competition Test for Exercise of Bus Functions by the Director

Part II of the Act provides for a number of measures to improve local transport particularly by bus, including quality partnership schemes to provide integrated services in a locality (Clause 113) and joint and through ticketing schemes (Clause 134). Sections 89 and 91 of the Transport Act 1985 provide for subsidised bus services (and a tendering system in relation to the award of contracts for providing such services). These matters are all within the functions of local authorities.

Clause 152 and Sched. 10 provide a distinct competition test in relation to these schemes and contracts. This test raises a presumption that where such a scheme or contract would:

(a)   secure improvements in the quality of vehicles or facilities used; or

(b)   secure other improvements in local services of substantial benefit to users of local services; or

(c)   reduce or limit traffic congestion, noise or air pollution.

The scheme or contract will meet the competition test unless:

(i)   it has a significantly adverse effect on competition; and

(ii)   its effect on competition is not likely to be proportionate to the achievement of one or more of the purposes set out in (a), (b) and (c) above.

This test could be satisfied by a scheme that has quite serious effects on competition if it brings proportionate benefits.

The Director is given a special role in enforcing the test, either at the request of a party or a local authority or of his own motion. This is the first official recognition of the Director's longstanding informal role as "OFBUS". Rather oddly, agreements which meet the competition test do not appear to be excluded from the Chapter I Prohibition although this may be intended and it could be done by statutory instrument under the Competition Act itself. If the test is intended to be more favourable than that for exemption from the Chapter I Prohibition, it would not achieve legal protection for the parties without an exclusion. If it is not intended to be more favourable it is doubtful that it is necessary at all.

17.3.3 Change in Scope of Rail Regulator's Jurisdiction

Clause 241 will change the Rail Regulator's concurrent competition jurisdiction for the purposes of the Competition Act 1998 by amendment to the Railways Act 1993, section 67. He will, once the amendment comes into force, have jurisdiction in relation to 'services related to railways" comprising:

(a)   "railway services" (his current jurisdiction, see Chapter 4, para. 4.4.8);

(b)   the provision or maintenance of rolling stock;

(c)   the development, maintenance or renewal of a network, station or light maintenance depot; and

(d)   the development, provision or maintenance of information systems designed wholly or mainly for facilitating the provision of railway services.

17.4   Competition in the Water Sector

17.4.1   Competition Act 1998

When the Competition Act 1998 was going through Parliament the Government rejected amendments which would have made it obligatory for water companies to grant access to their networks by expressly providing that a refusal to do so would be treated as a breach of the Chapter II Prohibition. Ministers responded by saying that sector-specific legislation would be a better means to ensure sensible arrangements were put into place which would allow for the effective development of competition while safeguarding social, environmental and public health objectives.

Guidance on the Competition Act issued by OFWAT and the OFT does however indicate that they see scope for the introduction of common carriage under the Competition Act, and OFWAT has asked the companies to draw up access codes.

17.4.2   Consultation on Sectoral Reform to Facilitate Common Carriage

In a Department for the Environment Consultation Paper: *Competition in the Water Industry in England & Wales* (Ref: OOEP0058) published by the Department of Environment, Transport and the Regions in April 2000, the Government states that it is not convinced that the Competition Act can deal with all the issues related to common carriage. It believes that there may be a need to create a specific institutional framework within which common carriage can develop most effectively for consumers, whilst protecting health, environmental and wider social policy interests. The Government is seeking comments on whether specific legislation or other measures for the water industry should be introduced.

17.5   The Financial Services and Markets Act 2000

17.5.1   New Legislation

The Financial Services and Markets Act 2000 ("FSA 2000"), which received royal assent on the June 14, 2000 and is expected to come into force during the summer of 2001 introduces some relevant changes to the previous regime.

The changes affecting exclusions are referred to in Chapter 7, para. 7.5 and Chapter 12, para. 12. 3.

17.5.2   Special Competition Reviews

The Act introduces a number of special procedures for competition scrutiny of bodies with regulatory functions in the field of financial services:

- Section 95 introduces the possibility of review of the practices and provisions of the authority responsible for the admission of securities for listing by statutory instrument;

- Chapter III of Part X introduces the possibility of competition scrutiny by the Director and Competition Commission of practices and regulating provisions of the Financial Services Authority itself which have "a significantly adverse effect on competition" in accordance with the special rules set out in that part;

- Chapter II of Part XVIII provides a similar regime regarding the practices and regulating provisions of investment exchanges and clearing houses.

Section 352 establishes that the improper disclosure of competition information gained in the course of proceedings may constitute a criminal offence.

17.6 Reform of Merger Control

17.6.1 Reduction in Role of Secretary of State

At the time of writing, the United Kingdom Government is embarked on consideration of the reform of merger control law. Its stated aim is to take the political dimension out of merger control and make the competition and economic assessment of primary importance. Certain sectors (defence, the media) are considered so politically sensitive that the Secretary of State intends to keep his present discretion and to take for all these sectors the power to over-rule a wholly favourable competition assessment — a power presently enjoyed only in relation to newspaper mergers (see *Mergers: A Consultation Document on Proposals for Reform,* DTI, August 1999). This approach is confirmed in the DTI document, *Mergers: the Response to the Consultation on Proposals for Reform,* October 2000 (consultation ends January 26, 2001), available from the DTI Website. Two changes are to take effect immediately:

- It is now the policy of the Secretary of State to accept the advice he receives from the Director on whether or not to refer merger cases to the Competition Commission, save in exceptional circumstances. Given that this is the normal practice of the Secretary of State and that he cannot lawfully fetter in advance the discretion given to him by the Act, this will not have much practical effect, although it should add very slightly to predictability.

- Fees for small and medium sized companies which fall within the merger regime are to be abolished. This is done by statutory instrument under the Act (the Merger (Fees) (Amendment) Regulations, published in draft on October 26, 2000, consultation ends on January 26, 2001). This will exempt businesses (whether or not incorporated) which are small or medium sized (or members of small or medium sized groups) by reference to the criteria set out in the Companies Act 1985, sub sections 247(3)–(5) and 249 (3)–(5). Given that such businesses will have a balance sheet total essentially of no more than £5.6 million (also a gross assets test), this will assist a very few of the companies presently liable for fees. It is estimated this would assist about 30 companies a year, although it is not clear that the number of mergers in that category would in fact be investigated by the OFT. It would have been simpler to abolish fees on all mergers not qualifying for investigation under the proposed new turnover test, which is likely to catch a higher proportion of mergers involving relatively small trading companies than will the current assets test.

17.6.2 The Proposals after Consultation

The Government has decided to retain the current division of duties between the OFT and the Competition Commission. The OFT will conduct first stage investigations and decide whether a reference to the Competition Commission should be made. It will also deal with undertakings in lieu of a reference. The Competition Commission will take the final decision and propose any remedies. Procedures for remedies will be developed to include greater public consultation. Undertakings will be negotiated by the OFT and approved by the Competition Commission. Pre-clearance, and use of the Merger Notice process, will remain optional, as at present, but timetables will be tightened slightly. The Secretary of State will retain decision-making powers in relation to sensitive areas, primarily defence. The special regime for press mergers will be considered in the context of a review of the media regulation presently proceeding and a harmonised regime for the media is likely to be introduced. The special regime for water mergers will continue.

The most important change is the modernisation of the regime to replace the wide ranging public interest test with a competition test. It is intended to depart from E.C. precedent and to test whether a merger "substantially lessens competition", in which case remedies may be imposed or the merger blocked, or required to be unwound. This test is essentially that used in the USA, Canada and Australia. Benefits of the merger (such as enhanced competition in some areas of the business or efficiency gains) will be considered only in the context of remedies. There are proposals for discussion that the Competition Commission should be able to consider whether other factors (not of a competition nature) outweigh the competition concerns. It will depend on the outcome of consultation how radical a departure from current practice results. The scheme laid out would operate very much as the current public interest test operates in practice. As it would be somewhat more prescriptive, it should be marginally more predictable.

Finally, there are proposals to replace the gross assets test (currently £70 million) with a turnover test (suggested at £45 million in the latest financial year) and to extend the market share test (aggregation of market share to 25 per cent or above) to catch more vertical mergers where one party has a very high market share (40 per cent or more). In practice, these jurisdictional changes may prove the ones which are most noticed by business. The figure of £45 million turnover is said to have been chosen to be neutral as to the number of affected businesses. However, it will undoubtedly shift the incidental regulatory burden in mergers which raise no competiton issues to smaller trading businesses (which are not asset rich, but have relatively high turnover) and away from property based businesses (which are asset rich). The 40 per cent market share test would make it simpler to look at strong businesses in local markets, but there will be few, if any, businesses with a market share of over 40 per cent in the United Kingdom as a whole that would have a turnover of under £45 million.

17.6.3 Comment on Proposed Reforms

The value of these reforms is uncertain. To some extent they are an attempt to modernise while minimising change in practice, except for the reduction of the role of the Secretary of State.

The changes do recognise the widespread acceptance of the present system, both procedurally and substantively, and seek to preserve the flexibility of the public interest test in the application of an inherently less flexible competition led test.

There must be some fear that the political element is not removed from ordinary merger control, but simply driven underground. It is unrealistic to think that there is not a political element in major merger control decisions, even when not expressly provided for in the system — e.g. the search by the E.C. Commission for a solution in the *Boeing/McDonnell Douglas* merger (Case No. IV/M.877 [1997] O.J. L336/16). More generally, DGIV is subject to the checks and balances of having to produce a decision acceptable to the majority of Commissioners, whereas the Competition Commission, once it ceases to be answerable to the Secretary of State, is unconstrained. This will place a heavy burden on it, but one better discharged if it can overtly deal with non-competition factors in its final decision.

17.7   Impact of the E.C. Reforms

17.7.1   Article 81(3) E.C. Directly Applicable

In April 1999 the E.C. Commission published its White Paper on the modernisation of the E.U. competition rules. The key elements of the Commission's proposals are the abolition of the notification and exemption system and its replacement by a Council Regulation which will render the exemption rule of Article 81(3) directly applicable without prior decision by the Commission. This should allow the Commission to focus its activities on the most serious infringements of Community law in cases with a Community interest. The E.C. Commission has now published a draft Council Regulation (COM (2000) 582 final of September 27, 2000, 2000/0243(CNS)). This would replace Regulation 17/62 and amend other Regulations dealing with the administration of Articles 81 and 82.

If these reforms are adopted, national courts and (with suitable national legislation) competition authorities will be in a position to apply Article 81(3) and will be much more involved in the day to day application of the E.C. competition rules.

The systems would be supported by high level block exemptions, such as the vertical agreements block exemption (discussed in Chapter 8).

Most importantly, the draft Regulation provides that, where an agreement or an abuse of a dominant position may affect trade between Member States, E.C. competition law shall apply, to the exclusion of national competition laws. This exclusion of national laws is to be at the substantive level. National authorities would be able to apply their own procedure and penalty regimes when dealing with breaches of Articles 81 and 82.

These proposals, if adopted in their present form, would require significant amendment of the Competition Act 1998. They would also limit the scope of application of the substantive provisions of the Act to minor agreements which do not affect trade between Member States. The proposals may also affect the workings of the Competition Commission under the monopoly provisions of the Fair Trading Act 1973 and could undermine the effectiveness of this legislation to address competition problems.

17.7.2   Impact on the Competition Act 1998

If Article 81(3) becomes directly effective, then the United Kingdom Government will have to decide how it is to be administered. The section 11 procedure (see Chapter 8, at 8.5.2), where the Secretary of State gives individual exemptions, would be cumbersome. Equally businesses would not be prepared to invest and leave it to the courts to deal with complaints at a later stage. This is particularly so because the market share and turnover thresholds which are a feature of the new generation of the E.C. block exemptions leave larger businesses exposed under Article 81 on investment intensive projects. Their financiers will wish to be assured that the risk of regulatory intervention has been ruled out so far as practicable.

It therefore seems likely that the Competition Act processes would be expanded to allow the Director to deal with Article 81 and 82 issues alongside the Chapter I and Chapter II Prohibitions. This would involve giving the Director and Regulators with concurrent powers the right to issue decisions on directly applicable provisions of Community competition law using the procedures of the Competition Act 1998 and imposing penalties in accordance with the United Kingdom regime.

Many important agreements that have their primary effects in the United Kingdom market may affect trade between Member States, a test which has been given a low threshold in E.C. decisions (see *Competition Law and Practice* paras 2.22–2.31). The same applies to much significant abusive conduct. There is to be no ability for national authorities to apply national laws in relation to effects within their own countries. Article 81 has frequently been a basis for remedies addressing effects on competition within a single Member State and the national authorities should have sufficient flexibility to deal with these concerns under Article 81. The same should apply to Article 82. The possibility for variations on the theme of Articles 81 and 82 in relation to the regulation of the same agreement or conduct in operation within the United Kingdom seems to be removed by the proposals. This would be welcome to business, even though the proposals open up the vista of variations on a theme in cases where an agreement or conduct has real affects in more than one Member State and the authorities in each regulate concurrently or consecutively (see 17.7.3 below).

In addition the draft regulation deals with enhanced powers of investigation for the E.C. Commission, including the right to enter private premises and the right for one national authority to carry out investigations on behalf of another. These will need to be incorporated into the sections of the Act which deal with investigations.

17.7.3 Allocation of Cases

It would seem that national authorities would be free, in cases where they are dealing with an agreement or conduct relating to the operation of a separate product and geographical market no wider than their own Member State, to apply national law to deal with issues at national level where this would not be justified under Article 81 or Article 82. In cases involving a wider geographical market, the Commission would mandate one authority to deal with the matter in co-operation with other Member State authorities (White Pater, paras 95–97): The Commission could withdraw major cases for its own consideration.

It is not clear how the United Kingdom system of notification would fit with the new unified approach to Article 81, where it is considered as a whole and only agreements that do not qualify for exemption are void. There would seem to be nothing to prevent a national authority continuing to offer a notification system where it makes rulings on the application of Article 81 or Article 82 at the request of the parties. The E.C. Commission proposes to introduce a registration process for the purpose of bringing to the attention of the authorities some types of agreement that fall outside the block exemptions.

It would be anomalous to retain for agreements that do not affect trade between Member States a prohibition system which is applied in such a way that agreements which infringe the Chapter I Prohibition are void unless exempted specifically or by block exemption. The Competition Act 1998 should be adapted to follow the same unified approach as the E.C. Regulation.

The draft regulation provides for the E.C. Commission to retain overall control. National authorities are to notify it of important steps in the cases that they handle and to consult on proposed decisions. At any time the E.C. Commission can commence proceedings, in which event the national authorities will no longer have the competence to apply Articles 81 and 82 in that case.

There seems to be no absolute bar to concurrent action by more than one national authority and this may lead to the imposition of multiple penalties or other remedies. It will, however, be open to a national authority or the E.C. Commission to decline jurisdiction where that one (or more) national authorities is already dealing with the case. It appears that decisions taken by a national authority or court will not bind other national authorities or courts and will not affect the ability of the E.C. Commission to take further action. No doubt, national decisions will be of persuasive authority.

The E.C. Commission clearly intends to reserve its own examination of cases to those of great importance to the Community and those where there is a major conflict of views between national authorities that cannot be resolved by the co-operation procedures provided for in the draft.

17.7.4   Effect on the Fair Trading Act 1973

The prohibition on the application of national competition laws to agreements and abusive conduct which may affect trade between Member States will also affect the application of the monopoly provisions of the Fair Trading Act 1973 and, possibly, also the application of the merger provisions to arrangements which are not a concentration for the purposes of the E.C. Merger Regulation. The Fair Trading Act system of examination looks primarily at structural issue and is intended to operate alongside the Competition Act 1998 and to complement it. It operates as an investigative procedure and does not normally consider whether the practices it is looking at are affected by Community competition law, although this arises from time to time, for example, in the recent investigation, *New Motor Cars* (2000) Cm. 4660. Many of the remedies followng *Beer* (1989) Cm. 651, for example, applied both to agreements to which Article 81 applied and those too small to affect trade between Member States.

One possible solution would be to give the Competition Commission power to recommend remedies for any breaches of Article 81 and 82 which it uncovers or which are referred to it by the OFT alongside its existing jurisdiction where Community law does not apply, such power to be dependent on the existence of a monopoly or merger situation. The Competition Commission would not deal with financial penalties, but refer back to the OFT or relevant sector Regulator any case where it considered financial penalties justified. This would, however, necessarily change its practices, since findings of breach of Article 81 and 82 carry severe financial penalties and the inquisitorial procedures of the Competition Commission are inappropriate to safeguard the rights of the defence and there is no fully effective right of appeal. This change may come, however, in any event, as a result of the Human Rights Act 1998.

It may be better to recognise that the end has arrived for this form of competition regulation and confine the reporting functions of the Competition Commission to cases where its functions are regulatory and not part of competition law. The E.C. Commission has recognised utility licence modifications as regulatory in nature. It also accepted the special comparative competition test for water mergers as regulatory in nature at the time of the merger of *Lyonnaise des Eaux and Northumbrian Water* [1996] O.J. C11; [1996] 4 C.M.L.R. 121, MMC report Cm. 2936. Some general industry reviews and consideration of public interest concerns of a prudential nature (not involving competition issues) would be possible. The Competition Commission is, however, far too well established as a competition authority for its present investigative activities to be readily regarded as outside the scope of the United Kingdom's national competition laws.

17.7.5 Comment

It is somewhat ironic that the abolition of the notification system at Community level is proposed just as virtually all Member States have replicated the system. The White Paper and the draft regulation states a case for a move to "*ex post*" regulation of competition law throughout the Community at national as well as E.C. Commission level. The United States operates an effective anti-trust policy on this basis.

There is a case that the savings in administrative costs and burdens on industry, coupled with a strong enforcement policy, would more than make up for the rather bureaucratic fine tuning that the notification system encourages with lengthy behavioural obligations (in some cases duplicating existing regulatory measures) becoming increasingly common.

There is no doubt that these E.C. reforms would require significant changes to be made to United Kingdom competition law in order to maintain consistency between the two systems.

Competition Act 1998
1998

CHAPTER 41

ARRANGEMENT OF SECTIONS

PART I

COMPETITION

CHAPTER I

ARRANGEMENTS

Introduction

The prohibition

Excluded agreements

Exemptions

Notification

CHAPTER II

ABUSE OF DOMINANT POSITION

Introduction

The prohibition

Excluded cases

Notification

CHAPTER III

INVESTIGATION AND ENFORCEMENT

Investigations

Enforcement

Offences

CHAPTER IV

THE COMPETITION COMMISSION AND APPEALS

The Commission

Appeals

CHAPTER V

MISCELLANEOUS

Vertical agreements and land agreements

Director's rules, guidance and fees

Regulators

Confidentiality and immunity from defamation

Findings of fact by Director

Interpretation and governing principles

PART II

INVESTIGATIONS IN RELATION TO ARTICLES 85 AND 86

PART III

MONOPOLIES

PART IV

SUPPLEMENTARY AND TRANSITIONAL

SCHEDULES:

An Act to make provision about competition and the abuse of a dominant position in the market; to confer powers in relation to investigations conducted in connection with Article 85 or 86 of the treaty establishing the European Community; to amend the Fair Trading Act 1973 in relation to information which may be required in connection with investigations under that Act; to make provision with respect to the meaning of "supply of services" in the Fair Trading Act 1973; and for connected purposes. [9th November 1998] BE IT ENACTED by the Queen's most Excellent Majesty, by and with the advice and consent of the Lords Spiritual and Temporal, and Commons, in this present Parliament assembled, and by the authority of the same, as follows:

Part I

COMPETITION

CHAPTER I

AGREEMENTS

Introduction

Enactments replaced

1. The following shall cease to have effect—

(a) the Restrictive Practices Court Act 1976 (c.33),

(b) the Restrictive Trade Practices Act 1976 (c.34),

(c) the Resale Prices Act 1976 (c.53), and

(d) the Restrictive Trade Practices Act 1977 (c.19).

The prohibition

Agreements etc. preventing, restricting or distorting competition

2.—(1) Subject to section 3, agreements between undertakings, decisions by associations of undertakings or concerted practices which—

(a) may affect trade within the United Kingdom, and

(b) have as their object or effect the prevention, restriction or distortion of competition within the United Kingdom,

are prohibited unless they are exempt in accordance with the provisions of this Part.

(2) Subsection (1) applies, in particular, to agreements, decisions or practices which—

(a) directly or indirectly fix purchase or selling prices or any other trading conditions;

(b) limit or control production, markets, technical development or investment;

(c) share markets or sources of supply;

(d) apply dissimilar conditions to equivalent transactions with other trading parties, thereby placing them at a competitive disadvantage;

(e) make the conclusion of contracts subject to acceptance by the other parties of supplementary obligations which, by their nature or according to commercial usage, have no connection with the subject of such contracts.

(3) Subsection (1) applies only if the agreement, decision or practice is, or is intended to be, implemented in the United Kingdom.

(4) Any agreement or decision which is prohibited by subsection (1) is void.

(5) A provision of this Part which is expressed to apply to, or in relation to, an agreement is to be read as applying equally to, or in relation to, a decision by an association of undertakings or a concerted practice (but with any necessary modifications).

(6) Subsection (5) does not apply where the context otherwise requires.

(7) In this section "the United Kingdom" means, in relation to an agreement which operates or is intended to operate only in a part of the United Kingdom, that part.

(8) The prohibition imposed by subsection (1) is referred to in this Act as "the Chapter I prohibition".

Excluded agreements

Excluded agreements

3.—(1) The Chapter I prohibition does not apply in any of the cases in which it is excluded by or as a result of—

(a) Schedule 1 (mergers and concentrations);

(b) Schedule 2 (competition scrutiny under other enactments);

(c) Schedule 3 (planning obligations and other general exclusions); or

(d) Schedule 4 (professional rules).

(2) The Secretary of State may at any time by order amend Schedule 1, with respect to the Chapter I prohibition, by—

(a) providing for one or more additional exclusions; or

(b) amending or removing any provision (whether or not it has been added by an order under this subsection).

(3) The Secretary of State may at any time by order amend Schedule 3, with respect to the Chapter I prohibition, by—

(a) providing for one or more additional exclusions; or

(b) amending or removing any provision—

(i)   added by an order under this subsection; or
(ii) included in paragraph 1, 2, 8 or 9 of Schedule 3.

(4) The power under subsection (3) to provide for an additional exclusion may be exercised only if it appears to the Secretary of State that agreements which fall within the additional exclusion—

(a) do not in general have an adverse effect on competition, or

(b) are, in general, best considered under Chapter II or the Fair Trading Act 1973.

(5) An order under subsection (2)(a) or (3)(a) may include provision (similar to that made with respect to any other exclusion provided by the relevant Schedule) for the exclusion concerned to cease to apply to a particular agreement.

(6) Schedule 3 also gives the Secretary of State power to exclude agreements from the Chapter I prohibition in certain circumstances.

Exemptions

Individual exemptions

4.—(1) The Director may grant an exemption from the Chapter I prohibition with respect to a particular agreement if—

(a) a request for an exemption has been made to him under section 14 by a party to the agreement; and

(b) the agreement is one to which section 9 applies.

(2) An exemption granted under this section is referred to in this Part as an individual exemption.

(3) The exemption—

(a) may be granted subject to such conditions or obligations as the Director considers it appropriate to impose; and

(b) has effect for such period as the Director considers appropriate.

(4) That period must be specified in the grant of the exemption.

(5) An individual exemption may be granted so as to have effect from a date earlier than that on which it is granted.

(6) On an application made in such way as may be specified by rules under section 51, the Director may extend the period for which an exemption has effect; but, if the rules so provide, he may do so only in specified circumstances.

Cancellation etc. of individual exemptions

5.—(1) If the Director has reasonable grounds for believing that there has been a material change of circumstances since he granted an individual exemption, he may by notice in writing—

(a) cancel the exemption;

(b) vary or remove any condition or obligation; or

(c) impose one or more additional conditions or obligations.

(2) If the Director has a reasonable suspicion that the information on which he based his decision to grant an individual exemption was incomplete, false or misleading in a material particular, he may by notice in writing take any of the steps mentioned in subsection (1).

(3) Breach of a condition has the effect of cancelling the exemption.

(4) Failure to comply with an obligation allows the Director, by notice in writing, to take any of the steps mentioned in subsection (1).

(5) Any step taken by the Director under subsection (1), (2) or (4) has effect from such time as may be specified in the notice.

(6) If an exemption is cancelled under subsection (2) or (4), the date specified in the notice cancelling it may be earlier than the date on which the notice is given.

(7) The Director may act under subsection (1), (2) or (4) on his own initiative or on a complaint made by any person.

Block exemptions

6.—(1) If agreements which fall within a particular category of agreement are, in the opinion of the Director, likely to be agreements to which section 9 applies, the Director may recommend that the Secretary of State make an order specifying that category for the purposes of this section.

(2) The Secretary of State may make an order ("a block exemption order") giving effect to such a recommendation—

(a) in the form in which the recommendation is made; or

(b) subject to such modifications as he considers appropriate.

(3) An agreement which falls within a category specified in a block exemption order is exempt from the Chapter I prohibition.

(4) An exemption under this section is referred to in this Part as a block exemption.

(5) A block exemption order may impose conditions or obligations subject to which a block exemption is to have effect.

(6) A block exemption order may provide—

(a) that breach of a condition imposed by the order has the effect of cancelling the block exemption in respect of an agreement;

(b) that if there is a failure to comply with an obligation imposed by the order, the Director may, by notice in writing, cancel the block exemption in respect of the agreement;

(c) that if the Director considers that a particular agreement is not one to which section 9 applies, he may cancel the block exemption in respect of that agreement.

(7) A block exemption order may provide that the order is to cease to have effect at the end of a specified period.

(8) In this section and section 7 "specified" means specified in a block exemption order.

Block exemptions: opposition

7.—(1) A block exemption order may provide that a party to an agreement which—

(a) does not qualify for the block exemption created by the order, but

(b) satisfies specified criteria, may notify the Director of the agreement for the purposes of subsection (2).

(2) An agreement which is notified under any provision included in a block exemption order by virtue of subsection (1) is to be treated, as from the end of the notice period, as falling within a category specified in a block exemption order unless the Director—

(a) is opposed to its being so treated; and

(b) gives notice in writing to the party concerned of his opposition before the end of that period.

(3) If the Director gives notice of his opposition under subsection (2), the notification under subsection (1) is to be treated as both notification under section 14 and as a request for an individual exemption made under subsection (3) of that section.

(4) In this section "notice period" means such period as may be specified with a view to giving the Director sufficient time to consider whether to oppose under subsection (2).

Block exemptions: procedure

8.—(1) Before making a recommendation under section 6(1), the Director must—

(a) publish details of his proposed recommendation in such a way as he thinks most suitable for bringing it to the attention of those likely to be affected; and

(b) consider any representations about it which are made to him.

(2) If the Secretary of State proposes to give effect to such a recommendation subject to modifications, he must inform the Director of the proposed modifications and take into account any comments made by the Director.

(3) If, in the opinion of the Director, it is appropriate to vary or revoke a block exemption order he may make a recommendation to that effect to the Secretary of State.

(4) Subsection (1) also applies to any proposed recommendation under subsection (3).

(5) Before exercising his power to vary or revoke a block exemption order (in a case where there has been no recommendation under subsection (3)), the Secretary of State must—

(a) inform the Director of the proposed variation or revocation; and

(b) take into account any comments made by the Director.

(6)A block exemption order may provide for a block exemption to have effect from a date earlier than that on which the order is made.

The criteria for individual and block exemptions

9. This section applies to any agreement which—

(a) contributes to—

(i) improving production or distribution, or

(ii) promoting technical or economic progress, while allowing consumers a fair share of the resulting benefit; but

(b) does not—

(i) impose on the undertakings concerned restrictions which are not indispensable to the attainment of those objectives; or

(ii) afford the undertakings concerned the possibility of eliminating competition in respect of a substantial part of the products in question.

Parallel exemptions

10.—(1) An agreement is exempt from the Chapter I prohibition if it is exempt from the Community prohibition—

(a) by virtue of a Regulation,

(b) because it has been given exemption by the Commission, or

    (c) because it has been notified to the Commission under the appropriate opposition or objection procedure and—

       (i) the time for opposing, or objecting to, the agreement has expired and the Commission has not opposed it; or

      (ii) the Commission has opposed, or objected to, the agreement but has withdrawn its opposition or objection.

(2) An agreement is exempt from the Chapter I prohibition if it does not affect trade between Member States but otherwise falls within a category of agreement which is exempt from the Community prohibition by virtue of a Regulation.

(3) An exemption from the Chapter I prohibition under this section is referred to in this Part as a parallel exemption.

(4) A parallel exemption—

    (a) takes effect on the date on which the relevant exemption from the Community prohibition takes effect or, in the case of a parallel exemption under subsection (2), would take effect if the agreement in question affected trade between Member States; and

    (b) ceases to have effect—

       (i) if the relevant exemption from the Community prohibition ceases to have effect; or

      (ii) on being cancelled by virtue of subsection (5) or (7).

(5) In such circumstances and manner as may be specified in rules made under section 51, the Director may—

    (a) impose conditions or obligations subject to which a parallel exemption is to have effect;

    (b) vary or remove any such condition or obligation;

    (c) impose one or more additional conditions or obligations;

    (d) cancel the exemption.

(6) In such circumstances as may be specified in rules made under section 51, the date from which cancellation of an exemption is to take effect may be earlier than the date on which notice of cancellation is given.

(7) Breach of a condition imposed by the Director has the effect of cancelling the exemption.

(8) In exercising his powers under this section, the Director may require any person who is a party to the agreement in question to give him such information as he may require.

(9) For the purpose of this section references to an agreement being exempt from the Community prohibition are to be read as including references to the prohibition being inapplicable to the agreement by virtue of a Regulation or a decision by the Commission.

(10) In this section—

"the Community prohibition" means the prohibition contained in—

    (a) paragraph 1 of Article 85;

    (b) any corresponding provision replacing, or otherwise derived from, that provision;

    (c) such other Regulation as the Secretary of State may by order specify; and

"Regulation" means a Regulation adopted by the Commission or by the Council.

(11) This section has effect in relation to the prohibition contained in paragraph 1 of Article 53 of the EEA Agreement (and the EFTA Surveillance Authority) as it has effect in relation to

the Community prohibition (and the Commission) subject to any modifications which the Secretary of State may by order prescribe.

Exemption for certain other agreements

11.—(1) The fact that a ruling may be given by virtue of Article 88 of the Treaty on the question whether or not agreements of a particular kind are prohibited by Article 85 does not prevent such agreements from being subject to the Chapter I prohibition.

(2) But the Secretary of State may by regulations make such provision as he considers appropriate for the purpose of granting an exemption from the Chapter I prohibition, in prescribed circumstances, in respect of such agreements.

(3) An exemption from the Chapter I prohibition by virtue of regulations under this section is referred to in this Part as a section 11 exemption.

Notification

Requests for Director to examine agreements

12.—(1) Sections 13 and 14 provide for an agreement to be examined by the Director on the application of a party to the agreement who thinks that it may infringe the Chapter I prohibition.

(2) Schedule 5 provides for the procedure to be followed—

(a) by any person making such an application; and

(b) by the Director, in considering such an application.

(3) The Secretary of State may by regulations make provision as to the application of sections 13 to 16 and Schedule 5, with such modifications (if any) as may be prescribed, in cases where the Director—

(a) has given a direction withdrawing an exclusion; or

(b) is considering whether to give such a direction.

Notification for guidance

13.—(1) A party to an agreement who applies for the agreement to be examined under this section must—

(a) notify the Director of the agreement; and

(b) apply to him for guidance.

(2) On an application under this section, the Director may give the applicant guidance as to whether or not, in his view, the agreement is likely to infringe the Chapter I prohibition. [In relation to an application for guidance or a decision in respect of an agreement to which a Chapter I prohibition does not apply for the reasons specified in SI 2000/263 reg.3:

"(2) On an application under this section, the Director may give the applicant guidance as to whether or not, in his view, the agreement is likely to infringe the Chapter I prohibition or would be likely to if the prohibition applied."]

(3) If the Director considers that the agreement is likely to infringe the prohibition if it is not exempt, his guidance may indicate—

    (a) whether the agreement is likely to be exempt from the prohibition under—

        (i) a block exemption;

        (ii) a parallel exemption; or

        (iii) a section 11 exemption; or

    (b) whether he would be likely to grant the agreement an individual exemption if asked to do so.

(4) If an agreement to which the prohibition applies has been notified to the Director under this section, no penalty is to be imposed under this Part in respect of any infringement of the prohibition by the agreement which occurs during the period—

    (a) beginning with the date on which notification was given; and

    (b) ending with such date as may be specified in a notice in writing given to the applicant by the Director when the application has been determined.

(5) The date specified in a notice under subsection (4)(b) may not be earlier than the date on which the notice is given.

Notification for a decision

14.—(1) A party to an agreement who applies for the agreement to be examined under this section must—

    (a) notify the Director of the agreement; and

    (b) apply to him for a decision.

(2) On an application under this section, the Director may make a decision as to—

    (a) whether the Chapter I prohibition has been infringed; and

    (b) if it has not been infringed, whether that is because of the effect of an exclusion or because the agreement is exempt from the prohibition. [In relation to an application for guidance or a decision in respect of an agreement to which a Chapter I prohibition does not apply for the reasons specified in SI 2000/263 reg.3:

"(2) On an application under this section, the Director may make a decision as to—

    (a) whether the Chapter I prohibition has been infringed; and

    (b) if it has not been infringed, whether that is because of the effect of an exclusion or because the agreement is exempt from the prohibition; or

    (c) if it has not been infringed, whether the Chapter I prohibition would be infringed if it applied to the agreement."]

(3) If an agreement is notified to the Director under this section, the application may include a request for the agreement to which it relates to be granted an individual exemption.

(4) If an agreement to which the prohibition applies has been notified to the Director under this section, no penalty is to be imposed under this Part in respect of any infringement of the prohibition by the agreement which occurs during the period—

    (a) beginning with the date on which notification was given; and

    (b) ending with such date as may be specified in a notice in writing given to the applicant by the Director when the application has been determined.

(5) The date specified in a notice under subsection (4)(b) may not be earlier than the date on which the notice is given.

Effect of guidance

15.—(1) This section applies to an agreement if the Director has determined an application under section 13 by giving guidance that—

   (a) the agreement is unlikely to infringe the Chapter I prohibition, regardless of whether or not it is exempt;

   (b) the agreement is likely to be exempt under—

       (i) a block exemption;

      (ii) a parallel exemption; or

     (iii) a section 11 exemption; or

   (c) he would be likely to grant the agreement an individual exemption if asked to do so. [In relation to an application for guidance or a decision in respect of an agreement to which a Chapter I prohibition does not apply for the reasons specified in SI 2000/263 reg.3:

"(1) This section applies to an agreement if the Director has determined an application under section 13 by giving guidance that—

    (a)   the agreement is unlikely to infringe the Chapter I prohibition, regardless of whether or not it is exempt;

   (aa)   the agreement would be unlikely to infringe the Chapter I prohibition if it applied;

    (b)   the agreement is likely to be exempt under—

       (i) a block exemption;

      (ii) a parallel exemption; or

     (iii) a section 11 exemption; or

    (c)   he would be likely to grant the agreement an individual exemption if asked to do so."]

(2) The Director is to take no further action under this Part with respect to an agreement to which this section applies, unless—

   (a) he has reasonable grounds for believing that there has been a material change of circumstances since he gave his guidance;

   (b) he has a reasonable suspicion that the information on which he based his guidance was incomplete, false or misleading in a material particular;

   (c) one of the parties to the agreement applies to him for a decision under section 14 with respect to the agreement; or

   (d) a complaint about the agreement has been made to him by a person who is not a party to the agreement.

(3) No penalty may be imposed under this Part in respect of any infringement of the Chapter I prohibition by an agreement to which this section applies.

(4) But the Director may remove the immunity given by subsection (3) if—

   (a) he takes action under this Part with respect to the agreement in one of the circumstances mentioned in subsection (2);

   (b) he considers it likely that the agreement will infringe the prohibition; and

   (c) he gives notice in writing to the party on whose application the guidance was given that he is removing the immunity as from the date specified in his notice.

(5) If the Director has a reasonable suspicion that information—

   (a) on which he based his guidance, and

   (b) which was provided to him by a party to the agreement, was incomplete, false or misleading in a material particular, the date specified in a notice under subsection (4)(c) may be earlier than the date on which the notice is given.

Effect of a decision that the Chapter I prohibition has not been infringed

16.—(1) This section applies to an agreement if the Director has determined an application under section 14 by making a decision that the agreement has not infringed the Chapter I prohibition. [In relation to an application for guidance or a decision in respect of an agreement to which a Chapter I prohibition does not apply for the reasons specified in SI 2000/263 reg.3:

"(1) This section applies to an agreement if the Director has determined an application under section 14 by making a decision that the agreement has not infringed the Chapter I prohibition or would not do so if the prohibition applied to the agreement."]

(2) The Director is to take no further action under this Part with respect to the agreement unless—

(a) he has reasonable grounds for believing that there has been a material change of circumstances since he gave his decision; or

(b) he has a reasonable suspicion that the information on which he based his decision was incomplete, false or misleading in a material particular.

(3) No penalty may be imposed under this Part in respect of any infringement of the Chapter I prohibition by an agreement to which this section applies.

(4) But the Director may remove the immunity given by subsection (3) if—

(a) he takes action under this Part with respect to the agreement in one of the circumstances mentioned in subsection (2);

(b) he considers that it is likely that the agreement will infringe the prohibition; and

(c) he gives notice in writing to the party on whose application the decision was made that he is removing the immunity as from the date specified in his notice.

(5) If the Director has a reasonable suspicion that information—

(a) on which he based his decision, and

(b) which was provided to him by a party to the agreement, was incomplete, false or misleading in a material particular, the date specified in a notice under subsection (4)(c) may be earlier than the date on which the notice is given.

CHAPTER II

ABUSE OF DOMINANT POSITION

Introduction

Enactments replaced

17. Sections 2 to 10 of the Competition Act 1980 (control of anti-competitive practices) shall cease to have effect.

The prohibition

Abuse of dominant position

18.—(1) Subject to section 19, any conduct on the part of one or more undertakings which amounts to the abuse of a dominant position in a market is prohibited if it may affect trade within the United Kingdom.

(2) Conduct may, in particular, constitute such an abuse if it consists in—

(a) directly, or indirectly imposing unfair purchase or selling prices or other unfair trading conditions;

(b) limiting production, markets or technical development to the prejudice of consumers;

(c) applying dissimilar conditions to equivalent transactions with other trading parties, thereby placing them at a competitive disadvantage;

(d) making the conclusion of contracts subject to acceptance by the other parties of supplementary obligations which, by their nature or according to commercial usage, have no connection with the subject of the contracts.

(3) In this section—

"dominant position" means a dominant position within the United Kingdom; and
"the United Kingdom" means the United Kingdom or any part of it.

(4) The prohibition imposed by subsection (1) is referred to in this Act as "the Chapter II prohibition"

Excluded cases

Excluded cases

19.—(1) The Chapter II prohibition does not apply in any of the cases in which it is excluded by or as a result of—

(a) Schedule 1 (mergers and concentrations); or

(b) Schedule 3 (general exclusions).

(2) The Secretary of State may at any time by order amend Schedule 1, with respect to the Chapter II prohibition, by—

(a) providing for one or more additional exclusions; or

(b) amending or removing any provisions (whether or not it has been added by an order under this subsection).

(3) The Secretary of State may at any time by order amend paragraph 8 of Schedule 3 with respect to the Chapter II prohibition.
(4) Schedule 3 also gives the Secretary of State power to provide that the Chapter II prohibition is not to apply in certain circumstances.

Notification

Requests for Director to consider conduct

20.—(1) Sections 21 and 22 provide for conduct of a person which that person thinks may infringe the Chapter II prohibition to be considered by the Director on the application of that person.

(2) Schedule 6 provides for the procedure to be followed—

(a) by any person making an application, and

(b) by the Director, in considering an application.

Notification for guidance

21.—(1) A person who applies for conduct to be considered under this section must—

(a) notify the Director of it; and

(b) apply to him for guidance.

(2) On an application under this section, the Director may give the applicant guidance as to whether or not, in his view, the conduct is likely to infringe the Chapter II prohibition.

Notification for a decision

22.—(1) A person who applies for conduct to be considered under this section must—

(a) notify the Director of it; and

(b) apply to him for a decision.

(2) On an application under this section, the Director may make a decision as to—

(a) whether the Chapter II prohibition has been infringed; and

(b) if it has not been infringed, whether that is because of the effect of an exclusion.

Effect of guidance

23.—(1) This section applies to conduct if the Director has determined an application under section 21 by giving guidance that the conduct is unlikely to infringe the Chapter II prohibition.
(2) The Director is to take no further action under this Part with respect to the conduct to which this section applies, unless—

(a) he has reasonable grounds for believing that there has been a material change of circumstances since he gave his guidance;

(b) he has a reasonable suspicion that the information on which he based his guidance was incomplete, false or misleading in a material particular; or

(c) a complaint about the conduct has been made to him.

(3) No penalty may be imposed under this Part in respect of any infringement of the Chapter II prohibition by conduct to which this section applies.
(4) But the Director may remove the immunity given by subsection (3) if—

(a) he takes action under this Part with respect to the conduct in one of the circumstances mentioned in subsection (2);

(b) he considers that it is likely that the conduct will infringe the prohibition; and

(c) he gives notice in writing to the undertaking on whose application the guidance was given that he is removing the immunity as from the date specified in his notice.

(5) If the Director has a reasonable suspicion that information—

(a) on which he based his guidance, and

(b) which was provided to him by an undertaking engaging in the conduct,
was incomplete, false or misleading in a material particular, the date specified in a notice under subsection (4)(c) may be earlier than the date on which the notice is given.

Effect of a decision that the Chapter II prohibition has not been infringed

24.—(1) This section applies to conduct if the Director has determined an application under section 22 by making a decision that the conduct has not infringed the Chapter II prohibition.

(2) The Director is to take no further action under this Part with respect to the conduct unless—

(a) he has reasonable grounds for believing that there has been a material change of circumstance since he gave his decision; or

(b) he has a reasonable suspicion that the information on which he based his decision was incomplete, false or misleading in a material particular.

(3) No penalty may be imposed under this Part in respect of any infringement of the Chapter II prohibition by conduct to which this section applies.

(4) But the Director may remove the immunity given by subsection (3) if—

(a) he takes action under this Part with respect to the conduct in one of the circumstances mentioned in subsection (2);

(b) he considers that it is likely that the conduct will infringe the prohibition; and

(c) he gives notice in writing to the undertaking on whose application the decision was made that he is removing the immunity as from the date specified in his notice.

(5) If the Director has a reasonable suspicion that information—

(a) on which he based his decision, and

(b) which was provided to him by an undertaking engaging in the conduct, was incomplete, false or misleading in a material particular, the date specified in a notice under subsection (4)(c) may be earlier than the date on which the notice is given.

CHAPTER III

INVESTIGATION AND ENFORCEMENT

Investigations

Director's power to investigate

25. The Director may conduct an investigation if there are reasonable grounds for suspecting—

(a) that the Chapter I prohibition has been infringed; or

(b) that the Chapter II prohibition has been infringed.

Powers when conducting investigations

26.—(1) For the purposes of an investigation under section 25, the Director may require any person to produce to him a specified document, or to provide him with specified information, which he considers relates to any matter relevant to the investigation.

(2) The power conferred by subsection (1) is to be exercised by a notice in writing.

(3) A notice under subsection (2) must indicate—

(a) the subject matter and purpose of the investigation; and

(b) the nature of the offences created by sections 42 to 44.

(4) In subsection (1) "specified" means —

(a) specified, or described, in the notice; or

(b) falling within a category which is specified, or described, in the notice.

(5) The Director may also specify in the notice—

(a) the time and place at which any document is to be produced or any information is to be provided;

(b) the manner and form in which it is to be produced or provided.

(6) The power under this section to require a person to produce a document includes power—

(a) if the document is produced—

(i) to take copies of it or extracts from it;
(ii) to require him, or any person who is a present or past officer of his, or is or was at any time employed by him, to provide an explanation of the document;

(b) if the document is not produced, to require him to state, to the best of his knowledge and belief, where it is.

Power to enter premises without a warrant

27.—(1) Any officer of the Director who is authorised in writing by the Director to do so ("an investigating officer") may enter any premises in connection with an investigation under section 25.

(2) No investigating officer is to enter any premises in the exercise of his powers under this section unless he has given to the occupier of the premises a written notice which—

(a) gives at least two working days' notice of the intended entry;

(b) indicates the subject matter and purpose of the investigation; and

(c) indicates the nature of the offences created by sections 42 to 44.

(3) Subsection (2) does not apply—

(a) if the Director has a reasonable suspicion that the premises are, or have been, occupied by—

(i) a party to an agreement which he is investigating under section 25(a); or
(ii) an undertaking the conduct of which he is investigating under section 25(b); or

(b) if the investigating officer has taken all such steps as are reasonably practicable to give notice but has not been able to do so.

(4) In a case falling within subsection (3), the power of entry conferred by subsection (1) is to be exercised by the investigating officer on production of—

(a) evidence of his authorisation; and

(b) a document containing the information referred to in subsection (2)(b) and (c) .

(5) An investigating officer entering any premises under this section may—

(a) take with him such equipment as appears to him to be necessary;

(b) require any person on the premises—

  (i) to produce any document which he considers relates to any matter relevant to the investigation; and
  (ii) if the document is produced, to provide an explanation of it;

(c) require any person to state, to the best of his knowledge and belief, where any such document is to be found;

(d) take copies of, or extracts from, any document which is produced;

(e) require any information which is held in a computer and is accessible from the premises and which the investigating officer considers relates to any matter relevant to the investigation, to be produced in a form—

  (i) in which it can be taken away, and
  (ii) in which it is visible and legible.

Power to enter premises under a warrant

28.—(1) On an application made by the Director to the court in accordance with rules of court, a judge may issue a warrant if he is satisfied that—

(a) there are reasonable grounds for suspecting that there are on any premises documents—

  (i) the production of which has been required under section 26 or 27; and
  (ii) which have not been produced as required;

(b) there are reasonable grounds for suspecting that—

  (i) there are on any premises documents which the Director has power under section 26 to require to be produced; and
  (ii) if the documents were required to be produced, they would not be produced but would be concealed, removed, tampered with or destroyed; or

(c) an investigating officer has attempted to enter premises in the exercise of his powers under section 27 but has been unable to do so and that there are reasonable grounds for suspecting that there are on the premises documents the production of which could have been required under that section.

(2) A warrant under this section shall authorise a named officer of the Director, and any other of his officers whom he has authorised in writing to accompany the named officer—

(a) to enter the premises specified in the warrant, using such force as is reasonably necessary for the purpose;

(b) to search the premises and take copies of, or extracts from, any document appearing to be of a kind in respect of which the application under subsection (1) was granted ("the relevant kind");

(c) to take possession of any documents appearing to be of the relevant kind if—

  (i) such action appears to be necessary for preserving the documents of preventing interference with them; or
  (ii) it is not reasonably practicable to take copies of the documents on the premises;

(d) to take any other steps which appear to be necessary for the purpose mentioned in paragraph (c)(i);

(e) to require any person to provide an explanation of any document appearing to be of the relevant kind or to state, to the best of his knowledge and belief, where it may be found;

(f) to require any information which is held in a computer and is accessible from the premises and which the named officer considers relates to any matter relevant to the investigation, to be produced in a form—

  (i) in which it can be taken away, and

(ii)   in which it is visible and legible.

(3) If, in the case of a warrant under subsection (1)(b), the judge is satisfied that it is reasonable to suspect that there are also on the premises other documents relating to the investigation concerned, the warrant shall also authorise action mentioned in subsection (2) to be taken in relation to any such document.

(4) Any person entering premises by virtue of a warrant under this section may take with him such equipment as appears to him to be necessary.

(5) On leaving any premises which he has entered by virtue of a warrant under this section, the named officer must, if the premises are unoccupied or the occupier is temporarily absent, leave them as effectively secured as he found them.

(6) A warrant under this section continues in force until the end of the period of one month beginning with the day on which it is issued.

(7) Any document of which possession is taken under subsection (2)(c) may be retained for a period of three months.

Entry of premises under warrant: supplementary

29.—(1) A warrant issued under section 28 must indicate—

(a)   the subject matter and purpose of the investigation;

(b)   the nature of the offences created by sections 42 to 44.

(2) The powers conferred by section 28 are to be exercised on production of a warrant issued under that section.

(3) If there is no one at the premises when the named officer proposes to execute such a warrant he must, before executing it—

(a)   take such steps as are reasonable in all the circumstances to inform the occupier of the intended entry; and

(b)   if the occupier is informed, afford him or his legal or other representative a reasonable opportunity to be present when the warrant is executed.

(4) If the named officer is unable to inform the occupier of the intended entry he must, when executing the warrant, leave a copy of it in a prominent place on the premises.

(5) In this section—

"named officer" means the officer named in the warrant; and
"occupier", in relation to any premises, means a person whom the named officer reasonably believes is the occupier of those premises.

Privileged communications

30.—(1) A person shall not be required, under any provision of this Part, to produce or disclose a privileged communication.

(2) "Privileged communication" means a communication—

(a)   between a professional legal adviser and his client, or

(b)   made in connection with, or in contemplation of, legal proceedings and for the purposes of those proceedings, which in proceedings in the High Court would be protected from disclosure on grounds of legal professional privilege.

(3) In the application of this section to Scotland—

(a)   references to the High Court are to be read as references to the Court of Session; and

(b) the reference to legal professional privilege is to be read as a reference to confidentiality of communications.

Decisions following an investigation

31.—(1) Subsection (2) applies if, as the result of an investigation conducted under section 25, the Director proposes to make—

(a) a decision that the Chapter I prohibition has been infringed, or

(b) a decision that the Chapter II prohibition has been infringed.

(2) Before making the decision, the Director must—

(a) give written notice to the person (or persons) likely to be affected by the proposed decision; and

(b) give that person (or those persons) an opportunity to make representations.

Enforcement

Directions in relation to agreements

32.—(1) If the Director has made a decision that an agreement infringes the Chapter I prohibition, he may give to such person or persons as he considers appropriate such directions as he considers appropriate to bring the infringement to an end.

(2) Subsection (1) applies whether the Director's decision is made on his own initiative or on an application made to him under this Part.

(3) A direction under this section may, in particular, include provision—

(a) requiring the parties to the agreement to modify the agreement; or

(b) requiring them to terminate the agreement.

(4) A direction under this section must be given in writing.

Directions in relation to conduct

33.—(1) If the Director has made a decision that conduct infringes the Chapter II prohibition, he may give to such person or persons as he considers appropriate such directions as he considers appropriate to bring the infringement to an end.

(2) Subsection (1) applies whether the Director's decision is made on his own initiative or on an application made to him under this Part.

(3) A direction under this section may, in particular, include provision—

(a) requiring the person concerned to modify the conduct in question; or

(b) requiring him to cease that conduct.

(4) A direction under this section must be given in writing.

Enforcement of directions

34.—(1) If a person fails, without reasonable excuse, to comply with a direction under section 32 or 33, the Director may apply to the court for an order—

(a) requiring the defaulter to make good his default within a time specified in the order; or

(b) if the direction related to anything to be done in the management or administration of an undertaking, requiring the undertaking or any of its officers to do it.

(2) An order of the court under subsection (1) may provide for all of the costs of, or incidental to, the application for the order to be borne by—

(a) the person in default; or

(b) any officer of an undertaking who is responsible for the default.

(3) In the application of subsection (2) to Scotland, the reference to "costs" is to be read as a reference to "expenses".

Interim measures

35.—(1) This section applies if the Director—

(a) has a reasonable suspicion that the Chapter I prohibition has been infringed, or

(b) has a reasonable suspicion that the Chapter II prohibition has been infringed, but has not completed his investigation into the matter.

(2) If the Director considers that it is necessary for him to act under this section as a matter of urgency for the purpose—

(a) of preventing serious, irreparable damage to a particular person or category of person, or

(b) of protecting the public interest,

he may give such directions as he considers appropriate for that purpose.
(3) Before giving a direction under this section, the Director must—

(a) give written notice to the person (or persons) to whom he proposes to give the direction; and

(b) give that person (or each of them) an opportunity to make representations.

(4) A notice under subsection (3) must indicate the nature of the direction which the Director is proposing to give and his reasons for wishing to give it.
(5) A direction given under this section has effect while subsection (1) applies, but may be replaced if the circumstances permit by a direction under section 32 or (as appropriate) section 33.
(6) In the case of a suspected infringement of the Chapter I prohibition, sections 32(3) and 34 also apply to directions given under this section.
(7) In the case of a suspected infringement of the Chapter II prohibition, sections 33(3) and 34 also apply to directions given under this section.

Penalty for infringing Chapter I or Chapter II prohibition

36.—(1) On making a decision that an agreement has infringed the Chapter I prohibition, the Director may require an undertaking which is a party to the agreement to pay him a penalty in respect of the infringement.
(2) On making a decision that conduct has infringed the Chapter II prohibition, the Director may require the undertaking concerned to pay him a penalty in respect of the infringement.
(3) The Director may impose a penalty on an undertaking under subsection (1) or (2) only if he is satisfied that the infringement has been committed intentionally or negligently by the undertaking.
(4) Subsection (1) is subject to section 39 and does not apply if the Director is satisfied that the undertaking acted on the reasonable assumption that that section gave it immunity in respect of the agreement.
(5) Subsection (2) is subject to section 40 and does not apply if the Director is satisfied that the

undertaking acted on the reasonable assumption that that section gave it immunity in respect of the conduct.

(6) Notice of a penalty under this section must—

(a) be in writing; and

(b) specify the date before which the penalty is required to be paid.

(7) The date specified must not be earlier than the end of the period within which an appeal against the notice may be brought under section 46.

(8) No penalty fixed by the Director under this section may exceed 10% of the turnover of the undertaking (determined in accordance with such provisions as may be specified in an order made by the Secretary of State).

(9) Any sums received by the Director under this section are to be paid into the Consolidated Fund.

Recovery of penalties

37.—(1) If the specified date in a penalty notice has passed and—

(a) the period during which an appeal against the imposition, or amount, of the penalty may be made has expired without an appeal having been made, or

(b) such an appeal has been made and determined,
the Director may recover from the undertaking, as a civil debt due to him, any amount payable under the penalty notice which remains outstanding.

(2) In this section—

"penalty notice" means a notice given under section 36; and
"specified date" means the date specified in the penalty notice.

The appropriate level of a penalty

38.—(1) The Director must prepare and publish guidance as to the appropriate amount of any penalty under this Part.

(2) The Director may at any time alter the guidance.

(3) If the guidance is altered, the Director must publish it as altered.

(4) No guidance is to be published under this section without the approval of the Secretary of State.

(5) The Director may, after consulting the Secretary of State, choose how he publishes his guidance.

(6) If the Director is preparing or altering guidance under this section he must consult such persons as he considers appropriate.

(7) If the proposed guidance or alteration relates to a matter in respect of which a regulator exercises concurrent jurisdiction, those consulted must include that regulator.

(8) When setting the amount of a penalty under this Part, the Director must have regard to the guidance for the time being in force under this section.

(9) If a penalty or a fine has been imposed by the Commission, or by a court or other body in another Member State, in respect of an agreement or conduct, the Director, an appeal tribunal or the appropriate court must take that penalty or fine into account when setting the amount of a penalty under this Part in relation to that agreement or conduct.

(10) In subsection (9) "the appropriate court" means—

(a) in relation to England and Wales, the Court of Appeal;

(b) in relation to Scotland, the Court of Session;

(c) in relation to Northern Ireland, the Court of Appeal in Northern Ireland;

(d) the House of Lords.

Limited immunity for small agreements

39.—(1) In this section "small agreement" means an agreement—

(a) which falls within a category prescribed for the purposes of this section; but

(b) is not a price fixing agreement.

(2) The criteria by reference to which a category of agreement is prescribed may, in particular, include—

(a) the combined turnover of the parties to the agreement (determined in accordance with prescribed provisions);

(b) the share of the market affected by the agreement (determined in that way).

(3) A party to a small agreement is immune from the effect of section 36(1); but the Director may withdraw that immunity under subsection (4).

(4) If the Director has investigated a small agreement, he may make a decision withdrawing the immunity given by subsection (3) if, as a result of his investigation, he considers that the agreement is likely to infringe the Chapter I prohibition.

(5) The Director must give each of the parties in respect of which immunity is withdrawn written notice of his decision to withdraw the immunity.

(6) A decision under subsection (4) takes effect on such date ("the withdrawal date") as may be specified in the decision.

(7) The withdrawal date must be a date after the date on which the decision is made.

(8) In determining the withdrawal date, the Director must have regard to the amount of time which the parties are likely to require in order to secure that there is no further infringement of the Chapter I prohibition with respect to the agreement.

(9) In subsection (1) "price fixing agreement" means an agreement which has as its object or effect, or one of its objects or effects, restricting the freedom of a party to the agreement to determine the price to be charged (otherwise than as between that party and another party to the agreement) for the product, service or other matter to which the agreement relates.

Limited immunity in relation to the Chapter II prohibition

40.—(1) In this section "conduct of minor significance" means conduct which falls within a category prescribed for the purposes of this section.

(2) The criteria by reference to which a category is prescribed may, in particular, include—

(a) the turnover of the person whose conduct it is (determined in accordance with prescribed provisions);

(b) the share of the market affected by the conduct (determined in that way).

(3) A person is immune from the effect of section 36(2) if his conduct is conduct of minor significance; but the Director may withdraw that immunity under subsection (4).

(4) If the Director has investigated conduct of minor significance, he may make a decision withdrawing the immunity given by subsection (3) if, as a result of his investigation, he considers that the conduct is likely to infringe the Chapter II prohibition.

(5) The Director must give the person, or persons, whose immunity has been withdrawn written notice of his decision to withdraw the immunity.

(6) A decision under subsection (4) takes effect on such date ("the withdrawal date") as may be specified in the decision.

(7) The withdrawal date must be a date after the date on which the decision is made.

(8) In determining the withdrawal date, the Director must have regard to the amount of time which the person or persons affected are likely to require in order to secure that there is no further infringement of the Chapter II prohibition.

Agreements notified to the Commission

41.—(1) This section applies if a party to an agreement which may infringe the Chapter I prohibition has notified the agreement to the Commission for a decision as to whether an exemption will be granted under Article 85 with respect to the agreement.

(2) A penalty may not be required to be paid under this Part in respect of any infringement of the Chapter I prohibition after notification but before the Commission determines the matter.

(3) If the Commission withdraws the benefit of provisional immunity from penalties with respect to the agreement, subsection (2) ceases to apply as from the date on which that benefit is withdrawn.

(4) The fact that an agreement has been notified to the Commission does not prevent the Director from investigating it under this Part.

(5) In this section "provisional immunity from penalties" has such meaning as may be prescribed.

Offences

Offences

42.—(1) A person is guilty of an offence if he fails to comply with a requirement imposed on him under section 26, 27 or 28.

(2) If a person is charged with an offence under subsection (1) in respect of a requirement to produce a document, it is a defence for him to prove—

(a) that the document was not in his possession or under his control; and

(b) that it was not reasonably practicable for him to comply with the requirement.

(3) If a person is charged with an offence under subsection (1) in respect of a requirement—

(a) to provide information,

(b) to provide an explanation of a document, or

(c) to state where a document is to be found, it is a defence for him to prove that he had a reasonable excuse for failing to comply with the requirement.

(4) Failure to comply with a requirement imposed under section 26 or 27 is not an offence if the person imposing the requirement has failed to act in accordance with that section.

(5) A person is guilty of an offence if he intentionally obstructs an officer acting in the exercise of his powers under section 27.

(6) A person guilty of an offence under subsection (1) or (5) is liable—

(a) on summary conviction, to a fine not exceeding the statutory maximum;

(b) on conviction on indictment, to a fine.

(7) A person who intentionally obstructs an officer in the exercise of his powers under a warrant issued under section 28 is guilty of an offence and liable—

(a) on summary conviction, to a fine not exceeding the statutory maximum;

(b) on conviction on indictment, to imprisonment for a term not exceeding two years or to a fine or to both.

Destroying or falsifying documents

43.—(1) A person is guilty of an offence if, having been required to produce a document under section 26, 27 or 28—

(a) he intentionally or recklessly destroys or otherwise disposes of it, falsifies it or conceals it, or

(b) he causes or permits its destruction, disposal, falsification or concealment.

(2) A person guilty of an offence under subsection (1) is liable—

(a) on summary conviction, to a fine not exceeding the statutory maximum;

(b) on conviction on indictment, to imprisonment for a term not exceeding two years or to a fine or to both.

False or misleading information

44.—(1) If information is provided by a person to the Director in connection with any function of the Director under this Part, that person is guilty of an offence if—

(a) the information is false or misleading in a material particular, and

(b) he knows that it is or is reckless as to whether it is.

(2) A person who—

(a) provides any information to another person, knowing the information to be false or misleading in a material particular, or

(b) recklessly provides any information to another person which is false or misleading in a material particular, knowing that the information is to be used for the purpose of providing information to the Director in connection with any of his functions under this Part, is guilty of an offence.

(3) A person guilty of an offence under this section is liable—

(a) on summary conviction, to a fine not exceeding the statutory maximum;

(b) on conviction on indictment, to imprisonment for a term not exceeding two years or to a fine or to both.

CHAPTER IV

The Competition Commission and Appeals

The Commission

The Competition Commission

45.—(1) There is to be a body corporate known as the Competition Commission.

(2) The Commission is to have such functions as are conferred on it by or as a result of this Act.

(3) The Monopolies and Mergers Commission is dissolved and its functions are transferred to the Competition Commission.

(4) In any enactment, instrument or other document, any reference to the Monopolies and Mergers Commission which has continuing effect is to be read as a reference to the Competition Commission.

(5) The Secretary of State may by order make such consequential, supplemental and incidental provision as he considers appropriate in connection with—

(a) the dissolution of the Monopolies and Mergers Commission; and

(b) the transfer of functions effected by subsection (3).

(6) An order made under subsection (5) may, in particular, include provision—

(a) for the transfer of property, rights, obligations and liabilities and the continuation of proceedings, investigations and other matters; or

(b) amending any enactment which makes provision with respect to the Monopolies and Mergers Commission or any of its functions.

(7) Schedule 7 makes further provision about the Competition Commission.

Appeals

Appealable decisions

46.—(1) Any party to an agreement in respect of which the Director has made a decision may appeal to the Competition Commission against, or with respect to, the decision.

(2) Any person in respect of whose conduct the Director has made a decision may appeal to the Competition Commission against, or with respect to, the decision.

(3) In this section "decision" means a decision of the Director—

(a) as to whether the Chapter I prohibition has been infringed,

(b) as to whether the Chapter II prohibition has been infringed,

(c) as to whether to grant an individual exemption,

(d) in respect of an individual exemption—

    (i) as to whether to impose any condition or obligation under section 4(3)(a) or 5(1)(c),

    (ii) where such a condition or obligation has been imposed, as to the condition or obligation,

    (iii) as to the period fixed under section 4(3)(b), or

    (iv) as to the date fixed under section 4(5),

(e) as to—

    (i) whether to extend the period for which an individual exemption has effect, or

    (ii) the period of any such extension,

(f) cancelling an exemption,

(g) as to the imposition of any penalty under section 36 or as to the amount of any such penalty,

(h) withdrawing or varying any of the decisions in paragraphs (a) to (f) following an application under section 47(1), and includes a direction given under section 32, 33 or 35 and such other decision as may be prescribed.

(4) Except in the case of an appeal against the imposition, or the amount, of a penalty, the making of an appeal under this section does not suspend the effect of the decision to which the appeal relates.

(5) Part I of Schedule 8 makes further provision about appeals.

Third party appeals

47.—(1) A person who does not fall within section 46(1) or (2) may apply to the Director asking him to withdraw or vary a decision ("the relevant decision") falling within paragraphs (a) to (f) of section 46(3) or such other decision as may be prescribed.

(2) The application must—

(a) be made in writing, within such period as the Director may specify in rules under section 51; and

(b) give the applicant's reasons for considering that the relevant decision should be withdrawn or (as the case may be) varied.

(3) If the Director decides—

(a) that the applicant does not have a sufficient interest in the relevant decision,

(b) that, in the case of an applicant claiming to represent persons who have such an interest, the applicant does not represent such persons, or

(c) that the persons represented by the applicant do not have such an interest, he must notify the applicant of his decision.

(4) If the Director, having considered the application, decides that it does not show sufficient reason why he should withdraw or vary the relevant decision, he must notify the applicant of his decision.

(5) Otherwise, the Director must deal with the application in accordance with such procedure as may be specified in rules under section 51.

(6) The applicant may appeal to the Competition Commission against a decision of the Director notified under subsection (3) or (4).

(7) The making of an application does not suspend the effect of the relevant decision.

Appeal tribunals

48.—(1) Any appeal made to the Competition Commission under section 46 or 47 is to be determined by an appeal tribunal.

(2) The Secretary of State may, after consulting the President of the Competition Commission Appeal Tribunals and such other persons as he considers appropriate, make rules with respect to appeals and appeal tribunals.

(3) The rules may confer functions on the President.

(4) Part II of Schedule 8 makes further provision about rules made under this section but is not to be taken as restricting the Secretary of State's powers under this section.

Appeals on point of law etc

49.—(1) An appeal lies—

(a) on a point of law arising from a decision of an appeal tribunal, or

(b) from any decision of an appeal tribunal as to the amount of a penalty.

(2) An appeal under this section may be made only—

(a) to the appropriate court;

(b) with leave; and

(c) at the instance of a party or at the instance of a person who has a sufficient interest in the matter.

(3) Rules under section 48 may make provision for regulating or prescribing any matters incidental to or consequential upon an appeal under this section.

(4) In subsection (2)—

"the appropriate court" means—

    (a) in relation to proceedings before a tribunal in England and Wales, the Court of Appeal;

    (b) in relation to proceedings before a tribunal in Scotland, the Court of Session;

    (c) in relation to proceedings before a tribunal in Northern Ireland, the Court of Appeal in Northern Ireland;

"leave" means leave of the tribunal in question or of the appropriate court; and

"party", in relation to a decision, means a person who was a party to the proceedings in which the decision was made.

CHAPTER V

MISCELLANEOUS

Vertical agreements and land agreements

Vertical agreements and land agreements

50.—(1) The Secretary of State may by order provide for any provision of this Part to apply in relation to—

    (a) vertical agreements, or

    (b) land agreements, with such modifications as may be prescribed.

(2) An order may, in particular, provide for exclusions or exemptions, or otherwise provide for prescribed provisions not to apply, in relation to—

    (a) vertical agreements, or land agreements, in general; or

    (b) vertical agreements, or land agreements, of any prescribed description.

(3) An order may empower the Director to give directions to the effect that in prescribed circumstances an exclusion, exemption or modification is not to apply (or is to apply in a particular way) in relation to an individual agreement.

(4) Subsection (2) and (3) are not to be read as limiting the powers conferred by section 71.

(5) In this section—

"land agreement" and "vertical agreement" have such meaning as may be prescribed; and

"prescribed" means prescribed by an order.

Director's rules, guidance and fees

Rules

51.—(1) The Director may make such rules about procedural and other matters in connection with the carrying into effect of the provisions of this Part as he considers appropriate.

(2) Schedule 9 makes further provisions about rules made under this section but is not to be taken as restricting the Director's powers under this section.

(3) If the Director is preparing rules under this section he must consult such persons as he considers appropriate.

(4) If the proposed rules relate to a matter in respect of which a regulator exercises concurrent jurisdiction, those consulted must include that regulator.

(5) No rule made by the Director is to come into operation until it has been approved by an order made by the Secretary of State.

(6) The Secretary of State may approve any rule made by the Director—

    (a) in the form in which it is submitted; or

    (b) subject to such modifications as he considers appropriate.

(7) If the Secretary of State proposes to approve a rule subject to modifications he must inform the Director of the proposed modifications and take into account any comments made by the Director.

(8) Subsections (5) to (7) apply also to any alteration of the rules made by the Director.

(9) The Secretary of State may, after consulting the Director, by order vary or revoke any rules made under this section.

(10) If the Secretary of State considers that rules should be made under this section with respect to a particular matter he may direct the Director to exercise his powers under this section and make rules about that matter.

Advice and information

52.—(1) As soon as is reasonably practicable after the passing of this Act, the Director must prepare and publish general advice and information about—

    (a) the application of the Chapter I prohibition and the Chapter II prohibition, and

    (b) the enforcement of those prohibitions.

(2) The Director may at any time publish revised, or new, advice or information.

(3) Advice and information published under this section must be prepared with a view to—

    (a) explaining provisions of this Part to persons who are likely to be affected by them; and

    (b) indicating how the Director expects such provisions to operate.

(4) Advice (or information) published by virtue of subsection (3)(b) may include advice (or information) about the factors which the Director may take into account in considering whether, and if so how, to exercise a power conferred on him by Chapter I, II or III.

(5) Any advice or information published by the Director under this section is to be published in such form and in such manner as he considers appropriate.

(6) If the Director is preparing any advice or information under this section he must consult such persons as he considers appropriate.

(7) If the proposed advice or information relates to a matter in respect of which a regulator exercises concurrent jurisdiction, those consulted must include that regulator.

(8) In preparing any advice or information under this section about a matter in respect of which he may exercise functions under this Part, a regulator must consult—

    (a) the Director;

    (b) the other regulators; and

    (c) such other persons as he considers appropriate.

Fees

53.—(1) The Director may charge fees, of specified amounts, in connection with the exercise by him of specified functions under this Part.

(2) Rules may, in particular, provide—

    (a) for the amount of any fee to be calculated by reference to matters which may include—

        (i) the turnover of any party to an agreement (determined in such manner as may be specified);

    (ii) the turnover of a person whose conduct the Director is to consider (determined in that way);

(b) for different amounts to be specified in connection with different functions;

(c) for the repayment by the Director of the whole or part of a fee in specified circumstances;

(d) that an application or notice is not to be regarded as duly made or given unless the appropriate fee is paid.

(3) In this section—

(a) "rules" means rules made by the Director under section 51; and

(b) "specified" means specified in rules.

Regulators

Regulators

54.—(1) In this Part "regulator" means any person mentioned in paragraphs (a) to (g) of paragraph 1 of Schedule 10.

(2) Parts II and III of Schedule 10 provide for functions of the Director under this Part to be exercisable concurrently by regulators.

(3) Parts IV and V of Schedule 10 make minor and consequential amendments in connection with the regulators' competition functions.

(4) The Secretary of State may make regulations for the purpose of coordinating the performance of functions under this Part ("Part I functions") which are exercisable concurrently by two or more competent persons as a result of any provision made by Part II or III of Schedule 10.

(5) The regulations may, in particular, make provision—

(a) as to the procedure to be followed by competent persons when determining who is to exercise Part I functions in a particular case;

(b) as to the steps which must be taken before a competent person exercise, in a particular case, such Part I functions as may be prescribed;

(c) as to the procedure for determining, in a particular case, questions arising as to which competent person is to exercise Part I functions in respect of the case;

(d) for Part I functions in a particular case to be exercised jointly—
    (i) by the Director and one or more regulators, or
    (ii) by two or more regulators,
and as to the procedure to be followed in such cases;

(e) as to the circumstances in which the exercise by a competent person of such Part I functions as may be prescribed in to preclude the exercise of such functions by another such person;

(f) for cases in respect of which Part I functions are being, or have been, exercised by a competent person to be transferred to another such person;

(g) for the person ("A") exercising Part I functions in a particular case—

    (i) to appoint another competent person ("B") to exercise Part I functions on A's behalf in relation to the case; or
    (ii) to appoint officers of B (with B's consent) to act as officers of A in relation to the case;

(h) for notification as to who is exercising Part I functions in respect of a particular case.

(6) Provision made by virtue of subsection (5)(c) may provide for questions to be referred to and determined by the Secretary of State or by such other person as may be prescribed.

(7) "Competent person" means the Director or any of the regulators.

Confidentiality and immunity from defamation

General restrictions on disclosure of information

55.—(1) No information which—

(a) has been obtained under or as a result of any provision of this Part, and

(b) relates to the affairs of any individual or to any particular business of an undertaking is to be disclosed during the lifetime of that individual or while that business continues to be carried on, unless the condition mentioned in subsection (2) is satisfied.

(2) The condition is that consent to the disclosure has been obtained from—

(a) the person from whom the information was initially obtained under or as a result of any provision of this Part (if the identity of that person is known); and

(b) if different—

(i) the individual to whose affairs the information relates, or
(ii) the person for the time being carrying on the business to which the information relates.

(3) Subsection (1) does not apply to a disclosure of information—

(a) made for the purpose of—

(i) facilitating the performance of any relevant functions of a designated person;
(ii) facilitating the performance of any functions of the Commission in respect of Community law about competition;
(iii) facilitating the performance by the Comptroller and Auditor General of any of his functions;
(iv) criminal proceedings in any part of the United Kingdom;

(b) made with a view to the institution of, or otherwise for the purposes of, civil proceedings brought under or in connection with this Part;

(c) made in connection with the investigation of any criminal offence triable in the United Kingdom or in any part of the United Kingdom; or

(d) which is required to meet a Community obligation.

(4) In subsection (3) "relevant functions" and "designated person" have the meaning given in Schedule 11.

(5) Subsection (1) also does not apply to a disclosure of information made for the purpose of facilitating the performance of specified functions of any specified person.

(6) In subsection (5) "specified" means specified in an order made by the Secretary of State.

(7) If information is disclosed to the public in circumstances in which the disclosure does not contravene subsection (1), that subsection does not prevent its further disclosure by any person.

(8) A person who contravenes this section is guilty of an offence and liable—

(a) on summary conviction, to a fine not exceeding the statutory maximum; or

(b) on conviction on indictment, to imprisonment for a term not exceeding two years or to a fine or to both.

Director and Secretary of State to have regard to certain matters in relation to the disclosure of information

56.—(1) This section applies if the Secretary of State or the Director is considering whether to disclose any information acquired by him under, or as a result of, any provision of this Part.

(2) He must have regard to the need for excluding, so far as is practicable, information the disclosure of which would in his opinion be contrary to the public interest.

(3) He must also have regard to—

(a) the need for excluding, so far as is practicable—

(i) commercial information the disclosure of which would, or might, in his opinion, significantly harm the legitimate business interests of the undertaking to which it relates, or

(ii) information relating to the private affairs of an individual the disclosure of which would, or might, in his opinion, significantly harm his interests; and

(b) the extent to which the disclosure is necessary for the purposes for which the Secretary of State or the Director is proposing to make the disclosure.

Defamation

57. For the purposes of the law relating to defamation, absolute privilege attaches to any advice, guidance, notice or direction given, or decision made, by the Director in the exercise of any of his functions under this Part.

Findings of fact by Director

Findings of fact by Director

58.—(1) Unless the court directs otherwise or the Director has decided to take further action in accordance with section 16(2) or 24(2), a Director's finding which is relevant to an issue arising in Part I proceedings is binding on the parties if—

(a) the time for bringing an appeal in respect of the finding has expired and the relevant party has not brought such an appeal; or

(b) the decision of an appeal tribunal on such an appeal has confirmed the finding.

(2) In this section—

"a Director's finding" means a finding of fact made by the Director in the course of—

(a) determining an application for a decision under section 14 or 22, or
(b) conducting an investigation under section 25;

"Part I proceedings" means proceedings—

(a) in respect of an alleged infringement of the Chapter I prohibition or of the Chapter II prohibition; but
(b) which are brought otherwise than by the Director;

"relevant party" means—

(a) in relation to the Chapter I prohibition, a party to the agreement which is alleged to have infringed the prohibition; and
(b) in relation to the Chapter II prohibition, the undertaking whose conduct is alleged to have infringed the prohibition.

(3) Rules of court may make provision in respect of assistance to be given by the Director to the court in Part I proceedings.

Interpretation and governing principles

Interpretation

59.—(1) In this Part—

"appeal tribunal" means an appeal tribunal established in accordance with the provisions of Part III of Schedule 7 for the purpose of hearing an appeal under section 46 or 47;

"Article 85" means Article 85 of the Treaty;

"Article 86" means Article 86 of the Treaty;

"block exemption" has the meaning given in section 6(4);

"block exemption order" has the meaning given in section 6(2);

"the Chapter I prohibition" has the meaning given in section 2(8);

"the Chapter II prohibition" has the meaning given in section 18(4);

"the Commission" (except in relation to the Competition Commission) means the European Commission;

"the Council" means the Council of the European Union;

"the court", except in sections 58 and 60 and the expression "European Court", means —

    (a) in England and Wales, the High Court;

    (b) in Scotland, the Court of Session; and

    (c) in Northern Ireland, the High Court;

"the Director" means the Director General of Fair Trading;

"document" includes information recorded in any form;

"the EEA Agreement" means the Agreement on the European Economic Area signed at Oporto on 2nd May 1992 as it has effect for the time being;

"the European Court" means the Court of Justice of the European Communities and includes the Court of First Instance;

"individual exemption" has the meaning given in section 4(2);

"information" includes estimates and forecasts;

"investigating officer" has the meaning given in section 27(1);

"Minister of the Crown" has the same meaning as in the Ministers of the Crown Act 1975;

"officer", in relation to a body corporate, includes a director, manager or secretary and, in relation to a partnership in Scotland, includes a partner;

"parallel exemption" has the meaning given in section 10(3);

"person", in addition to the meaning given by the Interpretation Act 1978, includes any undertaking;

"premises" does not include domestic premises unless—

    (a) they are also used in connection with the affairs of an undertaking, or

    (b) documents relating to the affairs of an undertaking are kept there,

but does include any vehicle;

"prescribed" means prescribed by regulations made by the Secretary of State;

"regulator" has the meaning given by section 54;

"section 11 exemption" has the meaning given in section 11(3); and

"the Treaty" means the treaty establishing the European Community.

(2) The fact that to a limited extent the Chapter I prohibition does not apply to an agreement, because of an exclusion provided by or under this Part or any other enactment, does not require those provisions of the agreement to which the exclusion relates to be disregarded when considering whether the agreement infringes the prohibition for other reasons.

(3) For the purposes of this Part, the power to require information, in relation to information recorded otherwise than in a legible form, includes power to require a copy of it in a legible form.

(4) Any power conferred on the Director by this Part to require information includes power to require any document which he believes may contain that information.

Principles to be applied in determining questions

60.—(1) The purposes of this section is to ensure that so far as is possible (having regard to any relevant differences between the provisions concerned), questions arising under this Part in relation to competition within the United Kingdom are dealt with in a manner which is consistent with the treatment of corresponding questions arising in Community law in relation to competition within the Community.

(2) At any time when the court determines a question arising under this Part, it must act (so far as is compatible with the provisions of this Part and whether or not it would otherwise be required to do so) with a view to securing that there is no inconsistency between—

(a) the principles applied, and decision reached, by the court in determining that question; and

(b) the principles laid down by the Treaty and the European Court, and any relevant decision of that Court, as applicable at that time in determining any corresponding question arising in Community law.

(3) The court must, in addition, have regard to any relevant decision or statement of the Commission.

(4) Subsections (2) and (3) also apply to—

(a) the Director; and

(b) any person acting on behalf of the Director, in connection with any matter arising under this Part.

(5) In subsections (2) and (3), "court" means any court or tribunal.

(6) In subsections (2)(b) and (3), "decision" includes a decision as to—

(a) the interpretation of any provision of Community law;

(b) the civil liability of an undertaking for harm caused by its infringement of Community law.

Part II

INVESTIGATIONS IN RELATION TO ARTICLES 85 AND 86

Introduction

61.—(1) In this Part—

"Article 85" and "Article 86" have the same meaning as in Part I;

"authorised officer", in relation to the Director, means an officer to whom an authorisation has been given under subsection (2);

"the Commission" means the European Commission;

"the Director" means the Director General of Fair Trading;

"Commission investigation" means an investigation ordered by a decision of the Commission under a prescribed provision of Community law relating to Article 85 or 86;

"Director's investigation" means an investigation conducted by the Director at the request of the Commission under a prescribed provision of Community law relating to Article 85 or 86;

"Director's special investigation" means a Director's investigation conducted at the request of the Commission in connection with a Commission investigation;

"prescribed" means prescribed by order made by the Secretary of State;

"premises" means—

(a) in relation to a Commission investigation, any premises, land or means of transport which an official of the Commission has power to enter in the course of the investigation; and

(b) in relation to a Director's investigation, any premises land or means of transport which an official of the Commission would have power to enter if the investigation were being conducted by the Commission.

(2) For the purposes of a Director's investigation, an officer of the Director to whom an authorisation has been given has the powers of an official authorised by the Commission in connection with a Commission investigation under the relevant provision.

(3) "Authorisation" means an authorisation given in writing by the Director which—

(a) identifies the officer;

(b) specifies the subject matter and purpose of the investigation; and

(c) draws attention to any penalties which a person may incur in connection with the investigation under the relevant provision of Community law.

Power to enter premises: Commission investigations

62.—(1) A judge of the High Court may issue a warrant if satisfied, on an application made to the High Court in accordance with rules of court by the Director, that a Commission investigation is being, or is likely to be, obstructed.

(2) A Commission investigation is being obstructed if—

(a) an official of the Commission ("the Commission official"), exercising his power in accordance with the provision under which the investigation is being conducted, has attempted to enter premises but has been unable to do so; and

(b) there are reasonable grounds for suspecting that there are books or records on the premises which the Commission official has power to examine.

(3) A Commission investigation is also being obstructed if there are reasonable grounds for suspecting that there are books or records on the premises—

(a) the production of which has been required by an official of the Commission exercising his power in accordance with the provision under which the investigation is being conducted; and

(b) which have not been produced as required.

(4) A Commission investigation is likely to be obstructed if—

(a) an official of the Commission ("the Commission official") is authorised for the purpose of the investigation;

(b) there are reasonable grounds for suspecting that there are books or records on the premises which the Commission official has power to examine; and

(c) there are also reasonable grounds for suspecting that, if the Commission official attempted to exercise his power to examine any of the books or records, they would not be produced but would be concealed, removed, tampered with or destroyed.

(5) A warrant under this section shall authorise—

(a) a named officer of the Director,

(b) any other of his officers whom he has authorised in writing to accompany the named officer; and

(c) any official of the Commission authorised for the purpose of the Commission investigation to enter the premises specified in the warrant, and search for books and records which the official has power to examine, using such force as is reasonably necessary for the purpose.

(6) Any person entering any premises by virtue of a warrant under this section may take with him such equipment as appears to him to be necessary.

(7) On leaving any premises entered by virtue of the warrant the named officer must, if the premises are unoccupied or the occupier is temporarily absent, leave them as effectively secured as he found them.

(8) A warrant under this section continues in force until the end of the period of one month beginning with the day on which it is issued.

(9) In the application of this section to Scotland, references to the High Court are to be read as references to the Court of Session.

Power to enter premises: Director's special investigations

63.—(1) A judge of the High Court may issue a warrant if satisfied, on an application made to the High Court in accordance with rules of court by the Director, that a Director's special investigation is being, or is likely to be, obstructed.

(2) A Director's special investigation is being obstructed if—

(a) an authorised officer of the Director has attempted to enter premises but has been unable to do so;

(b) the officer has produced his authorisation to the undertaking, or association of undertakings, concerned; and

(c) there are reasonable grounds for suspecting that there are books or records on the premises which the officer has power to examine.

(3) A Director's special investigation is also being obstructed if—

(a) there are reasonable grounds for suspecting that there are books or records on the premises which an authorised officer of the Director has power to examine;

(b) the officer has produced his authorisation to the undertaking, or association of undertakings, and has required production of the books or records; and

(c) the books and records have not been produced as required.

(4) A Director's special investigation is likely to be obstructed if—

(a) there are reasonable grounds for suspecting that there are books or records on the premises which an authorised officer of the Director has power to examine; and

(b) there are also reasonable grounds for suspecting that, if the officer attempted to exercise his power to examine any of the books or records, they would not be produced but would be concealed, removed, tampered with or destroyed.

(5) A warrant under this section shall authorise—

(a) a named authorised officer of the Director,

(b) any other authorised officer accompanying the named officer, and

(c) any named official of the Commission,
to enter the premises specified in the warrant, and search for books and records which the authorised officer has power to examine, using such force as is reasonably necessary for the purpose.

(6) Any person entering any premises by virtue of a warrant under this section may take with him such equipment as appears to him to be necessary.

(7) On leaving any premises which he has entered by virtue of the warrant the named officer must, if the premises are unoccupied or the occupier is temporarily absent, leave them as effectively secured as he found them.

(8) A warrant under this section continues in force until the end of the period of one month beginning with the day on which it is issued.

(9) In the application of this section to Scotland, references to the High Court are to be read as references to the Court of Session.

Entry of premises under sections 62 and 63: supplementary

64.—(1) A warrant issued under section 62 or 63 must indicate—

(a) the subject matter and purpose of the investigation;

(b) the nature of the offence created by section 65.

(2) The powers conferred by section 62 or 63 are to be exercised on production of a warrant issued under that section.

(3) If there is no one at the premises when the named officer proposes to execute such a warrant he must, before executing it—

(a) take such steps as are reasonable in all the circumstances to inform the occupier of the intended entry; and

(b) if the occupier is informed, afford him or his legal or other representative a reasonable opportunity to be present when the warrant is executed.

(4) If the named officer is unable to inform the occupier of the intended entry he must, when executing the warrant, leave a copy of it in a prominent place on the premises.

(5) In this section—

"named officer" means the officer named in the warrant; and
"occupier", in relation to any premises, means a person whom the named officer reasonably believes is the occupier of those premises.

Offences

65.—(1) A person is guilty of an offence if he intentionally obstructs any person in the exercise of his powers under a warrant issued under section 62 or 63.

(2) A person guilty of an offence under subsection (1) is liable—

(a) on summary conviction, to a fine not exceeding the statutory maximum;

(b) on conviction on indictment, to imprisonment for a term not exceeding two years or to a fine or to both.

Part III

MONOPOLIES

Monopoly investigations: general

66.—(1) Section 44 of the Fair Trading Act 1973 (power of the Director to require information about monopoly situations) is amended as follows.

(2) In subsection (1), for the words after paragraph (b) substitute—

"the Director may exercise the powers conferred by subsection (2) below for the purposes of assisting him in determining whether to take either of the following decisions with regard to that situation."

(3) After subsection (1) insert—
"(1A)Those decisions are—

    (a) whether to make a monopoly reference with respect to the existence or possible existence of the situation;

    (b) whether, instead, to make a proposal under section 56A below for the Secretary of State to accept undertakings".

(4) For subsection (2) substitute—

"(2) In the circumstances and for the purpose mentioned in subsection (1) above, the Director may—

    (a) require any person within subsection (3) below to produce to the Director, at a specified time and place—

        (i) any specified documents, or

        (ii) any document which falls within a specified category,

    which are in his custody or under his control and which are relevant;

    (b) require any person within subsection (3) below who is carrying on a business to give the Director specified estimates, forecasts, returns, or other information, and specify the time at which and the form and manner in which the estimates, forecasts, returns or information are to be given;

    (c) enter any premises used by a person within subsection (3) below for business purposes, and—

        (i) require any person on the premises to produce any documents on the premises which are in his custody or under his control and which are relevant;

        (ii) require any person on the premises to give the Director such explanation of the documents as he may require.

(3) A person is within this subsection if—

    (a) he produces goods of the description in question in the United Kingdom;

    (b) he supplies goods or (as the case may be) services of the description in question in the United Kingdom; or

    (c) such goods (or services) are supplied to him in the United Kingdom.

(4) The power to impose a requirement under subsection (2)(a) or (b) above is to be exercised by notice in writing served on the person on whom the requirement is imposed; and "specified" in those provisions means specified or otherwise described in the notice, and "specify" is to be read accordingly.

(5) The power under subsection (2)(a) above to require a person ("the person notified") to produce a document includes power—

    (a) if the document is produced—

        (i) to take copies of it or extracts from it;

  (ii) to require the person notified, or any person who is a present or past officer of his, or is or was at any time employed by him, to provide an explanation of the document;

 (b) if the document is not produced, to require the person notified to state, to the best of his knowledge and belief, where it is.

(6) Nothing in this section confers power to compel any person—

 (a) to produce any document which he could not be compelled to produce in civil proceedings before the High Court or, in Scotland, the Court of Session; or

 (b) in complying with any requirement for the giving of information, to give any information which he could not be compelled to give in evidence in such proceedings.

(7) No person has to comply with a requirement imposed under subsection (2) above by a person acting under an authorisation under paragraph 7 of Schedule 1 to this Act unless evidence of the authorisation has, if required, been produced.

(8) For the purposes of subsection (2) above—

 (a) a document is relevant if—

  (i) it is relevant to a decision mentioned in subsection (1A) above; and

  (ii) the powers conferred by this section are exercised in relation to the document for the purposes of assisting the Director in determining whether to take that decision;

 (b) "document" includes information recorded in any form; and

 (c) in relation to information recorded otherwise than in legible form, the power to require its production includes power to require production of it in legible form, so far as the means to do so are within the custody or under the control of the person on whom the requirement is imposed".

(5) The amendments made by this section and section 67 have effect in relation to sectoral regulators in accordance with paragraph 1 of Schedule 10.

Offences

67.—(1) Section 46 of the Fair Trading Act 1973 is amended as follows.

(2) Omit subsections (1) and (2).

(3) At the end insert—

"(4) Any person who refuses or wilfully neglects to comply with a requirement imposed under section 44(2) above is guilty of an offence and liable—

 (a) on summary conviction, to a fine not exceeding the prescribed sum, or

 (b) on conviction on indictment, to imprisonment for a term not exceeding two years or to a fine or to both.

(5) If a person is charged with an offence under subsection (4) in respect of a requirement to produce a document, it is a defence for him to prove—

 (a) that the document was not in his possession or under his control; and

 (b) that it was not reasonably practicable for him to comply with the requirement.

(6) If a person is charged with an offence under subsection (4) in respect of a requirement—

 (a) to provide an explanation of a document, or

 (b) to state where a document is to be found,

it is a defence for him to prove that he had a reasonable excuse for failing to comply with the requirement.

(7) A person who intentionally obstructs the Director in the exercise of his powers under section 44 is guilty of an offence and liable—

(a) on summary conviction, to a fine not exceeding the prescribed sum;

(b) on conviction on indictment, to a fine.

(8) A person who wilfully alters, suppresses or destroys any document which he has been required to produce under section 44(2) is guilty of an offence and liable—

(a) on summary conviction, to a fine not exceeding the prescribed sum;

(b) on conviction on indictment, to imprisonment for a term not exceeding two years or to a fine or to both."

Services relating to use of land

68. In section 137 of the Fair Trading Act 1973, after subsection (3) insert—

"(3A) The Secretary of State may by order made by statutory instrument—

(a) provide that "the supply of services" in the provisions of this Act is to include, or to cease to include, any activity specified in the order which consists in, or in making arrangements in connection with, permitting the use of land; and

(b) for that purpose, amend or repeal any of paragraphs (c), (d), (e) or (g) of subsection (3) above.

(3B) No order under subsection (3A) above is to be made unless a draft of the order has been laid before Parliament and approved by a resolution of each House of Parliament.

(3C) The provisions of Schedule 9 to this Act apply in the case of a draft of any such order as they apply in the case of a draft of an order to which section 91(1) above applies."

Reports: monopoly references

69. In section 83 of the Fair Trading Act 1973—

(a) in subsection (1), omit "Subject to subsection (1A) below"; and

(b) omit subsection (1A) (reports on monopoly references to be transmitted to certain persons at least twenty-four hours before laying before Parliament).

Part IV

SUPPLEMENTAL AND TRANSITIONAL

Contracts as to patented products etc.

70. Sections 44 and 45 of the Patents Act 1977 shall cease to have effect.

Regulations, orders and rules

71.—(1) Any power to make regulations or orders which is conferred by this Act is exercisable by statutory instrument.

(2) The power to make rules which is conferred by section 48 is exercisable by statutory instrument.

(3) Any statutory instrument made under this Act may—

(a) contain such incidental, supplemental, consequential and transitional provision as the Secretary of State considers appropriate; and

(b) make different provision for different cases.

(4) No order is to be made under—

(a) section 3,

(b) section 19,

(c) section 36(8),

(d) section 50, or

(e) paragraph 6(3) of Schedule 4,

unless a draft of the order has been laid before Parliament and approved by a resolution of each House.

(5) Any statutory instrument made under this Act, apart from one made—

(a) under any of the provisions mentioned in subsection (4), or

(b) under section 76(3),

shall be subject to annulment by a resolution of either House of Parliament.

Offences by bodies corporate etc.

72.—(1) This section applies to an offence under any of sections 42 to 44, 55(8) or 65.

(2) If an offence committed by a body corporate is proved—

(a) to have been committed with the consent or connivance of an officer, or

(b) to be attributable to any neglect on his part,

the officer as well as the body corporate is guilty of the offence and liable to be proceeded against and punished accordingly.

(3) In subsection (2) "officer", in relation to a body corporate, means a director, manager, secretary or other similar officer of the body, or a person purporting to act in any such capacity.

(4) If the affairs of a body corporate are managed by its members, subsection (2) applies in relation to the acts and defaults of a member in connection with his functions of management as if he were a director of the body corporate.

(5) If an offence committed by a partnership in Scotland is proved—

(a) to have been committed with the consent or connivance of a partner, or

(b) to be attributable to any neglect on his part,

the partner as well as the partnership is guilty of the offence and liable to be proceeded against and punished accordingly.

(6) In subsection (5) "partner" includes a person purporting to act as a partner.

Crown application

73.—(1) Any provision made by or under this Act binds the Crown except that—

(a) the Crown is not criminally liable as a result of any such provision;

(b) the Crown is not liable for any penalty under any such provision; and

(c) nothing in this Act affects Her Majesty in her private capacity.

(2) Subsection (1)(a) does not affect the application of any provision of this Act in relation to persons in the public service of the Crown.

(3) Subsection (1)(c) is to be interpreted as if section 38(3) of the Crown Proceedings Act 1947 (interpretation of references in that Act to Her Majesty in her private capacity) were contained in this Act.

(4) If, in respect of a suspected infringement of the Chapter I prohibition or of the Chapter II prohibition otherwise than by the Crown or a person in the public service of the Crown, an investigation is conducted under section 25—

(a) the power conferred by section 27 may not be exercised in relation to land which is occupied by a government department, or otherwise for purposes of the Crown, without the written consent of the appropriate person; and

(b) section 28 does not apply in relation to land so occupied.

(5) In any case in which consent is required under subsection (4), the person who is the appropriate person in relation to that case is to be determined in accordance with regulations made by the Secretary of State.

(6) Sections 62 and 63 do not apply in relation to land which is occupied by a government department, or otherwise for purposes of the Crown, unless the matter being investigated is a suspected infringement by the Crown or by a person in the public service of the Crown.

(7) In subsection (6) "infringement" means an infringement of Community law relating to Article 85 or 86 of the Treaty establishing the European Community.

(8) If the Secretary of State certifies that it appears to him to be in the interests of national security that the powers of entry—

(a) conferred by section 27, or

(b) that may be conferred by a warrant under section 28, 62 or 63,

should not be exercisable in relation to premises held or used by or on behalf of the Crown and which are specified in the certificate, those powers are not exercisable in relation to those premises.

(9) Any amendment, repeal or revocation made by this Act binds the Crown to the extent that the enactment amended, repealed or revoked binds the Crown.

Amendments, transitional provisions, savings and repeals

74.—(1) The minor and consequential amendments set out in Schedule 12 are to have effect.
(2) The transitional provisions and savings set out in Schedule 13 are to have effect.
(3) The enactments set out in Schedule 14 are repealed.

Consequential and supplementary provision

75.—(1) The Secretary of State may by order make such incidental, consequential, transitional or supplemental provision as he thinks necessary or expedient for the general purposes, or any particular purpose, of this Act or in consequence of any of its provisions or for giving full effect to it.

(2) An order under subsection (1) may, in particular, make provision—

(a) for enabling any person by whom any powers will become exercisable, on a date specified by or under this Act, by virtue of any provision made by or under this Act to take before that date any steps which are necessary as a preliminary to the exercise of those powers;

(b) for making savings, or additional savings, from the effect of any repeal made by or under this Act.

(3) Amendments made under this section shall be in addition, and without prejudice, to those made by or under any other provision of this Act.
(4) No other provision of this Act restricts the powers conferred by this section.

Short title, commencement and extent

76.—(1) This Act may be cited as the Competition Act 1998.
(2) Sections 71 and 75 and this section and paragraphs 1 to 7 and 35 of Schedule 13 come into force on the passing of this Act.
(3) The other provisions of this Act come into force on such day as the Secretary of State may by order appoint; and different days may be appointed for different purposes.
(4) This Act extends to Northern Ireland.

Schedules

SCHEDULE 1

Sections 3(1)(a) and 19(1)(a)

EXCLUSIONS: MERGERS AND CONCENTRATIONS

PART I

MERGERS

Enterprises ceasing to be distinct: the Chapter I prohibition

1.—(1) To the extent to which an agreement (either on its own or when taken together with another agreement) results, or if carried out would result, in any two enterprises ceasing to be distinct enterprises for the purposes of Part V of the Fair Trading Act 1973 ("the 1973 Act"), the Chapter I prohibition does not apply to the agreement.

(2) The exclusion provided by sub-paragraph (1) extends to any provision directly related and necessary to the implementation of the merger provisions.

(3) In sub-paragraph (2) "merger provisions" means the provisions of the agreement which cause, or if carried out would cause, the agreement to have the result mentioned in sub-paragraph (1).

(4) Section 65 of the 1973 Act applies for the purposes of this paragraph as if—

(a) in subsection (3) (circumstances in which a person or group of persons may be treated as having control of an enterprise), and

(b) in subsection (4) (circumstances in which a person or group of persons may be treated as bringing an enterprise under their control),

for "may" there were substituted "must".

Enterprises ceasing to be distinct: the Chapter II prohibition

2.—(1) To the extent to which conduct (either on its own or when taken together with other conduct)—

(a) results in any two enterprises ceasing to be distinct enterprises for the purposes of Part V of the 1973 Act), or

(b) is directly related and necessary to the attainment of the result mentioned in paragraph (a),

the Chapter II prohibition does not apply to that conduct.

(2) Sections 65 of the 1973 Act applies for the purposes of this paragraph as it applies for the purposes of paragraph 1.

Transfer of a newspaper or of newspaper assets

3.—(1) The Chapter I prohibition does not apply to an agreement to the extent to which it constitutes, or would if carried out constitute, a transfer of a newspaper or of newspaper assets for the purposes of section 57 of the 1973 Act.

(2) The Chapter II prohibition does not apply to conduct (either on its own or when taken together with other conduct) to the extent to which—

(a) it constitutes such a transfer, or

(b) it is directly related and necessary to the implementation of the transfer.

(3) The exclusion provided by sub-paragraph (1) extends to any provision directly related and necessary to the implementation of the transfer.

Withdrawal of the paragraph 1 exclusion

4.—(1) The exclusion provided by paragraph 1 does not apply to a particular agreement if the Director gives a direction under this paragraph to that effect.

(2) If the Director is considering whether to give a direction under this paragraph, he may by notice in writing require any party to the agreement in question to give him such information in connection with the agreement as he may require.

(3) The Director may give a direction under this paragraph only as provided in sub-paragraph (4) or (5).

(4) If at the end of such period as may be specified in rules under section 51 a person has failed, without reasonable excuse, to comply with a requirement imposed under sub-paragraph (2), the Director may give a direction under this paragraph.

(5) The Director may also give a direction under this paragraph if—

(a) he considers—

(i) that the agreement will, if not excluded, infringe the Chapter I prohibition; and

(ii) that he is not likely to grant it an unconditional individual exemption; and

(b) the agreement is not a protected agreement.

(6) For the purposes of sub-paragraph (5), an individual exemption is unconditional if no conditions or obligations are imposed in respect of it under section 4(3)(a).

(7) A direction under this paragraph—

(a) must be in writing;

(b) may be made so as to have effect from a date specified in the direction (which may not be earlier than the date on which it is given).

Protected agreements

5. An agreement is a protected agreement for the purposes of paragraph 4 if—

(a) the Secretary of State has announced his decision not to make a merger reference to the Competition Commission under section 64 of the 1973 Act in connection with the agreement;

(b) the Secretary of State has made a merger reference to the Competition Commission under section 64 of the 1973 Act in connection with the agreement and the Commission has found that the agreement has given rise to, or would if carried out give rise to, a merger situation qualifying for investigation;

(c) the agreement does not fall within sub-paragraph (a) or (b) but has given rise to, or would if carried out give rise to, enterprises to which it relates being regarded under section 65 of the 1973 Act as ceasing to be distinct enterprises (otherwise than as the result of subsection (3) or (4)(b) of that section); or

(d) the Secretary of State has made a merger reference to the Competition Commission under section 32 of the Water Industry Act 1991 in connection with the agreement and the Commission has found that the agreement has given rise to, or would if carried out give rise to, a merger of the kind to which that section applies.

PART II

CONCENTRATIONS SUBJECT TO EC CONTROLS

6.—(1) To the extent to which an agreement (either on its own or when taken together with another agreement) gives rise to, or would if carried out give rise to, a concentration, the Chapter

I prohibition does not apply to the agreement if the Merger Regulation gives the Commission exclusive jurisdiction in the matter.

(2) To the extent to which conduct (either on its own or when taken together with other conduct) gives rise to, or would if pursued give rise to, a concentration, the Chapter II prohibition does not apply to the conduct if the Merger Regulation gives the Commission exclusive jurisdiction in the matter.

(3) In this paragraph—

"concentration" means a concentration with a Community dimension within the meaning of Articles 1 and 3 of the Merger Regulation; and

"Merger Regulation" means Council Regulation (EEC) No. 4064/89 of 21st December 1989 on the control of concentrations between undertakings as amended by Council Regulation (EC) No. 1310/97 of 30th June 1997.

SCHEDULE 2

Section 3(1)(b)

EXCLUSIONS: OTHER COMPETITION SCRUTINY

PART I

FINANCIAL SERVICES

The Financial Services Act 1986 (c.60)[1]

1.—(1) The Financial Services Act 1986 is amended as follows.

(2) For section 125 (effect of the Restrictive Trade Practices Act 1976), substitute—

"The Competition Act 1998: Chapter I prohibition

125.—(1) The Chapter I prohibition does not apply to an agreement for the constitution of—

    (a)   a recognised self-regulating organisation,

    (b)   a recognised investment exchange, or

    (c)   a recognised clearing house,

to the extent to which the agreement relates to the regulating provisions of the body concerned.

(2) Subject to subsection (3) below, the Chapter I prohibition does not apply to an agreement for the constitution of—

    (a)   a self-regulating organisation,

    (b)   an investment exchange, or

    (c)   a clearing house,

to the extent to which the agreement relates to the regulating provisions of the body concerned.

(3) The exclusion provided by subsection (2) above applies only if—

    (a)   the body has applied for a recognition order in accordance with the provisions of this Act; and

---

[1] The Financial Services Act 1986 is to be superseded by the Financial Services and Markets Act 2000 on a day as yet to be appointed. New exclusions are introduced by the New Act (see Chapter 12 at 12.3).

(b) the application has not been determined.

(4) The Chapter I prohibition does not apply to a decision made by—

(a) a recognised self-regulating organisation,
(b) a recognised investment exchange, or
(c) a recognised clearing house,

to the extent to which the decision relates to any of that body's regulating provisions or specified practices.

(5) The Chapter I prohibition does not apply to the specified practices of—

(a) a recognised self-regulating organisation, a recognised investment exchange or a recognised clearing house; or
(b) a person who is subject to—

(i)   the rules of one of those bodies, or
(ii) the statements of principle, rules, regulations or codes of practice made by a designated agency in the exercise of functions transferred to it by a delegation order.

(6) The Chapter I prohibition does not apply to any agreement the parties to which consist of or include—

(a) a recognised self-regulating organisation, a recognised investment exchange or a recognised clearing house; or
(b) a person who is subject to—

(i)   the rules of one of those bodies, or
(ii) the statements of principle, rules, regulations or codes of practice made by a designated agency in the exercise of functions transferred to it by a delegation order,

to the extent to which the agreement consists of provisions the inclusion of which is required or contemplated by any of the body's regulating provisions or specified practices or by the statements of principle, rules, regulations or codes of practice of the agency.

(7) The Chapter I prohibition does not apply to—

(a) any clearing arrangements; or
(b) any agreement between a recognised investment exchange and a recognised clearing house, to the extent to which the agreement consists of provisions the inclusion of which in the agreement is required or contemplated by any clearing arrangements.

(8) If the recognition order in respect of a body of the kind mentioned in subsection (1)(a), (b) or (c) above is revoked, subsections (1) and (4) to (7) above are to have effect as if that body had continued to be recognised until the end of the period of six months beginning with the day on which the revocation took effect.

(9) In this section—

"the Chapter I prohibition" means the prohibition imposed by section 2(1) of the Competition Act 1998;
"regulating provisions" means—
(a) in relation to a self-regulating organisation, any rules made, or guidance issued, by the organisation;
(b) in relation to an investment exchange, any rules made, or guidance issued, by the exchange;
(c) in relation to a clearing house, any rules made, or guidance issued, by the clearing house;

"specified practices" means—

(a) in the case of a recognised self-regulating organisation, the practices mentioned in section 119(2)(a)(ii) and (iii) above (read with section 119(5) and (6)(a));

(b) in the case of a recognised investment exchange, the practices mentioned in section 119(2)(b)(ii) and (iii) above (read with section 119(5) and (6)(b));

(c) in the case of a recognised clearing house, the practices mentioned in section 119(2)(c)(ii)and (iii) above (read with section 119(5) and (6)(b));

(d) in the case of a person who is subject to the statements of principle, rules, regulations or codes of practice issued or made by a designated agency in the exercise of functions transferred to it by a delegation order, the practices mentioned in section 121(2)(c) above (read with section 121(4));

and expressions used in this section which are also used in Part I of the Competition Act 1998 are to be interpreted in the same way as for the purposes of that Part of that Act."

(3) Omit section 126 (certain practices not to constitute anti-competitive practices for the purposes of the Competition Act 1980).

(4) For section 127 (modification of statutory provisions in relation to recognised professional bodies), substitute—

"Application of Competition Act 1998 in relation to recognised professional bodies: Chapter I prohibition

127.—(1) This section applies to—

(a) any agreement for the constitution of a recognised professional body to the extent to which it relates to the rules or guidance of that body relating to the carrying on of investment business by persons certified by it ("investment business rules"); and

(b) any other agreement, the parties to which consist of or include—

(i) a recognised professional body,
(ii) a person certified by such a body, or
(iii) a member of such a body,

and which contains a provision required or contemplated by that body's investment business rules.

(2) If it appears to the Treasury, in relation to some or all of the provisions of an agreement to which this section applies—

(a) that the provisions in question do not have, and are not intended or likely to have, to any significant extent the effect of restricting, distorting or preventing competition; or

(b) that the effect of restricting, distorting or preventing competition which the provisions in question do have, or are intended or are likely to have, is not greater than is necessary for the protection of investors,

the Treasury may make a declaration to that effect.

(3) If the Treasury make a declaration under this section, the Chapter I prohibition does not apply to the agreement to the extent to which the agreement consists of provisions to which the declaration relates.

(4) If the Treasury are satisfied that there has been a material change of circumstances, they may—

(a) revoke a declaration made under this section, if they consider that the grounds on which it was made no longer exist;

(b) vary such a declaration, if they consider that there are grounds for making a different declaration; or

(c) make a declaration even though they have notified the Director of their intention not to do so.

(5) If the Treasury make, vary or revoke a declaration under this section they must notify the Director of their decision.

(6) If the Director proposes to exercise any Chapter III powers in respect of any provisions of an agreement to which this section applies, he must—

(a) notify the Treasury of his intention to do so; and

   (b)   give the Treasury particulars of the agreement and such other information—

        (i)   as he considers will assist the Treasury to decide whether to exercise their powers under this section; or

       (ii)   as the Treasury may request.

(7) The Director may not exercise his Chapter III powers in respect of any provisions of an agreement to which this section applies, unless the Treasury—

   (a)   have notified him that they have not made a declaration in respect of those provisions under this section and that they do not intend to make such a declaration; or

   (b)   have revoked a declaration under this section and a period of six months beginning with the date on which the revocation took effect has expired.

(8) A declaration under this section ceases to have effect if the agreement to which it relates ceases to be one to which this section applies.

(9) In this section—

"the Chapter I prohibition" means the prohibition imposed by section 2(1) of the Competition Act 1998,

"Chapter III powers" means the powers given to the Director by Chapter III of Part I of that Act so far as they relate to the Chapter I prohibition, and

expressions used in this section which are also used in Part I of the Competition Act 1998 are to be interpreted in the same way as for the purposes of that Part of that Act.

(10) In this section references to an agreement are to be read as applying equally to, or in relation to, a decision or concerted practice.

(11) In the application of this section to decisions and concerted practices, references to provisions of an agreement are to be read as references to elements of a decision or concerted practice."

PART II

COMPANIES

The Companies Act 1989 (c.40)

2.—(1) The Companies Act 1989 is amended as follows.

(2) In Schedule 14, for paragraph 9 (exclusion of certain agreements from the Restrictive Trade Practices Act 1976), substitute—

"The Competition Act 1998

9.—(1) The Chapter I prohibition does not apply to an agreement for the constitution of a recognised supervisory or qualifying body to the extent to which it relates to—

   (a)   rules of, or guidance issued by, the body; and

   (b)   incidental matters connected with the rules or guidance.

(2) The Chapter I prohibition does not apply to an agreement the parties to which consist of or include—

   (a)   a recognised supervisory or qualifying body, or

   (b)   any person mentioned in paragraph 3(5) or (6) above,

to the extent to which the agreement consists of provisions the inclusion of which in the agreement is required or contemplated by the rules or guidance of that body.

(3) The Chapter I prohibition does not apply to the practices mentioned in paragraph 3(4)(a) and (b) above.

(4) Where a recognition order is revoked, sub-paragraphs (1) to (3) above are to continue to apply for a period of six months beginning with the day on which the revocation takes effect, as if the order were still in force.

(5) In this paragraph—

    (a) "the Chapter I prohibition" means the prohibition imposed by section 2(1) of the Competition Act 1998,

    (b) references to an agreement are to be read as applying equally to, or in relation to, a decision or concerted practice,

and expressions used in this paragraph which are also used in Part I of the Competition Act 1998 are to be interpreted in the same way as for the purposes of that Part of that Act.

(6) In the application of this paragraph to decisions and concerted practices, references to provisions of an agreement are to be read as references to elements of a decision or concerted practice."

The Companies (Northern Ireland) Order 1990 (S.I. 1990/593 (N.I. 5))

3.—(1) The Companies (Northern Ireland) Order 1990 is amended as follows.

(2) In Schedule 14, for paragraph 9 (exclusion of certain agreements from the Restrictive Trade Practices Act 1976), substitute—

"The Competition Act 1998

9.—(1) The Chapter I prohibition does not apply to an agreement for the constitution of a recognised supervisory or qualifying body to the extent to which it relates to—

    (a) rules of, or guidance issued by, the body; and

    (b) incidental matters connected with the rules or guidance.

(2) The Chapter I prohibition does not apply to an agreement the parties to which consist of or include—

    (a) a recognised supervisory or qualifying body, or

    (b) any person mentioned in paragraph 3(5) or (6),

to the extent to which the agreement consists of provisions the inclusion of which in the agreement is required or contemplated by the rules or guidance of that body.

(3) The Chapter I prohibition does not apply to the practices mentioned in paragraph 3(4)(a) and (b).

(4) Where a recognition order is revoked, sub-paragraphs (1) to (3) are to continue to apply for a period of 6 months beginning with the day on which the revocation takes effect, as if the order were still in force.

(5) In this paragraph—

    (a) "the Chapter I prohibition" means the prohibition imposed by section 2(1) of the Competition Act 1998,

    (b) references to an agreement are to be read as applying equally to, or in relation to, a decision or concerted practice,

and expressions used in this paragraph which are also used in Part I of the Competition Act 1998 are to be interpreted in the same way as for the purposes of that Part of that Act.

(6) In the application of this paragraph to decisions and concerted practices, references to provisions of an agreement are to be read as references to elements of a decision or concerted practice."

PART III

BROADCASTING

The Broadcasting Act 1990 (c.42)

4.—(1) The Broadcasting Act 1990 is amended as follows.

(2) In section 194A (which modifies the Restrictive Trade Practices Act 1976 in its

application to agreements relating to Channel 3 news provision), for subsections (2) to (6), substitute—

"(2)If, having sought the advice of the Director, it appears to the Secretary of State, in relation to some or all of the provisions of a relevant agreement, that the conditions mentioned in subsection (3) are satisfied, he may make a declaration to that effect.

(3) The conditions are that—

(a) the provisions in question do not have, and are not intended or likely to have, to any significant extent the effect of restricting, distorting or preventing competition; or

(b) the effect of restricting, distorting or preventing competition which the provisions in question do have or are intended or are likely to have, is not greater than is necessary—

    (i) in the case of a relevant agreement falling within subsection (1)(a), for securing the appointment by holders of regional Channel 3 licences of a single body corporate to be the appointed news provider for the purposes of section 31(2), or

    (ii) in the case of a relevant agreement falling within subsection (1)(b), for compliance by them with conditions included in their licences by virtue of section 31(1) and (2).

(4) If the Secretary of State makes a declaration under this section, the Chapter I prohibition does not apply to the agreement to the extent to which the agreement consists of provisions to which the declaration relates.

(5) If the Secretary of State is satisfied that there has been a material change of circumstances, he may—

(a) revoke a declaration made under this section, if he considers that the grounds on which it was made no longer exist;

(b) vary such a declaration, if he considers that there are grounds for making a different declaration; or

(c) make a declaration, even though he has notified the Director of his intention not to do so.

(6) If the Secretary of State makes, varies or revokes a declaration under this section, he must notify the Director of his decision.

(7) The Director may not exercise any Chapter III powers in respect of a relevant agreement, unless—

(a) he has notified the Secretary of State of his intention to do so; and

(b) the Secretary of State—

    (i) has notified the Director that he has not made a declaration in respect of the agreement, or provisions of the agreement, under this section and that he does not intend to make such a declaration; or

    (ii) has revoked a declaration under this section and a period of six months beginning with the date on which the revocation took effect has expired.

(8) If the Director proposes to exercise any Chapter III powers in respect of a relevant agreement, he must give the Secretary of State particulars of the agreement and such other information—

(a) as he considers will assist the Secretary of State to decide whether to exercise his powers under this section; or

(b) as the Secretary of State may request.

(9) In this section—

"the Chapter I prohibition" means the prohibition imposed by section 2(1) of the Competition Act 1998;

"Chapter III powers" means the powers given to the Director by Chapter III of Part I of that Act so far as they relate to the Chapter I prohibition;

"Director" means the Director General of Fair Trading;

"regional Channel 3 licence" has the same meaning as in Part I;

and expressions used in this section which are also used in Part I of the Competition Act 1998 are to be interpreted in the same way as for the purposes of that Part of that Act.

(10) In this section references to an agreement are to be read as applying equally to, or in relation to, a decision or concerted practice.

(11) In the application of this section to decisions and concerted practices, references to provisions of an agreement are to be read as references to elements of a decision or concerted practice."

Networking arrangements under the Broadcasting Act 1990 (c.42)

5.—(1) The Chapter I prohibition does not apply in respect of any networking arrangements to the extent to which they—

(a)   are subject to Schedule 4 to the Broadcasting Act 1990 (competition references with respect to networking arrangements); or

(b)   contain provisions which have been considered under that Schedule.

(2) The Independent Television Commission ("ITC") must publish a list of the networking arrangements which in their opinion are excluded from the Chapter I prohibition by virtue of sub-paragraph (1).

(3) The ITC must—

(a)   consult the Director before publishing the list, and

(b)   publish the list in such a way as they think most suitable for bringing it to the attention of persons who, in their opinion, would be affected by, or likely to have an interest in, it.

(4) In this paragraph "networking arrangements" means —

(a)   any arrangements entered into as mentioned in section 39(4) or (7)(b) of the Broadcasting Act 1990, or

(b)   any agreements—

(i)   which do not constitute arrangements of the kind mentioned in paragraph (a), but

(ii)   which are made for the purpose mentioned in section 39(1) of that Act, or

(c)   any modification of the arrangements or agreements mentioned in paragraph (a) or (b).

PART IV

ENVIRONMENTAL PROTECTION

Producer responsibility obligations

6.—(1) The Environment Act 1995 is amended as follows.

(2) In section 94(1) (supplementary provisions about regulations imposing producer responsibility obligations on prescribed persons), after paragraph (o), insert—

"(oa) the exclusion or modification of any provision of Part I of the Competition Act 1998 in relation to exemption schemes or in relation to any agreement, decision or concerted practice at least one of the parties to which is an operator of an exemption scheme;".

(3)After section 94(6), insert—

"(6A) Expressions used in paragraph (oa) of subsection (1) above which are also used in

Part I of the Competition Act 1998 are to be interpreted in the same way as for the purposes of that Part of that Act."

(4) After section 94, insert—

"Producer responsibility: competition matters

94A.—(1) For the purposes of this section, the relevant paragraphs are paragraphs (n), (o), (oa) and (ya) of section 94(1) above.

(2) Regulations made by virtue of any of the relevant paragraphs may include transitional provision in respect of agreements or exemption schemes—

(a) in respect of which information has been required for the purposes of competition scrutiny under any regulation made by virtue of paragraph (ya);

(b) which are being, or have been, considered for the purposes of competition scrutiny under any regulation made by virtue of paragraph (n) or (ya); or

(c) in respect of which provisions of the Restrictive Trade Practices Acts 1976 and 1977 have been modified or excluded in accordance with any regulation made by virtue of paragraph (o).

(3) Subsections (2), (3), (5) to (7) and (10) of section 93 above do not apply to a statutory instrument which contains only regulations made by virtue of any of the relevant paragraphs or subsection (2) above.

(4) Such a statutory instrument shall be subject to annulment in pursuance of a resolution of either House of Parliament."

SCHEDULE 3

Sections 3(1)(c) and 19(1)(b)

GENERAL EXCLUSIONS

Planning obligations

1.—(1) The Chapter I prohibition does not apply to an agreement—

(a) to the extent to which it is a planning obligation;

(b) which is made under section 75 (agreements regulating development or use of land) or 246 (agreements relating to Crown land) of the Town and Country Planning (Scotland) Act 1997; or

(c) which is made under Article 40 of the Planning (Northern Ireland) Order 1991.

(2) In sub-paragraph (1)(a), "planning obligation" means —

(a) a planning obligation for the purposes of section 106 of the Town and Country Planning Act 1990; or

(b) a planning obligation for the purposes of section 299A of that Act.

Section 21(2) agreements

2.—(1) The Chapter I prohibition does not apply to an agreement in respect of which a direction under section 21(2) of the Restrictive Trade Practices Act 1976 is in force immediately before the coming into force of section 2 ("a section 21(2) agreement").

(2) If a material variation is made to a section 21(2) agreement, sub-paragraph (1) ceases to apply to the agreement on the coming into force of the variation.

(3) Sub-paragraph (1) does not apply to a particular section 21(2) agreement if the Director gives a direction under this paragraph to that effect.

(4) If the Director is considering whether to give a direction under this paragraph, he may by notice in writing require any party to the agreement in question to give him such information in connection with the agreement as he may require.

(5) The Director may give a direction under this paragraph only as provided in sub-paragraph (6) or (7).

(6) If at the end of such period as may be specified in rules under section 51 a person has failed, without reasonable excuse, to comply with a requirement imposed under sub-paragraph (4), the Director may give a direction under this paragraph.

(7) The Director may also give a direction under this paragraph if he considers—

(a) that the agreement will, if not excluded, infringe the Chapter I prohibition; and

(b) that he is not likely to grant it an unconditional individual exemption.

(8) For the purposes of sub-paragraph (7) an individual exemption is unconditional if no conditions or obligations are imposed in respect of it under section 4(3)(a).

(9) A direction under this paragraph—

(a) must be in writing;

(b) may be made so as to have effect from a date specified in the direction (which may not be earlier than the date on which it is given).

EEA Regulated Markets

3.—(1) The Chapter I prohibition does not apply to an agreement for the constitution of an EEA regulated market to the extent to which the agreement relates to any of the rules made, or guidance issued, by that market.

(2) The Chapter I prohibition does not apply to a decision made by an EEA regulated market, to the extent to which the decision relates to any of the market's regulating provisions.

(3) The Chapter I prohibition does not apply to—

(a) any practices of an EEA regulated market; or

(b) any practices which are trading practices in relation to an EEA regulated market.

(4) The Chapter I prohibition does not apply to an agreement the parties to which are or include—

(a) an EEA regulated market, or

(b) a person who is subject to the rules of that market,

to the extent to which the agreement consists of provisions the inclusion of which is required or contemplated by the regulating provisions of that market.

(5) In this paragraph—

"EEA regulated market" is a market which—

(a) is listed by an EEA State other than the United Kingdom pursuant to article 16 of Council Directive No. 93/22/EEC of 10th May 1993 on investment services in the securities field; and

(b) operates without any requirement that a person dealing on the market should have a physical presence in the EEA State from which any trading facilities are provided or on any trading floor that the market may have;

"EEA State" means a State which is a contracting party to the EEA Agreement;

"regulating provisions", in relation to an EEA regulated market, means—

(a) rules made, or guidance issued, by that market,

(b)　practices of that market, or

(c)　practices which, in relation to that market, are trading practices;

"trading practices", in relation to an EEA regulated market, means practices of persons who are subject to the rules made by that market, and—

(a)　which relate to business in respect of which those persons are subject to the rules of that market, and which are required or contemplated by those rules or by guidance issued by that market; or

(b)　which are otherwise attributable to the conduct of that market as such.

Services of general economic interest etc.

4. Neither the Chapter I prohibition nor the Chapter II prohibition applies to an undertaking entrusted with the operation of services of general economic interest or having the character of a revenue-producing monopoly in so far as the prohibition would obstruct the performance, in law or in fact, of the particular tasks assigned to that undertaking.

Compliance with legal requirements

5.—(1) The Chapter I prohibition does not apply to an agreement to the extent to which it is made in order to comply with a legal requirement.

(2) The Chapter II prohibition does not apply to conduct to the extent to which it is engaged in an order to comply with a legal requirement.

(3) In this paragraph "legal requirement" means a requirement—

(a)　imposed by or under any enactment in force in the United Kingdom;

(b)　imposed by or under the Treaty or the EEA Agreement and having legal effect in the United Kingdom without further enactment; or

(c)　imposed by or under the law in force in another Member State and having legal effect in the United Kingdom.

Avoidance of conflict with international obligations

6.—(1) If the Secretary of State is satisfied that, in order to avoid a conflict between provisions of this Part and an international obligation of the United Kingdom, it would be appropriate for the Chapter I prohibition not to apply to—

(a)　a particular agreement, or

(b)　any agreement of a particular description,
    he may by order exclude the agreement, or agreements of that description, from the Chapter I prohibition.

(2) An order under sub-paragraph (1) may make provision for the exclusion of the agreement or agreements to which the order applies, or of such of them as may be specified, only in specified circumstances.

(3) An order under sub-paragraph (1) may also provide that the Chapter I prohibition is to be deemed never to have applied in relation to the agreement or agreements, or in relation to such of them as may be specified.

(4) If the Secretary of State is satisfied that, in order to avoid a conflict between provisions of this Part and an international obligation of the United Kingdom, it would be appropriate for the Chapter II prohibition not to apply in particular circumstances, he may by order provide for it not to apply in such circumstances as may be specified.

(5) An order under sub-paragraph (4) may provide that the Chapter II prohibition is to be deemed never to have applied in relation to specified conduct.

(6) An international arrangement relating to civil aviation and designated by an order made by the Secretary of State is to be treated as an international obligation for the purposes of this paragraph.

(7) In this paragraph and paragraph 7 "specified" means specified in the order.

Public policy

7.—(1) If the Secretary of State is satisfied that there are exceptional and compelling reasons of public policy why the Chapter I prohibition ought not to apply to—

(a) a particular agreement, or

(b) any agreement of a particular description,

he may by order exclude the agreement, or agreements of that description, from the Chapter I prohibition.

(2) An order under sub-paragraph (1) may make provision for the exclusion of the agreement or agreements to which the order applies, or of such of them as may be specified, only in specified circumstances.

(3) An order under sub-paragraph (1) may also provide that the Chapter I prohibition is to be deemed never to have applied in relation to the agreement or agreements, or in relation to such of them as may be specified.

(4) If the Secretary of State is satisfied that there are exceptional and compelling reasons of public policy why the Chapter II prohibition ought not to apply in particular circumstances, he may by order provide for it not to apply in such circumstances as may be specified.

(5) An order under sub-paragraph (4) may provide that the Chapter II prohibition is to be deemed never to have applied in relation to specified conduct.

Coal and steel

8.—(1) The Chapter I prohibition does not apply to an agreement which relates to a coal or steel product to the extent to which the ECSC Treaty gives the Commission exclusive jurisdiction in the matter.

(2) Sub-paragraph (1) ceases to have effect on the date on which the ECSC Treaty expires ("the expiry date").

(3) The Chapter II prohibition does not apply to conduct which relates to a coal or steel product to the extent to which the ECSC Treaty gives the Commission exclusive jurisdiction in the matter.

(4) Sub-paragraph (3) ceases to have effect on the expiry date.

(5) In this paragraph—

"coal or steel product" means any product of a kind listed in Annex I to the ECSC Treaty; and

"ECSC Treaty" means the Treaty establishing the European Coal and Steel Community.

Agricultural products

9.—(1) The Chapter I prohibition does not apply to an agreement to the extent to which it relates to production of or trade in an agricultural product and—

(a) forms an integral part of a national market organisation;

(b) is necessary for the attainment of the objectives set out in Article 39 of the Treaty; or

(c) is an agreement of farmers or farmers' associations (or associations of such associations) belonging to a single member State which concerns—

(i) the production or sale of agricultural products, or

(ii) the use of joint facilities for the storage, treatment or processing of agricultural products,

and under which there is no obligation to charge identical prices.

(2) If the Commission determines that an agreement does not fulfil the conditions specified by

the provision for agricultural products for exclusion from Article 85(1), the exclusion provided by this paragraph ("the agriculture exclusion") is to be treated as ceasing to apply to the agreement on the date of the decision.

(3) The agriculture exclusion does not apply to a particular agreement if the Director gives a direction under this paragraph to that effect.

(4) If the Director is considering whether to give a direction under this paragraph, he may by notice in writing require any party to the agreement in question to give him such information in connection with the agreement as he may require.

(5) The Director may give a direction under this paragraph only as provided in sub-paragraph (6) or (7).

(6) If at the end of such period as may be specified in rules under section 51 a person has failed, without reasonable excuse, to comply with a requirement imposed under sub-paragraph (4), the Director may give a direction under this paragraph.

(7) The Director may also give a direction under this paragraph if he considers that an agreement (whether or not he considers that it infringes the Chapter I prohibition) is likely, or is intended, substantially and unjustifiably to prevent, restrict or distort competition in relation to an agricultural product.

(8) A direction under this paragraph—

(a)   must be in writing;

(b)   may be made so as to have effect from a date specified in the direction (which may not be earlier than the date on which it is given).

(9) In this paragraph—

"agricultural product" means any product of a kind listed in Annex II to the Treaty; and
"provision for agricultural products" means Council Regulation (EEC) No. 26/62 of 4th April 1962 applying certain rules of competition to production of and trade in agricultural products.

SCHEDULE 4

Section 3(1)(d)

PROFESSIONAL RULES

PART I

EXCLUSION

General

1.—(1) To the extent to which an agreement (either on its own or when taken together with another agreement)—

(a)   constitutes a designated professional rule,

(b)   imposes obligations arising from designated professional rules, or

(c)   constitutes an agreement to act in accordance with such rules,

the Chapter I prohibition does not apply to the agreement.

(2) In this Schedule—

"designated" means designated by the Secretary of State under paragraph 2;
"professional rules" means rules regulating a professional service or the persons providing, or wishing to provide, that service;

"professional service" means any of the service described in Part II of this Schedule; and "rules" includes regulations, codes of practice and statements of principle.

Designated rules

2.—(1) The Secretary of State must establish and maintain a list designating, for the purposes of this Schedule, rules—

(a) which are notified to him under paragraph 3; and

(b) which, in his opinion, are professional rules.

(2) The list is to be established, and any alteration in the list is to be effected, by an order made by the Secretary of State.

(3) The designation of any rule is to have effect from such date (which may be earlier than the date on which the order listing it is made) as may be specified in that order.

Application for designation

3.—(1) Any body regulating a professional service or the persons who provide, or wish to provide, that service may apply to the Secretary of State for rules of that body to be designated.

(2) An application under this paragraph must—

(a) be accompanied by a copy of the rules to which it relates; and

(b) be made in the prescribed manner.

Alterations

4.—(1) A rule does not cease to be a designated professional rule merely because it is altered.

(2) If such a rule is altered (whether by being modified, revoked or replaced), the body concerned must notify the Secretary of State and the Director of the alteration as soon as is reasonably practicable.

Reviewing the list

5.—(1) The Secretary of State must send to the Director—

(a) a copy of any order made under paragraph 2; and

(b) a copy of the professional rules to which the order relates.

(2) The Director must—

(a) retain any copy of a professional rule which is sent to him under sub-paragraph (1)(b) so long as the rule remains in force;

(b) maintain a copy of the list, as altered from time to time; and

(c) keep the list under review.

(3) If the Director considers—

(a) that, with a view to restricting the exclusion provided by this Schedule, some or all of the rules of a particular body should no longer be designated, or

(b) that rules which are not designated should be designated,

he must advise the Secretary of State accordingly.

Removal from the list

6.—(1) This paragraph applies if the Secretary of State receives advice under paragraph 5(3)(a).

(2) If it appears to the Secretary of State that another Minister of the Crown has functions in relation to the professional service concerned, he must consult that Minister.

(3) If it appears to the Secretary of State, having considered the Director's advice and the advice of any other Minister resulting from consultation under sub-paragraph (2), that the rules in question should no longer be designated, he may by order revoke their designation.

(4) Revocation of a designation is to have effect from such date as the order revoking it may specify.

Inspection

7.—(1) Any person may inspect, and take a copy of—

(a) any entry in the list of designated professional rules as kept by the Director under paragraph 5(2); or

(b) any copy of professional rules retained by him under paragraph 5(1).

(2) The right conferred by sub-paragraph (1) is to be exercised only—

(a) at a time which is reasonable;

(b) on payment of such fee as the Director may determine; and

(c) at such offices of his as the Director may direct.

PART II

PROFESSIONAL SERVICES

Legal

8. The services of barristers, advocates or solicitors.

Medical

9. The provision of medical or surgical advice or attendance and the performance of surgical operations.

Dental

10. Any services falling within the practice of dentistry within the meaning of the Dentists Act 1984.

Ophthalmic

11. The testing of sight.

Veterinary

12. Any services which constitute veterinary surgery within the meaning of the Veterinary Surgeons Act 1966.

Nursing

13. The services of nurses.

Midwifery

14. The services of midwives.

Physiotherapy

15. The services of physiotherapists.

Chiropody

16. The services of chiropodists.

Architectural

17. The services of architects.

Accounting and auditing

18. The making or preparation of accounts or accounting records and the examination, verification and auditing of financial statements.

Insolvency

19. Insolvency services within the meaning of section 428 of the Insolvency Act 1986.

Patent agency

20. The services of registered patent agents (within the meaning of Part V of the Copyright, Designs and Patents Act 1988).

21. The services of persons carrying on for gain in the United Kingdom the business of acting as agents or other representatives for or obtaining European patents or for the purpose of conducting proceedings in relation to applications for or otherwise in connection with such patents before the European Patent Office or the comptroller and whose names appear on the European list (within the meaning of Part V of the Copyright, Designs and Patents Act 1988).

Parliamentary agency

22. The services of parliamentary agents entered in the register in either House of Parliament as agents entitled to practise both in promoting and in opposing Bills.

Surveying

23. The services of surveyors of land, of quantity surveyors, of surveyors of buildings or other structures and of surveyors of ships.

Engineering and technology etc.

24. The services of persons practising or employed as consultants in the field of—

(a) civil engineering;

(b) mechanical, aeronautical, marine, electrical or electronic engineering;

(c) mining, quarrying, soil analysis or other forms of mineralogy or geology;

(d) agronomy, forestry, livestock rearing or ecology;

(e) metallurgy, chemistry, biochemistry or physics; or

(f) any other form of engineering or technology analogous to those mentioned in sub-paragraphs (a) to (e).

Educational

25. The provision of education or training.

Religious

26. The services of ministers of religion.

SCHEDULE 5

Section 12(2)

NOTIFICATION UNDER CHAPTER I: PROCEDURE

Terms used

1. In this Schedule—

"applicant" means the person making an application to which this Schedule applies;

"application" means an application under section 13 or an application under section 14;

"application for guidance" means an application under section 13;

"application for a decision" means an application under section 14;

"rules" means rules made by the Director under section 51; and

"specified" means specified in the rules.

General rules about applications

2.—(1) An application must be made in accordance with rules.

(2) A party to an agreement who makes an application must take all reasonable steps to notify all other parties to the agreement of whom he is aware—

(a) that the application has been made; and

(b) as to whether it is for guidance or a decision.

(3) Notification under sub-paragraph (2) must be in the specified manner.

Preliminary investigation

3.—(1) If, after a preliminary investigation of an application, the Director considers that it is likely—

(a) that the agreement concerned will infringe the Chapter I prohibition, and

(b) that it would not be appropriate to grant the agreement an individual exemption,

he may make a decision ("a provisional decision") under this paragraph. [In relation to an application for guidance or a decision in respect of an agreement to which a Chapter I prohibition does not apply for the reasons specified in SI 2000/263 reg.3:

" (1) If, after a preliminary investigation of an application, the Director considers that it is likely—

(a)   that the agreement concerned will infringe the Chapter I prohibition, and (aa) or that the agreement concerned would infringe the Chapter I prohibition if it applied,

(b) that it would not be appropriate to grant the agreement an individual exemption, he may make a decision ("a provisional decision") under this paragraph."]

(2) If the Director makes a provisional decision—

(a) the Director must notify the applicant in writing of his provisional decision; and

(b) section 13(4) or (as the case may be) section 14(4) is to be taken as never having applied.

(3) When making a provisional decision, the Director must follow such procedure as may be specified.

(4) A provisional decision does not affect the final determination of an application.

(5) If the Director has given notice to the applicant under sub-paragraph (2) in respect of an application for a decision, he may continue with the application under section 14.

Procedure on application for guidance

4. When determining an application for guidance, the Director must follow such procedure as may be specified.

Procedure on application for a decision

5.—(1) When determining an application for a decision, the Director must follow such procedure as may be specified.

(2) The Director must arrange for the application to be published in such a way as he thinks most suitable for bringing it to the attention of those likely to be affected by it, unless he is satisfied that it will be sufficient for him to seek information from one or more particular persons other than the applicant.

(3) In determining the application, the Director must take into account any representations made to him by persons other than the applicant.

Publication of decisions

6. If the Director determines an application for a decision he must publish his decision, together with his reasons for making it, in such manner as may be specified.

Delay by the Director

7.—(1) This paragraph applies if the court is satisfied, on the application of a person aggrieved by the failure of the Director to determine an application for a decision in accordance with the specified procedure, that there has been undue delay on the part of the Director in determining the application.

(2) The court may give such directions to the Director as it considers appropriate for securing that the application is determined without unnecessary further delay.

SCHEDULE 6

Section 20(2)

NOTIFICATION UNDER CHAPTER II: PROCEDURE

Terms used

1. In this Schedule—

"applicant" means the person making an application to which this Schedule applies;

"application" means an application under section 21 or an application under section 22;
"application for guidance" means an application under section 21;
"application for a decision" means an application under section 22;
"other party", in relation to conduct of two or more persons, means one of those persons other than the applicant;
"rules" means rules made by the Director under section 51; and
"specified" means specified in the rules.

General rules about applications

2.—(1) An application must be made in accordance with rules.

(2) If the conduct to which an application relates is conduct of two or more persons, the applicant must take all reasonable steps to notify all of the other parties of whom he is aware—

(a) that the application has been made; and

(b) as to whether it is for guidance or a decision.

(3) Notification under sub-paragraph (2) must be in the specified manner.

Preliminary investigation

3.—(1) If, after a preliminary investigation of an application, the Director considers that it is likely that the conduct concerned will infringe the Chapter II prohibition, he may make a decision ("a provisional decision") under this paragraph.

(2) If the Director makes a provisional decision, he must notify the applicant in writing of that decision.

(3) When making a provisional decision, the Director must follow such procedure as may be specified.

(4) A provisional decision does not affect the final determination of an application.

(5) If the Director has given notice to the applicant under sub-paragraph (2) in respect of an application for a decision, he may continue with the application under section 22.

Procedure on application for guidance

4. When determining an application for guidance, the Director must follow such procedure as may be specified.

Procedure on application for a decision

5.—(1) When determining an application for a decision, the Director must follow such procedure as may be specified.

(2) The Director must arrange for the application to be published in such a way as he thinks most suitable for bringing it to the attention of those likely to be affected by it, unless he is satisfied that it will be sufficient for him to seek information from one or more particular persons other than the applicant.

(3) In determining the application, the Director must take into account any representations made to him by persons other than the applicant.

Publication of decisions

6. If the Director determines an application for a decision he must publish his decision, together with his reasons for making it, in such manner as may be specified.

Delay by the Director

7.—(1) This paragraph applies if the court is satisfied, on the application of a person aggrieved by the failure of the Director to determine an application for a decision in accordance with the specified procedure, that there has been undue delay on the part of the Director in determining the application.

(2) The court may give such directions to the Director as it considers appropriate for securing that the application is determined without unnecessary further delay.

SCHEDULE 7

Section 45(7)

THE COMPETITION COMMISSION

PART I

GENERAL

Interpretation

1. In this Schedule—

"the 1973 Act" means the Fair Trading Act 1973;
"appeal panel member" means a member appointed under paragraph 2(1)(a);
"Chairman" means the chairman of the Commission;
"the Commission" means the Competition Commission;
"Council" has the meaning given in paragraph 5;
"general functions" means any functions of the Commission other than functions—

(a) in connection with appeals under this Act; or
(b) which are to be discharged by the Council;

"member" means a member of the Commission;
"newspaper merger reference" means a newspaper merger reference under section 59 of the 1973 Act;
"President" has the meaning given by paragraph 4(2);
"reporting panel member" means a member appointed under paragraph 2(1)(b);
"secretary" means the secretary of the Commission appointed under paragraph 9; and
"specialist panel member" means a member appointed under any of the provisions mentioned in paragraph 2(1)(d).

Membership of the Commission

2.—(1) The Commission is to consist of—

(a) members appointed by the Secretary of State to form a panel for the purposes of the Commission's functions in relation to appeals;

(b) members appointed by the Secretary of State to form a panel for the purposes of the Commission's general functions;

(c) members appointed (in accordance with paragraph 15(5)) from the panel maintained under paragraph 22;

(d) members appointed by the Secretary of State under or by virtue of—

(i) section 12(4) or 14(8) of the Water Industry Act 1991;
(ii) section 12(9) of the Electricity Act 1989[2];
(iii) section 13(10) of the Telecommunications Act 1984;
(iv) Article 15(9) of the Electricity (Northern Ireland) Order 1992.

(2) A person who is appointed as a member of a kind mentioned in one of paragraphs (a) to (c) of sub-paragraph (3) may also be appointed as a member of either or both of the other kinds mentioned in those paragraphs.

(3) The kinds of member are—

(a) an appeal panel member;

(b) a reporting panel member;

[2] As amended by s.104(3) of the Utilities Act 2000 as from a day to be appointed.

(c)   a specialist panel member.

(4) Before appointing a person who is qualified for appointment to the panel of chairmen (see paragraph 26(2)), the Secretary of State must consult the Lord Chancellor or Lord Advocate, as he considers appropriate.

(5) The validity of the Commission's proceedings is not affected by a defect in the appointment of a member.

Chairman and deputy chairmen

3.—(1) The Commission is to have a chairman appointed by the Secretary of State from among the reporting panel members.

(2) The Secretary of State may appoint one or more of the reporting panel members to act as deputy chairman.

(3) The Chairman, and any deputy chairman, may resign that office at any time by notice in writing addressed to the Secretary of State.

(4) If the Chairman (or a deputy chairman) ceases to be a member he also ceases to be Chairman (or a deputy chairman).

(5) If the Chairman is absent or otherwise unable to act, or there is no chairman, any of his functions may be performed—

(a)   if there is one deputy chairman, by him;

(b)   if there is more than one—

(i)   by the deputy chairman designated by the Secretary of State; or
(ii)   if no such designation has been made, by the deputy chairman designated by the deputy chairmen;

(c)   if there is no deputy chairman able to act—

(i)   by the member designated by the Secretary of State; or
(ii)   if no such designation has been made, by the member designated by the Commission.

President

4.—(1) The Secretary of State must appoint one of the appeal panel members to preside over the discharge of the Commission's functions in relation to appeals.

(2) The member so appointed is to be known as the President of the Competition Commission Appeal Tribunals (but is referred to in this Schedule as "the President").

(3) The Secretary of State may not appoint a person to be the President unless that person—

(a)   has a ten year general qualification within the meaning of section 71 of the Courts and Legal Services Act 1990,

(b)   is an advocate or solicitor in Scotland of at least ten years' standing, or

(c)   is—

(i)   a member of the Bar of Northern Ireland of at least ten years' standing, or
(ii)   a solicitor of the Supreme Court of Northern Ireland of at least ten years' standing,

and appears to the Secretary of State to have appropriate experience and knowledge of competition law and practice.

(4) Before appointing the President, the Secretary of State must consult the Lord Chancellor or Lord Advocate, as he considers appropriate.

(5) If the President ceases to be a member he also ceases to be President.

The Council

5.—(1) The Commission is to have a management board to be known as the Competition Commission Council (but referred to in this Schedule as "the Council").

(2) The Council is to consist of—

    (a) the Chairman;

    (b) the President;

    (c) such other members as the Secretary of State may appoint; and

    (d) the secretary.

(3) In exercising its functions under paragraphs 3 and 7 to 12 and paragraph 5 of Schedule 8, the Commission is to act through the Council.

(4) The Council may determine its own procedure including, in particular, its quorum.

(5) The Chairman (and any person acting as Chairman) is to have a casting vote on any question being decided by the Council.

Term of office

6.—(1) Subject to the provisions of this Schedule, each member is to hold and vacate office in accordance with the terms of his appointment.

(2) A person is not to be appointed as a member for more than five years at a time.

(3) Any member may at any time resign by notice in writing addressed to the Secretary of State.

(4) The Secretary of State may remove a member on the ground of incapacity or misbehaviour.

(5) No person is to be prevented from being appointed as a member merely because he has previously been a member.

Expenses, remuneration and pensions

7.—(1) The Secretary of State shall pay to the Commission such sums as he considers appropriate to enable it to perform its functions.

(2) The Commission may pay, or make provision for paying, to or in respect of each member such salaries or other remuneration and such pensions, allowances, fees, expenses or gratuities as the Secretary of State may determine.

(3) If a person ceases to be a member otherwise than on the expiry of his term of office and it appears to the Secretary of State that there are special circumstances which make it right for him to receive compensation, the Commission may make a payment to him of such amount as the Secretary of State may be determine.

(4) The approval of the Treasury is required for—

    (a) any payment under sub-paragraph (1);

    (b) any determination of the Secretary of State under sub-paragraph (2) or (3).

The Commission's powers

8. Subject to the provisions of this Schedule, the Commission has power to do anything (except borrow money)—

    (a) calculated to facilitate the discharge of its functions; or

    (b) incidental or conducive to the discharge of its functions.

Staff

9.—(1) The Commission is to have a secretary, appointed by the Secretary of State on such terms and conditions of service as he considers appropriate.

(2) The approval of the Treasury is required as to those terms and conditions.

(3) Before appointing a person to be secretary, the Secretary of State must consult the Chairman and the President.

(4) Subject to obtaining the approval of—

    (a) the Secretary of State, as to numbers, and

(b) the Secretary of State and Treasury, as to terms and conditions of service,

the Commission may appoint such staff as it thinks appropriate.

Procedure

10. Subject to any provision made by or under this Act, the Commission may regulate its own procedure.

Application of seal and proof of instruments

11.—(1) The application of the seal of the Commission must be authenticated by the signature of the secretary or of some other person authorised for the purpose.

(2) Sub-paragraph (1) does not apply in relation to any document which is or is to be signed in accordance with the law of Scotland.

(3) A document purporting to be duly executed under the seal of the Commission—

(a) is to be received in evidence; and

(b) is to be taken to have been so executed unless the contrary is proved.

Accounts

12.—(1) The Commission must—

(a) keep proper accounts and proper records in relation to its accounts;

(b) prepare a statement of accounts in respect of each of its financial years; and

(c) send copies of the statement to the Secretary of State and to the Comptroller and Auditor General Before the end of the month of August next following the financial year to which the statement relates.

(2) The statement of accounts must comply with any directions given by the Secretary of State with the approval of the Treasury as to—

(a) the information to be contained in it,

(b) the manner in which the information contained in it is to be presented, or

(c) the methods and principles according to which the statement is to be prepared,

and must contain such additional information as the Secretary of State may with the approval of the Treasury require to be provided for informing Parliament.

(3) The Comptroller and Auditor General must—

(a) examine, certify and report on each statement received by him as a result of this paragraph; and

(b) lay copies of each statement and of his report before each House of Parliament.

(4) In this paragraph "financial year" means the period beginning with the date on which the Commission is established and ending with March 31st next, and each successive period of twelve months.

Status

13.—(1) The Commission is not to be regarded as the servant or agent of the Crown or as enjoying any status, privilege or immunity of the Crown.

(2) The Commission's property is not to be regarded as property of, or held on behalf of, the Crown.

PART II

PERFORMANCE OF THE COMMISSION'S GENERAL FUNCTIONS

Interpretation

14. In this Part of this Schedule "group" means a group selected under paragraph 15.

Discharge of certain functions by groups

15.—(1) Except where sub-paragraph (7) gives the Chairman power to act on his own, any general function of the Commission must be performed through a group selected for the purpose by the Chairman.

(2) The group must consist of at least three persons one of whom may be the Chairman.

(3) In selecting the members of the group, the Chairman must comply with any requirement as to its constitution imposed by any enactment applying to specialist panel members.

(4) If the functions to be performed through the group relate to a newspaper merger reference, the group must, subject to sub-paragraph (5), consist of such reporting panel members as the Chairman may select.

(5) The Secretary of State may appoint one, two or three persons from the panel maintained under paragraph 22 to be members and, if he does so, the group—

(a)   must include that member or those members; and

(b)   if there are three such members, may (if the Chairman so decides) consist entirely of those members.

(6) Subject to sub-paragraphs (2) to (5), a group must consist of reporting panel members or specialist panel members selected by the Chairman.

(7) While a group is being constituted to perform a particular general function of the Commission, the Chairman may—

(a)   take such steps (falling within that general function) as he considers appropriate to facilitate the work of the group when it has been constituted; or

(b)   exercise the power conferred by section 75(5) of the 1973 Act (setting aside references).

Chairmen of groups

16. The Chairman must appoint one of the members of a group to act as the chairman of the group.

Replacement of member of group

17.—(1) If, during the proceedings of a group—

(a)   a member of the group ceases to be a member of the Commission,

(b)   the Chairman is satisfied that a member of the group will be unable for a substantial period to perform his duties as a member of the group, or

(c)   it appears to the Chairman that because of a particular interest of a member of the group it is inappropriate for him to remain in the group,

the Chairman may appoint a replacement.

(2) The Chairman may also at any time appoint any reporting panel member to be an additional member of a group.

Attendance of other members

18.—(1) At the invitation of the chairman of a group, any reporting panel member who is not a member of the group may attend meetings or otherwise take part in the proceedings of the group.

(2) But any person attending in response to such an invitation may not—

(a) vote in any proceedings of the group; or

(b) have a statement of his dissent from a conclusion of the group included in a report made by them.

(3) Nothing in sub-paragraph (1) is to be taken to prevent a group, or a member of a group, from consulting any member of the Commission with respect to any matter or question with which the group is concerned.

Procedure

19.—(1) Subject to any special or general directions given by the Secretary of State, each group may determine its own procedure.

(2) Each group may, in particular, determine its quorum and determine—

(a) the extent, if any, to which persons interested or claiming to be interested in the subject-matter of the reference are allowed—

    (i)   to be present or to be heard, either by themselves or by their representatives;
    (ii) to cross-examine witnesses; or
    (iii) otherwise to take part; and

(b) the extent, if any, to which sittings of the group are to be held in public.

(3) In determining its procedure a group must have regard to any guidance issued by the Chairman.

(4) Before issuing any guidance for the purposes of this paragraph the Chairman must consult the members of the Commission.

Effect of exercise of functions by group

20.—(1) Subject to sub-paragraph (2), anything done by or in relation to a group in, or in connection with, the performance of functions to be performed by the group is to have the same effect as if done by or in relation to the Commission.

(2) For the purposes of—

(a) sections 56 and 73 of the 1973 Act,

(b) section 19A of the Agricultural Marketing Act 1958.

(c) Articles 23 and 42 of the Agricultural Marketing (Northern Ireland) Order 1982.

a conclusion contained in a report of a group is to be disregarded if the conclusion is not that of at least two-thirds of the members of the group.

Casting votes

21. The chairman of a group is to have a casting vote on any question to be decided by the group.

Newspaper merger references

22. The Secretary of State must maintain a panel of persons whom he regards as suitable for selection as members of a group constituted in connection with a newspaper merger reference.

PART III

APPEALS

Interpretation

23. In this Part of this Schedule—

"panel of chairmen" means the panel appointed under paragraph 26; and
"tribunal" means an appeal tribunal constituted in accordance with paragraph 27.

Training of appeal panel members

24. The President must arrange such training for appeal panel members as he considers appropriate.

Acting President

25. If the President is absent or otherwise unable to act, the Secretary of State may appoint as acting president an appeal panel member who is qualified to act as chairman of a tribunal.

Panel of tribunal chairmen

26.—(1) There is to be a panel of appeal panel members appointed by the Secretary of State for the purposes of providing chairmen of appeal tribunals established under this Part of this Schedule.
(2) A person is qualified for appointment to the panel of chairmen only if—

    (a) he has a seven year general qualification within the meaning of section 71 of the Courts and Legal Services Act 1990,

    (b) he is an advocate or solicitor in Scotland of at least seven years' standing, or

    (c) he is—

        (i) a member of the Bar of Northern Ireland of at least seven years' standing, or
        (ii) a solicitor of the Supreme Court of Northern Ireland of at least seven years' standing,

and appears to the Secretary of State to have appropriate experience and knowledge of competition law and practice.

Constitution of tribunals

27.—(1) On receipt of a notice of appeal, the President must constitute an appeal tribunal to deal with the appeal.
(2) An appeal tribunal is to consist of—

    (a) a chairman, who must be either the President or a person appointed by him to be chairman from the panel of chairmen; and

(b) two other appeal panel members appointed by the President.

PART IV

MISCELLANEOUS

Disqualification of members for House of Commons

28. In Part II of Schedule 1 to the House of Commons Disqualification Act 1975 (bodies of which all members are disqualified) insert at the appropriate place—

"The Competition Commission".

Disqualification of members for Northern Ireland Assembly

29. In Part II of Schedule 1 to the Northern Ireland Assembly Disqualification Act 1975 (bodies of which all members are disqualified) insert at the appropriate place—

"The Competition Commission".

PART V

TRANSITIONAL PROVISIONS

Interpretation

30. In this Part of this Schedule—

"commencement date" means the date on which section 45 comes into force; and
"MMC" means the Monopolies and Mergers Commission.

Chairman

31.—(1) The person who is Chairman of the MMC immediately before the commencement date is on that date to become both a member of the Commission and its chairman as if he had been duly appointed under paragraphs 2(1)(b) and 3.

(2) He is to hold office as Chairman of the Commission for the remainder of the period for which he was appointed as Chairman of the MMC and on the terms on which he was so appointed.

Deputy chairmen

32. The persons who are deputy chairmen of the MMC immediately before the commencement date are on that date to become deputy chairmen of the Commission as if they had been duly appointed under paragraph 3(2).

Reporting panel members

33.—(1) The persons who are members of the MMC immediately before the commencement date are on that date to become members of the Commission as if they had been duly appointed under paragraph 2(1)(b).

(2) Each of them is to hold office as a member for the remainder of the period for which he was appointed as a member of the MMC and on the terms on which he was so appointed.

Specialist panel members

34.—(1) The persons who are members of the MMC immediately before the commencement date by virtue of appointments made under any of the enactments mentioned in paragraph 2(1)(d) are on that date to become members of the Commission as if they had been duly appointed to the Commission under the enactment in question.

(2) Each of them is to hold office as a member for such period and on such terms as the Secretary of State may determine.

Secretary

35. The person who is the secretary of the MMC immediately before the commencement date is on that date to become the secretary of the Commission as if duly appointed under paragraph 9, on the same terms and conditions.

Council

36.—(1) The members who become deputy chairmen of the Commission under paragraph 32 are also to become members of the Council as if they had been duly appointed under paragraph 5(2)(c).

(2) Each of them is to hold office as a member of the Council for such period as the Secretary of State determines.

SCHEDULE 8

Sections 46(5) and 48(4)

APPEALS

PART I

GENERAL

Interpretation

1. In this Schedule—

"the chairman" means a person appointed as chairman of a tribunal in accordance with paragraph 27(2)(a) of Schedule 7;
"the President" means the President of the Competition Commission Appeal Tribunals appointed under paragraph 4 of Schedule 7;
"rules" means rules made by the Secretary of State under section 48;
"specified" means specified in rules;
"tribunal" means an appeal tribunal constituted in accordance with paragraph 27 of Schedule 7.

General procedure

2.—(1) An appeal to the Competition Commission must be made by sending a notice of appeal to the Commission within the specified period.

(2) The notice of appeal must set out the grounds of appeal in sufficient detail to indicate—

(a) under which provision of this Act the appeal is brought;

(b) to what extent (if any) the appellant contends that the decision against, or with respect to which, the appeal is brought was based on an error of fact or was wrong in law; and

(c) to what extent (if any) the appellant is appealing against the Director's exercise of his discretion in making the disputed decision.

(3) The tribunal may give an appellant leave to amend the grounds of appeal identified in the notice of appeal.

Decisions of the tribunal

3.—(1) The tribunal must determine the appeal on the merits by reference to the grounds of appeal set out in the notice of appeal.

(2) The tribunal may confirm or set aside the decision which is the subject of the appeal, or any part of it, and may—

(a) remit the matter to the Director,

(b) impose or revoke, or vary the amount of, a penalty,

(c) grant or cancel an individual exemption or vary any conditions or obligations imposed in relation to the exemption by the Director,

(d) give such directions, or take such other steps, as the Director could himself have given or taken, or

(e) make any other decision which the Director could himself have made.

(3) Any decision of the tribunal on an appeal has the same effect, and may be enforced in the same manner, as a decision of the Director.

(4) If the tribunal confirms the decision which is the subject of the appeal it may nevertheless set aside any finding of fact on which the decision was based.

4.—(1) A decision of the tribunal may be taken by a majority.

(2) The decision must—

(a) state whether it was unanimous or taken by a majority; and

(b) be recorded in a document which—

(i)   contains a statement of the reasons for the decision; and
(ii) is signed and dated by the chairman of the tribunal.

(3) When the tribunal is preparing the document mentioned in sub-paragraph (2)(b), section 56 is to apply to the tribunal as it applies to the Director.

(4) The President must make such arrangements for the publication of the tribunal's decision as he considers appropriate.

PART II

RULES

Registrar of Appeal Tribunals

5.—(1) Rules may provide for the appointment by the Competition Commission, with the approval of the Secretary of State, of a Registrar of Appeal Tribunals.

(2) The rules may, in particular—

    (a) specify the qualifications for appointment as Registrar; and

    (b) provide for specified functions relating to appeals to be exercised by the Registrar in specified circumstances.

Notice of appeal

6. Rules may make provision—

    (a) as to the period within which appeals must be brought;

    (b) as to the form of the notice of appeal and as to the information which must be given in the notice;

    (c) with respect to amendment of a notice of appeal;

    (d) with respect to acknowledgement of a notice of appeal.

Response to the appeal

7. Rules may provide for the tribunal to reject an appeal if—

    (a) it considers that the notice of appeal reveals no valid ground of appeal; or

    (b) it is satisfied that the appellant has habitually and persistently and without any reasonable ground—

        (i) instituted vexatious proceedings, whether against the same person or against different persons; or

       (ii) made vexatious applications in any proceedings.

Pre-hearing reviews and preliminary matters

8.—(1) Rules may make provision—

    (a) for the carrying-out by the tribunal of a preliminary consideration of proceedings (a "pre-hearing review"); and

    (b) for enabling such powers to be exercised in connection with a pre-hearing review as may be specified.

(2) If rules make provision of the kind mentioned in sub-paragraph (1), they may also include—

    (a) provision for security; and

    (b) supplemental provision.

(3) In sub-paragraph (2) "provision for security" means provision authorising a tribunal carrying out a pre-hearing review under the rules, in specified circumstances, to make an order requiring a party to the proceedings, if he wishes to continue to participate in them, to pay a deposit of an amount not exceeding such sum—

    (a) as may be specified; or

    (b) as may be calculated in accordance with specified provisions.

(4) In sub-paragraph (2) "supplemental provision" means any provision as to—

    (a) the manner in which the amount of such a deposit is to be determined;

    (b) the consequences of non-payment of such a deposit; and

    (c) the circumstances in which any such deposit, or any part of it, may be—

        (i) refunded to the person who paid it; or

(ii)   paid to another party to the proceedings.

Conduct of the hearing

9.—(1) Rules may make provision—

(a)   as to the manner in which appeals are to be conducted, including provision for any hearing to be held in private if the tribunal considers it appropriate because it may be considering information of a kind to which section 56 applies;

(b)   as to the persons entitled to appear on behalf of the parties;

(c)   for requiring persons to attend to give evidence and produce documents and for authorising the administration of oaths to witnesses;

(d)   as to the evidence which may be required or admitted in proceedings before the tribunal and the extent to which it should be oral or written;

(e)   allowing the tribunal to fix time limits with respect to any aspect of the proceedings before it and to extend any time limit (whether or not it has expired);

(f)   for enabling the tribunal to refer a matter back to the Director if it appears to the tribunal that the matter has not been adequately investigated;

(g)   for enabling the tribunal, on the application of any party to the proceedings before it or on its own initiative—

(i)   in England and Wales or Northern Ireland, to order the disclosure between, or the production by, the parties of documents or classes of documents;
(ii)   in Scotland, to order such recovery or inspection of documents as might be ordered by a sheriff;

(h)   for the appointment of experts for the purposes of any proceedings before the tribunal;

(i)   for the award of costs or expenses, including any allowances payable to persons in connection with their attendance before the tribunal;

(j)   for taxing or otherwise settling any costs or expenses directed to be paid by the tribunal and for the enforcement of any such direction.

(2) A person who without reasonable excuse fails to comply with—

(a)   any requirement imposed by virtue of sub-paragraph (1)(c), or

(b)   any requirement with respect to the disclosure, production, recovery or inspection of documents which is imposed by virtue of sub-paragraph (1)(g),

is guilty of an offence and liable on summary conviction to a fine not exceeding level 3 on the standard scale.

Interest

10.—(1) Rules may make provision—

(a)   as to the circumstances in which the tribunal may order that interest is payable;

(b)   for the manner in which and the periods by reference to which interest is to be calculated and paid.

(2) The rules may, in particular, provide that compound interest is to be payable if the tribunal—

(a)   upholds a decision of the Director to impose a penalty, or

(b)   does not reduce a penalty so imposed by more than a specified percentage,

but in such a case the rules may not provide that interest is to be payable in respect of any period before the date on which the appeal was brought.

Fees

11.—(1) Rules may provide—

    (a) for fees to be chargeable in respect of specified costs of proceedings before the tribunal;

    (b) for the amount of such costs to be determined by the tribunal.

(2) Any sums received in consequence of rules under this paragraph are to be paid into the Consolidated Fund.

Withdrawing an appeal

12. Rules may make provision—

    (a) that a party who has brought an appeal may not withdraw it without the leave of—

        (i) the tribunal, or
        (ii) in specified circumstances, the President or the Registrar;

    (b) for the tribunal to grant leave to withdraw the appeal on such conditions as it considers appropriate;

    (c) enabling the tribunal to publish any decision which it could have made had the appeal not been withdrawn;

    (d) as to the effect of withdrawal of an appeal;

    (e) as to any procedure to be followed if parties to proceedings on an appeal agree to settle.

Interim orders

13.—(1) Rules may provide for the tribunal to make an order ("an interim order") granting, on an interim basis, any remedy which the tribunal would have power to grant in its final decision.

(2) An interim order may, in particular, suspend the effect of a decision made by the Director or vary the conditions or obligations attached to an exemption.

(3) Rules may also make provision giving the tribunal powers similar to those given to the Director by section 35.

Miscellaneous

14. Rules may make provision—

    (a) for a person who is not a party to proceedings on an appeal to be joined in those proceedings;

    (b) for appeals to be consolidated on such terms as the tribunal thinks appropriate in such circumstances as may be specified.

SCHEDULE 9

Section 51(2)

DIRECTOR'S RULES

General

1. In this Schedule—

"application for guidance" means an application for guidance under section 13 or 21;

"application for a decision" means an application for a decision under section 14 or 22;
"guidance" means guidance given under section 13 or 21;
"rules" means rules made by the Director under section 51; and
"specified" means specified in rules.

Applications

2. Rules may make provision—

(a) as to the form and manner in which an application for guidance or an application for a decision must be made;

(b) for the procedure to be followed in dealing with the application;

(c) for the application to be dealt with in accordance with a timetable;

(d) as to the documents and information which must be given to the Director in connection with the application;

(e) requiring the applicant to give such notice of the application, to such other persons, as may be specified;

(f) as to the consequences of a failure to comply with any rule made by virtue of sub-paragraph (e);

(g) as to the procedure to be followed when the application is subject to the concurrent jurisdiction of the Director and a regulator.

Provisional decisions

3. Rules may make provision as to the procedure to be followed by the Director when making a provisional decision under paragraph 3 of Schedule 5 or paragraph 3 of Schedule 6.

Guidance

4. Rules may make provision as to—

(a) the form and manner in which guidance is to be given;

(b) the procedure to be followed if—

    (i) the Director takes further action with respect to an agreement after giving guidance that it is not likely to infringe the Chapter I prohibition; or

    (ii) the Director takes further action with respect to conduct after giving guidance that it is not likely to infringe the Chapter II prohibition.

Decisions

5.—(1) Rules may make provisions as to—

(a) the form and manner in which notice of any decision is to be given;

(b) the person or persons to whom the notice is to be given;

(c) the manner in which the Director is to publish a decision;

(d) the procedure to be followed if—

    (i) the Director takes further action with respect to an agreement after having decided that it does not infringe the Chapter I prohibition; or

    (ii) the Director takes further action with respect to conduct after having decided that it does not infringe the Chapter II prohibition.

(2) In this paragraph "decision" means a decision of the Director (whether or not made on an application)—

(a) as to whether or not an agreement has infringed the Chapter I prohibition, or

(b) as to whether or not conduct has infringed the Chapter II prohibition,

and, in the case of an application for a decision under section 14 which includes a request for an individual exemption, includes a decision as to whether or not to grant the exemption.

Individual exemptions

6. Rules may make provision as to—

(a) the procedure to be followed by the Director when deciding whether, in accordance with section 5—

  (i)   to cancel an individual exemption that he has granted,
  (ii) to vary or remove any of its conditions or obligations, or
  (iii) to impose additional conditions or obligations;

(b) the form and manner in which notice of such a decision is to be given.

7. Rules may make provision as to—

(a) the form and manner in which an application under section 4(6) for the extension of an individual exemption is to be made;

(b) the circumstances in which the Director will consider such an application;

(c) the procedure to be followed by the Director when deciding whether to grant such an application;

(d) the form and manner in which notice of such a decision is to be given.

Block exemptions

8. Rules may make provision as to—

(a) the form and manner in which notice of an agreement is to be given to the Director under subsection (1) of section 7;

(b) the procedure to be followed by the Director if he is acting under subsection (2) of that section;

(c) as to the procedure to be followed by the Director if he cancels a block exemption.

Parallel exemptions

9. Rules may make provision as to—

(a) the circumstances in which the Director may—

  (i)   impose conditions or obligations in relation to a parallel exemption,
  (ii) vary or remove any such conditions or obligations,
  (iii) impose additional conditions or obligations, or
  (iv) cancel the exemption;

(b) as to the procedure to be followed by the Director if he is acting under section 10(5);

(c) the form and manner in which notice of a decision to take any of the steps in sub-paragraph (a) is to be given;

(d) the circumstances in which an exemption may be cancelled with retrospective effect.

Section 11 exemptions

10. Rules may, with respect to any exemption provided by regulations made under section 11, make provision similar to that made with respect to parallel exemptions by section 10 or by rules under paragraph 9.

Directions withdrawing exclusions

11. Rules may make provision as to the factors which the Director may take into account when he is determining the date on which a direction given under paragraph 4(1) of Schedule 1 or paragraph 2(3) or 9(3) of Schedule 3 is to have effect.

Disclosure of information

12.—(1) Rules may make provision as to the circumstances in which the Director is to be required, before disclosing information given to him by a third party in connection with the exercise of any of the Director's functions under Part I, to give notice, and an opportunity to make representations, to the third party.

(2) In relation to the agreement (or conduct) concerned, "third party" means a person who is not a party to the agreement (or who has not engaged in the conduct).

Applications under section 47

13. Rules may make provision as to—

(a) the period within which an application under section 47(1) must be made;

(b) the procedure to be followed by the Director in dealing with the application;

(c) the person or persons to whom notice of the Director's response to the application is to be given.

Enforcement

14. Rules may make provision as to the procedure to be followed when the Director takes action under any of sections 32 to 41 with respect to the enforcement of the provisions of this Part.

SCHEDULE 10

Sections 54 and 66(5)

REGULATORS

PART I

MONOPOLIES

1. The amendments of the Fair Trading Act 1973 made by sections 66 and 67 of this Act are to have effect, not only in relation to the jurisdiction of the Director under the provisions amended, but also in relation to the jurisdiction under those provisions of each of the following—

(a) the Director General of Telecommunications;

(b)   the Director General of Electricity Supply;

(c)   the Director General of Electricity Supply for Northern Ireland;

(d)   the Director General of Water Services;

(e)   the Rail Regulator;

(f)   the Director General of Gas Supply; and

(g)   the Director General of Gas for Northern Ireland.

PART II

THE PROHIBITIONS

Telecommunications

2.—(1) In consequence of the repeal by this Act of provisions of the Competition Act 1980, the functions transferred by subsection (3) of section 50 of the Telecommunications Act 1984 (functions under 1973 and 1980 Acts) are no longer exercisable by the Director General of Telecommunications.

(2) Accordingly, that Act is amended as follows.

(3) In section 3 (general duties of Secretary of State and Director), in subsection (3)(b), for "section 50" substitute "section 50(1) or (2)".

(4) In section 3, after subsection (3A), insert—

"(3B)Subsections (1) and (2) above do not apply in relation to anything done by the Director in the exercise of functions assigned to him by section 50(3) below ("Competition Act functions").

(3C)The Director may nevertheless, when exercising any Competition Act function, have regard to any matter in respect of which a duty is imposed by subsection (1) or (2) above ("a general matter"), if it is a matter to which the Director General of Fair Trading could have regard when exercising that function; but that is not to be taken as implying that, in relation to any of the matters mentioned in subsection (3) or (3A) above, regard may not be had to any general matter."

(5) Section 50 is amended as follows.

(6) For subsection (3) substitute—

"(3) The Director shall be entitled to exercise, concurrently with the Director General of Fair Trading, the functions of that Director under the provisions of Part I of the Competition Act 1998 (other than sections 38(1) to (6) and 51), so far as relating to—

(a)   agreements, decisions or concerted practices of the kind mentioned in section 2(1) of that Act, or

(b)   conduct of the kind mentioned in section 18(1) of that Act,

which relate to commercial activities connected with telecommunications.

(3A)So far as necessary for the purposes of, or in connection with, the provisions of subsection (3) above, references in Part I of the Competition Act 1998 to the Director General of Fair Trading are to be read as including a reference to the Director (except in sections 38(1) to (6), 51, 52(6) and (8) and 54 of that Act and in any other provision of that Act where the context otherwise requires)."

(7)In subsection (4), omit paragraph (c) and the "and" immediately after it.

(8) In subsection (5), omit "or (3)".

(9) In subsection (6), for paragraph (b) substitute—

"(b) Part I of the Competition Act 1998 (other than sections 38(1) to (6) and 51)."

(10) In subsection (7), omit "or the 1980 Act".

Gas

3.—(1) In consequence of the repeal by this Act of provisions of the Competition Act 1980, the functions transferred by subsection (3) of section 36A of the Gas Act 1986 (functions with respect to competition) are no longer exercisable by the Director General of Gas Supply.

(2) Accordingly, that Act is amended as follows.

(3) In section 4 (general duties of Secretary of State and Director), after subsection (3), insert—

"(3A) Subsections (1) to (3) above and section 4A below do not apply in relation to anything done by the Director in the exercise of functions assigned to him by section 36A below ("Competition Act functions").

(3B) The Director may nevertheless, when exercising any Competition Act function, have regard to any matter in respect of which a duty is imposed by any of subsection (1) to (3) above or section 4A below, if it is a matter to which the Director General of Fair Trading could have regard when exercising that function."

(4) Section 36A is amended as follows.

(5) For subsection (3) substitute—

"(3) The Director shall be entitled to exercise, concurrently with the Director General of Fair Trading, the functions of that Director under the provisions of Part I of the Competition Act 1998 (other than sections 38(1) to (6) and 51), so far as relating to—

   (a)   agreements, decisions or concerted practices of the kind mentioned in section 2(1) of that Act, or

   (b)   conduct of the kind mentioned in section 18(1) of that Act,

which relate to the carrying on of activities to which this subsection applies.

(3A) So far as necessary for the purposes of, or in connection with, the provisions of subsection (3) above, references in Part I of the Competition Act 1998 to the Director General of Fair Trading are to be read as including a reference to the Director (except in sections 38(1) to (6), 51, 52(6) and (8) and 54 of that Act and in any other provision of that Act where the context otherwise requires)."

(6) In subsection (5)—

   (a)   for "transferred by", in each place, substitute "mentioned in";

   (b)   after paragraph (b), insert "and";

   (c)   omit paragraph (d) and the "and" immediately before it.

(7) In subsection (6), omit "or (3)".

(8) In subsection (7), for paragraph (b) substitute—

"(b) Part I of the Competition Act 1998 (other than sections 38(1) to (6) and 51),"

(9) In subsection (8)—

   (a)   omit "or under the 1980 Act";

   (b)   for "or (3) above" substitute "above and paragraph 1 of Schedule 10 to the Competition Act 1998".

(10) In subsection (9), omit "or the 1980 Act".

(11) In subsection (10), for the words from "transferred" to the end substitute "mentioned in subsection (2) or (3) above."

Electricity

4.—(1) In consequence of the repeal by this Act of provisions of the Competition Act 1980, the functions transferred by subsection (3) of section 43 of the Electricity Act 1989 (functions with respect to competition) are no longer exercisable by the Director General of Electricity Supply.

(2) Accordingly, that Act is amended as follows.

(3) In section 3 (general duties of Secretary of State and Director), after subsection (6), insert—

"(6A) Subsections (1) to (5) above do not apply in relation to anything done by the Director in the exercise of functions assigned to him by section 43(3) below ("Competition Act functions").

(6B) The Director may nevertheless, when exercising any Competition Act function, have regard to any matter in respect of which a duty is imposed by any of subsections (1) to (5) above ("a general matter"), if it is a matter to which the Director General of Fair Trading could have regard when exercising that function; but that is not to be taken as implying that, in the exercise of any function mentioned in subsection (6) above, regard may not be had to any general matter."

(4) Section 43 is amended as follows.

(5) For subsection (3) substitute—

"(3) The Director shall be entitled to exercise, concurrently with the Director General of Fair Trading, the functions of that Director under the provisions of Part I of the Competition Act 1998 (other than sections 38(1) to (6) and 51), so far as relating to—

(a) agreements, decisions or concerted practices of the kind mentioned in section 2(1) of that Act, or

(b) conduct of the kind mentioned in section 18(1) of that Act,

which relate to commercial activities connected with the generation, transmission or supply of electricity.

(3A) So far as necessary for the purposes of, or in connection with, the provisions of subsection (3) above, references in Part I of the Competition Act 1998 to the Director General of Fair Trading are to be read as including a reference to the Director (except in sections 38(1) to (6), 51, 52(6) and (8) and 54 of that Act and in any other provision of that Act where the context otherwise requires)."

(6) In subsection (4), omit paragraph (c) and the "and" immediately after it.

(7) In subsection (5), omit "or (3)".

(8) In subsection (6), for paragraph (b) substitute—

"(b) Part I of the Competition Act 1998 (other than sections 38(1) to (6) and 51),".

(9) In subsection (7), omit "or the 1980 Act".

Water

5.—(1) In consequence of the repeal by this Act of provisions of the Competition Act 1980, the functions exercisable by virtue of subsection (3) of section 31 of the Water Industry Act 1991 (functions of Director with respect to competition) are no longer exercisable by the Director General of Water Services.

(2) Accordingly, that Act is amended as follows.

(3) In section 2 (general duties with respect to water industry), in subsection (6)(a), at the beginning, insert "subject to subsection (6A) below".

(4) In section 2, after subsection (6), insert—

"(6A) Subsections (2) to (4) above do not apply in relation to anything done by the Director in the exercise of functions assigned to him by section 31(3) below ("Competition Act functions").

(6B) The Director may nevertheless, when exercising any Competition Act function, have regard to any matter in respect of which a duty is imposed by any of subsections (2) to

(4) above, if it is a matter to which the Director General of Fair Trading could have regard when exercising that function."

(5)Section 31 is amended as follows.
(6) For subsection (3) substitute—

"(3) The Director shall be entitled to exercise, concurrently with the Director General of Fair Trading, the functions of that Director under the provisions of Part I of the Competition Act 1998 (other than sections 38(1) to (6) and 51), so far as relating to—

    (a)   agreements, decisions or concerted practices of the kind mentioned in section 2(1) of that Act, or
    (b)   conduct of the kind mentioned in section 18(1) of that Act,

which relate to commercial activities connected with the supply of water or securing a supply of water or with the provision or securing of sewerage services."

(7) In subsection (4)—

    (a)   for "to (3)" substitute "and (2)";

    (b)   omit paragraph (c) and the "and" immediately before it.
       (8) After subsection (4), insert—

"(4A) So far as necessary for the purposes of, or in connection with, the provisions of subsection (3) above, references in Part I of the Competition Act 1998 to the Director General of Fair Trading are to be read as including a reference to the Director (except in sections 38(1) to (6), 51, 52(6) and (8) and 54 of that Act and in any other provision of that Act where the context otherwise requires)."

(9)In subsection (5), omit "or in subsection (3) above".
(10) In subsection (6), omit "or in subsection (3) above".
(11) In subsection (7), omit "or (3)".
(12) In subsection (8), for paragraph (b) substitute—

"(b) Part I of the Competition Act 1998 (other than sections 38(1) to (6) and 51),".

(13)In subsection (9), omit "or the 1980 Act".

Railways

6.—(1) In consequence of the repeal by this Act of provisions of the Competition Act 1980, the functions transferred by subsection (3) of section 67 of the Railways Act 1993 (respective functions of the Regulator and the Director etc.) are no longer exercisable by the Rail Regulator.
   (2) Accordingly, that Act is amended as follows.
   (3) In section 4 (general duties of the Secretary of State and the Regulator), after subsection (7), insert—

"(7A)Subsections (1) to (6) above do not apply in relation to anything done by the Regulator in the exercise of functions assigned to him by section 67(3) below ("Competition Act functions").
   (7B) The Regulator may nevertheless, when exercising any Competition Act function, have regard to any matter in respect of which a duty is imposed by any of subsections (1) to (6) above, if it is a matter to which the Director General of Fair Trading could have regard when exercising that function."

(4) Section 67 is amended as follows.

(5) For subsection (3) substitute—

"(3) The Regulator shall be entitled to exercise, concurrently with the Director, the functions of the Director under the provisions of Part I of the Competition Act 1998 (other than sections 38(1) to (6) and 51), so far as relating to—

(a)   agreements, decisions or concerted practices of the kind mentioned in section 2(1) of that Act, or

(b)   conduct of the kind mentioned in section 18(1) of that Act,

which relate to the supply of railway services.

(3A)So far as necessary for the purposes of, or in connection with, the provisions of subsection (3) above, references in Part I of the Competition Act 1998 to the Director are to be read as including a reference to the Regulator (except in sections 38(1) to (6), 51, 52(6) and (8) and 54 of that Act and in any other provision of that Act where the context otherwise requires)."

(6) In subsection (4), omit paragraph (c) and the "and" immediately after it.
(7) In subsection (6)(a), omit "or (3)".
(8) In subsection (8), for paragraph (b) substitute—

"(b) Part I of the Competition Act 1998 (other than sections 38(1) to (6) and 51),".

(9) In subsection (9)—

(a)   omit "or under the 1980 Act";

(b)   for "or (3) above" substitute "above and paragraph 1 of Schedule 10 to the Competition Act 1998".

PART III

THE PROHIBITIONS: NORTHERN IRELAND

Electricity

7.—(1) In consequence of the repeal by this Act of provisions of the Competition Act 1980, the functions transferred by paragraph (3) of Article 46 of the Electricity (Northern Ireland) Order 1992 (functions with respect to competition) are no longer exercisable by the Director General of Electricity Supply for Northern Ireland.

(2) Accordingly, that Order is amended as follows.
(3) In Article 6 (general duties of the Director), after paragraph (2), add—

"(3) Paragraph (1) does not apply in relation to anything done by the Director in the exercise of functions assigned to him by Article 46(3) ("Competition Act functions").

(4) The Director may nevertheless, when exercising any Competition Act function, have regard to any matter in respect of which a duty is imposed by paragraph (1) ("a general matter"), if it is a matter to which the Director General of Fair Trading could have regard when exercising that function; but that is not to be taken as implying that, in the exercise of any function mentioned in Article 4(7) or paragraph (2), regard may not be had to any general matter."

(4) Article 46 is amended as follows.
(5) For paragraph (3) substitute—

"(3) The Director shall be entitled to exercise, concurrently with the Director General of Fair Trading, the functions of that Director under the provisions of Part I of the Competition Act 1998 (other than sections 38(1) to (6) and 51), so far as relating to—

(a) agreements, decisions or concerted practices of the kind mentioned in section 2(1) of that Act, or

(b) conduct of the kind mentioned in section 18(1) of that Act,

which relate to commercial activities connected with the generation, transmission or supply of electricity.

(3A) So far as necessary for the purposes of, or in connection with, the provisions of paragraph (3), references in Part I of the Competition Act 1998 to the Director General of Fair Trading are to be read as including a reference to the Director (except in sections 38(1) to (6), 51, 52(6) and (8) and 54 of that Act and in any other provision of that Act where the context otherwise requires)."

(6) In paragraph (4), omit sub-paragraph (c) and the "and" immediately after it.

(7) In paragraph (5), omit "or (3)".

(8) In paragraph (6), for sub-paragraph (b) substitute—

"(b) Part I of the Competition Act 1998 (other than sections 38(1) to (6) and 51),".

(9) In paragraph (7), omit "or the 1980 Act".

Gas

8.—(1) In consequence of the repeal by this Act of provisions of the Competition Act 1980, the functions transferred by paragraph (3) of Article 23 of the Gas (Northern Ireland) Order 1996 (functions with respect to competition) are no longer exercisable by the Director General of Gas for Northern Ireland.

(2) Accordingly, that Order is amended as follows.

(3) In Article 5 (general duties of the Department and Director), after paragraph (4), insert—

"(4A) Paragraphs (2) to (4) do not apply in relation to anything done by the Director in the exercise of functions assigned to him by Article 23(3) ("Competition Act functions").

(4B) The Director may nevertheless, when exercising any Competition Act function, have regard to any matter in respect of which a duty is imposed by any of paragraphs (2) to (4), if it is a matter to which the Director General of Fair Trading could have regard when exercising that function."

(4) Article 23 is amended as follows.

(5) For paragraph (3) substitute—

"(3) The Director shall be entitled to exercise, concurrently with the Director General of Fair Trading, the functions of that Director under the provisions of Part I of the Competition Act 1998 (other than sections 38(1) to (6) and 51), so far as relating to—

(a) agreements, decisions or concerted practices of the kind mentioned in section 2(1) of that Act, or

(b) conduct of the kind mentioned in section 18(1) of that Act,

connected with the conveyance, storage or supply of gas.

(3A) So far as necessary for the purposes of, or in connection with, the provisions of paragraph (3), references in Part I of the Competition Act 1998 to the Director General of Fair Trading are to be read as including a reference to the Director (except in sections 38(1) to (6), 51, 52(6) and (8) and 54 of that Act and in any other provision of that Act where the context otherwise requires)."

(6) In paragraph (4)—

(a) for "transferred by", in each place, substitute "mentioned in";

(b) after sub-paragraph (b), insert "and";

(c) omit sub-paragraph (d) and the "and" immediately before it.

(7) In paragraph (5), omit "or (3)".

(8) In paragraph (6), for sub-paragraph (b) substitute—

"(b) Part I of the Competition Act 1998 (other than sections 38(1) to (6) and 51),".

(9) In paragraph (7)—

(a) omit "or under the 1980 Act";

(b) for "or (3)" substitute "and paragraph 1 of Schedule 10 to the Competition Act
      1998".

(10) In paragraph (8), omit "or the 1980 Act".

(11) In paragraph (9), for the words from "transferred" to the end substitute "mentioned in
paragraph (2) or (3)."

PART IV

UTILITIES: MINOR AND CONSEQUENTIAL AMENDMENTS

The Telecommunications Act 1984 (c.12)

9.—(1) The Telecommunications Act 1984 is amended as follows.

(2) In section 13 (licence modification references to Competition Commission), for
subsections (9) and (10) substitute—

"(9) The provisions mentioned in subsection (9A) are to apply in relation to references
under this section as if—

(a) the functions of the Competition Commission in relation to those references were
     functions under the Fair Trading Act 1973 [1973 c. 41] (in this Act referred to as
     "the 1973 Act");

(b) the expression "merger reference" included a reference under this section;

(c) in section 70 of the 1973 Act—

    (i) references to the Secretary of State were references to the Director, and

    (ii) the reference to three months were a reference to six months.

(9A) The provisions are—

(a) sections 70 (time limit for report on merger) and 85 (attendance of witnesses
     and production of documents) of the 1973 Act;

(b) Part II of Schedule 7 to the Competition Act 1998 (performance of the
     Competition Commission's general functions); and

(c) section 24 of the Competition Act 1980 [1980 c. 21] (modification of
     provisions about performance of such functions).

(10) For the purposes of references under this section, the Secretary of State is to appoint
not less than three members of the Competition Commission.

(10A) In selecting a group to perform the Commission's functions in relation to any such
reference, the chairman of the Commission must select up to three of the members
appointed under subsection (10) to be members of the group."

(3) In section 14, omit subsection (2) (which falls with the repeal of the Restrictive Trade
Practices Act 1976).

(4) In section 16 (securing compliance with licence conditions), in subsection (5), after
paragraph (a), omit "or" and after paragraph (b), insert—

"or

  (c) that the most appropriate way of proceeding is under the Competition Act 1998."

(5) In section 50 (functions under 1973 and 1980 Acts), after subsection (6), insert—

"(6A) Section 93B of the 1973 Act (offences of supplying false or misleading information) is to have effect so far as relating to functions exercisable by the Director by virtue of—

  (a) subsection (2) above and paragraph 1 of Schedule 10 to the Competition Act 1998, or

  (b) paragraph 1 of Schedule 2 to the Deregulation and Contracting Out Act 1994 [1994 c. 40],

as if the reference in section 93B(1)(a) to the Director General of Fair Trading included a reference to the Director."

(6) In section 95 (modification by orders under other enactments)—

  (a) in subsection (1), omit "or section 10(2)(a) of the 1980 Act";

  (b) in subsection (2)—

    (i) after paragraph (a), insert "or";
    (ii) omit paragraph (c) and the "or" immediately before it;

  (c) in subsection (3), omit "or the 1980 Act".

(7) In section 101(3) (general restrictions on disclosure of information)—

  (a) omit paragraphs (d) and (e) (which refer to the Restrictive Trade Practices Act 1976 and the Resale Prices Act 1976);

  (b) after paragraph (m), insert—

"(n) the Competition Act 1998".

(8) At the end of section 101, insert—

"(6) Information obtained by the Director in the exercise of functions which are exercisable concurrently with the Director General of Fair Trading under Part I of the Competition Act 1998 is subject to sections 55 and 56 of that Act (disclosure) and not to subsections (1) to (5) of this section."

The Gas Act 1986 (c.44)

10.—(1) The Gas Act 1986 is amended as follows.
(2) In section 24 (modification references to the Competition Commission), for subsection (7) substitute—

"(7) The provisions mentioned in subsection (7A) are to apply in relation to references under this section as if—

  (a) the functions of the Competition Commission in relation to those references were functions under the Fair Trading Act 1973; [1973 c. 41]
  (b) the expression "merger reference" included a reference under this section:

(c)   in section 70 of the Fair Trading Act 1973 [1973 c. 41]—

(i)   references to the Secretary of State were references to the Director, and
(ii) the reference to three months were a reference to six months.

(7A)The provisions are—

(a)   sections 70 (time limit for report on merger) and 85 (attendance of witnesses and production of documents) of the Fair Trading Act 1973;
(b)   Part II of Schedule 7 to the Competition Act 1998 (performance of the Competition Commission's general functions); and
(c)   section 24 of the Competition Act 1980 [1980 c. 21] (modification of provisions about performance of such functions)."

(3) In section 25, omit subsection (2) (which falls with the repeal of the Restrictive Trade Practices Act 1976).

(4) In section 27 (modification by order under other enactments)—

(a)   in subsection (1), omit "or section 10(2)(a) of the Competition Act 1980";

(b)   in subsection (3)(a), omit from "or" to "competition reference";

(c)   in subsection (6), omit "or the said Act of 1980".

(5) In section 28 (orders for securing compliance with certain provisions), in subsection (5), after paragraph (aa), omit "or" and after paragraph (b), insert

"or

(c)   that the most appropriate way of proceeding is under the Competition Act 1998."

(6) In section 42(3) (general restrictions on disclosure of information)—

(a)   omit paragraphs (e) and (f) (which refer to the Restrictive Trade Practices Act 1976 and the Resale Prices Act 1976);

(b)   after paragraph (n), insert—

"(o) the Competition Act 1998".

(7) At the end of section 42, insert—

"(7) Information obtained by the Director in the exercise of functions which are exercisable concurrently with the Director General of Fair Trading under Part I of the Competition Act 1998 is subject to sections 55 and 56 of that Act (disclosure) and not to subsections (1) to (6) of this section."

The Water Act 1989 (c.15)

11. In section 174(3) of the Water Act 1989 (general restrictions on disclosure of information)—

(a)   omit paragraphs (d) and (e) (which refer to the Restrictive Trade Practices Act 1976 and the Resale Prices Act 1976);

(b)   after paragraph (l), insert—

"(ll) the Competition Act 1998".

The Electricity Act 1989 (c.29)

12.—(1) The Electricity Act 1989 is amended as follows.

(2) In section 12 (modification references to Competition Commission), for subsections (8) and (9) substitute—

"(8) The provisions mentioned in subsection (8A) are to apply in relation to references under this section as if—

(a)   the functions of the Competition Commission in relation to those references were functions under the 1973 Act;

(b)   the expression "merger reference" included a reference under this section;

(c)   in section 70 of the 1973 Act—

(i)   references to the Secretary of State were references to the Director, and

(ii)   the reference to three months were a reference to six months.

(8A) The provisions are—

(a)   sections 70 (time limit for report on merger) and 85 (attendance of witnesses and production of documents) of the 1973 Act;

(b)   Part II of Schedule 7 to the Competition Act 1998 (performance of the Competition Commission's general functions); and

(c)   section 24 of the 1980 Act (modification of provisions about performance of such functions).

(9) For the purposes of references under this section, the Secretary of State is to appoint not less than eight members of the Competition Commission.

(9A) In selecting a group to perform the Commission's functions in relation to any such reference, the chairman of the Commission must select up to three of the members appointed under subsection (9) to be members of the group."

(3) In section 13, omit subsection (2) (which falls with the repeal of the Restrictive Trade Practices Act 1976).

(4) In section 15 (modification by order under other enactments)—

(a)   in subsection (1), omit paragraph (b) and the "or" immediately before it;

(b)   in subsection (2)—

(i)   after paragraph (a), insert "or";

(ii)   omit paragraph (c) and the "or" immediately before it;

(c)   in subsection (3), omit "or the 1980 Act".

(5) In section 25 (orders for securing compliance), in subsection (5), after paragraph (b), omit "or" and after paragraph (c), insert

"or

(d)   that the most appropriate way of proceeding is under the Competition Act 1998."

(6) In section 43 (functions with respect to competition), after subsection (6), insert—

"(6A) Section 93B of the 1973 Act (offences of supplying false or misleading information) is to have effect so far as relating to functions exercisable by the Director by virtue of—

(a)   subsection (2) above and paragraph 1 of Schedule 10 to the Competition Act 1998, or

(b)   paragraph 4 of Schedule 2 to the Deregulation and Contracting Out Act 1994 [1994 c. 40],

as if the reference in section 93B(1)(a) to the Director General of Fair Trading included a reference to the Director."

(7) In section 57(3) (general restrictions on disclosure of information)—

(a)   omit paragraphs (d) and (e) (which refer to the Restrictive Trade Practices Act 1976 and the Resale Prices Act 1976);

(b)   after paragraph (no), insert—

"(nop) the Competition Act 1998".

(8) At the end of section 57, insert—

"(7) Information obtained by the Director in the exercise of functions which are exercisable concurrently with the Director General of Fair Trading under Part I of the Competition Act 1998 is subject to sections 55 and 56 of that Act (disclosure) and not to subsections (1) to (6) of this section."

The Water Industry Act 1991 (c.56)

13.—(1) The Water Industry Act 1991 is amended as follows.
(2) In section 12(5) (determinations under conditions of appointment)—

(a)   after "this Act", insert "or";

(b)   omit "or the 1980 Act".

(3) In section 14 (modification references to Competition Commission), for subsections (7) and (8) substitute—

"(7) The provisions mentioned in subsection (7A) are to apply in relation to references under this section as if—

(a)   the functions of the Competition Commission in relation to those references were functions under the 1973 Act;
(b)   the expression "merger reference" included a reference under this section;
(c)   in section 70 of the 1973 Act—

(i)   references to the Secretary of State were references to the Director, and
(ii)   the reference to three months were a reference to six months.

(7A) The provisions are—

(a)   sections 70 (time limit for report on merger) and 85 (attendance of witnesses and production of documents) of the 1973 Act;
(b)   Part II of Schedule 7 to the Competition Act 1998 (performance of the Competition Commission's general functions); and
(c)   section 24 of the 1980 Act (modification of provisions about performance of such functions).

(8) For the purposes of references under this section, the Secretary of State is to appoint not less than eight members of the Competition Commission.
(8A) In selecting a group to perform the Commission's functions in relation to any such reference, the chairman of the Commission must select one or more of the members appointed under subsection (8) to be members of the group."

(4) In section 15, omit subsection (2) (which falls with the repeal of the Restrictive Trade Practices Act 1976).
(5) In section 17 (modification by order under other enactments)—

(a)   in subsection (1), omit paragraph (b) and the "or" immediately before it;

(b)   in subsection (2)—

(i)   after paragraph (a), insert "or";

(ii) omit paragraph (c) and the "or" immediately before it;

(c) in subsection (4), omit "or the 1980 Act".

(6) In section 19 (exceptions to duty to enforce), after subsection (1), insert—

"(1A) The Director shall not be required to make an enforcement order, or to confirm a provisional enforcement order, if he is satisfied that the most appropriate way of proceeding is under the Competition Act 1998."

(7) In section 19(3), after "subsection (1) above", insert "or, in the case of the Director, is satisfied as mentioned in subsection (1A) above,"

(8) In section 31 (functions of Director with respect to competition), after subsection (8), insert—

"(8A) Section 93B of the 1973 Act (offences of supplying false or misleading information) is to have effect so far as relating to functions exercisable by the Director by virtue of—

(a)   subsection (2) above and paragraph 1 of Schedule 10 to the Competition Act 1998, or

(b)   paragraph 8 of Schedule 2 to the Deregulation and Contracting Out Act 1994 [1994 c. 40], as if the reference in section 93B(1)(a) to the Director General of Fair Trading included a reference to the Director."

(9) After section 206(9) (restriction on disclosure of information), insert—

"(9A) Information obtained by the Director in the exercise of functions which are exercisable concurrently with the Director General of Fair Trading under Part I of the Competition Act 1998 is subject to sections 55 and 56 of that Act (disclosure) and not to subsections (1) to (9) of this section."

(10)In Schedule 15 (disclosure of information), in Part II (enactments in respect of which disclosure may be made)—

(a)   omit the entries relating to the Restrictive Trade Practices Act 1976 and the Resale Prices Act 1976;

(b)   after the entry relating to the Railways Act 1993, insert the entry—

"The Competition Act 1998".

The Water Resources Act 1991 (c.57)

14. In Schedule 24 to the Water Resources Act 1991 (disclosure of information), in Part II (enactments in respect of which disclosure may be made)—

(a)   omit the entries relating to the Restrictive Trade Practices Act 1976 and the Resale Prices Act 1976;

(b)   after the entry relating to the Coal Industry Act 1994, insert the entry—

"The Competition Act 1998".

The Railways Act 1993 (c.43)

15.—(1) The Railways Act 1993 is amended as follows.

(2) In section 13 (modification references to the Competition Commission), for subsection (8) substitute—

"(8) The provisions mentioned in subsection (8A) are to apply in relation to references under this section as if—

    (a)   the functions of the Competition Commission in relation to those references were functions under the 1973 Act;

    (b)   the expression "merger reference" included a reference under this section;

    (c)   in section 70 of the 1973 Act—

        (i) references to the Secretary of State were references to the Director, and

        (ii) the reference to three months were a reference to six months.

(8A) The provisions are—

    (a)   sections 70 (time limit for report on merger) and 85 (attendance of witnesses and production of documents) of the 1973 Act;

    (b)   Part II of Schedule 7 to the Competition Act 1998 (performance of the Competition Commission's general functions); and

    (c)   section 24 of the Competition Act 1980 [1980 c. 21] (in this Part referred to as "the 1980 Act") (modification of provisions about performance of such functions).

(3) In section 14, omit subsection (2) (which falls with the repeal of the Restrictive Trade Practices Act 1976).

(4) In section 16 (modification by order under other enactments)—

    (a) in subsection (1), omit paragraph (b) and the "or" immediately before it;

    (b) in subsection (2)—

        (i) after paragraph (a), insert "or";

        (ii) omit paragraph (c) and the "or" immediately before it;

    (c) in subsection (5), omit "or the 1980 Act".

(5) In section 22, after subsection (6), insert—

"(6A) Neither the Director General of Fair Trading nor the Regulator may exercise, in respect of an access agreement, the powers given by section 32 (enforcement directions) or section 35(2) (interim directions) of the Competition Act 1998.

(6B) Subsection (6A) does not apply to the exercise of the powers given by section 35(2) in respect of conduct—

    (a) which is connected with an access agreement; and

    (b) in respect of which section 35(1)(b) of that Act applies."

(6) In section 55 (orders for securing compliance), after subsection (5), insert—

"(5A) The Regulator shall not make a final order, or make or confirm a provisional order, in relation to a licence holder or person under closure restrictions if he is satisfied that the most appropriate way of proceeding is under the Competition Act 1998."

(7) In section 55—

    (a) in subsection (6), after "subsection (5)", insert "or (5A)";

    (b) in subsection (11), for "subsection (10)" substitute "subsections (5A) and (10)".

(8) Omit section 131 (modification of Restrictive Trade Practices Act 1976).

(9) In section 145(3) (general restrictions on disclosure of information)—

    (a) omit paragraphs (d) and (e) (which refer to the Restrictive Trade Practices Act 1976 and the Resale Prices Act 1976);

    (b) after paragraph (q), insert—

"(qq) the Competition Act 1998."

(10) After section 145(6), insert—

"(6A) Information obtained by the Regulator in the exercise of functions which are exercisable concurrently with the Director General of Fair Trading under Part I of the Competition Act 1998 is subject to sections 55 and 56 of that Act (disclosure) and not to subsections (1) to (6) of this section."

The Channel Tunnel Rail Link Act 1996 (c.61)

16.—(1) The Channel Tunnel Rail Link Act 1996 is amended as follows.

(2) In section 21 (duties as to exercise of regulatory functions), in subsection (6), at the end of the paragraph about regulatory functions, insert—

"other than any functions assigned to him by virtue of section 67(3) of that Act ("Competition Act functions").

(7) The Regulator may, when exercising any Competition Act function, have regard to any matter to which he would have regard if—

(a) he were under the duty imposed by subsection (1) or (2) above in relation to that function; and

(b) the matter is one to which the Director General of Fair Trading could have regard if he were exercising that function."

(3) In section 22 (restriction of functions in relation to competition etc.), for subsection (3) substitute—

"(3) The Rail Regulator shall not be entitled to exercise any functions assigned to him by section 67(3) of the Railways Act 1993 [1993 c. 43] (by virtue of which he exercises concurrently with the Director General of Fair Trading certain functions under Part I of the Competition Act 1998 so far as relating to matters connected with the supply of railway services) in relation to—

(a) any agreements, decisions or concerted practices of the kind mentioned in section 2(1) of that Act that have been entered into or taken by, or

(b) any conduct of the kind mentioned in section 18(1) of that Act that has been engaged in by,

a rail link undertaker in connection with the supply of railway services, so far as relating to the rail link."

PART V

MINOR AND CONSEQUENTIAL AMENDMENTS: NORTHERN IRELAND

The Electricity (Northern Ireland) Order 1992

17.—(1) The Electricity (Northern Ireland) Order 1992 is amended as follows.

(2) In Article 15 (modification references to Competition Commission), for paragraphs (8) and (9) substitute—

"(8) The provisions mentioned in paragraph (8A) are to apply in relation to references under this Article as if—

(a) the functions of the Competition Commission in relation to those references were functions under the 1973 Act;

(b) "merger reference" included a reference under this Article;

(c) in section 70 of the 1973 Act—

(i) references to the Secretary of State were references to the Director, and

(ii) the reference to three months were a reference to six months.

(8A) The provisions are—

    (a) sections 70 (time limit for report on merger) and 85 (attendance of witnesses and production of documents) of the 1973 Act;

    (b) Part II of Schedule 7 to the Competition Act 1998 (performance of the Competition Commission's general functions); and

    (c) section 24 of the 1980 Act (modification of provisions about performance of such functions).

(9) The Secretary of State may appoint members of the Competition Commission for the purposes of references under this Article.

(9A) In selecting a group to perform the Commission's functions in relation to any such reference, the chairman of the Commission must select up to three of the members appointed under paragraph (9) to be members of the group."

(3) In Article 16, omit paragraph (2) (which falls with the repeal of the Restrictive Trade Practices Act 1976).

(4) In Article 18 (modification by order under other statutory provisions)—

  (a) in paragraph (1), omit sub-paragraph (b) and the "or" immediately before it;

  (b) in paragraph (2)—

    (i) after sub-paragraph (a), insert "or";

    (ii) omit sub-paragraph (c) and the "or" immediately before it;

  (c) in paragraph (3), omit "or the 1980 Act".

(5) In Article 28 (orders for securing compliance), in paragraph (5), after sub-paragraph (b), omit "or" and after sub-paragraph (c), insert

"or

    (d) that the most appropriate way of proceeding is under the Competition Act 1998."

(6) In Article 46 (functions with respect to competition), after paragraph (6), insert—

"(6A) Section 93B of the 1973 Act (offences of supplying false or misleading information) is to have effect so far as relating to functions exercisable by the Director by virtue of—

    (a) paragraph (2) and paragraph 1 of Schedule 10 to the Competition Act 1998, or

    (b) paragraph 5 of Schedule 2 to the Deregulation and Contracting Out Act 1994 [1994 c. 40],

as if the reference in section 93B(1)(a) to the Director General of Fair Trading included a reference to the Director."

(7) In Article 61(3) (general restrictions on disclosure of information)—

  (a) omit sub-paragraphs (f) and (g) (which refer to the Restrictive Trade Practices Act 1976 and the Resale Prices Act 1976);

  (b) after sub-paragraph (t), add—

"(u) the Competition Act 1998".

(8) At the end of Article 61, insert—

"(7) Information obtained by the Director in the exercise of functions which are exercisable concurrently with the Director General of Fair Trading under Part I of the Competition Act 1998 is subject to sections 55 and 56 of that Act (disclosure) and not to paragraphs (1) to (6)."

(9) In Schedule 12, omit paragraph 16 (which amends the Restrictive Trade Practices Act 1976).

The Gas (Northern Ireland) Order 1996

18.—(1) The Gas (Northern Ireland) Order 1996 is amended as follows.

(2) In Article 15 (modification references to the Competition Commission), for paragraph (9) substitute—

"(9) The provisions mentioned in paragraph (9A) are to apply in relation to references under this Article as if—

    (a)   the functions of the Competition Commission in relation to those references were functions under the 1973 Act;

    (b)   "merger reference" included a reference under this Article;

    (c)   in section 70 of the 1973 Act—

        (i) references to the Secretary of State were references to the Director; and

        (ii) the reference to three months were a reference to six months.

(9A) The provisions are—

    (a)   sections 70 (time limit for report on merger) and 85 (attendance of witnesses and production of documents) of the 1973 Act;

    (b)   Part II of Schedule 7 to the Competition Act 1998 (performance of the Competition Commission's general functions); and

    (c)   section 24 of the 1980 Act (modification of provisions about performance of such functions)."

(3) In Article 16, omit paragraph (2) (which falls with the repeal of the Restrictive Trade Practices Act 1976).

(4) In Article 18 (modification by order under other statutory provisions)—

    (a) in paragraph (1), omit sub-paragraph (b) and the "or" immediately before it;

    (b) in paragraph (3)—

        (i) after sub-paragraph (a), insert "or";

        (ii) omit sub-paragraph (c) and the "or" immediately before it;

    (c) in paragraph (5), omit "or the 1980 Act".

(5) In Article 19 (orders for securing compliance), in paragraph (5), after subparagraph (b), omit "or" and after sub-paragraph (c), insert

"or

    (d)   that the most appropriate way of proceeding is under the Competition Act 1998."

(6) In Article 44(4) (general restrictions on disclosure of information)—

    (a) omit sub-paragraphs (f) and (g) (which refer to the Restrictive Trade Practices Act 1976 and the Resale Price Act 1976);

    (b) after sub-paragraph (u), add—

"(v) the Competition Act 1998".

(7) At the end of Article 44, insert—

"(8) Information obtained by the Director in the exercise of functions which are exercisable concurrently with the Director General of Fair Trading under Part I of the Competition Act 1998 is subject to sections 55 and 56 of that Act (disclosure) and not to paragraphs (1) to (7)."

SCHEDULE 11

Section 55(4)

INTERPRETATION OF SECTION 55

Relevant functions

1. In section 55(3) "relevant functions" means any function under—

(a) Part I or any enactment repealed in consequence of Part I;

(b) the Fair Trading Act 1973 (c. 41) or the Competition Act 1980 (c. 21);

(c) the Estate Agents Act 1979 (c. 38);

(d) the Telecommunications Act 1984 (c. 12);

(e) the Gas Act 1986 (c.44) or the Gas Act 1995 (c. 45);

(f) the Gas (Northern Ireland) Order 1996;

(g) the Airports Act 1986 (c. 31) or Part IV of the Airports (Northern Ireland) Order 1994;

(h) the Financial Services Act 1986 (c. 60);

(i) the Electricity Act 1989 (c. 29) or the Electricity (Northern Ireland) Order 1992;

(j) the Broadcasting Act 1990 (c. 42) or the Broadcasting Act 1996 (c. 55);

(k) the Courts and Legal Services Act 1990 (c. 41);

(l) the Water Industry Act 1991 (c. 56), the Water Resources Act 1991 (c. 57), the Statutory Water Companies Act 1991 (c. 58), the Land Drainage Act 1991 (c. 59) and the Water Consolidation (Consequential Provisions) Act 1991 (c. 60);

(m) the Railways Act 1993 (c. 43);

(n) the Coal Industry Act 1994 (c. 21);

(o) the EC Competition Law (Articles 88 and 89) Enforcement Regulations 1996;

(p) any subordinate legislation made (whether before or after the passing of this Act) for the purpose of implementing Council Directive No. 91/440/EEC of 29th July 1991 on the development of the Community's railways, Council Directive No. 95/18/EC of 19th June 1995 on the licensing of railway undertaking or Council Directive No. 95/19/EC of 19th June 1995 on the allocation of railway infrastructure capacity and the charging of infrastructure fees.

Designated persons

2. In section 55(3) "designated person" means any of the following—

(a) the Director;

(b) the Director General of Telecommunications;

(c) the Independent Television Commission;

(d) the Director General of Gas Supply;

(e) the Director General of Gas for Northern Ireland;

(f) the Civil Aviation Authority;

(g) the Director General of Water Services;

(h) the Director General of Electricity Supply;

(i) the Director General of Electricity Supply for Northern Ireland;

(j) the Rail Regulator;

(k) the Director of Passenger Rail Franchising;

(l) the International Rail Regulator;

(m) the Authorised Conveyancing Practitioners Board;

(n) the Scottish Conveyancing and Executory Services Board;

(o) the Coal Authority;

(p) the Monopolies and Mergers Commission;

(q) the Competition Commission;

(r) the Securities and Investments Board;

(s) any Minister of the Crown or any Northern Ireland department.

SCHEDULE 12

Section 74(1)

MINOR AND CONSEQUENTIAL AMENDMENTS

The Fair Trading Act 1973 (c.41)

1.—(1) The Fair Trading Act 1973 is amended as follows.

(2) Omit section 4 and Schedule 3 (which make provision in respect of the Monopolies and Mergers Commission).

(3) Omit—

(a) section 10(2),

(b) section 54(5),

(c) section 78(3),

(d) paragraph 3(1) and (2) of Schedule 8,

(which fall with the repeal of the Restrictive Trade Practices Act 1976).

(4) In section 10 (supplementary provisions about monopoly situations), in subsection (8), for "to (7)" substitute "and (3) to (7)".

(5) In sections 35 and 37 to 41, for "the Restrictive Practices Court", in each place, substitute "a relevant Court".

(6) After section 41, insert—

"Meaning of "relevant Court"

"41A. In this Part of this Act, "relevant Court", in relation to proceedings in respect of a course of conduct maintained in the course of a business, means any of the following courts in whose jurisdiction that business is carried on—

(a) in England and Wales or Northern Ireland, the High Court;

(b) in Scotland, the Court of Session."

(7) In section 42 (appeals from decisions or orders of courts under Part III)—

(a) in subsection (1), at the end, add "; but this subsection is subject to subsection (3) of this section";

(b) in subsection (2)(b), after "Scotland," insert "from the sheriff court"; and

(c) after subsection (2), and—

"(3) A decision or order of the Court of Session as the relevant Court may be reviewed, whether on a question of fact or on a question of law, by reclaiming to the Inner House."

(8) Omit section 45 (power of the Director to require information about complex monopoly situations).

(9) In section 81 (procedure in carrying out investigations)—

(a) in subsection (1)—

   (i) in the words before paragraph (a), omit from "and the Commission" to "of this Act)";

   (ii) in paragraph (b), omit "or the Commission, as the case may be," and "or of the Commission";

(b) in subsection (2), omit "or the Commission" and "or of the Commission"; and

(c) in subsection (3), omit from "and, in the case" to "85 of this Act" and "or the Commission, as the case may be,".

(10) In section 85 (attendance of witnesses and production of documents on investigations by Competition Commission of references under the Fair Trading Act 1973), in subsection (1)(b)—

(a) after "purpose", insert "(i)";

(b) after the second "notice", insert—

"or

   (ii) any document which falls within a category of document which is specified, or described, in the notice,".

(11) In section 85, in subsection (1)(c), after "estimates" (in both places), insert "forecasts".

(12) In section 85, after subsection (1), insert—

"(1A) For the purposes of subsection (1) above—

(a) "document" includes information recorded in any form;

(b) the power to require the production of documents includes power to take copies of, or extracts from, any document produced; and

(c) in relation to information recorded otherwise than in legible form, the power to require it to be produced includes power to require it to be produced in legible form, so far as the means to do so are within the custody or under the control of the person on whom the requirement is imposed."

(13) In section 85(2), for "any such investigation" substitute "an investigation of the kind mentioned in subsection (1)".

(14) In section 133 (general restrictions on disclosure of information), in subsection (2)(a), after "the Coal Industry Act 1994" insert "or the Competition Act 1998".

(15) In section 135(1) (financial provisions)—

(a) in the words before paragraph (a) and in paragraph (b), omit "or the Commission"; and

(b) omit paragraph (a).

The Energy Act 1976 (c.76)

2. In the Energy Act 1976, omit section 5 (temporary relief from restrictive practices law in relation to certain agreements connected with petroleum).

The Estate Agents Act 1979 (c.38)

3. In section 10(3) of the Estate Agents Act 1979 (restriction on disclosure of information), in paragraph (a)—

(a) omit "or the Restrictive Trade Practices Act 1976"; and

(b) after "the Coal Industry Act 1994", insert "or the Competition Act 1998".

The Competition Act 1980 (c.21)

4.—(1) The Competition Act 1980 is amended as follows.

(2) In section 11(8) (public bodies and other persons referred to the Commission), omit paragraph (b) and the "and" immediately before it.

(3) For section 11(9) (which makes provision for certain functions of the Competition Commission under the Fair Trading Act 1973 to apply in relation to references under the Competition Act 1980) substitute—

"(9) The provisions mentioned in subsection (9A) are to apply in relation to a reference under this section as if—

(a) the functions of the Competition Commission under this section were functions under the Fair Trading Act 1973;

(b) the expression "merger reference" included a reference to the Commission under this section; and

(c) in paragraph 20(2)(a) of Schedule 7 to the Competition Act 1998, the reference to section 56 of the Fair Trading Act 1973 were a reference to section 12 below.

(9A) The provisions are—

(a) sections 70 (time limit for report on merger), 84 (public interest) and 85 (attendance of witnesses and production of documents) of the Fair Trading Act 1973; and

(b) Part II of Schedule 7 to the Competition Act 1998 (performance of the Competition Commission's general functions)."

(4) In section 13 (investigation of prices directed by Secretary of State)—

(a) in subsection (1), omit from "but the giving" to the end;

(b) for subsection (6) substitute—

"(6) For the purposes of an investigation under this section the Director may, by notice in writing signed by him—

(a) require any person to produce—

(i) at a time and a place specified in the notice,
(ii) to the Director or to any person appointed by him for the purpose,
any documents which are specified or described in the notice and which are documents in his custody or under his control and relating to any matter relevant to the investigation; or

(b) require any person carrying on any business to—

(i) furnish to the Director such estimates, forecasts, returns or other information as may be specified or described in the notice; and
(ii) specify the time, manner and form in which any such estimates, forecasts, returns or information are to be furnished.

(7) No person shall be compelled, for the purpose of any investigation under this section—

    (a)   to produce any document which he could not be compelled to produce in civil proceedings before the High Court or, in Scotland, the Court of Session; or

    (b)   in complying with any requirement for the furnishing of information, to give any information which he could not be compelled to give in evidence in such proceedings.

(8) Subsections (6) to (8) of section 85 of the Fair Trading Act 1973 (enforcement provisions relating to notices requiring production of documents etc.) shall apply in relation to a notice under subsection (6) above as they apply in relation to a notice under section 85(1) but as if, in section 85(7), for the words from "any one" to "the Commission" there were substituted "the Director" "

(5) In section 15 (special provisions for agricultural schemes) omit subsections (2)(b), (3) and (4).

(6) In section 16 (reports), omit subsection (3).

(7) In section 17 (publication etc. of reports)—

    (a) in subsections (1) and (3) to (5), omit "8(1)";

    (b) in subsection (2), omit "8(1) or"; and

    (c) in subsection (6), for "sections 9, 10 or" substitute "section".

(8) In section 19(3) (restriction on disclosure of information), omit paragraphs (d) and (e).

(9) In section 19(3), after paragraph (q), insert—

"(r) the Competition Act 1998."

(10) In section 19(5)(a), omit "or in anything published under section 4(2)(a) above".

(11) Omit section 22 (which amends the Fair Trading Act 1973).

(12) In section 24(1) (modifications of provisions about performance of Commission's functions), for from "Part II" to the first "Commission" substitute "Part II of Schedule 7 to the Competition Act 1998 (performance of the Competition Commission's general functions)".

(13) Omit sections 25 to 30 (amendments of the Restrictive Trade Practices Act 1976).

(14) In section 31 (orders and regulations)—

    (a) omit subsection (2); and

    (b) in subsection (3), omit "10".

(15) In section 33 (short title etc.)—

    (a) in subsection (2), for "sections 2 to 24" substitute "sections 11 to 13 and sections 15 to 24";

    (b) omit subsections (3) and (4).

Magistrates' Courts (Northern Ireland) Order 1981 (S.I. 1981/1675 (N.I. 26))

5. In Schedule 6 to the Magistrates' Courts (Northern Ireland) Order 1981, omit paragraphs 42 and 43 (which amend the Restrictive Trade Practices Act 1976).

Agricultural Marketing (Northern Ireland) Order 1982 (S.I. 1982/ 1080 (N.I. 12))

6. In Schedule 8 to the Agricultural Marketing (Northern Ireland) Order 1982—

    (a) omit the entry relating to paragraph 16(2) of Schedule 3 to the Fair Trading Act 1973; and

    (b) in the entry relating to the Competition Act 1980—

(i) for "sections" substitute "section";
(ii) omit "and 15(3)".

The Airports Act 1986 (c. 31)

7.—(1) The Airports Act 1986 is amended as follows.

(2) In section 44 (which makes provision about references by the CAA to the Competition Commission), for subsection (3) substitute—

"(3) The provisions mentioned in subsection (3A) are to apply in relation to references under this section as if—

(a) the functions of the Competition Commission in relation to those references were functions under the 1973 Act;

(b) the expression "merger reference" included a reference under this section;

(c) in section 70 of the 1973 Act—

(i) references to the Secretary of State were references to the CAA, and
(ii) the reference to three months were a reference to six months.

(3A) The provisions are—

(a) sections 70 (time limit for report on merger) and 85 (attendance of witnesses and production of documents) of the 1973 Act;

(b) Part II of Schedule 7 to the Competition Act 1998 (performance of the Competition Commission's general functions); and

(c) section 24 of the 1980 Act (modification of provisions about performance of such functions)."

(3) In section 45, omit subsection (3) (which falls with the repeal of the Restrictive Trade Practices Act 1976).

(4) In section 54 (orders under the 1973 Act or 1980 Act modifying or revoking conditions)—

(a) in subsection (1), omit "or section 10(2)(a) of the 1980 Act";

(b) in subsection (3), omit paragraph (c) and the "or" immediately before it;

(c) in subsection (4), omit "or the 1980 Act".

(5) In section 56 (co-ordination of exercise of functions by CAA and Director General of Fair Trading), in paragraph (a)(ii), omit "or the 1980 Act".

The Financial Services Act 1986 (c.60)

8. In Schedule 11 to the Financial Services Act 1986, in paragraph 12—

(a) in sub-paragraph (1), omit "126";

(b) omit sub-paragraph (2).

The Companies Consolidation (Consequential Provisions) (Northern Ireland) Order 1986 (S.I. 1986/1035 (N.I. 9))

9. In Part II of Schedule 1 to the Companies Consolidation (Consequential Provisions) (Northern Ireland) Order 1986, omit the entries relating to the Restrictive Trade Practices Act 1976 and the Resale Prices Act 1976.

The Consumer Protection Act 1987 (c.43)

10. In section 38(3) of the Consumer Protection Act 1987 (restrictions on disclosure of information)—

(a) omit paragraphs (e) and (f); and

(b) after paragraph (o), insert—

"(p) the Competition Act 1998."

The Channel Tunnel Act 1987 (c.53)

11. In section 33 of the Channel Tunnel Act 1987—

(a) in subsection (2), omit paragraph (c) and the "and" immediately before it;

(b) in subsection (5), omit paragraphs (b) and (c).

The Road Traffic (Consequential Provisions) Act 1988 (c.54)

12. In Schedule 3 to the Road Traffic (Consequential Provisions) Act 1988 (consequential amendments), omit paragraph 19.

The Companies Act 1989 (c.40)

13. In Schedule 20 to the Companies Act 1989 (amendments about mergers and related matters), omit paragraphs 21 to 24.

The Broadcasting Act 1990 (c.42)

14.—(1) The Broadcasting Act 1990 is amended as follows.
(2) In section 193 (modification of networking arrangements in consequence of reports under competition legislation)—

(a) in subsection (2), omit paragraph (c) and the "and" immediately before it;

(b) in subsection (4), omit "or the Competition Act 1980".

(3) In Schedule 4 (which makes provision for references to the Director or the Competition Commission in respect of networking arrangements), in paragraph 4, for sub-paragraph (7) substitute—

"(7) The provisions mentioned in sub-paragraph (7A) are to apply in relation to references under this paragraph as if—

(a) the functions of the Competition Commission in relation to those references were functions under the Fair Trading Act 1973;
(b) the expression "merger reference" included a reference under this paragraph.

(7A) The provisions are—

(a) section 85 of the Fair Trading Act 1973 (attendance of witnesses and production of documents);
(b) Part II of Schedule 7 to the Competition Act 1998 (performance of the Competition Commission's general functions); and
(c) section 24 of the Competition Act 1980 (modification of provisions about performance of such functions)."

The Tribunals and Inquiries Act 1992 (c.53)

15. In Schedule 1 to the Tribunals and Inquiries Act 1992 (tribunals under the supervision of the Council on Tribunals), after paragraph 9, insert—

"Competition
9A. An appeal tribunal established under section 48 of the Competition Act 1998."

The Osteopaths Act 1993 (c.21)

16. Section 33 of the Osteopaths Act 1993 (competition and anti-competitive practices) is amended as follows—

(a) in subsection (4), omit paragraph (b) and the "or" immediately before it;

(b) in subsection (5), omit "or section 10 of the Act of 1980".

The Chiropractors Act 1994 (c.17)

17. Section 33 of the Chiropractors Act 1994 (competition and anti-competitive practices) is amended as follows—

(a) in subsection (4), omit paragraph (b) and the "or" immediately before it;

(b) in subsection (5), omit "or section 10 of the Act of 1980".

The Coal Industry Act 1994 (c. 21)

18. In section 59(4) of the Coal Industry Act 1994 (information to be kept confidential by the Coal Authority)—

(a) omit paragraphs (e) and (f); and

(b) after paragraph (m), insert—

"(n) the Competition Act 1998."

The Deregulation and Contracting Out Act 1994 (c.40)

19.—(1) The Deregulation and Contracting Out Act 1994 is amended as follows.
(2) Omit—

(a) section 10 (restrictive trade practices: non-notifiable agreements); and

(b) section 11 (registration of commercially sensitive information).

(3) In section 12 (anti-competitive practices: competition references), omit subsections (1) to (6).
(4) In Schedule 4, omit paragraph 1.
(5) In Schedule 11 (miscellaneous deregulatory provisions: consequential amendments), in paragraph 4, omit sub-paragraphs (3) to (7).

The Airports (Northern Ireland) Order 1994 (S.I. 1994/426 (N.I. 1))

20.—(1) The Airports (Northern Ireland) Order 1994 is amended as follows.
(2) In Article 35 (which makes provision about references by the CAA to the Competition Commission), for paragraph (3) substitute—

"(3) The provisions mentioned in paragraph (3A) are to apply in relation to references under Article 34 as if—

(a) the functions of the Competition Commission in relation to those references were functions under the 1973 Act;
(b) the expression "merger reference" included a reference under that Article;
(c) in section 70 of the 1973 Act—

(i) references to the Secretary of State were references to the Director, and
(ii) the reference to three months were a reference to six months.

(3A) The provisions are—

(a) sections 70 (time limit for report on merger) and 85 (attendance of witnesses and production of documents) of the 1973 Act;

(b) Part II of Schedule 7 to the Competition Act 1998 (performance of the Competition Commission's general functions); and

(c) section 24 of the 1980 Act (modification of provisions about performance of such functions)."

(3) In Article 36, omit paragraph (3) (which falls with the repeal of the Restrictive Trade Practices Act 1976).

(4) In Article 45 (orders under the 1973 Act or 1980 Act modifying or revoking conditions)—

(a) in paragraph (1), omit "or section 10(2)(a) of the 1980 Act";

(b) in paragraph (3), omit sub-paragraph (c) and the "or" immediately before it;

(c) in paragraph (4), omit "or the 1980 Act".

(5) In Article 47 (co-ordination of exercise of functions by CAA and Director of Fair Trading), in paragraph (a)(ii), omit "or the 1980 Act".

(6) In Schedule 9, omit paragraph 5 (which amends the Restrictive Trade Practices Act 1976).

The Broadcasting Act 1996 (c.55)

21. In section 77 of the Broadcasting Act 1996 (which modifies the Restrictive Trade Practices Act 1976 in its application to agreements relating to Channel 3 news provision), omit subsection (2).

SCHEDULE 13

Section 74(2)

TRANSITIONAL PROVISIONS AND SAVINGS

PART I

General

Interpretation

1.—(1) In this Schedule—

"RPA" means the Resale Prices Act 1976;
"RTPA" means the Restrictive Trade Practices Act 1976;
"continuing proceedings" has the meaning given by paragraph 15;
"the Court" means the Restrictive Practices Court;
"Director" means the Director General of Fair Trading;
"document" includes information recorded in any form;
"enactment date" means the date on which this Act is passed;
"information" includes estimates and forecasts;
"interim period" means the period beginning on the enactment date and ending immediately before the starting date;
"prescribed" means prescribed by an order made by the Secretary of State;
"regulator" means any person mentioned in paragraphs (a) to (g) of paragraph 1 of Schedule 10;
"starting date" means the date on which section 2 comes into force;
"transitional period" means the transitional period provided for in Chapters III and IV of Part IV of this Schedule.

(2) Sections 30, 44, 51, 53, 55, 56, 57 and 59(3) and (4) and paragraph 12 of Schedule 9 ("the applied provisions") apply for the purposes of this Schedule as they apply for the purposes of Part I of this Act.

(3) Section 2(5) applies for the purposes of any provisions of this Schedule which are concerned with the operation of the Chapter I prohibition as it applies for the purposes of Part I of this Act.

(4) In relation to any of the matters in respect of which a regulator may exercise powers as a result of paragraph 35(1), the applied provisions are to have effect as if references to the Director included references to the regulator.

(5) The fact that to a limited extent the Chapter I prohibition does not apply to an agreement, because a transitional period is provided by virtue of this Schedule, does not require those provisions of the agreement in respect of which there is a transitional period to be disregarded when considering whether the agreement infringes the prohibition for other reasons.

General power to make transitional provision and savings

2.—(1) Nothing in this Schedule affects the power of the Secretary of State under section 75 to make transitional provisions or savings.

(2) An order under that section may modify any provision made by this Schedule.

Advice and information

3.—(1) The Director may publish advice and information explaining provisions of this Schedule to persons who are likely to be affected by them.

(2) Any advice or information published by the Director under this paragraph is to be published in such form and manner as he considers appropriate.

PART II

DURING THE INTERIM PERIOD

Block exemptions

4.—(1) The Secretary of State may, at any time during the interim period, make one or more orders for the purpose of providing block exemptions which are effective on the starting date.

(2) An order under this paragraph has effect as if properly made under section 6.

Certain agreements to be non-notifiable agreements

5. An agreement which—

(a) is made during the interim period, and

(b) satisfies the conditions set out in paragraphs (a), (c) and (d) of section 27A(1) of the RTPA.

is to be treated as a non-notifiable agreement for the purposes of the RTPA.

Application of RTPA during the interim period

6. In relation to agreements made during the interim period—

(a) the Director is no longer under the duty to take proceedings imposed by section 1(2)(c) of the RTPA but may continue to do so;

(b)   section 21 of that Act has effect as if subsections (1) and (2) were omitted; and

(c)   section 35(1) of that Act has effect as if the words "or within such further time as the Director may, upon application made within that time, allow" were omitted.

Guidance

7.—(1) Sub-paragraphs (2) to (4) apply in relation to agreements made during the interim period.

(2) An application may be made to the Director in anticipation of the coming into force of section 13 in accordance with directions given by the Director and such an application is to have effect on and after the starting date as if properly made under section 13.

(3) The Director may, in response to such an application—

(a)   give guidance in anticipation of the coming into force of section 2; or

(b)   on and after the starting date, give guidance under section 15 as if the application had been properly made under section 13.

(4) Any guidance so given is to have effect on and after the starting date as if properly given under section 15.

PART III

ON THE STARTING DATE

Applications which fall

8.—(1) Proceedings in respect of an application which is made to the Court under any of the provisions mentioned in sub-paragraph (2), but which is not determined before the starting date, cease on that date.

(2) The provisions are—

(a)   sections 2(2), 35(3), 37(1) and 40(1) of the RTPA and paragraph 5 of Schedule 4 to that Act;

(b)   section 4(1) of the RTPA so far as the application relates to an order under section 2(2) of that Act; and

(c)   section 25(2) of the RPA.

(3) The power of the Court to make an order for costs in relation to any proceedings is not affected by anything in this paragraph or by the repeals made by section 1.

Orders and approvals which fall

9.—(1) An order in force immediately before the starting date under—

(a)   section 2(2), 29(1), 30(1), 33(4), 35(3) or 37(1) of the RTPA; or

(b)   section 25(2) of the RPA,

ceases to have effect on that date.

(2) An approval in force immediately before the starting date under section 32 of the RTPA ceases to have effect on that date.

PART IV

ON AND AFTER THE STARTING DATE

CHAPTER I

GENERAL

Duty of Director to maintain register etc.

10.—(1) This paragraph applies even though the relevant provisions of the RTPA are repealed by this Act.

(2) The Director is to continue on and after the starting date to be under the duty imposed by section 1(2)(a) of the RTPA to maintain a register in respect of agreements—

(a) particulars of which are, on the starting date, entered or filed on the register;

(b) which fall within sub-paragraph (4);

(c) which immediately before the starting date are the subject of proceedings under the RTPA which do not cease on that date by virtue of this Schedule; or

(d) in relation to which a court gives directions to the Director after the starting date in the course of proceedings in which a question arises as to whether an agreement was, before that date—

(i) one to which the RTPA applied;

(ii) subject to registration under that Act;

(iii) a non-notifiable agreement for the purposes of that Act.

(3) The Director is to continue on and after the starting date to be under the duties imposed by section 1(2)(a) and (b) of the RTPA of compiling a register of agreements and entering or filing certain particulars in the register, but only in respect of agreements of a kind referred to in paragraph (b), (c) or (d) of sub-paragraph (2).

(4) An agreement falls within this sub-paragraph if—

(a) it is subject to registration under the RTPA but—

(i) is not a non-notifiable agreement within the meaning of section 27A of the RTPA, or

(ii) is not one to which paragraph 5 applies;

(b) particulars of the agreement have been provided to the Director before the starting date; and

(c) as at the starting date no entry or filing has been made in the register in respect of the agreement.

(5) Sections 23 and 27 of the RTPA are to apply after the starting date in respect of the register subject to such modifications, if any, as may be prescribed.

(6) In sub-paragraph (2)(d) "court" means —

(a)   the High Court;

(b)   the Court of Appeal;

(c)   the Court of Session;

(d)   the High Court of Court of Appeal in Northern Ireland; or

(e)   the House of Lords.

RTPA section 3 applications

11.—(1) Even though section 3 of the RTPA is repealed by this Act, its provisions (and so far as necessary that Act) are to continue to apply, with such modifications (if any) as may be prescribed—

(a)   in relation to a continuing application under that section; or

(b)   so as to allow an application to be made under that section on or after the starting date in respect of a continuing application under section 1(3) of the RTPA.

(2) "Continuing application" means an application made, but not determined, before the starting date.

RTPA section 26 applications

12.—(1) Even though section 26 of the RTPA is repealed by this Act, its provisions (and so far as necessary that Act) are to continue to apply, with such modifications (if any) as may be prescribed, in relation to an application which is made under that section, but not determined, before the starting date.

(2) If an application under section 26 is determined on or after the starting date, this Schedule has effect in relation to the agreement concerned as if the application had been determined immediately before that date.

Right to bring civil proceedings

13.—(1) Even though section 35 of the RTPA is repealed by this Act, its provisions (and so far as necessary that Act) are to continue to apply in respect of a person who, immediately before the starting date, has a right by virtue of section 27ZA or 35(2) of that Act to bring civil proceedings in respect of an agreement (but only so far as that right relates to any period before the starting date or, where there are continuing proceedings, the determination of the proceedings).

(2) Even though section 25 of the RPA is repealed by this Act, the provisions of that section (and so far as necessary that Act) are to continue to apply in respect of a person who, immediately before the starting date, has a right by virtue of subsection (3) of that section to bring civil proceedings (but only so far as that right relates to any period before the starting date or, where there are continuing proceedings, the determination of the proceedings).

CHAPTER II

CONTINUING PROCEEDINGS

The general rule

14.—(1) The Chapter I prohibition does not apply to an agreement at any time when the agreement is the subject of continuing proceedings under the RTPA.

(2) The Chapter I prohibition does not apply to an agreement relating to goods which are the subject to continuing proceedings under section 16 or 17 of the RPA to the extent to which the agreement consists of exempt provisions.

(3) In sub-paragraph (2) "exempt provisions" means those provisions of the agreement which would, disregarding section 14 of the RPA, be—

(a) void as a result of section 9(1) of the RPA; or

(b) unlawful as a result of section 9(2) or 11 of the RPA.

(4) If the Chapter I prohibition does not apply to an agreement because of this paragraph, the provisions of, or made under, the RTPA or the RPA are to continue to have effect in relation to the agreement.

(5) The repeals made by section 1 do not affect—

(a) continuing proceedings; or

(b) proceedings of the kind referred to in paragraph 11 or 12 of this Schedule which are continuing after the starting date.

Meaning of "continuing proceedings"

15.—(1) For the purposes of this Schedule "continuing proceedings" means proceedings in respect of an application made to the Court under the RTPA or the RPA, but not determined, before the starting date.

(2) But proceedings under section 3 or 26 of the RTPA to which paragraph 11 or 12 applies are not continuing proceedings.

(3) The question whether (for the purposes of Part III, or this Part, of this Schedule) an application has been determined is to be decided in accordance with sub-paragraphs (4) and (5).

(4) If an appeal against the decision on the application is brought, the application is not determined until—

(a) the appeal is disposed of or withdrawn; or

(b) if as a result of the appeal the case is referred back to the Court—

    (i) the expiry of the period within which an appeal ("the further appeal") in respect of the Court's decision on that reference could have been brought had this Act not been passed; or

    (ii) if later, the date on which the further appeal is disposed of or withdrawn.

(5) Otherwise, the application is not determined until the expiry of the period within which any party to the application would have been able to bring an appeal against the decision on the application had this Act not been passed.

RTPA section 4 proceedings

16. Proceedings on an application for an order under section 4 of the RTPA are also continuing proceedings if—

(a) leave to make the application is applied for before the starting date but the proceedings in respect of that application for leave are not determined before that date; or

(b) leave to make an application for an order under that section is granted before the starting date but the application itself is not made before that date.

RPA section 16 or 17 proceedings

17. Proceedings on an application for an order under section 16 or 17 of the RPA are also continuing proceedings if—

(a) leave to make the application is applied for before the starting date but the proceedings in respect of that application for leave are not determined before that date; or

(b) leave to make an application for an order under section 16 or 17 of the RPA is granted before the starting date, but the application itself is not made before that date.

Continuing proceedings which are discontinued

18.—(1) On an application made jointly to the Court by all the parties to any continuing proceedings, the Court must, if it is satisfied that the parties wish it to do so, discontinue the proceedings.

(2) If, on an application under sub-paragraph (1) or for any other reason, the Court orders the proceedings to be discontinued, this Schedule has effect (subject to paragraphs 21 and 22) from the date on which the proceedings are discontinued as if they had never been instituted.

CHAPTER III

THE TRANSITIONAL PERIOD

The general rule

19.—(1) Except where this Chapter or Chapter IV provides otherwise, there is a transitional period, beginning on the starting date and lasting for one year, for any agreement made before the starting date.

(2) The Chapter I prohibition does not apply to an agreement to the extent to which there is a transitional period for the agreement.

(3) The Secretary of State may by regulations provide for sections 13 to 16 and Schedule 5 to apply with such modifications (if any) as may be specified in the regulations, in respect of applications to the Director about agreements for which there is a transitional period.

Cases for which there is no transitional period

20.—(1) There is no transitional period for an agreement to the extent to which, immediately before the starting date, it is—

(a) void under section 2(1) or 35(1)(a) of the RTPA;

(b) the subject of an order under section 2(2) or 35(3) of the RTPA; or

(c) unlawful under section 1, 2 or 11 of the RPA or void under section 9 of that Act.

(2) There is no transitional period for an agreement to the extent to which, before the starting date, a person has acted unlawfully for the purposes of section 27ZA(2) or (3) of the RTPA in respect of the agreement.

(3) There is no transitional period for an agreement to which paragraph 25(4) applies.

(4) There is no transitional period for—

(a) an agreement in respect of which there are continuing proceedings, or

(b) an agreement relating to goods in respect of which there are continuing proceedings,

to the extent to which the agreement is, when the proceedings are determined, void or unlawful.

Continuing proceedings under the RTPA

21. In the case of an agreement which is the subject of continuing proceedings under the RTPA, the transitional period begins—

(a) if the proceedings are discontinued, on the date of discontinuance;

(b) otherwise, when the proceedings are determined.

Continuing proceedings under the RPA

22.—(1) In the case of an agreement relating to goods which are the subject of continuing proceedings under the RPA, the transitional period for the exempt provisions of the agreement begins—

(a) if the proceedings are discontinued, on the date of discontinuance;

(b) otherwise, when the proceedings are determined.

(2) In sub-paragraph (1) "exempt provisions" has the meaning given by paragraph 14(3).

Provisions not contrary to public interest

23.—(1) To the extent to which an agreement contains provisions which, immediately before the starting date, are provisions which the Court has found not to be contrary to the public interest, the transitional period lasts for five years.

(2) Sub-paragraph (1) is subject to paragraph 20(4).

(3) To the extent to which an agreement which on the starting date is the subject of continuing proceedings is, when the proceedings are determined, found by the Court not to be contrary to the public interest, the transitional period lasts for five years.

Goods

24.—(1) In the case of an agreement relating to goods which, immediately before the starting date, are exempt under section 14 of the RPA, there is a transitional period for the agreement to the extent to which it consists of exempt provisions.

(2) Sub-paragraph (1) is subject to paragraph 20(4).

(3) In the case of an agreement relating to goods—

(a) which on the starting date are the subject of continuing proceedings, and

(b) which, when the proceedings are determined, are found to be exempt under section 14 of the RPA,

there is a transitional period for the agreement, to the extent to which it consists of exempt provisions.

(4) In each case, the transitional period lasts for five years.

(5) In sub-paragraphs (1) and (3) "exempt provisions" means those provisions of the agreement which would, disregarding section 14 of the RPA, be—

(a) void as a result of section 9(1) of the RPA; or

(b) unlawful as a result of section 9(2) or 11 of the RPA.

Transitional period for certain agreements

25.—(1) This paragraph applies to agreements—

(a) which are subject to registration under the RTPA but which—

(i) are not non-notifiable agreements within the meaning of section 27A of the RTPA, or

(ii) are not agreements to which paragraph 5 applies; and

(b) in respect of which the time for furnishing relevant particulars as required by or under the RTPA expires on or after the starting date.

(2) "Relevant particulars" means—

(a) particulars which are required to be furnished by virtue of section 24 of the RTPA; or

(b) particulars of any variation of an agreement which are required to be furnished by virtue of sections 24 and 27 of the RTPA.

(3) There is a transitional period of one year for an agreement to which this paragraph applies if—

(a) relevant particulars are furnished before the starting date; and

(b) no person has acted unlawfully (for the purposes of section 27ZA(2) or (3) of the RTPA) in respect of the agreement.

(4) If relevant particulars are not furnished by the starting date, section 35(1)(a) of the RTPA does not apply in relation to the agreement (unless subparagraph (5) applies).

(5) This sub-paragraph applies if a person falling within section 27ZA(2) or (3) of the RTPA has acted unlawfully for the purposes of those subsections in respect of the agreement.

Special cases

26.—(1) In the case of an agreement in respect of which—

(a) a direction under section 127(2) of the Financial Services Act 1986 ("the 1986 Act") is in force immediately before the starting date, or

(b) a direction under section 194A(3) of the Broadcasting Act 1990 ("the 1990 Act") is in force immediately before the starting date,

the transitional period lasts for five years.

(2) To the extent to which an agreement is the subject of a declaration—

(a) made by the Treasury under section 127(3) of the 1986 Act, and

(b) in force immediately before the starting date,

the transitional period lasts for five years.

(3) Sub-paragraphs (1) and (2) do not affect the power of—

(a) the Treasury to make a declaration under section 127(2) of the 1986 Act (as amended by Schedule 2 to this Act),

(b) the Secretary of State to make a declaration under section 194A of the 1990 Act (as amended by Schedule 2 to this Act),

in respect of an agreement for which there is a transitional period.

CHAPTER IV

THE UTILITIES

General

27. In this Chapter "the relevant period" means the period beginning with the starting date and ending immediately before the fifth anniversary of the date.

Electricity

28.—(1) For an agreement to which, immediately before the starting date, the RTPA does not apply by virtue of a section 100 order, there is a transitional period—

(a) beginning on the starting date; and

(b) ending at the end of the relevant period.

(2) For an agreement which is made at any time after the starting date and to which, had the RTPA not been repealed, that Act would not at the time at which the agreement is made have applied by virtue of a section 100 order, there is a transitional period—

(a) beginning on the date on which the agreement is made; and

(b) ending at the end of the relevant period.

(3) For an agreement (whether made before or after the starting date) which, during the relevant period, is varied at any time in such a way that it becomes an agreement which, had the RTPA not been repealed, would at that time have been one to which that Act did not apply by virtue of a section 100 order, there is a transitional period—

(a) beginning on the date on which the variation is made; and

(b) ending at the end of the relevant period.

(4) If an agreement for which there is a transitional period as a result of subparagraph (1), (2) or (3) is varied during the relevant period, the transitional period for the agreement continues if, had the RTPA not been repealed, the agreement would have continued to be one to which that Act did not apply by virtue of a section 100 order.

(5) But if an agreement for which there is a transitional period as a result of sub-paragraph (1), (2) or (3) ceases to be one to which, had it not been repealed, the RTPA would not have applied by virtue of a section 100 order, the transitional period ends on the date on which the agreement so ceases.

(6) Sub-paragraph (3) is subject to paragraph 20.

(7) In this paragraph and paragraph 29—

   "section 100 order" means an order made under section 100 of the Electricity Act 1989; and

expressions which are also used in Part I of the Electricity Act 1989 have the same meaning as in that Part.

Electricity: power to make transitional orders

29.—(1) There is a transitional period for an agreement (whether made before or after the starting date) relating to the generation, transmission or supply of electricity which—

(a) is specified, or is of a description specified, in an order ("a transitional order") made by the Secretary of State (whether before or after the making of the agreement but before the end of the relevant period); and

(b) satisfies such conditions as may be specified in the order.

(2) A transitional order may make provision as to when the transitional period in respect of such an agreement is to start or to be deemed to have started.

(3) The transitional period for such an agreement ends at the end of the relevant period.

(4) But if the agreement—

(a) ceases to be one to which a transitional order applies, or

(b) ceases to satisfy one or more of the conditions specified in the transitional order,

the transitional period ends on the date on which the agreement so ceases.

(5) Before making a transitional order, the Secretary of State must consult the Director General of Electricity Supply and the Director.

(6) The conditions specified in a transitional order may include conditions which refer any matter to the Secretary of State for determination after such consultation as may be so specified.

(7) In the application of this paragraph to Northern Ireland, the reference in sub-paragraph (5) to the Director General of Electricity Supply is to be read as a reference to the Director General of Electricity Supply for Northern Ireland.

Gas

30.—(1) For an agreement to which, immediately before the starting date, the RTPA does not apply by virtue of section 62 or a section 62 order, there is a transitional period—

    (a) beginning on the starting date; and

    (b) ending at the end of the relevant period.

(2) For an agreement which is made at any time after the starting date and to which, had the RTPA not been repealed, that Act would not at the time at which the agreement is made have applied by virtue of section 62 or a section 62 order, there is a transitional period—

    (a) beginning on the date on which the agreement is made; and

    (b) ending at the end of the relevant period.

(3) For an agreement (whether made before or after the starting date) which, during the relevant period, is varied at any time in such a way that it becomes an agreement which, had the RTPA not been repealed, would at that time have been one to which that Act did not apply by virtue of section 62 or a section 62 order, there is a transitional period—

    (a) beginning on the date on which the variation is made; and

    (b) ending at the end of the relevant period.

(4) If an agreement for which there is a transitional period as a result of subparagraph (1), (2) or (3) is varied during the relevant period, the transitional period for the agreement continues if, had the RTPA not been repealed, the agreement would have continued to be one to which that Act did not apply by virtue of section 62 or a section 62 order.

(5) But if an agreement for which there is a transitional period as a result of sub-paragraph (1), (2) or (3) ceases to be one to which, had it not been repealed, the RTPA would not have applied by virtue of section 62 or a section 62 order, the transitional period end on the date on which the agreement so ceases.

(6) Sub-paragraph (3) also applies in relation to a modification which is treated as an agreement made on or after 28th November 1985 by virtue of section 62(4).

(7) Sub-paragraph (3) is subject to paragraph 20.

(8) In this paragraph and paragraph 31—

    "section 62" means section 62 of the Gas Act 1986;
    "section 62 order" means an order made under section 62.

Gas: power to make transitional orders

31.—(1) There is a transitional period for an agreement of a description falling within section 62(2)(a) and (b) or section 62(2A)(a) and (b) which—

    (a) is specified, or is of a description specified, in an order ("a transitional order") made by the Secretary of State (whether before or after the making of the agreement but before the end of the relevant period); and

    (b) satisfies such conditions as may be specified in the order.

(2) A transitional order may make provision as to when the transitional period in respect of such an agreement is to start or to be deemed to have started.

(3) The transitional period for such an agreement ends at the end of the relevant period.
(4) But if the agreement—

(a) ceases to be one to which a transitional order applies, or

(b) ceases to satisfy one or more of the conditions specified in the transitional order,

the transitional period ends on the date when the agreement so ceases.
(5) Before making a transitional order, the Secretary of State must consult the Director General of Gas Supply and the Director.
(6) The conditions specified in a transitional order may include—

(a) conditions which are to be satisfied in relation to a time before the coming into force of this paragraph;

(b) conditions which refer any matter (which may be the general question whether the Chapter I prohibition should apply to a particular agreement) to the Secretary of State, the Director or the Director General of Gas Supply for determination after such consultation as may be so specified.

Gas: Northern Ireland

32.—(1) For an agreement to which, immediately before the starting date, the RTPA does not apply by virtue of an Article 41 order, there is a transitional period—

(a) beginning on the starting date; and

(b) ending at the end of the relevant period.

(2) For an agreement which is made at any time after the starting date and to which, had the RTPA not been repealed, that Act would not at the time at which the agreement is made have applied by virtue of an Article 41 order, there is a transitional period—

(a) beginning on the date on which the agreement is made; and

(b) ending at the end of the relevant period.

(3) For an agreement (whether made before or after the starting date) which, during the relevant period, is varied at any time in such a way that it becomes an agreement which, had the RTPA not been repealed, would at that time have been one to which that Act did not apply by virtue of an Article 41 order, there is a transitional period—

(a) beginning on the date on which the variation is made; and

(b) ending at the end of the relevant period.

(4) If an agreement for which there is a transitional period as a result of sub-paragraph (1), (2) or (3) is varied during the relevant period, the transitional period for the agreement continues if, had the RTPA not been repealed, the agreement would have continued to be one to which that Act did not apply by virtue of an Article 41 order.

(5) But if an agreement for which there is a transitional period as a result of sub-paragraph (1), (2) or (3) ceases to be one to which, had it not been repealed, the RTPA would not have applied by virtue of an Article 41 order, the transitional period ends on the date on which the agreement so ceases.

(6) Sub-paragraph (3) is subject to paragraph 20.

(7) In this paragraph and paragraph 33—

"Article 41 order" means an order under Article 41 of the Gas (Northern Ireland) Order 1996;

"Department" means the Department of Economic Development.

Gas: Northern Ireland - power to make transitional orders

33.—(1) There is a transitional period for an agreement of a description falling within Article 41(1) which—

(a) is specified, or is of a description specified, in an order ("a transitional order") made by the Department (whether before or after the making of the agreement but before the end of the relevant period); and

(b) satisfies such conditions as may be specified in the order.

(2) A transitional order may make provision as to when the transitional period in respect of such an agreement is to start or to be deemed to have started.

(3) The transitional period for such an agreement ends at the end of the relevant period.

(4) But if the agreement—

(a) ceases to be one to which a transitional order applies, or

(b) ceases to satisfy one or more of the conditions specified in the transitional order,

the transitional period ends on the date when the agreement so ceases.

(5) Before making a transitional order, the Department must consult the Director General of Gas for Northern Ireland and the Director.

(6) The conditions specified in a transitional order may include conditions which refer any matter (which may be the general question whether the Chapter I prohibition should apply to a particular agreement) to the Department for determination after such consultation as may be so specified.

Railways

34.—(1) In this paragraph—

"section 131" means section 131 of the Railways Act 1993 ("the 1993 Act");

"section 131 agreement" means an agreement—

(a) to which the RTPA does not apply immediately before the starting date by virtue of section 131(1); or

(b) in respect of which a direction under section 131(3) is in force immediately before that date;

"non-exempt agreement" means an agreement relating to the provision of railway services (whether made before or after the starting date) which is not a section 131 agreement; and

"railway services" has the meaning given by section 82 of the 1993 Act.

(2) For a section 131 agreement there is a transitional period of five years.

(3) There is a transitional period for a non-exempt agreement to the extent to which the agreement is at any time before the end of the relevant period required or approved—

(a) by the Secretary of State or the Rail Regulator in pursuance of any function assigned or transferred to him under or by virtue of any provision of the 1993 Act;

(b) by or under any agreement the making of which is required or approved by the Secretary of State or the Rail Regulator in the exercise of any such function; or

(c) by or under a licence granted under Part I of the 1993 Act.

(4) The transitional period conferred by sub-paragraph (3)—

(a) is to be taken to have begun on the starting date; and

(b) ends at the end of the relevant period.

(5) Sub-paragraph (3) is subject to paragraph 20.

(6) Any variation of a section 131 agreement on or after the starting date is to be treated, for the purposes of this paragraph, as a separate non-exempt agreement.

The regulators

35.—(1) Subject to sub-paragraph (3), each of the regulators may exercise, in respect of sectoral matters and concurrently with the Director, the functions of the Director under paragraph 3, 7, 19(3), 36, 37, 38 or 39.

(2) In sub-paragraph (1) "sectoral matters" means—

(a) in the case of the Director General of Telecommunications, the matters referred to in section 50(3) of the Telecommunications Act 1984;

(b) in the case of the Director General of Gas Supply, the matters referred to in section 36A(3) and (4) of the Gas Act 1986;

(c) in the case of the Director General of Electricity Supply, the matters referred to in section 43(3) of the Electricity Act 1989;

(d) in the case of the Director General of Electricity Supply for Northern Ireland, the matters referred to in Article 46(3) of the Electricity (Northern Ireland) Order 1992;

(e) in the case of the Director General of Water Services, the matters referred to in section 31(3) of the Water Industry Act 1991;

(f) in the case of the Rail Regulator, the matters referred to in section 67(3) of the Railways Act 1993;

(g) in the case of the Director General of Gas for Northern Ireland, the matters referred to in Article 23(3) of the Gas (Northern Ireland) Order 1996.

(3) The power to give directions in paragraph 7(2) is exercisable by the Director only but if the Director is preparing directions which relate to a matter in respect of which a regulator exercises concurrent jurisdiction, he must consult that regulator.

(4) Consultations conducted by the Director before the enactment date, with a view to preparing directions which have effect on or after that date, are to be taken to satisfy sub-paragraph (3).

(5) References to enactments in sub-paragraph (2) are to the enactments as amended by or under this Act.

CHAPTER V

EXTENDING THE TRANSITIONAL PERIOD

36.—(1) A party to an agreement for which there is a transitional period may apply to the Director, not less than three months before the end of the period, for the period to be extended.

(2) The Director may (on his own initiative or on an application under sub-paragraph (1))—

(a) extend a one-year transitional period by not more than twelve months;

(b) extend a transitional period of any period other than one year by not more than six months.

(3) An application under sub-paragraph (1) must—

(a) be in such form as may be specified; and

(b) include such documents and information as may be specified.

(4) If the Director extends the transitional period under this paragraph, he must give notice in such form, and to such persons, as may be specified.

(5) The Director may not extend a transitional period more than once.

(6) In this paragraph—

"person" has the same meaning as in Part I; and
"specified" means specified in rules made by the Director under section 51.

CHAPTER VI

TERMINATING THE TRANSITIONAL PERIOD

General

37.—(1) Subject to sub-paragraph (2), the Director may by a direction in writing terminate the transitional period for an agreement, but only in accordance with paragraph 38.

(2) The Director may not terminate the transitional period, nor exercise any of the powers in paragraph 38, in respect of an agreement which is excluded from the Chapter I prohibition by virtue of any of the provisions of Part I of this Act other than paragraph 1 of Schedule 1 or paragraph 2 or 9 of Schedule 3 or the Competition Act 1998 (Land and Vertical Agreements Exclusion) Order 2000.

Circumstances in which the Director may terminate the transitional period

38.—(1) If the Director is considering whether to give a direction under paragraph 37 ("a direction"), he may in writing require any party to the agreement concerned to give him such information in connection with that agreement as he may require.

(2) If at the end of such period as may be specified in rules made under section 51, a person has failed, without reasonable excuse, to comply with a requirement imposed under sub-paragraph (1), the Director may give a direction.

(3) The Director may also give a direction if he considers—

(a) that the agreement would, but for the transitional period or a relevant exclusion, infringe the Chapter I prohibition; and

(b) that he would not be likely to grant the agreement an unconditional individual exemption.

(4) For the purposes of sub-paragraph (3) an individual exemption is unconditional if no conditions or obligations are imposed in respect of it under section 4(3)(a).

(5) In this paragraph—

"person" has the same meaning as in Part I;
"relevant exclusion" means an exclusion under paragraph 1 of Schedule 1 or paragraph 2 or 9 of Schedule 3.

Procedural requirements on giving a paragraph 37 direction

39.—(1) The Director must specify in a direction under paragraph 37 ("a direction") the date on which it is to have effect (which must not be less than 28 days after the direction is given).

(2) Copies of the direction must be given to—

(a) each of the parties concerned, and

(b) the Secretary of State,

not less than 28 days before the date on which the direction is to have effect.

(3) In relation to an agreement to which a direction applies, the transitional period (if it has not already ended) ends on the date specified in the direction unless, before that date, the direction is revoked by the Director or the Secretary of State.

(4) If a direction is revoked, the Director may give a further direction in respect of the same agreement only if he is satisfied that there has been a material change of circumstance since the revocation.

(5) If, as a result of paragraph 24(1) or (3), there is a transitional period in respect of provisions of an agreement relating to goods—

(a) which immediately before the starting date are exempt under section 14 of the RPA, or

(b) which, when continuing proceedings are determined, are found to be exempt under section 14 of the RPA,

the period is not affected by paragraph 37 or 38.

PART V

THE FAIR TRADING ACT 1973

References to the Monopolies and Mergers Commission

40.—(1) If, on the date on which the repeal by this Act of a provision mentioned in sub-paragraph (2) comes into force, the Monopolies and Mergers Commission has not completed a reference which was made to it before that date, continued consideration of the reference may include consideration of a question which could not have been considered if the provision had not been repealed.

(2) The provisions are—

(a) sections 10(2), 54(5) and 78(3) and paragraph 3(1) and (2) of Schedule 8 to the Fair Trading Act 1973 (c.41);

(b) section 11(8)(b) of the Competition Act 1980 (c.21);

(c) section 14(2) of the Telecommunications Act 1984 (c.12);

(d) section 45(3) of the Airports Act 1986 (c. 31);

(e) section 25(2) of the Gas Act 1986 (c. 44);

(f) section 13(2) of the Electricity Act 1989 (c. 29);

(g) section 15(2) of the Water Industry Act 1991 (c. 56);

(h) article 16(2) of the Electricity (Northern Ireland) Order 1992;

(i) section 14(2) of the Railways Act 1993 (c. 43);

(j) article 36(3) of the Airports (Northern Ireland) Order 1994;

(k) article 16(2) of the Gas (Northern Ireland) Order 1996.

Orders under Schedule 8

41.—(1) In this paragraph—

"the 1973 Act" means the Fair Trading Act 1973;

"agreement" means an agreement entered into before the date on which the repeal of the limiting provisions comes into force;

"the order" means an order under section 56 or 73 of the 1973 Act;

"the limiting provisions" means sub-paragraph (1) or (2) of paragraph 3 of Schedule 8 to the 1973 Act (limit on power to make orders under paragraph 1 or 2 of that Schedule) and includes any provisions of the order included because of either of those sub-paragraphs; and

"transitional period" means the period which—

(a) begins on the day on which the repeal of the limiting provisions comes into force; and

(b) ends on the first anniversary of the starting date.

(2) Sub-paragraph (3) applies to any agreement to the extent to which it would have been unlawful (in accordance with the provisions of the order) but for the limiting provisions.

(3) As from the end of the transitional period, the order is to have effect in relation to the agreement as if the limiting provisions had never had effect.

Part III of the Act

42.—(1) The repeals made by section 1 do not affect any proceedings in respect of an application which is made to the Court under Part III of the Fair Trading Act 1973, but is not determined, before the starting date.

(2) The question whether (for the purposes of sub-paragraph (1)) an application has been determined is to be decided in accordance with sub-paragraphs (3) and (4).

(3) If an appeal against the decision on the application is brought, the application is not determined until—

(a) the appeal is disposed of or withdrawn; or

(b) if as a result of the appeal the case is referred back to the Court—

(i) the expiry of the period within which an appeal ("the further appeal") in respect of the Court's decision on that reference could have been brought had this Act not been passed; or

(ii) if later, the date on which the further appeal is disposed of or withdrawn.

(4) Otherwise, the application is not determined until the expiry of the period within which any party to the application would have been able to bring an appeal against the decision on the application had this Act not been passed.

(5) Any amendment made by Schedule 12 to this Act which substitutes references to a relevant Court for references to the Court is not to affect proceedings of the kind referred to in sub-paragraph (1).

PART VI

THE COMPETITION ACT 1980

Undertakings

43.—(1) Subject to sub-paragraph (2), an undertaking accepted by the Director under section 4 or 9 of the Competition Act 1980 ceases to have effect on the coming into force of the repeal by this Act of that section.

(2) If the undertaking relates to an agreement which on the starting date is the subject of continuing proceedings, the undertaking continues to have effect for the purposes of section 29 of the Competition Act 1980 until the proceedings are determined.

Application of sections 25 and 26

44. The repeals made by section 1 do not affect—

(a) the operation of section 25 of the Competition Act 1980 in relation to an application under section 1(3) of the RTPA which is made before the starting date;

(b) an application under section 26 of the Competition Act 1980 which is made before the starting date.

PART VII

MISCELLANEOUS

Disclosure of information

45.—(1) Section 55 of this Act applies in relation to information which, immediately before the starting date, is subject to section 41 of the RTPA as it applies in relation to information obtained under or as a result of Part I.

(2) But section 55 does not apply to any disclosure of information of the kind referred to in sub-paragraph (1) if the disclosure is made—

(a) for the purpose of facilitating the performance of functions of a designated person under the Control of Misleading Advertisements Regulations 1988; or

(b) for the purposes of any proceedings before the Court or of any other legal proceedings under the RTPA or the Fair Trading Act 1973 or the Control of Misleading Advertisements Regulations 1988.

(3) Section 56 applies in relation to information of the kind referred to in sub-paragraph (1) if particulars containing the information have been entered or filed on the special section of the register maintained by the Director under, or as a result of, section 27 of the RTPA or paragraph 10 of this Schedule.

(4) Section 55 has effect, in relation to the matters as to which section 41(2) of the RTPA had effect, as if it contained a provision similar to section 41(2).

The Court

46. If it appears to the Lord Chancellor that a person who ceases to be a non-judicial member of the Court as a result of this Act should receive compensation for loss of office, he may pay to him out of moneys provided by Parliament such sum as he may with the approval of the Treasury determine.

Section 74(3)   **SCHEDULE 14**

REPEALS AND REVOCATIONS

PART I

REPEALS

Chapter	Short title	Extent of repeal
1973 c. 41	The Fair Trading Act 1973.	Section 4. Section 10(2). Section 45. Section 54(5). Section 78(3). In section 81(1), in the words before paragraph (a), from "and the Commission" to "of this Act)"; in paragraph (b), "or the Commission, as the case may be" and "or of the Commission"; in subsection (2), "or the Commission" and "or of the Commission" and in subsection (3), from "and, in the case," to "85 of this Act", and "or the Commission, as the case may be,". In section 83, in subsection (1) "Subject to subsection (1A) below" and subsection (1A). In section 135(1), in the words before paragraph (a) and in paragraph (b), "or the Commission", and paragraph (a). Schedule 3. In Schedule 8, paragraph 3(1) and (2).
1976 c. 33	The Restrictive Practices Court Act 1976.	The whole Act.
1976 c. 34	The Restrictive Trade Practices Act 1976.	The whole Act.
1976 c. 53	The Resale Prices Act 1976.	The whole Act.
1976 c. 76	The Energy Act 1976.	Section 5.
1977 c. 19	The Restrictive Trade Practices Act 1977.	The whole Act.
1977 c. 37	The Patents Act 1977.	Sections 44 and 45.
1979 c. 38	The Estate Agents Act 1979.	In section 10(3), "or the Restrictive Trade Practices Act 1976.".
1980 c. 21	The Competition Act 1980.	Sections 2 to 10. In section 11(8), paragraph (b) and the "and" immediately before it. In section 13(1), from "but the giving" to the end.

Chapter	Short title	Extent of repeal
		In section 15, subsections (2)(b), (3) and (4).
		Section 16(3).
		In section 17, "8(1)" in subsections (1) and (3) to (5) and in subsection (2) "8(1) or".
		In section 19(3), paragraph (d).
		In section 19(5)(a), "or in anything published under section 4(2)(a) above".
		Section 22.
		Sections 25 to 30.
		In section 31, subsection (2) and "10" in subsection (3).
		Section 33(3) and (4).
1984 c. 12	The Telecommunications Act 1984.	Section 14(2).
		In section 16(5), the "or" immediately after paragraph (a).
		In section 50(4), paragraph (c) and the "and" immediately after it.
		In section 50(5), "or (3)".
		In section 50(7), "or the 1980 Act".
		In section 95(1), "or section 10(2)(a) of the 1980 Act".
		In section 95(2), paragraph (c) and the "or" immediately before it.
		In section 95(3), "or the 1980 Act".
		In section 101(3), paragraphs (d) and (e).
1986 c. 31	The Airports Act 1986.	Section 45(3).
		In section 54(1), "or section 10(2)(a) of the 1980 Act".
		In section 54(3), paragraph (c) and the "or" immediately before it.
		In section 54(4), "or the 1980 Act".
		In section 56(a)(ii), "or the 1980 Act".
1986 c. 44	The Gas Act 1986.	Section 25(2).
		In section 27(1), "or section 10(2)(a) of the Competition Act 1980".
		In section 27(3)(a), from "or" to "competition reference".
		In section 27(6), "or the said Act of 1980".
		In section 28(5), the "or" immediately after paragraph (aa).
		In section 36A(5), paragraph (d) and the "and" immediately before it.
		In section 36A(6), "or (3)".
		In section 36A(8), "or under the 1980 Act".
		In section 36A(9), "or the 1980 Act".
		In section 42(3), paragraphs (e) and (f).
1986 c. 60	The Financial Services Act 1986.	Section 126.
1987 c. 43	The Consumer Protection Act 1987.	In section 38(3), paragraphs (e) and (f).

Chapter	Short title	Extent of repeal
1987 c. 53	The Channel Tunnel Act 1987.	In section 33(2), paragraph (c) and the "and" immediately before it. In section 33(5), paragraphs (b) and (c).
1988 c. 54	The Road Traffic (Consequential Provisions) Act 1988.	In Schedule 3, paragraph 19.
1989 c. 15	The Water Act 1989.	In section 174(3), paragraphs (d) and (e).
1989 c. 29	The Electricity Act 1989.	Section 13(2). In section 15(1), paragraph (b) and the "or" immediately before it. In section 15(2), paragraph (c) and the "or" immediately before it. In section 15(3), "or the 1980 Act". In section 25(5), the "or" immediately after paragraph (b). In section 43(4), paragraph (c) and the "and" immediately after it. In section 43(5), "or (3)". In section 43(7), "or the 1980 Act". In section 57(3), paragraphs (d) and (e).
1989 c. 40	The Companies Act 1989.	In Schedule 20, paragraphs 21 to 24.
1990 c. 42	The Broadcasting Act 1990.	In section 193(2), paragraph (c) and the "and" immediately before it. In section 193(4), "or the Competition Act 1980".
1991 c. 56	The Water Industry Act 1991.	In section 12(5), "or the 1980 Act". Section 15(2). In section 17(1), paragraph (b) and the "or" immediately before it. In section 17(2), paragraph (c) and the "or" immediately before it. In section 17(4), "or the 1980 Act". In section 31(4), paragraph (c) and the "and" immediately before it. In section 31(5), "or in subsection (3) above". In section 31(6), "or in subsection (3) above". In section 31(7), "or (3)". In section 31(9), "or the 1980 Act". In Part II of Schedule 15, the entries relating to the Restrictive Trade Practices Act 1976 and the Resale Prices Act 1976.
1991 c. 57	The Water Resources Act 1991.	In Part II of Schedule 24, the entries relating to the Restrictive Trade Practices Act 1976 and the Resale Prices Act 1976.
1993 c. 21	The Osteopaths Act 1993.	In section 33(4), paragraph (b) and the "or" immediately before it. In section 33(5), "or section 10 of the Act of 1980".

Chapter	Short title	Extent of repeal
1993 c. 43	The Railways Act 1993.	Section 14(2). In section 16(1), paragraph (b) and the "or" immediately before it. In section 16(2), paragraph (c) and the "or" immediately before it. In section 16(5), "or the 1980 Act". In section 67(4), paragraph (c) and the "and" immediately after it. In section 67(6)(a), "or (3)". In section 67(9), "or under the 1980 Act". Section 131. In section 145(3), paragraphs (d) and (e).
1994 c. 17	The Chiropractors Act 1994.	In section 33(4), paragraph (b) and the "or" immediately before it. In section 33(5), "or section 10 of the Act of 1980".
1994 c. 21	The Coal Industry Act 1994.	In section 59(4), paragraphs (e) and (f).
1994 c. 40	The Deregulation and Contracting Out Act 1994.	Sections 10 and 11. In section 12, subsections (1) to (6). In Schedule 4, paragraph 1. In Schedule 11, in paragraph 4, sub-paragraphs (3) to (6).
1996 c. 55	The Broadcasting Act 1996.	Section 77(2).

PART II

REVOCATIONS

Reference	Title	Extent of revocation
S.I. 1981/1675 (N.I. 26).	The Magistrates' Courts (Northern Ireland) Order 1981.	In Schedule 6, paragraphs 42 and 43.
S.I. 1982/1080 (N.I. 12).	The Agricultural Marketing (Northern Ireland) Order 1982.	In Schedule 8, the entry relating to paragraph 16(2) of Schedule 3 to the Fair Trading Act 1973 and in the entry relating to the Competition Act 1980, "and 15(3)".
S.I. 1986/1035 (N.I. 9).	The Companies Consolidation (Consequential Provisions) (Northern Ireland) Order 1986.	In Part II of Schedule 1, the entries relating to the Restrictive Trade Practices Act 1976 and the Resale Prices Act 1976.

Reference	Title	Extent of revocation
S.I. 1992/231 (N.I. 1).	The Electricity (Northern Ireland) Order 1992.	Article 16(2). In Article 18— (a) in paragraph (1), sub-paragraph (b) and the "or" immediately before it; (b) in paragraph (2), sub-paragraph (c) and the "or" immediately before it; (c) in paragraph (3) "or the 1980 Act". In Article 28(5), the "or" immediately after sub-paragraph (b). In Article 46— (a) in paragraph (4), sub-paragraph (c) and the "and" immediately after it; (b) in paragraph (5), "or (3)"; (c) in paragraph (7), "or the 1980 Act". Article 61(3)(f) and (g). In Schedule 12, paragraph 16.
S.I. 1994/426 (N.I. 1).	The Airports (Northern Ireland) Order 1994.	Article 36(3). In Article 45— (a) in paragraph (1), "or section 10(2)(a) of the 1980 Act"; (b) in paragraph (3), sub-paragraph (c) and the "or" immediately before it; (c) in paragraph (4), "or the 1980 Act". In Article 47(a)(ii), "or the 1980 Act". In Schedule 9, paragraph 5.
S.I. 1996/275 (N.I. 2).	The Gas (Northern Ireland) Order 1996.	Article 16(2). In Article 18— (a) in paragraph (1), sub-paragraph (b) and the "or" immediately before it; (b) in paragraph (3), sub-paragraph (c) and the "or" immediately before it; (c) in paragraph (5), "or the 1980 Act". In Article 19(5), the "or" immediately after sub-paragraph (b). In Article 23— (a) in paragraph (4), sub-paragraph (d) and the "and" immediately before it; (b) in paragraph (5), "or (3)";

Reference	Title	Extent of revocation
		(c) in paragraph (7), "or under the 1980 Act"; (d) in paragraph (8), "or the 1980 Act". Article 44(4)(f) and (g).

Index